foreigners

Marcus Klein

*f*oreigners

*The Making of
American Literature
1900–1940*

The University of Chicago Press   Chicago and London

THE UNIVERSITY OF CHICAGO PRESS, CHICAGO 60637
THE UNIVERSITY OF CHICAGO PRESS, LTD., LONDON
©1981 by The University of Chicago
All rights reserved. Published 1981
Printed in the United States of America
85 84 83 82 81   5 4 3 2 1

MARCUS KLEIN is professor of English at the State University of New York
at Buffalo. He is the editor of *The American Novel since World War II*
and the author of *After Alienation: American Novels in Mid-Century,* the latter
published by the University of Chicago Press.

LIBRARY OF CONGRESS CATALOGING IN PUBLICATION DATA

Klein, Marcus.
  Foreigners: the making of American literature,
1900–1940.

  Includes bibliographical references and index.
  1. American literature—20th century—History
and criticism. I. Title.
PS223.K5   810′.9′0052   80–28711
ISBN 0–226–43956–9

For Nelson and Lena Klein

Contents

Preface

I had intended to write a book about American literature in the 1930s, thus to present myself with a tidy problem in the ways in which literary expression is related to social fact. The 1930s seemed to offer an eminently convenient and obvious case for study. From *terminus a quo* to *terminus ad quem*, the crash of the stock market in 1929 to the beginning of the Second World War in 1939, the dates had a rare specificity, and for the first time ever, in all of recorded history, God had seemed to be working His way in terms of decimals. Moreover, and as everyone knows, social fact in the 1930s imposed itself on all kinds of expression more generally and more forcefully than it has in any subsequent time in America excepting perhaps for the time of the Second World War. I did suspect from the beginning, however, that writing in the 1930s was not to be defined with any adequacy by reference merely to the more overt categories of public event and reflexive literary response. I did not think that I would get very far by contemplating the materials in terms—to use the names of some currently popular anthologies—of *Years of Protest* or *Hard Times* or *Proletarian Writers* or *Writers in Revolt*. Even in the most public of times, the act of writing is of course a lonely and intimate business, and I suspected that the true connectives between literature and social fact were to be discovered in some commonalities of experience both underlying and broader than the public events.

The following pages will indicate that my suspicions overrode my original intentions, to the point where my subject became a larger and a less obviously coherent segment of history. Keeping in mind the fact that after all an individual self is present in any piece of formal writing—unto blatant potboilers, occasional philippics, cartoon strips, and ghost-written autobiographies—I had to recognize this among some other things, that my writers in revolt during the years of protest were born and often had had literary careers in other, previous years. I was also forced to recognize that what happened in literature in the 1930s was happening in prior decades as well, although under the auspices of a somewhat lesser amount of public recognition. By the beginning of the 1930s there existed, for instance, a well-established tradition of a literature not only of protest, but specifically of socialist protest. And I was led further to suspect that my writers who were engaged in protest on the left had some interesting correspondences with writers who were their opposites in temperament, literary commitment, and politics, but who with their different faces were facing the same history. Meanwhile, and engaged still in the same history, there were a great number of writers in the middle.

As is indicated by the following pages, I came to think that the historical facts which were pertinent to my uses were the very large but nonetheless particular ones of the several decades of the beginning of this century: industrialism, urbanization, political radicalism, and immigration. These were not events, but pervasive and continuous developments, of a sort which might well have compelled writers (left, right, and middle) to new dubieties of apprehension.

God does not work in decimals, and I would not wish to be insistent about dates, but it was some time approximately and conveniently at the turn of the twentieth century that an America which had had definitions in myth and idea—variable definitions but nevertheless antique and accepted ones—all but disappeared. Therefore I begin in 1900. What had been a facsimile of culture was chaos within which everybody was a foreigner, including the native-born and the millions of authentic foreigners. And there were consequences for the making of literature. Having no culture in which to be at home, writers made one—or, rather, they fabricated many versions of a culture depending on their various kinds of knowledge of what they had been dispossessed from and what reasonably they could come into possession of. Not unreasonably, as perhaps I have made clear in the following pages, children of the Mayflower tended to invent Western culture, and children of the immigrants, who seem to me to present the more interesting case, tended to invent America.

Acknowledgments

As I planned and prepared this book I had the advantage of having some extraordinarily challenging and generous students at the State University of New York at Buffalo. They led me to new subjects for consideration, provided me with materials for research, and not infrequently commanded my thinking by putting texts before me. I am especially indebted to Charles Banning, Kerry Driscoll, Sally Drucker, Finvola Drury, Susan Handleman, Vicki Hill, Richard Kopley, David Porush, Michael Sartisky, Roy Zipris, and Lynda Zwinger.

I have also had the advantage of some wise and skilled colleagues who have educated me much more broadly than might be indicated by an occasional footnote in this book. I wish to thank Raymond Federman, Leslie Fiedler, William Fischer, David Hollinger, Jay Martin, Irving Sanes, and Herbert Schneidau.

I owe gratitude to the staff of the Poetry Room of Lockwood Library, without whose aid I could not have written this book.

Hilda Ludwig typed my manuscript again and again. She also read the manuscript and declared an interest in my subject. Her interest sustained me wonderfully, and I thank her.

Part One

traditions

Full fathom five your Bleistein lies

T. S. Eliot

God is making the American

Israel Zangwill

Emerson said, in a famous and typical instance: "We have listened too long to the courtly muses of Europe. The spirit of the American freeman is already suspected to be timid, imitative, tame.... We will walk on our own feet; we will work with our own hands; we will speak our own minds." And Thoreau, insolent and exquisite, observed: "as for England, almost the last significant scrap of news from that quarter was the revolution of 1649.... If one may judge who rarely looks into the newspapers, nothing new does ever happen in foreign parts, a French revolution not excepted." And Whitman, so late as 1871, in *Democratic Vistas,* exhorted: "Mark the roads, the processes, through which these States have arrived, standing easy, henceforth ever-equal, ever-compact, in their range to-day. European adventures? the most antique? Asiatic or African? old history—miracles— romances? Rather, our own unquestion'd facts. They hasten, incredible, blazing bright as fire." The American, all in all, was, properly, that "new man" who had been discovered or invented by St. John Crèvecoeur so long before as 1782, "who acts upon new principles," and who would therefore "entertain new ideas, and form new opinions."

> From involuntary idleness, servile dependence, penury, and
> useless labour, he has passed to toils of a very different nature,
> rewarded by ample subsistence.—This is an American.

Of course not everyone concurred and, moreover, both the dilatation and the blatancy of the proposition might have been understood really to betray an uneasiness, but the idea of the *new man,* unfettered and unbeholden and disregardful of all prior traditions, was asserted so frequently and so eminently during the classic period of American letters as to comprise indisputably one of the distinguishing signs of the American recognition of the American civilization. For a period of approximately one hundred years, America was the name of the cultural ideal which stood for conscientious opposition to that idea Matthew Arnold was to call "Culture." ("The word of the modern," said Whitman, having Arnold in mind, "is the word Culture. We find ourselves abruptly in close quarters with the enemy.") And America was, indeed, not only a new thing in the world, but a perpetually self-renewing new thing, always and on principle breaking from its own past. "Old deeds for old people," said Thoreau, "and new deeds for new." "Life only avails," said Emerson, "not the having lived." And Whitman: "Do I contradict myself / Very well then I contradict myself."

But the past which was being rejected, whether cultural or even personal, was after all a very present past. Even as he was invoking the strategies of a godly self-reliance, Emerson could advise that we "enter into the state of war and wake Thor and Woden, courage and constancy, in our Saxon breasts," assuming that most of us did have Saxon breasts. The place of the thriving of the rebellion against tradition, meaning chiefly the tradition of the English, was called New England. By measure of a latter-day state of things—industry and urbanization and corporate business and poverty and institutionalized political corruption and political radicalism and massive immigration, all coming into being in the late years of the nineteenth century—the America of the "new man" was quite wonderfully homogeneous and stable. Even the arch-bohemian Walt Whitman, with his infinite posturings and his real problems of knowing who he was in the world, knew very well who he was not, what aristocratic or "feudal" or generally European heritage was available to him for the discarding, and was able to exploit his repudiation of the manners to be inferred from that heritage. The traditional past was to be rejected but not questioned.

By the end of the nineteenth century, such luxury was no longer so readily available. The known past was for Americans at the least hugely miscellaneous, including among other problematics the American cultural past itself, which had been so largely defined by its discountenancing of an anterior past. The traditional past could no longer authorize the nontraditional present because there could no longer be general agreement as to what the traditional past was. In these circumstances, especially after the turn of the new century, "tradition" secured a peculiar importance, both for those who wanted to reclaim a privilege and for those who wanted for the first time in their American history to claim a status. In a time of rapid changes, rapid degradations, "tradition" was a metaphor for a place in the world. And if in fact there was no longer any consensus about the nature of tradition as a thing in history, then it could be and had to be made up—obviously within history.

one

Tradition and History

In his editorial for the July 1929 issue of the *Criterion* T. S. Eliot attended to the dispute between communism and fascism.

Eliot was equable, cautious, and meticulous, as always. He would certainly not fully commit himself to either the one side or the other. Both of these new "doctrines," he said, enunciated really very conventional ideas insofar as they presented *ideas* at all. "A revolutionary idea," he said, "is one which requires a reorganization of the mind; fascism or communism is now the natural idea for the thoughtless person." He did not see a genuine difference between the two even in their theories of economics. Nonetheless he was understanding; he sensed the enthusiasms—the unexamined enthusiasms, albeit—which they provoked, and he did feel compelled to say that at the end he was himself not susceptible:

> The objections of fascists and communists to each other are mostly quite irrational. I confess to a preference for fascism in practice, which I dare say most of my readers share; and I will not admit that this preference is itself wholly irrational. I believe that the fascist form of unreason is less remote from my own than is that of the communists, but that my form is a more reasonable form of unreason.[1]

And who would have been astonished? Either by the decision of Eliot's instincts or by the tonalities of the expression—the intricate litotes, the lack of ardor suggesting both whimsy and a deliberate superciliousness? As insouciant as the statement was, it merely discovered a new political term for an attitude toward history which Eliot had implied from the beginning. Indeed, and as was plain to be noted in the current instance, in one way Eliot had by this time gone quite beyond fascism. He believed in royalism, cagily but still with a considerable literalness. He believed in the idea if not the plausibility of divine right. The political party which did in fact claim his support was *l'Action française*, of which he said in this same instance that its "vital dogma" was not the demotic nationalism which fascism claimed, "but royalism . . . the reintroduction of the idea of loyalty to a King, who incarnates the idea of the Nation.''[2] From which perspective both communism and fascism were almost identical in—although he did not quite use the term—their vulgarity.

But meanwhile, however unaccountably, men were dying for these other doctrines. The *Criterion* was not, could not, be unaware. Certainly at Eliot's own instigation, for he was absolute monarch of that magazine, it had already run two full-length essays, one on communism and one on fascism. The times demanded and the vocabulary was insistent. Eliot as maker of criteria might well feel himself forced to make a choice, and so forced he would of course—although he did not say this at all—have found the superior emotional appeal in the doctrine which was more frankly antidemocratic and which, besides, had its current locus, in Italy, in a richly traditional and also accessible national culture.

Nor was he in error, certainly, in assuming the agreement of most of the readers of the *Criterion*. They, in particular, did not sway in the wind like a field of ripe corn. They were an elite to whom, in particular, the political conformations of high culture had been repreatedly revealed. A few months prior to reading Eliot on fascism, readers of the *Criterion* had been reading John Gould Fletcher on Marx:

> It is impossible to grasp the reason for Marx's naive dismissal of man's finest achievements, without first understanding his own peculiarly racial psychology. Marx was, as is known, a Jew, and his greatest confusion of thought, that of the wage-earning class with the producing class, as well as his apocalyptic "world revolution," are products of specifically Jewish psychology. If we study history closely, it is apparent that the Jews, as an independent race, were as deeply despised by the Egyptians, the Babylonian-Assyrians, the Romans, as, since the dispersal, they have remained on bad terms with the various Christian communities in which they lived.[3]

And a few months before that they had been reading a translation of an essay by Henri Massis, "Defense of the West," in which it was suggested that the future of Western civilization was in jeopardy because the colored nations of Asia and Africa, "united by Bolshevism," were ranged against Western civilization.[4]

But in fact Eliot's readers, likely sharers in both his literary and his political preferences, were by now very numerous and not limited to those few who received their criteria by direct subscription to the *Criterion*.[5] By 1929 Eliot could with utter confidence assume that when he spoke, he spoke in behalf of a well-defined and moreover a victorious sensibility. More than anyone else who wrote in English, he represented that revolution in thought and feeling which was called modernism, and which had achieved its exemplary expression in *The Waste Land*. And what was now confirmed by the spokesmen in his discovery of a local term—"fascism"—was that since, say, the "lyric year" of 1912, modernism had contained suggestion of a revolution in a narrower, explicitly political sense also, that at the very least the style of thought and feeling had exact political connotations which would become conspicuous when the times demanded. Modernism had been a strategy for the making of literature *and* it had been from the beginning an implicit ideology.

As a literary strategy it had had its obvious justifications. New writers in a moment of what was indeed crucial historical change, circa 1912, had put themselves to the invention of new expression: a new language (which, in the words of Eliot, struggled "to express new objects, new groups of objects, new feelings, new aspects")[6] and new techniques, new freedoms, new conventions, the pressure in poetry of original observation, "direct treatment of the 'thing,'"[7] original discovery, and experiment above all. The strategy in turn had demanded an attitude toward history. And what was invented by Pound and Eliot and some others was an ingenious paradox: lacking a plausible Golden Age or a relevant Augustan Age, there could be a *new tradition,* which would serve as a tactical base for an attack upon the present. The present was conceived to be the desuetude of romanticism. (Said T. E. Hulme, the philosopher prince of modernism: "Each field of artistic activity is exhausted by the first great artist who gathers a full harvest from it. This period of exhaustion seems to me to have been reached in romanticism.")[8] Pound, by way of direct assault on the "emotional slither" of most poetry written since 1450,[9] discovered the true classics in Anglo-Saxon, Provençal, early Italian, and then subsequently Chinese and Japanese literatures. Eliot assumed leadership of the revival of the metaphysical poets when he reviewed Herbert Grierson's anthology in 1921, and took the occasion to eliminate from the canon most poets from Milton through Tennyson. And by how much the new tradition was a tactic, conceived for its present usefulness in liberating poetry from the immediate past, was to be indicated by the fact that Eliot not so long afterward, in the period after 1933, read back into the canon many of those poets whom he primarily had succeeded in banishing.

But this discovered tradition, no matter where discovered and no matter how arbitrary or fleeting its contents, had never been only a congeries of serviceable inventions. For one thing, it had enjoined a tremendous amount of scholarship or, more exactly, a taste for the supposed authority of traditional literary-historical scholarship—from which followed the virtual definition of literature as the enterprise of an intellectual aristocracy. Like modern science, as was quite part of the general intention, literature was to require special academic training, and of course not everyone went to the university. To a remarkable extent, the modernism made by Americans had a Harvard education.

More important, the new tradition, conceived to allow a new progress for poetry, in fact denied progress as, for all of its recovery of historical fragments, it denied history. History became static omnipresence. In "Tradition and the Individual Talent," that singularly influential essay, Eliot had put the matter most directly. The "historical sense," he said, was "nearly indispensable to any one who would continue to be a poet beyond his twenty-fifth year," but then he had gone on to define the key term in such a way that history was neither sequential nor consequential, but a kind of completeness in itself, unmoving and immovable:

> the historical sense involves a perception, not only of the pastness of the past, but of its presence; the historical sense compels a man to write not merely with his own generation in his bones, but with a feeling that the whole of the literature of Europe from Homer and within it the whole of the literature of his own country has a simultaneous existence and composes a simultaneous order. This historical sense, which is a sense of the timeless as well as of the temporal and of the timeless and of the temporal together, is what makes a writer traditional. And it is at the same time what makes a writer most acutely conscious of his place in time, of his own contemporaneity.[10]

And it followed that the writer who was to be traditional and contemporaneous at the same time had also to be reactionary, in the pure sense that he would approach the present and define himself in the present by asserting the presentness of the past, which was to say, precisely, the tradition of the past.

The new "tradition" was not merely a tactic but also a value. The tradition was a reconstituting of the past in such a way that the past was neither the flow of recorded historical events nor, in the terms of another theory currently popular, a dialectical process which might be ascertained scientifically. The past of the tradition did not contain time at all, but was antagonistic to change. "The existing monuments," Eliot wrote, "form an ideal order among themselves," and it was the duty of the individual artist, while his success *might* change the configuration of that order ever so slightly, to find this propriety within it. The past so conceived was a kind of State, which impelled—Eliot went so far—the elimination of individuality in behalf of the ideal order. Hence Eliot's famous proscription, "Poetry is not a turning loose of emotion, but an escape from emotion; it is not the expression of personality, but an escape from personality."[11] The poet was one who was privileged to yield his personality to the ideal order.

Which is not to suggest that Eliot's modernism was disguised fascism. It may indeed be said, as has been said, that it was the kind of emotional excess against which Eliot arranged his aesthetic that led to the actual practices of fascists in history. But this modernism did implicate both a sensibility and a value system to which fascism was amenable when it came along, and to which theoretical communism—given the importuning of the current political terms—was not. Eliot's particular sources for information would probably have indicated to him that Marxist history was open-ended and insistent that nothing was permanent.[12] Moreover, although in fact Soviet communism had by this time become fully totalitarian—it was in 1929 that Trotsky was expelled from Russia—communism of course meant opposition to vested authority. Perhaps it was not truly revolutionary, but it was manifestly antitraditional. Its center of energy was, theoretically, in the declassed, hence the ignorant. Its peculiar distinction as philosophy was the importance it placed on materialism. Fascism, on the other hand, envisioned a millennium based on "order, loyalty, realization of the individual in the life of the State"—words Eliot found to be of "good implication and good report."[13] Fascism was above everything opposed to anarchy. Although the form of its nationalism was in some ways unfortunate, still because it was nationalistic it was traditional, its symbol and its very name deriving from memory of the ancient Empire. It bred a mystique of the leader which was almost sacral, and it did support the Church, for whatever reasons.[14]

And while Eliot's temperament was not everybody's, Eliot's idea of a changeless past coming to bear on the present was fundamental to modernism. This device of perspective by which the degeneration of the culture of the present might be measured, if it began solely as that,[15] was in itself the value and the politics which assembled quite heterogeneous personalities into a literary generation. The "tradition" was for everybody something, finally, like a rearguard action against any Revolution subsequent to the fifteenth century—Protestant, American, French, Industrial—or it was a belated piece of sabotage. The "tradition" was an organization of society, offering a contrast to the present by being immobile, hierarchical, and holistic. It had its own urgency, insisting when it was literalized, as it very often was, that the present not take place.

The "tradition" after all had much the same information for Ernest Hemingway, to take the case of a writer of absolutely dissimilar temperament. With all of his astonishing adeptness in creating contemporaneity, Hemingway secured his emotional force by his manipulation of modes of elegy. The present generation was, in the words Hemingway sloganized, a "lost generation," meaning that once in the past young people had known where they were, that once in the past young people had been old people. The stories of *In Our Time* celebrated not our time, but past time. *The Sun Also Rises* implied directly that the glorious day was gone, that the sun had set. The past to which Hemingway so continuously pointed, and with such cunning reticence, was imagined variously, to be sure, but in fact that sensibility which found refuge in American pastoral, as in the Nick Adams stories, was equally attuned to a concept of the "tradition" quite in Eliot's Christian terms. The unrooted, aimless, fragmented society of *The Sun Also Rises* after all achieved definition by being measured against its opposite, and not definition only, but also its brief sustenance. The movement of the novel is from contemporary secular Paris, where Jake Barnes with his Fisher-King wound is so out of place, to a locale of solemn Christian ritual:

> Now on the day of the starting of the fiesta of San Fermin [the peasants] had been in the wine-shops of the narrow streets of the town since early morning. Going down the streets in the morning on the way to mass in the cathedral, I heard them singing through the open doors of the shops. They were warming up. There were many people at the eleven o'clock mass. San Fermin is also a religious festival.[16]

The various protagonists as they are sent forth to the bullfights are subscribed by their author to a pilgrimage. That is their adventure. And when they arrive at the shrine, they secure or lose value by the amounts of their aptitude for participating in the religious tradition. They are tested along the way. Jake and Bill, after the episode of their holy fishing, stop to visit the monastery at Roncesvalles, the shrine of the place where Roland saved Christianity. Jake and Brett are, explicitly, failed Catholics who go to cathedrals and try to pray. They want to be real Catholics.

That is not to emphasize the fact that the novel works with Catholic metaphors, but that the metaphors are expressly sacerdotal. The issue was not a sectarian one. Nor was the issue even belief in God. Brett's eventual opting for decency and sacrifice with regard to Romero will really do as well. Hemingway's response to the present was not God but the way of life represented in the fiesta of San Fermin: peasants organized for a traditional form of worship. By the amount that Brett is affected—specifically by Romero, the chief actor in the rites of the fiesta—she feels "good." Jake Barnes with his superior equipment, or his superior lack of equipment, is wiser and better than the others in his crowd by the amount that, as an outsider, he is skilled in the fiesta life. He knows the forms. Indeed, because he knows them, he can lead a life which is marginal to his own place and time, in good part outside of history.

Like many another hero within the major canon of modern literature, Jake Barnes was a spiritual aristocrat. While Hemingway himself emphatically, too emphatically, was disassociated from the scholarly overbearingness of, for instance, Pound and Eliot, the modern movement as a whole offered an implication of a spiritual aristocracy being defined by an intellectual aristocracy.

And there was a likelihood in that implication because in fact the American makers of the modern movement were with remarkable uniformity of a certain class, one which might well think of itself as a dispossessed *social* aristocracy. Besides Eliot, Pound, and Hemingway, the makers included Gertrude Stein, Wallace Stevens, E. E. Cummings, Marianne Moore, F. Scott Fitzgerald, Hilda Doolittle, John Dos Passos (in his earlier career), John Gould Fletcher, perhaps Faulkner, and some dozens of others in supporting roles—Margaret Anderson, Sylvia Beach, Gorham Munson, and so on. They were the inventors. They were all of a distinct generation, all with the exception of Stein and Stevens born in the 1880s and 1890s.[17] (Gertrude Stein was born in 1874, Stevens in 1879.) More to the point, by actual fact of birth they tended—as in the cases of Eliot, Pound, Cummings, Stevens, Moore, Faulkner, Fitzgerald, and Stein and Dos Passos—to come from old American stock. (Gertrude Stein was Jewish, but from an old American family nonetheless; her *Making of Americans* was in one aspect a monograph on that subject. Dos Passos was a bastard, but raised in such circumstances that he had standing in elevated society; he was a kind of royal bastard.) The American Eliots, as T. S. Eliot well knew, dated back to the year 1670. Ezra Pound, as Pound well knew, went back somewhat further, on the Pound side to the 1630s and on his mother's side back to circa 1623.[18] Moreover, the various makers almost without exception came from families which either were wealthy or had been wealthy. These inventors constituted, whether by actual fact of birth or not, a beleaguered gentry, forced quite abruptly, by real history, to assert a glamorous antiquity. It was another function of the "tradition," then, that it provided a homeland for upper-class aliens.

The post hoc myth, adduced principally by Malcolm Cowley in *Exiles' Return,* was that a generation's exile, metaphorical and literal, was consequent upon disillusion: the American makers of modern literature were refugees from an America that suddenly had lost its old idealisms and that had in the period after the First World War gone wildly, grubbily commercial. But that case for the matter was at best an ideal approximation. For one thing, the commercialism which putatively had disillusioned these idealists had been as much a fact of the 1880s, say, as of the 1910s and 1920s. If anything, the sheer business thrust of American civilization had been the more blatant in the years of the robber barons, prior to the turn of the century. For another thing, it was precisely in the time of the coming-of-age of these idealists that the muckrakers were revealing the symbiotic corruption of the leading businessmen and the leading politicians in Eliot's St. Louis, Ezra Pound's Philadelphia, Hemingway's Chicago, and the Minneapolis next door to F.Scott Fitzgerald's St. Paul. And those fine old American values (to which, most particularly, Fitzgerald had alluded) would have been difficult to corroborate in the contemporary knowledge of these particular persons.

But these persons were exiles truly, nonetheless. The country had changed, and in such a way as to rob them of what they very well might have assumed to be their cultural security, their cultural standing, their cultural rights.

Civilization in America was not even where it had been before, and therefore was not what it had been before. The Jeffersonian ideal of a country of small farmers, which Ezra Pound in particular was to invoke, had long ago been betrayed by history. Now as this generation came of age, its successor, the America of the comfortable, quite homogeneous small town, after the turn of the century just beginning to be idealized, was also in process of being betrayed. The fact, if not yet quite the realization, was exactly contemporary with this generation. In the single decade of the 1880s, the urban population of the United States increased by more than 50 percent. In the next decade it increased by another (exponential) approximately 36 percent, and then, after the turn of the century, in the decade 1900–1910, by an additional approximately 40 percent, and then by still another 30 percent in each of the following two decades. By 1922, when, in *The Waste Land,* Eliot published his discovery that the mythical waste land was the modern

city (using London as his specific example, to be sure, but having
America in mind),[19] well over half of that country from which he was
exiled lived in the modern city. And that was perhaps the last moment
in which it could have been conceived that the city was a mistake, or an
imposition, rather than a fatality, and that the underlying reality of the
nation was something else. In the same year, 1922, the author of the
essay "The Small Town" in Harold Stearns's *Civilization in the United
States* did say with great positiveness that "the civilization of America
is predominantly the civilization of the small town." Although the
small-town culture might be somewhat disguised in the cities, he said,
it predominated there too. But then the author of the parallel essay in
Stearns's *America Now,* published in 1938, was to speak of the small
town just as positively as being a "completed episode," existing, if at
all, contingent upon hazy recollections. The small town, he said, had
lost its inhabitants, its economic base, and its isolation.[20]

Not that the particular Americans who made the modern movement were small towners—a good number of them were, in fact,
already suburbanites—but they were by and large so situated in their
individual growings-up that they might be greatly threatened by the
particular form of American urbanization. It was another cause of their
exile that their country had been invaded, occupied, and culturally
ravaged, by barbarians.

In terms of its personnel, the primary fact of American urbanization was the so-called Second, or New, or Great Immigration, beginning in the 1880s and reaching its peak in the years 1905–10. Except for
the unfortunate incursions of the Irish on the East Coast and the
Chinese on the West Coast and the Scandanavians in the middle, immigration for a half century heretofore had been largely a cultural
beneficence. Now the country was being overrun by immigrants in
numbers far surpassing anything that had been known and, more to the
point, of nationalities (if these landless peasants, these ghetto refugees
could be said to have nationality) scarcely available to imagination.
These Sicilians and Greeks and Slavs and Polish-Russian Jews who
filled the cities spoke in tongues which in themselves were an affront,
except perhaps that an amount of sophistication might perceive them to
be comic. Having no law, these immigrants had no society. Having no
cultivation, they had no culture. Being southern and eastern Europeans, they were not northern and western Europeans. And they made
the de facto culture of American cities. They arrived in such numbers
that it became difficult, and indeed an urgent, question to determine
what an American was, and then they insisted upon clustering and
spawning. In 1930, when the episode of the New Immigration had

stabilized, some 14 million persons living in the United States had been born elsewhere, very largely in southern and eastern Europe, and another 25-million-plus persons were first-generation native born. Another 12 million persons, it might be added, were black, so that between 40 and 50 percent of the entire population of the United States consisted of persons who had at best an ambivalent relationship to any such essentialized, mainstream American tradition as anybody might propose. (Southern blacks began arriving in the northern cities in large numbers when northern industry began to subsidize the war in Europe; the so-called Great Migration began in 1916, when a million southern blacks went North. In the decade of the 1920s the black population of the northern cities was compounded by an additional 64 percent.) Civilization in the United States was located in the cities, and the cities were ghetto conglomerates. By 1930 the "great cities," those with a total population of a million or more, were made up of persons *two-thirds* of whom were either foreign born or first-generation native born.[21]

After such assault, what gentry assumptions any old Americans might have had could have had no more than dubious pertinence in America.[22]

On the other hand, the loss of America conferred peculiar opportunity. The young sons of the old stock, growing up in the time of the assault, might find themselves to be not only dispossessed but also a glamorously defeated nobility, having old values (not otherwise specific) to be honored and a lineage (not necessarily detailed) to be invoked. Suggestions for the literary exploitation of such loss were already plentiful at the turn of the century, in modes ranging from popular chivalric romances to high decadence. And then shortly afterward there was the Henry Adams of the *Education,* who more pertinently than anyone else—more so certainly than Jules Laforgue or Tristan Corbière—defined the *cultural authority* of American modernism. Adams of course had rare authority indeed. He could make unique claim to a prominent American heritage which the America of the new age had betrayed. The insult was personal and conveyed plausible privilege. Adams was eloquently credible when he said of himself in the *Education:*

> His world was dead. Not a Polish Jew fresh from Warsaw or
> Cracow—not a furtive Yacoob [sic] or Ysaac still reeking of the
> Ghetto, snarling a weird Yiddish to the officers of the
> customs—but had a keener instinct, an intenser energy, and a
> freer hand than he—American of Americans, with Heaven knew
> how many Puritans and Patriots behind him, and an education
> that had cost a civil war. He made no complaint and found no

fault with his time; he was not worse off than the Indians or the buffalo who had been ejected from their heritage.[23]

But if Adams was particularly privileged, still the young generation of the modern masters—engaged in inventing themselves, it happened, just when the *Education* became public—could very well participate, and in accents not very much different. Ezra Pound could suggest, with just a small amount of self-conscious irony, that "one"—that is, Pound himself—"could write the whole social history of the United States from one's family annals." To do so, moreover, would be to illustrate the abrupt contemporary mongrelization of that history. A Philadelphia neighbor of his youth "was not only a gentleman but the fine old type. And his son is a stockbroker, roaring himself hoarse every day in the Wheat Pit . . . and *his* son will look like a Jew, and his grandson . . . will talk Yiddish. And this dissolution is taking place in hundreds of American families who have not thought of it as a decadence."[24] And for Eliot there was a family feeling of what must be called dynasty, now assaulted if not yet quite defeated. His mother had written a biography of her father-in-law, William Greenleaf Eliot. (Had her subject been her own father, then her motive might presumably have been merely filial.) The lost cause became high principle, "tradition" precisely, especially when Eliot could address those fine few who might be presumed to understand. So his series of lectures to the University of Virginia in 1933 was conceived as further reflections on "Tradition and the Individual Talent," and Eliot would say to these southerners:

> You have here, I imagine, at least some recollection of a 'tradition,' such as the influx of foreign populations has almost effaced in some parts of the North, and such as never established itself in the West: though it is hardly to be expected that a tradition here, any more than anywhere else, should be found in healthy and flourishing growth. . . . Yet I think that the chances for the re-establishment of a native culture are perhaps better here than in New England. You are farther away from New York; you have been less industrialized and less invaded by foreign races.

And again, a true traditionalism would require that

> The population should be homogeneous; where two or more cultures exist in the same place they are likely either to be fiercely self-conscious or both to become adulterate. What is still more important is unity of religious background; and reasons of race and religion combine to make any large number of free-thinking Jews undesirable.[25]

This statement, soon to become notorious, was personal without doubt, and was a reflection on the education of T. S. Eliot. Underlying the elegant dogmatism there was Second Empire conviction and yearning. A few years prior to the Virginia lectures, in 1928, Eliot had been writing to Sir Herbert Read:

> Some day I want to write an essay about the point of view of an American who wasn't an American, because he was born in the South and went to school in New England as a small boy with a nigger drawl, but who wasn't a southerner in the South because his people were northerners in a border state and looked down on all southerners and Virginians, and who so was never anything anywhere and who therefore felt himself to be more a Frenchman than an American and more an Englishman than a Frenchman and yet felt that the U.S.A. up to a hundred years ago was a family extension.[26]

Which point of view incidentally covered all possibilities: the Eliots had been New England aristocrats, southern cavaliers, and in the conjunction of circumstances *not* "never anything anywhere" but the owners of America. And in this literary generation as a whole there was a suggestion of a similar sensibility, only not necessarily quite so immoderate in its pretensions.

The Mongols were at the gates. Meanwhile, say, Mr. and Mrs. Edward Fitzgerald of St. Paul, Minnesota, she the daughter of an Irish immigrant but he on his mother's side the descendant of colonial Marylanders, named their boy Francis Scott Key in order to memorialize what might have seemed to someone else to be a ludicrous blood connection with American history. And their handsome boy grew up to learn beautiful manners, the implications of which education he stood for until the end and despite whatever rambunctiousness of charming rue. "The very rich," he was to say in his famous fragment of conversation with Hemingway, "are different from you and me." But the very rich, as Hemingway did not reply, were not nearly so different as the very poor.

Although perhaps not very rich, "you and me" and some others still had a conspicuous exclusiveness. There was the imputation of a coherent, more-or-less credible past—the "tradition" variously conceived.

This literary generation was a social class, defined as American social classes tend to be defined, along ethnic and racial lines. Hence the "tradition," which however conceived—whether rooted in Eliot's Anglo-Catholicism or Fitzgerald's mythical Middle West or Hemingway's Michigan woods or Faulkner's magnolia South, or wherever—had the effect of excluding all of the abrupt barbarians.

Hence also a mode of social references in the literary discourse of this generation which occasionally made blatant the relationship between the "tradition" and an ethnic exclusiveness. There was, for convenient instance, the celebrated comic moment in *The Great Gatsby* when Fitzgerald told the names, in a half-dozen paragraphs, of the people who came to Gatsby's parties:

> From farther out on the Island came the Cheadles and O.R.P. Schraeders, and the Stonewall Jackson Abrams of Georgia, and the Fishguards and the Ripley Snells. Snell was there three days before he went to the penitentiary, so drunk out on the gravel drive that Mrs. Ulysses Swett's automobile ran over his right hand. The Dancies came, too, and S. B. Whitebait, who was well over sixty, and Maurice A. Flink, and the Hammerheads, and Beluga the tobacco importer, and Beluga's girls.

And so on. Who were the Cheadles and the Stonewall Jackson Abrams of Georgia and the Fishguards and the Snells? The answer, in all obviousness, was that they were mongrels. They were debasers of the social coin: imagine a man named Abrams who has dared to call himself Stonewall Jackson and who has also dared to come from (American) Georgia. Such names were very funny, and not only to Francis Scott Key Fitzgerald, because the class implication to which Fitzgerald was appealing was after all understood by most of his readers.

Hence, more forthrightly, an early trifle by E. E. Cummings (the rebellious son of a rebellious father who, although rebellious, was still minister of the South Congregational Church of Boston):

> IKEY (GOLDBERG)'S WORTH I'M TOLD $ SEVERAL MILLION
> FINKELSTEIN (FRITZ) LIVE
> AT THE RITZ WEAR
> earl & wilson COLLARS[29]

Hence Ezra Pound's principled anti-Semitism, only the later virulence of which was plausibly insane. Hence, more seriously, Eliot's stock characters Sweeney and Bleistein. Eliot was indeed ambivalent about the former, although never about the latter, and about the former never in such a way as to confer fellow-feeling: Sweeney was to be envied his animality, perhaps. But Sweeney and Bleistein were metaphors, plainly, by which a traditionalist measured the decline of the West. And it would have required some peculiar effort or naiveté to regard Eliot's metaphors as being fortuitous or idiosyncratic, as though he might just as well have named his characters by other names. The metaphor functioned because Sweeney was the name for an Irishman and Bleistein was the name for a Jew. More precisely still, what was plainly meant was a shanty Irishman with low appetites and the slimy Jew whose

> lustreless protrusive eye
> Stares from the protozoic slime
> At a perspective of Canaletto.

Of course no specific slur was intended. Some of everybody's best friends were Irish, Jewish, or whatever. (Sir) Jacob Epstein had come to London from New York's Lower East Side, and everybody knew and liked him. T. S. Eliot wrote fan letters to Groucho Marx. Such utterance did not have a literal bearing. It did, however, affirm a convention by which a literal society was to be known. An American gentry might have been dispossessed, but it was therefore—asserting its exclusiveness. It might have been exiled from America, but it still owned and could defend civilization. The property was plainly posted: No Irish Permitted, Jews Not Welcome, Caucasians Only. And given the actualities of the contemporary history of American culture, these postings were to a considerable extent the device by which the property—Civilization, Culture, Kulcher, Tradition—was to be defined.

BARBARISM

On the other side there were the barbarians themselves and their unremitting progeny, some of whom chose to write literature under the auspices of an American culture. Despite the predominance of the modern movement and despite many other considerable odds, these others did manage to exist. They, too, composed a literary generation, almost exactly coeval with the modern movement and quite as self-conscious and quite as distinguishable as the modern movement. Given some conspirings of history, these others even managed their own moment of predominance, in the 1930s, and then beyond that moment, and despite many gaffes and gropings, they did alter some of the suppositions of an American literature.

In ways potentially very telling for literature, they were different from "you and me."

These others tended to have peculiar names, often manifestly even to their own way of thinking: Itzok Granich, who became Michael Gold; George Goetz, who became—resoundingly—V. F. Calverton; Elmer Reizenstein, who became Elmer Rice. Anzia Yezierska. Or, born a few years later, just after the turn of the century, they were Daniel Fuchs or Louis Zukofsky or Harry Roskolenko or Nathan Weinstein, who became Nathanael West, with some dozens of others in supporting roles. Isidor Schneider, Henry Potamkin, Herman Spector, Lester Cohen, Samuel Ornitz.[28] Or their names were as flagrantly Irish-mick as that of Eliot's Sweeney: Jack Conroy, James Farrell. Or, if nominally Anglo-Saxon—Langston Hughes, Richard Wright—they were black.

They were no less exiles, of course, than Ezra Pound and T. S. Eliot, et alia, but they were exiled in the opposite direction. They broached at least as complicated a task in discovering assumptions by which literature might be written and justified, one of the complications being that all of these came of age either during the time when the modern movement was being made or, worse, just after it had consolidated its pretensions. What was to be considered the major canon of modern literature had been in large part completed by the mid-1920s. Pound and Eliot and the *aspirants* were by no means the only contemporary source for literary instruction, but Pound and Eliot—and Hemingway, it happened, more pertinently—were assertively, imperatively present. Largely by their doing, as could not be denied, literature now was an enterprise of perhaps unprecedented excitement. Stunning possibilities were being demonstrated or just had been. There was no denying the accomplishment, but then there was also no accepting of the attitudes upon which the accomplishment depended.

It could not but be known that those attitudes began by dismissing the vulgar, by which, ever more clearly and precisely, was meant just these others. The best of Americans, the most commonsensical and the most goodwilled, tended to think of them in terms of animal images—visiting the Lower East Side in the 1890s, William Dean Howells commented charitably on "the inmates of the dens and lairs about me."[29] What was the geography of wasted land for Eliot was home for most of them. *They* were the polluters. If more pointed proof were needed, in 1922, the year of *The Waste Land,* Eliot was discussing Marxist literary criticism. The trouble with Marxism, he said, was that it terribly restricted a critic's ambition. The Marxist could not find delight in Homer or Virgil. The end of "his precipitous ascent" would be his estimation "of Sam Ornitz, Lester Cohen, and Granville Hicks"—by which was meant, plainly, two Jews of crashing inconsequence and an unaccountable Granville Hicks.[30] And in fact and as these others were likely to know instinctively, Eliot was mistaken only in general and not in the more important particulars. Marxism was not the proper issue, although almost all of these others were or were to become Marxists. By the plausible amount that Karl Marx, for one, had been a Marxist, Marxism loved the ancients. But truly, Eliot's "tradition" was not the tradition of, say, Itzok Granich.

It was the truth that (not unlike Eliot and Pound) these others had no tradition at all other than what they could forage from readings in an inchoate past. What they had uniquely was a desperately confusing personal experience, a part of which was the demand of loyalty to an alien, arbitrary, and currently useless version of tradition.

Quite reasonably from an Eliotic point of view, these others were simply beyond the Pale. But then from the opposite point of view, also, they were beyond the Pale, and in some nearly literal way. The Pale—in America, the urban ghetto—was where they were most likely to have come from. They were of it inevitably, and yet not of it. They were likely to have become exiles from home, such as it was, as soon as they had individually conceived of literary ambitions in America. It was a blunt likelihood that the people of the Pale—which would have been to say, one's father and mother and one's childhood friends and neighbors, the whole of society in any intimate definition—not only were not accessible to the cultural assumptions of contemporary literature, but also simply did not know English. To be a writer (in English) in itself was an act of emigration, and therefore an act of hostility directed against a most peculiarly sensitive and imposing society.

On the other hand, the inheritance proffered by home was nothing if not ambiguous. If home in the immediate sense—the place where one grew up—was an urban ghetto, then home was at best and in its most generous aspects a kind of receiving station, a society defined by its transitoriness. Or so it might have seemed if one were allowed some perspective, but then if one were oneself fully involved in the transition, even that amount of definition was very hard to come by. The ghetto did not at all encourage perspective from the future.

The ghetto was clingingly conservative, and for a reason which was so unassailable, so obvious, so pertinent to one's daily life as to be an ethical absolute. The American Pales of Settlement (numerously plural) were situated in a nation which had suggested and which continued to suggest great promises, and which was at the same time only not quite officially hostile. Aside from instances of Brahmin arrogance or low-caste racism, the nation which was making promises to its immigrants, external and internal, was at the same time busily engaged in discovering that the immigrants were not and could never be Americans. It was in the beginning of the last quarter of the nineteenth century, contemporary with the New Immigration, that American public spokesmen began to fashion ideology from the idea that America had an essential ethnic identity, namely Western-European and, more specifically, Anglo-Saxon or Nordic or English-speaking.[31] The idea was romantic and fragile, but it came to have the force virtually of public policy, and in the ghetto it had the effect of making retrenchment a virtue. The primary social fact of the ghettos was that, being isolated, they defensively isolated themselves.

In further consequence, they imposed intricate obligations on their young, the fulfillment of which would mean isolation precisely, just as denial would constitute treachery. The true patrimony of the ghetto therefore was guilt, for the manufacture of which the ghetto was perfectly shaped and organized.

The ghetto obliged honor to the old ways, the traditional ways. Those traditional ways, however, not only were conspicuously non-American but also contained very little in the way of substantial history or myth or romance. Tradition, as always, was memorialization of "our old home." In Hawthorne's phrase. But *our* old home was not at all those charming British Isles which Hawthorne had been satisfied to recover, and there was a consequent distinction between Hester Street and Hester Prynne. Home was to the contrary an impoverished county in Ireland or in Mississippi, or it was a *gbernya* somewhere within the shifting frontiers of Russia and Poland, or it was a peasant village on the Hungarian side of Austria-Hungary, or at best it was another ghetto—now in fact all too faithfully reproduced and in a way to make tradition a conspiracy. The discovery of America might well incur two large frustrations, first that there was no America and second that America was a nation of immigrants. So in an apparently autobiographical novel of 1904, *The Fugitive,* by Ezra S. Brudno, the young Russian-Jewish hero describes his arrival in New York in the mid-1880s:

> At length I found myself in the Jewish settlement. I then had no further need for inquiry. The muddy, murky, filthy streets; the squalid tenement blocks, with bedclothes on the fire-escapes and various Hebrew signs dangling beneath them; stooped and sallow-faced creatures with "hurry-up" expression in every feature; the fruit-sellers and fishmongers and hawkers of suspenders and handkerchiefs crying their merchandise—all these proclaimed to me that I had arrived in a new Ghetto. It reminded me of Vilno.[32]

It happens that this fugitive has previously known cultural confusions; his further adventures in New York will now teach him that the confusions which were inherent in the old home are insistences in the new. So, again, in 1917 Marcus Ravage, having become a real American intellectual—he wrote for the *Nation* and the *New Republic*—recalled his immigrant past:

Of that greater and remoter world in which the native resides we immigrants are for a long time hardly aware. What rare flashes of it do come within range of our blurred vision reveal a planet so alien and far removed from our experience that they strike us as merely comical or fantastic—a set of phenomena so odd that we can only smile over them, but never be greatly concerned with them.

I needed sadly to readjust myself when I arrived in New York. But the incredible thing is that my problem was to fit myself in with the people of Vaslui and Rumania, my erstwhile fellow-townsmen and my fellow-countrymen. It was not America in the large sense, but the East Side Ghetto that upset all my calculations, reversed all my values, and set my head swimming.[33]

There might have been some quaintness, at the least, in the odd memorialization of the old home places except that those places were much too close and much too desperately memorialized to be quaint. Certainly, moreover, there was no esteem to be had in America, no glamor, no social subsidy to be gained in considering oneself to be an exile from, say, Vilna or Vaslui, where—furthermore—one's family really had been despised outcastes. There was no allure in dim distant shades of the past.

There was instead the importunate presentness of a construction of the immediate past. In the ghetto, tradition was an intense parochialism, the pretensions of which were largely unjustified by history. The immigrants in the ghettos for the most part had not been foreign nationals in the first place, in the usual sense. Whether from the American South or from southern or eastern Europe, they had not been acknowledged to be citizens. Indeed, in the case of the eastern Europeans, new nationalisms precisely, and attendant persecutions and military conscriptions (especially the so-called May Laws of 1882), had been a large part of the reason for coming to America. Tradition in these circumstances was the imagined refuge of displaced peasants or realienated aliens, but for that reason also—because in fact there was so little to fall back upon—traditionalism was still more important and much more demanding than matters of separate language and accretions of national customs.

The past existed in the present, in effect, much more constrictingly than it had ever existed in the past, when it had been defined by external authority. The new ghetto went far toward defining itself ever more narrowly. There were newspapers in the ghetto, but they were not windows on the world; they devoted large portions of their space to intimate news of the hometown folks one thousand or five thousand miles away. Neighborliness within the ghettos was based largely on hometown ties, as were the institutions of neighborliness, the Associations and Fraternal Orders and Circles and Mutual Aid Societies and saloons and halls and coffeehouses and churches and synagogues. Tradition in these circumstances was not a structure of beliefs or antique wisdom, but a desperate assertion of kinship.

The assertion was continuously reinforced, moreover, because the displacement which had generated it was continuous. The lives of the residents of the urban ghettos in the basic components of daily life—housing arrangements, household budgets—were attached to the demands of the hometown. The episode of the creation of the ghettos lasted a long time, during which time there was a constant incoming flow of cousins and friends of cousins and acquaintances of friends, and total strangers who claimed the hometown tie, all of them having needs, the first of which was a bed but there were no extra beds. Growing up in the ghetto, one was likely to know kinship as something enforced and most exceedingly intimate. The hometowners were in one's home, serially. Nor was there any extra money in the household, but money nonetheless flowed back to the hometown.

Any young person coming of age in the ghetto might know in his bones that there was something preposterous in this assertion of kinship. He was called upon to honor a way of life which had little inherent meaning but which nevertheless was the more intense by the amount that it had no larger relevance. The focus of tradition was a small, backward community off somewhere in another world.

And even insofar as that other place did signify values, these values, as has been observed, most notably by Oscar Handlin, were likely to be ones which most present experience exactly contravened.[34] The other place was likely to have made a virtue of family interdependency; the present experience of the ghetto was a struggle for space. In a situation in which one acre of land was occupied by more than seven hundred persons (as was the case in the Tenth Ward of the Lower East Side of Manhattan in 1900), the claims of second and third and fourth cousins were grotesque. The other place in perhaps most instances was a village or rural hamlet, implying a closeness to nature; in the present experience of America, nature was a sentimentality if not altogether incredible. The old home acknowledged paternal authority; one's own father, in the American ghetto, was likely to be a poor and an intermittent provider, if he was present at all and not usurped by that figure ubiquitous in ghetto fiction, "the boarder." The old home meant communitarianism, while the ghetto, with its crowdedness, filth, disease, and high incidence of crime and insanity, in every way suggested the necessary disintegration of community life.[35] In all instances the old home meant the centrality of religion and consequently a lesser role for material motives. It meant fatalism. It meant stability purchased by obedience, by the acknowledgment of hierarchy, by restricted opportunities and curtailed ambitions, and altogether by a hermetic view of life. But success in America was to be achieved by just the reverse of all of these values. Religion in America was not central, and anyway it was a far different religion in all of its tonalities as well as its dogma. America was materialistic; more immediately to the point, a young person growing up in the ghetto *had* to earn money, and as early as possible, by the measure of which necessity religious idealisms might well seem to be either manifestly hypocritical or hopelessly arcane. The virtues of fatalism, obedience, and stability, meanwhile, were sabotaged at once by the American promise of mobility and by the fact that the one certain choice made by all of those who had come to the ghetto had been their specific rejection of those virtues. The old virtues might be honored—severely honored—in the ghetto, but it was still the case that only the obviously defeated were without desire to escape from them.

Nonetheless, all close relationships conspired to make a young person tradition-minded. One's mother and father and neighbors, and the putative *Landzleute* or the folks from down-home, were necessarily imperative models. Moreover, it had been with all the authority of their real hardships and needs that they had established the range of institutions that would make such a young person a faithful, respectable member of the hamlet, the *gbernya*, the county, or wherever. The authority was not only imperative but ethical.

And indeed, the inheritance proffered by home was still more complicated. A young man growing up in the ghetto was likely to suffer at least three attempts on his cultural definition, not counting whatever was suggested by "America in the large sense," each of them being quite discrete in its demands and all of them being equally impossible. In addition to his hometown-oriented family life, there was school and there was the street, each enforcing quite different criteria of respectability.

The school figured very large and as something more than an academic curriculum. In the case of the internal—black—immigrants, school was the primary agency for a supposed integration with the larger community.[36] In the case of the external immigrants, it was the primary agency for what in the 1910s came to be called "Americanization." In both instances it at once had great authority and was likely greatly to confuse its clients.

For one thing, it was, with all benign goodwill where that existed, an exact counterauthority to everything that family life demanded. Despite some profusion of factory schools and day schools for immigrants and night schools and the efforts of many private social agencies and many private entrepreneurs who went into the schooling-for-immigrants business,[37] the public elementary school throughout the period of the immigrations had de facto charge of integrating or Americanizing not only the children but also their parents. The children were to take their lessons home. The child was to become father to the man, mother to the woman, with consequences which had to be intensely uncomfortable for everybody. So Mary Antin in 1912, reflecting on the process of her Americanization in the ghettos of Boston, inquired rhetorically,

> did I not begin to make my father and mother, as truly as they had ever made me? Did I not become the parent and they the children, in those relations of teacher and learner? . . . In my parents' bewilderment and uncertainty they needs must trust us children to learn from such models as the tenements afforded. More than this, they must step down from their throne of parental authority, and take the law from their children's mouths; for they had no other means of finding out what was good American form. The result was that laxity of domestic organization, that inversion of normal relations which makes for friction, and which sometimes ends in breaking up a family that was formerly united and happy.[38]

Again, in Abraham Cahan's typifying novel of 1917, *The Rise of David Levinsky,* a mother drives herself into learning English so that she will not feel inferior to her school-age daughter.

> "I kept saying to myself, 'She'll grow up and be an educated American lady and she'll be ashamed to walk in the street with me.' Don't we see things like that? People will beggar themselves to send their children to college, only to be treated as fools and greenhorns by them. I call that terrible. Don't you?"

The daughter's grammar school, meanwhile, is the source of everything that is "real Yankee," while everything else is "greenhorn."[39] And this sense of a *necessary* inversion of parent-child relationship, if not always so consciously realized, went very deep. So a Lower East Side play produced in 1926, called *We Americans,* purported "to portray with photographic truth the immigrant Jew who clings to his European traditions and who fails to respond in any marked degree to Americanizing influences." The play was frank propaganda, urging the immigrant parents of Americanized children to attend night school, but it reached a climax of certainly unintended poignance when Mrs. Levine, finally reunited with her daughter, says, "It was our fault. Parents should improve themselves for the sake of their children."[40]

Without anybody's having specifically intended it so, a young person growing up in the ghetto who was conscientious about school was taught to be ashamed of his parents. He was an American, meaning not only that he knew English while his parents probably did not, but also that he was their superior in a set of loyalties. He knew about George Washington and the Fourth of July, and each morning he saluted the flag. Indeed, teachers on the scene seem to have been very much impressed by their students' progress in "patriotism."[41]

For another thing, the sympathetic goodwill of teachers who were doing the daily work of the ghetto schools was not a dependable resource. In the moment in history, the ladies who became public school teachers in the ghettos were likely to be too truly representative of American expectations and mores.[42]

White schoolteachers were not prepared to cope with black children. An investigation in New York City in the years immediately prior to the Great Migration revealed, not surprisingly, that teachers typically knew nothing about the special conditions of the families of their black pupils, and it also revealed that, with some considerable frankness, they did not like the black children in their classes. The teachers felt "degraded."[43] The particular investigation was conducted in the years 1911–15. In 1916 and the years immediately thereafter, those same teachers were the official receivers of masses of black children from the rural South, children who not only were black and rural but were also retarded academically, and who therefore confirmed beliefs to the effect that blacks were lazy, stupid, and generally inferior.[44]

Antecedent prejudices against the eastern Europeans were not necessarily so well defined, but such as they were, they, too, were encouraged. Everybody knew that the fabled intelligence of Jews was a function of their acquisitiveness and that Jews were pushy. So in 1905 J. K. Paulding, an educator whose motives were absolutely benign—he was an educator who in fact was famous for his concern and helpfulness—commented, "The instinct of success, so strong in the Jewish people, accounts for much prize-taking and high standing in the class-room, but for the formation of a finer type of scholarship there is necessary the cultivation of a greater degree of disinterestedness." And again:

> One of the great aims of all education, undoubtedly, is to develop the true individuality of the child; and it is not surprising that but little attention can be devoted to this in the overcrowded class-rooms of our public schools. But sometimes di-

rectly wrong methods are adopted, as when a teacher encour-
ages in a forward or self-conscious child the tendencies that require stimulation in an unduly retiring or modest one. There
seems to be a smaller proportion of bashfulness among Jewish
children than among those of other nationalities, and therefore
less need to have to resort to devices, such as public declama-
tion and quotation-citing, designed to overcome this evil. I have
often been present at such exhibitions in down-town
schoolhouses where the display of vanity and of a certain self-
conscious forwardness inconsistent with the modesty of childhood was painful in the extreme.[45]

Moreover, among the many things lacking in the households of these
immigrant children were, as a usual matter, toilets. (A report published
in 1903 stated that 20 percent of the tenement-house apartments in New
York City had water closets. The usual arrangement was a water closet
in the hall or in the cellar, or a "school sink"—that is, a multiseated
privy—in the yard, which incidentally abutted on the next tenement.)
Nor was washing an easy matter. In 1902, a survey indicated, only 8
percent of the Russian Jews of the Lower East Side of New York had
apartments with baths, not necessarily with hot water, and at the same
time, according to another report, there was a woeful insufficiency of
public bath facilities.[46] These children were dirty—perhaps less so than
the children of some other nationalities, as was sometimes pointed out,
but dirty nonetheless. They had an odor. They had vermin. Teachers,
as missionaries from civilization, found themselves having to wash
these children first of all, and then, time permitting, to teach them
rudiments and right attitudes.[47] Willing and apt as the children might
be, furthermore, their teachers could not but know that they were
among heathen. There was little hope of appeal to the understanding of
the parents, although authority might be invoked. Coming to school
each morning, these teachers put themselves in a place where, as they
could not help but know, *they* were different; they were *Krisht* while
the children were natives.[48] For one who was a missionary, it followed
that, as one might have suspected, the eastern Europeans generally
were physically offensive, morally recalcitrant, and latently defiant.

The schools were, despite everything, very effective and teaching
did occur, but when it did, what was taught, beyond the rudiments, was
a right attitude which might well begin in insult and end in impressive,
incongruous pieties, small and large. In Anzia Yezierska's autobiographical novel of 1925, *Bread Givers,* the little girl who is yearning for
and on her way to the promise of the real America reflects in an instance, "The school teacher's rule, 'A place for everything, and

everything in its place,' was no good for us, because there weren't enough places."[49] In larger measure, immigration prompted the invention of "Americanization," and Americanization in turn prompted invention of a set of terms by which America could be regarded as having some kind of predefinition. The terms of the predefinition were potentially meaningful, obviously, by the amount that they distinguished Americans from immigrants. If the immigrants were eastern and southern Europeans, then it followed that America was by genealogical definition western and northern European. (Northeastern Europeans—Finns—might have presented a problem, but did not. In the 1920s a St. Paul district attorney argued that Finns were not to be allowed American citizenship because "a Finn...is a Mongolian and not a 'white person.'")[50] The immigrants were "illiterate, docile, lacking in self-reliance and initiative," in the words of Professor Ellwood P. Cubberly of Stanford, writing in 1909, and they did not possess "the Anglo-Teutonic conceptions of law, order, and government." It was therefore the task of education, he said, to implant in the children of the immigration "the Anglo-Saxon conception of righteousness, law and order.[51] "It cannot be emphasized too strongly or repeated too often," said Peter Roberts, Ph.D., writing in the lyric year of 1912, "that we must look to Americans for the preservation of American civilization. There is no holier duty, no more sacred mission given to the heirs of the founders of this democracy than that of transmitting in its integrity the heritage of ethnic endowment gained by the white men through generations of struggle, toil, and suffering."[52] Roberts, it should be said, seems by the testimony of his book to have been a man who was genuinely concerned for the plight of the new immigrants and emphatically liberal in his attitudes. He seems to have been challenging an ensconced scholarship which did not allow even the possibility that these aliens might be integrated into American life. In 1901 Woodrow Wilson, for particular instance, in the final volume of his monumental *History of the American People,* had reflected monumentally on just this matter of American ethnic identity and the present danger thereto. Speaking of the immigration of the 1890s, he had said:

> Immigrants poured steadily in as before, but with an alteration
> of stock which students of affairs marked with uneasiness.
> Throughout the century men of the sturdy stocks of the north of
> Europe had made up the main strain of foreign blood which was
> every year added to the vital working force of the country, or
> else men of the Latin-Gallic stocks of France and northern Italy;
> but now there came multitudes of men of the lowest class from
> the south of Italy and men of the meaner sort out of Hungary

and Poland, men out of the ranks where there was neither skill nor energy nor any initiative of quick intelligence; and they came in numbers which increased from year to year, as if the countries of the south of Europe were disburdening themselves of the more sordid and hapless elements of their population.[53]

"Americanization" was a necessity, officially sanctioned and formulated and imposed, but at the same time basically so defined as to be a flat contradiction. Real Americans were a different people. It followed logically and in fact that the immigrant who did accept the imposition of Americanization invited contempt from both immigrants and Americans, for the more urgent or even distinguished his perform- ance as an American, the more obvious that he was aping a manner and adopting a history to neither of which he had any inherent right. On the one hand, on the Lower East Side the largest and the most energetic of the voluntary missionizing institutions was the Educational Alliance, founded in 1893. It was hugely successful in terms of the numbers of its clients, the volume and variety of its activities, and the careers of some of its Americanized graduates (ranging from Morris Raphael Cohen to David Sarnoff to Arthur Murray), and on the Lower East Side it was ridiculed. So the *Jewish Daily Forward* reported a Thanksgiving cere- mony conducted by the Alliance's director, Dr. David Blaustein:

> He gathered over fifty *green* children, put them on the stage, gave each one an American flag and paraded them on the stage like monkeys.... Blaustein told the greeners to raise their heads toward the flag on the stage and repeat a declaration of loyalty. The *Greeners* then marched on the stage several times, and Blaustein explained to them the significance of Thanksgiving Day and called on them to observe it in every detail, even up to the eating of turkeys which they have not got.[54]

On the other hand, one of the most successful careers in Americaniza- tion was that of Mary Antin. She was a girl from Plotzk, and she came to have the respect and the aid of established letters in America. Her particular sponsor was none less than Barrett Wendell, a man nobly liberal in his attitudes toward both literature and immigrants. But after all, in both instances, he was liberal only up to a point, and he did complain of Antin's habit "of describing herself and her people as Americans, in distinction from such folks as Edith and me who have been here for three hundred years."[55]

"Americanization" was not an imposition only; it was also an issue. There was another party to the debate, including spokesmen for immigrants' groups who advanced the melting-pot idea of American civilization. But this latter party was not likely to be doing the job of teaching the children of the immigrants in the public schools, and those who did do the job were in every probability likely to insinuate a remarkably remote formulation of the higher, or the essential, American civilization.

Their lesson in the all-important matter of literacy, in particular, in all goodwill, was that the high literature of the Americans was mostly British, and so even was the proper language of the Americans. American literature in general was distinctly low-caste. (As was the opinion generally. It was not until the turn of the century, when Barrett Wendell offered a series of lectures at Harvard, that American literature had any academic recognition whatsoever.) Appropriately enough, American literature was for the greatest part left to be the discovery of the immigrants themselves, among the Russian Jews through the ghetto press and theater and educational alliances. William Dean Howells was translated in the Yiddish-language journals of the Lower East Side (along with such other foreigners as Flaubert, Zola, Tolstoy, and Turgenev).[56] Mark Twain was dramatized. In the autobiography he called *An American Testament,* Joseph Freeman, a first-generation son of immigrant parents, was to remember that the first American book he read when he was growing up in the Williamsburg section of Brooklyn was *The Last of the Mohicans,* which he read in Hebrew translation. At school, however, in the same moment he was learning *Stepping Stones to Literature* and "an English so pure, so lofty, so poetic that it seemed to bear no relation to the language of the street." Of course it also bore no relationship to the language—Yiddish—spoken in his home. When he began to write poems, he said, "I suddenly realized that my parents could not read them."[57] And the evidence quite aside from Freeman's direct testament is that his subsequent literary career was a long, difficult, and ideologically confusing retreat from *Stepping Stones to Literature.*

And then there was the street, where—vide Freeman—still another language was used and where a different citizenship was adumbrated, which did not mediate between school and home. The street had its own demanding cultural criteria. The street was a metaphor for territory. It was something to be possessed and defended, and sometimes extended. Since the urban ghetto was in fact a warren of ghettos, one's own street—meaning one or two city blocks—was likely to have an ethnic definition created by the ethnic differences of the neighboring streets. Children organize into gangs. With lesser and greater degrees of organization, some quite intricate and formal, the purpose of the gangs was to fight other gangs from other streets. The street therefore was the place where ethnic warfare was most candid. In Chicago, where the ghetto stretched in a semicircular zone around the downtown Loop, the children from "Pojay Town" fought the children from "Dago Town," who fought the "Coons from Lake Street," who fought the "Mickies," who fought the "Jews from Twelfth Street," and so on, with assorted Slavs, Swedes, Bohemians, Germans, and Lithuanians participating.[58] New York's Lower East Side was by 1890 an eastern-European Jewish ghetto in large predominance, but within the concentrated area there were also Italian and Irish ghettos, and the Jews themselves were divided, geographically, between Hungarians, Galicians, Rumanians, Russo-Poles, Lithuanians, Byelorussians, Ukrainians, and so on.[59] The Ridge-Streeters (Galicians) fought with the Chrystie-Streeters (Rumanians), and everybody fought with the Italians and the Irish. The war was still going on some twenty-five years later, according to a memoirist:

> On Cherry Street, we grew up with our fists—the Jewish boys fighting the Poles, the Poles the Irish, the Irish the Italians, and all of them usually against the Jews.... When it was not purely racist, it was often terribly mixed up as to why the Micks were fighting the Sheenies—or we were all cooperating against the Wops.... We loaded our stocking hats with glass and stones and charged away, slugging until a dozen kids were left sprawled and bleeding in the gutters—their eyes half-blinded, their arms or legs broken—and we were gone when the cops arrived with the ambulances from Gouverneur Hospital. When the losers had recuperated, the violence—everything short of murder—was on again.[60]

Not that the warfare was constant, but the danger was. The street organized children for battle. A boy growing up in the ghetto was perforce loyal to his own one or two city blocks. He did not wander elsewhere if he could help it, because the neighboring gangs would beat him up.

And the street might offer rewards for good citizenship much more tangible, much more vivid than could be had from any other cultural agency. Although education did tender promise, despite everything, and although a young man might aspire to individuality through great achievement perhaps in sports[61] or in music, a more obvious way was through politics and the rackets, both of which were come to through the neighborhood gangs. Crime of the shopkeeping variety—gambling and prostitution—was familiar neighborhood enterprise,[62] for the simple reason that it could secure better concealment in the ghetto than elsewhere. The more affluent, and violent, enterprise of

labor racketeering was indigenous to the ghetto; it was a ghetto business and did some service. Labor bosses or contractors were men who
knew English and had connections, and thereby got jobs for their
clients and also monopolized labor markets. Recruitment in the various
enterprises was from the gangs. The various entrepreneurs were able to
do favors and were able therefore to deliver votes; hence they were
political leaders. And they were attractive. Dominating their neighborhoods, they were in a measure outside the curtailment and in-
timidation of the ghetto; by selling the ghetto, they in a measure had
escaped from it. They had influence in high places.[63] By so much they
participated in a larger world. At the same time they participated fully
in the small community and were likely to be exemplars of the old
hometown virtues. They had an allure, not with any necessity connected with violence. And their invitation was not to be easily denied.
So Mike Gold was to recall, in *Jews without Money,* that one of the two
models of success in his Lower East Side neighborhood was Harry the
Pimp. "People envied him. He had a big pull with Tammany Hall. He
owned a gambling house, and spoke perfect English."[64] The other
model of success was Jake Wolf, the saloonkeeper. So, looking from
the top at the same scene in the same moment, the racketeer-hero of
Samuel Ornitz's *Haunch Paunch and Jowl* reflects:

> As I pass it seems as though the very tenements bow in def-
> erence. The pushcart peddlers humbly tip their hats. I am their
> protector and advisor. The gang greets me as boss. . . . Business
> men greet me, respectfully, as their accelerator in certain affairs.
> Everywhere I meet respect and gratitude. The bearded orthodox
> *schule* people praise my faithful attendance and the way I serve
> the *schule* and the poor.

And he will end up in "*Allrightnicks* Row, Riverside Drive."[65]

Ornitz's book particularly, it may be added, illuminates and was
capstone to an inside knowledge of the promise of the street, in measure just because the validity of the book as memoir was somewhat
suspect. Subtitled "An Anonymous Autobiography," it was supposedly an edited version of the autobiography of a New York City
politician. The matter of authenticity was attested and sworn to by the
publisher, Horace Liveright,[66] but the politician was never identified;
moreover, Ornitz's own politics might well have dictated an amount of
exposé at the expense of truth. The book was unremittingly cynical.
But if untrue in its specific reference, it did have its mythic credibility;
it romanticized and essentialized a general knowledge. Ornitz's hero,
Meyer Hirsch, begins his rise in life at the age of nine, when he is

accepted into the Ludlow Street Gang. He becomes a strategist in wars with the (Jewish) Essex Street Guerrillas and with the (Irish) Jackson Street Gang. At the age of ten he sells protection to shopkeepers. Later, as a law student, he sells the services of his gang to Tammany Hall. He organizes the pushcart peddlers. He organizes the hoodlums who will in effect control the unions of the garment industry. And so forth, until he is judge of the Superior Criminal Court of New York.

Some such in general was the knowledge that the children of the barbarians brought to the writing of literature.

Not, of course, that the typical experience would have been anybody's complete experience. The ghetto itself, if it was ingenious in establishing institutions which confirmed cultural isolation, also invented institutions which had an opposite implication. In New York's Lower East Side, in particular, there was from the earliest period of the immigration an availability of culture in the formal sense. There were literary societies, which had a social function but also a literary function. There were libraries. There was a publishing and translating industry. There was the Yiddish theater, which was in great part tawdry and banal and mawkish, in a word provincial, but which also offered in its standard and popular repertoire adaptations—sometimes peculiar—of Molière and Tolstoy and Schiller and Shakespeare.[67] The theater of the Lower East Side reached beyond itself, moreover; throughout the period of the immigration it established branches in the serially newer Yiddish ghettos in Brownsville, Harlem, and the Bronx, as well as in Philadelphia, Newark, Cleveland, Detroit, and Chicago. And even, perhaps especially, in its lower forms, in vaudeville and burlesque, the theater breached the ghetto precisely by parodying the cultural discordance of ghetto life; such was the probable implication of coon songs and of the tunes of Smith and Dale (née Sulzer and Marks).[68]

And the particularities of individual experiences were of course heterogeneously particular. Even Michael Gold, who in *Jews without Money* was to publish the exemplary Lower East Side novel of the 1930s, was not in all specific detail the child of the ghetto whom, through his protagonist, he pretended to be. At least by the standards of the Lower East Side just prior to the turn of the century, Gold's family was well off and cultivated. Other writers from other places had their other particularities of intimate background. Nathanael West, Gold's younger contemporary and occasional friend, was the son of Russian-Jewish immigrants, but his family lived in the Upper West Side of New York and was affluent by any standards. Daniel Fuchs grew up in Williamsburg in Brooklyn, but in a neighborhood within

Williamsburg which he was to identify as being a new one. James Farrell, a second-generation American, was the son of parents who could not afford him, but he was boarded out with grandparents who did have some money, and he grew up in a social geography which, in successive moves, was always just on the edge of the ghetto proper. Jack Conroy (according to the evidence of his autobiographical novel, *The Disinherited*) was the son of an Irish immigrant, but he grew up in a mining camp which, despite crudities and hardships, had some nearness to rural countryside. Richard Wright, who in *Native Son* was to publish the exemplary novel of the Chicago Black Belt, was already nineteen years old when he came to Chicago, and Langston Hughes, who in the "Simple" series was to propose the authentic, domestic, intimate voice of Harlem, was nineteen when he first arrived in New York, having been born in Joplin, Missouri, and having lived in half a dozen places in the Midwest and in Mexico.

And of course the amounts of the individual separatenesses from the ghetto typicality did matter. But in an America divided culturally between new aristocrats and new immigrants, the ghetto was a given, and it was the ultimate home of all of these latter—including even Nathanael West, to note the most complicated instance. (The fact of West's peculiar and studied anti-Semitism implicated him.) West perhaps excluded, they did recognize that given condition, moreover, in the most obvious of ways. The inheritance of the ghetto was their fundamental subject. The ghetto might be seen in its blatancies or in its ironies, might be studied as socioeconomic instance (vide Richard Wright) or experienced as fatality (vide Henry Roth, *Call It Sleep*), might be denied or celebrated. Whatever the individualities of attitude, however, the ghetto was the distinction these writers had. It was their subject. They tended, in fact, to suppress individualities of attitude for the sake, precisely, of typicality. It is one of the peculiarities of the fiction they wrote that their protagonists have little personality, little of such a sense of prior definition as is in, say, Hemingway's Jake Barnes, but are defined by the exemplary social experience. It is a peculiarity of the same significance in these writers that they tended to write about the growing-up—the emigration, as it were—of children and adolescents.

It happened also that within the peculiar given there were hidden some riches, some special means of access to America in general. History conspired. These writers were of a generation, all of them born in the 1890s or in the first decade after the turn of the century. They all secured their varied amounts of major recognition in one certain and significant decade: Michael Gold published *Jews without Money* in

1930, Richard Wright published *Native Son* in 1940. They achieved their major reputations at that time in the national history when the subject they had had from their beginnings, in the 1900s–1920s, was suddenly of general relevance. Their relationships to the American or to the Western past had been entirely dubious, but these writers held altogether a peculiarly native place in what was to be the major event of history in the 1930s. When the Depression came along, they were ready for it, having had their experience. Moreover, they had an amount of current closeness to the Depression which others were not likely to have. The 13 million people who were to be out of work shortly after the Crash in October 1929 were in the main just those urban immigrants from whom these writers secured identification. In the new circumstances, poverty was no longer merely a tug on conscience (as Jacob Riis, for instance, had made it to be), nor quaint (as Israel Zangwill, writing for the most part about London, had made it to be), nor a betrayal of higher things (vide Abraham Cahan), nor such a source of lonely bravado as it had been when, in 1923, Anzia Yezierska, the Russian-Jewish immigrant and novelist, had declared, "I stand on solid ground when I write of the poor, the homeless, and the hungry."[69] Poverty was now a plausible universal, and therefore for a writer poverty was wealth. It was a subject-matter, validated by the enormous factuality of the Depression, to which these writers had an inside track. Poverty was even an aesthetic justification.

For others the factuality of the Depression might come to be a confrontation with art. So it was to be for Wallace Stevens, for conveniently specific example, in *Owl's Clover* in 1936. Stevens, with severe honesty, found himself having to grope for a conception that would reconcile art of the tradition (the "tradition" much in Eliot's sense) with the abrupt happening of beggared masses. The primary emblems of his poem, a statue in a public park on one hand and a destitute old woman on the other, posed for Stevens an absolute discordance. The statue's sculptor had foreseen and defined much, "But her he had not foreseen: the bitter mind / In a flapping cloak." In her presence, "The mass of stone collapsed to marble hulk." And it cannot be said that in his final postulate in the poem, of a kind of Ur-imagination, Stevens found the true principle that would make the two congenial. (Apparently he did not himself think that he had succeeded. He never reprinted the poem in its original version.)[70] But that old woman, putatively "black by thought that could not understand," could herself, ironically, have had a much more succinct idea of what was the meaning of art. From the perspective over on her side of the proposed discordance, art was the assertion of current reality, in the most immediate, obvious, and forthright sense. She had unassailable presence and meaning. The old woman, in her circumstances, was herself art. By the given of current history, she exemplified, not perhaps the eternal will of things, but the truth of things exactly as they were, in time and place. Being poor, she was authoritative.

For those who knew her, it should be said, she was also imperious. Stevens's old woman addressed Stevens, specifically and by his own statement, as "a symbol of those who suffered during the depression".[71] She made demands on a man of conscience. For the others, however, she was kith and kin, undeniable in any time but most especially now in this hour of her special humiliation. She was conspicuously needy. She demanded intimate sympathy, even while her poverty turned out to be a valuable legacy.

And history conspiring, there were riches in the ghetto beyond poverty. The ghetto was suddenly the opposite of itself. It became an American archetype.

It had been a rabble of individuals in transit to America or a swarm in process of being dissipated, however slowly or recalcitrantly, into the general life of America. America-in-the-large-sense had demanded Americanization, no matter that the term was so ambiguous or that America also established formidable barriers to assimilation. The essential business of the immigrants, on their side, had been to try to become Americans, no matter with what recalcitrance or frustrations. (So, around 1910, the Yiddish-language *Forward* had been publishing instructions on the game of baseball. So the makers of Yiddish fiction and poetry in America had received special acclaims for writing about the American South, the American prairie, and tennis.)[72] In all logic and seeming inevitability, the future of the ghetto had always been upward and outward, up toward wealth and out into a presumed mainstream. The Depression reversed the future, however. Now, from the perspective from the bottom, the poverty of the ghetto was a seeming ineluctability and the way of life of the ghetto might seem to be fatally stabilized. From the perspective from above, the Depression made the ghetto seem to be, not of course a goal, but a root definition. The Depression meant in general, and enormously, a shutting down of private anticipations. Not everyone was poor, but poverty was much more perceptible than it had ever been before and much more a matter for individual contemplating. The poor were no longer the forgotten poor. They had the appearance—and the glamour, too, as it turned out—of destiny.

With the general canceling of expectation of reward for private initiative, the poor were transformed from a rabble into a class. They were no longer assorted Rumanians and Poles and blacks and Sicilians and Lithuanian Jews, but "the people." They were therefore accessible to literary, and ideological, construction. For a writer emergent from the milieu, all of that alien and polyglot value which home had represented could now be defended, generalized, and *used,* even while conscience demanded that it be honored. All of America could now be seen in terms of the ghetto, as a broad land populated everywhere by discrete clusters of the despised aliens. These latter could be seen, indeed, to be more native than the natives. They constituted not merely a class, after all, but the working class, on whom everything depended[73]—and it was also a fact easily accessible to recognition, after all, that all of the old natives really were immigrants. America was *essentially* polyglot. It had been demanded that the immigrants become Americans; now by the new dispensation Americans could be transformed into immigrants.

In any event it did happen that a great amount of the literature which was to be written during and just after the years of the Depression took for its concern the American-ness of non-Americans or, what amounted to the same material for drama, of "forgotten Americans"—the irony being registered in such titles as Richard Wright's *Native Son,* Sherwood Anderson's *Puzzled America* and *Hometown,* Theodore Dreiser's *Tragic America,* Louise Armstrong's *We Too Are the People,* Erskine Caldwell's *Say! Is This the U.S.A.?* and *Some American People,* Paul S. Taylor's *An American Exodus,* Nathan Asch's *The Road: In Search of America,* Eleanor Roosevelt's *This Is America,* Benjamin Appel's *The People Talk,* James Agee's *Let Us Now Praise Famous Men,* Walker Evans's *American Photographs,* Louis Adamic's *My America,* Joseph Freeman's *An American Testament,* the WPA's *These Are Our Lives,* and the Federal Writers' Project's *American Stuff.*[74] The point in all of these, as in literally hundreds of other plays, pamphlets, poems, "reportages," novels, movies, stories, and popular songs, was that the characters being memorialized were the true Americans, first appearances to the contrary: these were ghetto blacks, midwestern "bohunks," Lower East Side Jews, or the rural poor of the South, and so forth, and altogether they were the people.

Incipient in the heritage of the ghetto there was also one authentically revolutionary idea, even according to T. S. Eliot's definition of a revolutionary idea as a requirement for the reorganization of the mind. The culture that had been formulated by the great modernists had enabled them to propose the idea of an elite against the presumption of a rabble. The function of the rabble was to despoil; that of the elite was to conserve, and since the despoilment was an occurrence in history, it was a function of the elite to deny history. When on the other hand the rabble itself could be conceived to be a culture—and not only that, but the basic, emblematic integer of society—then an entirely different aesthetic was required. The idea that came into being, affecting literature and politics and entertainments and graphic arts, and every form of expression, was that of a mass, or, in a modulation of the same thing, a folk. The mass became "tradition." Certainly there was irony in that because within contemporary history the masses were a field full of Sweeneys and Bleisteins, and the irony was the greater because the idea of the mass could be seen *almost* by definition to be the same thing as the idea of democracy, which latter was the *American* "tradition" if anything was.

This other idea of the tradition had in fact not gone unrecognized as a justification for the making of literature. It had been asserted and explored quite during the time of the growing-up of the children of the barbarians, by authentic (English-speaking, second- and third- and fifth-generation) Americans, and when Itzok Granich, for instance, was ready to enter literature, there was a strictly American and contemporary body of instructions available to him.

two

Tradition on the Left

"Modernism" was one response to the dislocations of modern history in America, but it was not unique in its conveying of an apprehension of a changed situation for literature. Ezra Pound and T. S. Eliot wonderfully exploited but did not create the moment of opportunity, nor was the excitement transmitted exclusively by the passionate little journals of modernist experiment—*Poetry* (by the amount of Pound's influence on it), the *Dial, Little Review, transatlantic review, Broom,* and their like. "Modernism" was a tacit concordance of attitudes—not a movement or a school—taking shape within a larger context of cultural challenge and possibilities, which context also encouraged another set of literary attitudes, once again diverse in many particulars and not constituting a school or a movement, but certainly different. The sense of the necessity for a new literary enterprise, incurring new forms, new responsibilities, new dignities, and a new tradition, was available to quite other formulation.

These other attitudes were distinguishable at the least by their oppositeness. The participants in the Pound Era nominated themselves to be conservators of the grand western European cultural past, and not incidentally they were conservatives in their social and political choices—fascists, some of the best of them, when the crunch came. On the other side were such writers and critics as Van Wyck Brooks, Paul Rosenfeld, Lewis Mumford, Waldo Frank, Sherwood Anderson, Randolph Bourne, Max Eastman, Floyd Dell, John Reed, and others, who created and sustained such journals as *Seven Arts,* the *Freeman, Modern Quarterly,* the *Masses,* the *Liberator,* and then latterly and for a short while *New Masses.* They, too, were engaged in creating a tradition—in fabricating a past from random oddments of history, that is to say, which might sanction and direct present aspirations. While they among themselves (people and journals) assumed separate, sometimes merely accidental associations, they had in common first of all a commitment to an American rather than a Western culture, and then not incidentally they all considered themselves to be socialists. "Modernism" tended inevitably to the right; these others formed a literary left and an alternative of very considerable presence. From an Eliotic point of view they were hopelessly provincial, but these provincials did create a version of tradition so sufficiently expansive as not only to allow but also to encourage the participation of current barbarians, who could be conceived to be a new American generation.

VAN WYCK BROOKS

The maker and finder was the young Van Wyck Brooks. He was of the generation of Pound and Eliot—born in 1886, thus a few months younger than Pound, a couple of years older than Eliot. Like them, he came from a very old, pre-Revolutionary American family, which in this time was aware of its own history, was secure in its place and its manners and its comforts, yet aware of intimations of change. Like Pound and Eliot, and presumably impelled by motives similar to theirs, Brooks was an early seeker after a version of history which later, with a nice precision, he was to call a "usable past." What he discovered, however, and somewhat despite his own apparent intentions, was not an "ideal order" but a historical dynamics, a tradition in the shape of a set of active contradictions. It happened for reasons not ever likely to be known fully that the discovery was not finally sustaining for Brooks himself; when he was in his mid-forties he was to begin anew, this time writing about the history of American letters in terms of a mild pastoral which contained neither radical antinomies nor lasting monuments.[1] The earlier tradition did, however, prove to be eminently usable by many others.

The important discovery came very early and prior to the published activities of Pound and Eliot. In 1908 in his first book, *The Wine of the Puritans,* Brooks was already broaching the matter of tradition as the primary problem for contemporary American writers: "As for originality," he said, in a vocabulary which was not merely echoed but virtually repeated by Eliot a decade later, "it seems to me that all true originality immediately reconciles itself with tradition, has in itself the elements of tradition, and is really the shadow of tradition thrown across the future. The proof of new ideas is that they become traditional in exact ratio to their vitality."[2] Unlike Eliot, however, Brooks found in that realization not a goal or a propriety, but rather a dilemma. Assuming without question that the locale of tradition for an American writer was in the American past, he turned to that past and saw only Puritanism. The American artist could not falsify by pretending to a tradition which was not his own. Great and lasting work might be produced "only out of the materials which exist in him by instinct and which constitute racial fibre, the accretion of countless generations of ancestors, trained to one deep, local, indigenous attitude toward life."[3] But Puritanism was, simply, not enough. It had not been adequate to create a civilization broader than that of provincial New England.

Lacking any other genuine American past, what then? Brooks's paradoxical, rather whimsical resolution of the dilemma in this instance was to advise his American contemporaries to become founding fathers. Somehow, without being self-conscious about their activity, they were to sacrifice themselves to establishing a tradition which later generations might enjoy.

But the formula of resolution did not exhaust the implication that was in Brooks's discovery. Quite contrary to the stated objective, Brooks was not really engaged in examining the Puritan tradition for its potential usefulness; he was, rather, attacking a certain kind of American traditionalism: that which, precisely, was associated with New England, claimed the Puritan inheritance, and was defined by a genteel snobbery which was patently irrelevant to American life in the twentieth century. By negative implication, then, but also forthrightly, Brooks defined the general area in which the *usable* tradition might be discovered. It was not to be found in Boston. The tradition was—had to be—immanent in the actualities of American life. The usable tradition would be one which, when discovered, would be concordant with and would explain such facts as the imperialist expansion westward, prosperity, cosmopolitanism, and also the fact that "nations of foreigners came to our ports desiring to be called American." It would acknowledge the cultural possibilities of all of that America which was most foreign to New England. "I think a day will come when the names of Denver and Sioux City will have a traditional and antique dignity like Damascus and Perugia—and when it will not seem to us grotesque that they have."[4] And this usable past would have the advantage—although Brooks did not quite say so much—that it would make comprehensible, and that it would sanction, and that it would give mythic stature to the vulgate realities of present American life.

As was always to be the case, Brooks's diagnosis was much more pertinent than the projected cure, but indeed the diagnosis was the thing which was sought. It put forth the dynamics of a social history for American writers and thereby created a possibility for relating writers to contemporary American society. Brooks did not in fact entirely reject what he took to be the Puritan inheritance, but in this early essay he constructed a vital opposition to it, composed of some of the lowlier elements of American life. The implications were galvanic, perhaps even revolutionary. No less than that tradition which was to be discovered by Pound and Eliot, Brooks's conception established a

moral base for assault on the inherited culture, but with the difference
that moral authority was seen to have a social definition.

Hereafter, until the mid-1930s, Brooks was to explore the opportunities for literature inherent in that authority, assembling a significant
following as he did so. So in "America's Coming-of-Age" in 1915, he
essentially repeated the argument of *The Wine of the Puritans*, but he
sharpened the argument by naming the *two* American inheritances;
"Highbrow" and "Lowbrow." Once again he projected an equable
resolution, this time by calling on the example of Walt Whitman, but
once again his real achievement was the conception of an adversary
dynamics in American culture. In effect he reminded Highbrows of the
equal existence of Lowbrows, thus to put intellectuals in touch with the
context of society. "If something vibrates in the air, it is without doubt
the expectation of a social ideal that shall act upon us as the sun acts
upon a photographic plate, that shall work as a magnet upon all these
energies which are on the point of being released." And it was to be the
invigorating task of intellectuals to locate and define the field of force,
and even more, perhaps, to imagine it. "Issues that make the life of a
society do not spring spontaneously out of the mass. They exist in it—a
thousand potential currents and crosscurrents; but they have to be
discovered like principles of science, they have almost to be created
like works of art." What, then, was to be achieved, was a sense of deep
cleavage in American life, and with that sense an opportunity to take
sides.[5]

Here and hereafter, Brooks's name for the social ideal was
"socialism." It was a term he never defined with any exactness, so as
to convey the idea of a particular form of political organization.
Nonetheless he did use it frequently. It signified not a distinct politics
but rather an insistence on the relatedness of modern social movements
to literary practice. The models from the past whom he invoked most
frequently were not "writers" at all, or if writers, then only incidentally: Nietzsche, Renan, William Morris, Rodin, Marx, and John
Stuart Mill. They were the great rebels who, "revolting against the
facts of their environment, kept alive the tradition of a great society."
It was the function of the contemporary American writer to be of their
company. "For poets and novelists and critics are the pathfinders of
society; to them belongs the vision without which the people perish."
And if Brooks did not mean "socialism," exactly, when he spoke the
name—he was far removed from the actual sectarian politics of the
1910s and 1920s—he did mean in every literal way that the poet's goal
was not the poem but the good society. "Socialism" was a term of
convenience, but it was not merely a metaphor. However vaguely
addressed, the appeal was to a conception of poetry as a social instru-

ment. Therein was the glory and the challenge of literary life. More particularly, poetry was the device which would create a humane civilization from the materials of the industrial age. Poetry was therefore progressive, liberal, involved within a general social ferment. The younger generation, Brooks would say, "have been taught to speak a certain language in common by the social movements of the last twenty years." Again, the dream and the necessity of Young America was "to live creatively, to live completely, to live in behalf of some great corporate purpose."[6]

It is true that intricate with Brooks's progressivism was a romantic nostalgia for an ideal past, as it is true that his Americanism had much to do with his romantic idea of the richer European civilizations,[7] but still his response to these preconceptions ended in his joining literature to a broad contemporary social effort. He would say about H. G. Wells that "socialism is to him at bottom an artistic idea."[8] To the same degree of truth—somewhat limited, certainly—art was for Brooks at bottom a socialist idea.

Brooks represented not merely an alternative to the right wing of modernism. For one thing, modernism was still in its incipience in the time of his early career. The enemy was not yet T. S. Eliot, whom indeed he later came to despise, but the orthodoxy represented variously by Stuart Sherman, and by Paul Elmer More and Irving Babbitt—"the somewhat repellent writings of Messrs. More and Babbitt."[9] Far from being a mere alternative, however, for a number of important years—from about 1915 until the early part of the 1920s—Brooks was the most prominent critic in America and the recognized captain of a distinct party. As late as 1924 Edmund Wilson, in a mock dialogue between Brooks and F. Scott Fitzgerald, while he derogated the legitimacy of Brooks's role as a spokesman, acknowledged still that Brooks was the authoritative possessor of American literature. ("I suppose," says a wide-eyed and suppliant Fitzgerald, "you must know more about American literature than anybody else in the world, don't you?")[10] For the while of his prominence, Brooks was the undisputed leader of Young America, a party which included, among others, Alfred Stieglitz, Waldo Frank, Paul Rosenfeld, Sherwood Anderson, Lewis Mumford, and Randolph Bourne. And it is of some significance that with the exception of Anderson, none of these persons who were most closely associated with Brooks took literature to be their primary domain of activity. The composite field of their interests included photography, painting, history, anthropology, music, architecture, city planning, technology in general, philosophy, social service, and politics. The common aim demanded at least so much diversity; the aim, in the words of one of Frank's titles, was *The Re-Discovery of America.*

Nothing less. The rediscovery of America was to be conducted in behalf, moreover, of a new generation, in all of its traditionalism quite conscious of a break with the past and in revolt against the Americans of—in the words of one of Randolph Bourne's titles—"This Older Generation."

So Mumford would end his study of American letters and culture, *The Golden Day,* saying:

> We must rectify the abstract framework of ideas which we have used, in lieu of a full culture, these last few centuries. . . . To take advantage of our experience and our social heritage and to help in creating this new idolum is not the smallest adventure our generation may know. It is more imaginative than the dreams of the transcendentalists, more practical than the work of the pragmatists, more drastic than the criticisms of the old social revolutionists, and more deeply cultural than all our early attempts to possess the simulacra of culture. It is nothing less than the effort to conceive a new world.
> *Allons! the road is before us!*[11]

And so Randolph Bourne, the most impassioned, the most radical, and by dint of personality the youngest member of Young America, would call forth a new generation of dedicated malcontents:

> These malcontents will be more or less of the American tribe of talent who used either to go immediately to Europe, or starved submissively at home. But these people will neither go to Europe, nor starve submissively. They are too much entangled emotionally in the possibilities of American life to leave it, and they have no desire whatever to starve. So they are likely to go ahead beating their heads at the wall until they are either bloody or light appears. They will give offense to their elders who cannot see what all the concern is about, and they will hurt the more middle-aged sense of adventure upon which the better integrated minds of the younger generation will have compromised. . . . A more skeptical, malicious, desperate, ironical mood may actually be the sign of more vivid and more stirring life fermenting in America to-day.[12]

Their note was sounded again and again, and when Ezra Pound greeted the American *Risorgimento* of the years following 1912, he was in fact recognizing an effect largely created by the Young Americans. "Renaissance" was the more obvious label for the goal they sought, or, more accurately, for the general social ferment in which they believed themselves involved, but in any event they shared at least equally with the modernist movement in the singular mobilization of energies of the 1910s and 1920s. More to the point, nationalists though they were, they allowed a sense of range and breadth, a sense of large participation, in their celebration of the new energies. So one of the initial journals in which they gathered, the *Seven Arts,* began its short life (November 1916–October 1917) by announcing:

> It is our faith and the faith of many, that we are living in the first days of a renascent period, a time which means for America the coming of that national self-consciousness which is the beginning of greatness. In all such epochs the arts cease to be private matters; they become not only the expression of the national life but a means to its enhancement.
>
> It is the aim of *The Seven Arts* to become a channel for the flow of these new tendencies: an expression of our American arts which shall be fundamentally an expression of our American life.
>
> We have no tradition to continue; we have no school of style to build up. What we ask of the writer is simply self-expression. . . .
>
> In short, *The Seven Arts* is not a magazine for artists, but an expression of artists for the community.[13]

Like the manifestos of the dozens of other little magazines of the "epoch," the statement hedged on specifics. Nonetheless it implied an attitude toward the cultural enterprise which was distinct, and which was to become more distinct with the emergence of the other party to the renaissance. It may be compared with Jane Heap's rueful, rather snappish envoi to *Little Review,* that most catholic, and in terms of longevity that most successful, of the modernist journals. She was to say in her article called "Lost: A Renaissance": "For years we offered the *Little Review* as a trial-track for racers. . . . But you can't get race horses from mules. I do not believe that the conditions of our life can produce men who can give us masterpieces. Masterpieces are not made from chaos. If there is confusion of life there will be confusion of art." And she went on to say that in the fifteen years of its existence (1914–29), the magazine had given space to twenty-three new systems of art—"all now dead"—from nineteen countries. In all of this, it had not brought forward anything approaching a masterpiece except for Joyce's *Ulysses,* and even that experiment was flawed. "It is too personal, too tortured, too special a document to be a masterpiece in the true sense of the word."[14]

The one statement as much as the other finally rested in its platitudes, but in that appalling record of twenty-three new systems of art, a little better than 1.5 each year, and in that narrowing ambition to produce "a masterpiece in the true sense of the word"—the true sense of the word having something to do with stasis—was an implication which gave definition to the Young Americans.

Jane Heap to the contrary, the putative chaos in the surrounding life was not of such degree as to demand acknowledgment. It was after all a contented nation that had elected Woodrow Wilson, Warren G. Harding, and Calvin Coolidge to the presidency, and then Herbert Hoover—to isolate one major mode of American cultural self-expression. From the point of view of those equipped with a special taste for drastic social change, or born to a set of circumstances requiring change, it was the dreadful placidity of the surrounding life that was remarkable. Those writers, therefore, who sought the feeling of being "employed by civilization"—in Brooks's phrase—might take disturbance, just for itself, to be the primary task of letters.

Not paradoxically, the socialist left marched with the banners of individualism and freedom, even while it espoused or just somehow, vaguely, made reference to the ideal of the organized, equitable society. The point was agitation and affront, and assault on all manner of equability, "irritation at things as they are," in the words of Bourne, "disgust at the continual frustrations and aridities of American life."[15] And the broad purpose would contain all manner of parties and temperaments—even, in a later moment, Ezra Pound, who was to write some essays for *New Masses,* as well as Allen Tate, who was to be one of the consultants involved in the planning of *New Masses* and would for a while be an irregular contributor to that magazine.[16]

FLOYD DELL, MAX EASTMAN, AND THE *Masses*

Meanwhile, the Young Americans were in fact, for all of their principled disgust, rather high-toned in the practice of their effrontery. Bourne was the angriest of the Young Americans, but he was angry for the most part within terms of an acknowledgment of an intellectual elite. At his most strident he was engaged in lecturing his own mentors, chiefly John Dewey, whom nonetheless he continued to respect and whom he sought to convince. Brooks, the founder, was often sarcastic, but not infrequently also very sage. "The great critics," he would counsel, "have always convinced the world in spite of the prepossessions of the world . . . for unless they speak with reasonableness and human understanding they confess in their own words that they do not possess that in the name of which they speak," and he would, wisely, repeat the wisdom of Amiel, "Truth should not merely conquer, it should win."[17] Again, in his book on H. G. Wells, Brooks had declared that the whole trend of Matthew Arnold's social criticism had been in a straight line with socialism, from which observation it might well have been inferred that the true hero of socialism for Brooks would be such a one as would demonstrate the temper and manner and accent of a new Matthew Arnold.[18]

But the left was broader than that and could encourage other accents and manners. For a while, in particular, a literary commitment to socialism did not contradict a taste for, or even an ideology of, Bohemianism. Among writers, perhaps no one spoke for socialism more insistently than Floyd Dell, at least until the mid-1920s, but at the same time no one spoke so eloquently in behalf of Greenwich Village and Free Love. Max Eastman's late account of his early radical days was to be called *Love and Revolution,* with alternate chapters devoted to each of these interests.

Dell and Eastman represented another party, which was, simply, much less solemn than the Young Americans, notwithstanding its somewhat more pragmatic and literal commitment to the politics of socialism. Their most nearly perfect hero and therefore their most appropriate emblem was their own John Reed, that joyous, reckless young man who might have been the Richard Harding Davis of journalism except that his sincerity of purpose was so clear, that free-spirited genius, a classmate of T. S. Eliot by chance, whose master-pieces were the Madison Square Garden rally of 1913 in behalf of the Paterson silk strikers and his inside report on the *Ten Days That Shook the World.* Reed was a brilliant journalist who had sacrificed fortune and, probably, a kind of official fame for the sake of political conscience. More than that, he was available to a preconception. He fulfilled for the socialist Bohemians the image of the soul of the artist, something finely luminous, some quantum of energy which radiated both art and justice. In behalf of both art and justice, moreover, he had chosen to become a criminal. "We pay our tribute to John Reed," Max Eastman said in his memorial oration, "because he was an outlaw."[19] If anything else were needed, the fact that he died young made the quality of his heroism mythic. And beyond all of that, gratuitously, there was his canonization by the Bolsheviks, making his role in legend unassailable even by strong imputations that at the end he had changed his mind about the Bolsheviks.[20] He was at once Percy Shelley, François Villon, and an American roughneck.

Floyd Dell and Max Eastman were in the end—or in mid-career, really—to be damned on all sides. Eastman attacked the modernist Right in two principal essays, "The Cult of Unintelligibility" and

"Poets Talking to Themselves," with the result, as he was to say much later, that "I disappeared under a cloud of awfully overwhelming language called the New Criticism, and as a critic of poetry I have not been heard of since."[21] On the other side, the Brooksian socialists were to find Eastman in particular to be insufficiently sensitive to the idea of culture. And on still another side, the younger generation of literary socialists who began to emerge in the mid-1920s, who had enjoyed the sponsorship of Dell and Eastman, found both of them to be at once insufficiently committed to the working classes and untrustworthy according to the requirements of political discipline.

In truth, Dell and Eastman represented an assemblance of ideas and attitudes which would not bear much scrutiny or withstand much historical pressure. Sinclair Lewis, a friend and a fellow socialist, was to refer to Dell with tantamount accuracy as "a faun at the barricades." But on the other hand the confusion of their enthusiasms in itself created much of their usefulness. Without a great deal of rationalizing, they could be sympathetic at once to young romantic poets, older muckrakers, sectarian Socialists, radical labor organizers, feminists, urban immigrants, and prairie bards—and so forth through a broad spectrum of rebels and outsiders. What they lacked in theoretical strictness, they made up for in the greater range and adventurousness of their sensitivity. Dell and Eastman were not, indeed, the self-conscious leaders of a movement, which in any event lacked formulated definition. They were little self-conscious at all about the idea of mission. They were not identical with each other, either, in their attitudes and views, nor were they collaborators except fortuitously. They did, for all of that, however, provide for a while extending from about 1912 to the mid-1920s the possibility of a coherence for many kinds of new disturbances and disturbers within the culture. And, somewhat fortuitously, they were in large part responsible for the series of the more important journals which for the while made this tenuous coherence *look* like a movement: the *Masses*, the *Liberator*, and also, despite some explicit disclaimer, the early *New Masses*.

The *Masses*, especially, comprehended a latitude in which impertinence became polemical and polemics were fun. What it lacked in theoretical strictness, it made up for in an ebullience which served better as an organizing principle. The magazine had been founded in 1911 by a man named Piet Vlag, a Greenwich Village restaurant owner who had ideas about consumers' cooperatives. It had quickly run out of money, and Vlag had left for Florida. Eastman had just left his teaching job in the philosophy department at Columbia University, and so was available to revive the magazine. He became editor in the summer of 1912. Floyd Dell, who had been the manager of a literary review in Chicago, arrived in Greenwich Village in 1913 and was looking for something to do. He became Eastman's associate editor. Together, then, they teased, wheedled, mediated, and charmed impossible contraries into a temporary unity. And that unity could be discovered again and again each month, with each issue, because everyone who was closely connected with the magazine—Art Young, John Sloan, John Reed, Louis Untermeyer, Mary Heaton Vorse, Arturo Giovannitti, Robert Minor, William English Walling, latterly Michael Gold, among others—believed in it, at least for the while. The magazine did establish limits, in theory and in practice. There was room for anyone's individuality, according to Eastman, except that the "principles of socialism" were not to be transgressed.[22] More pointedly, and in practice, the *Masses* was as antipathetic to the hard left as it was to the right. It was sometimes doubtful about anarchists like Emma Goldman—Eastman and Goldman finally just did not like each other. It antagonized the left labor movement. It was very friendly to the Socialist party, but it refused to be a party organ. In literature, it was not on principle opposed to formal innovation, but it was not very accepting either.[23] What remained nevertheless was a not inconsiderable eclecticism, suffused and buoyed by the spirit of revolution. Somehow throughout the years of its existence, until 1917, it managed to be true to Eastman's initial statement of purpose, despite fervid paradoxes in his statement. The *Masses,* he had said in a manifesto written in collaboration with Reed, was to be "A revolutionary and not a reform magazine; a magazine with a sense of humor and no respect for the respectable; frank; arrogant; impertinent; searching for the true causes; a magazine directed against rigidity and dogma wherever it is found; printing what is too naked or true for a money-making press; a magazine whose final policy is to do as it pleases and conciliate nobody, not even its readers."[24]

The revolution which was to be conducted with a sense of humor was at all conceivable, in turn, because, first, it was sustained by the peculiar moment of its history, and because, second, the revolutionists themselves were not really aliens to the culture at large: they had the security of a sense of native tradition and could afford to be hospitable.

Evidences testify that, circa 1912, there was an attitude or a spirit, or a recognition, abroad in the land, of the being and the activity of an American mass, to which a magazine called the *Masses*—rather than, specifically, the *Criterion*—might appeal, a recognition manifest at the levels both of popular politics and serious art. The year 1912, when Eastman took over the *Masses,* was a presidential year besides being the lyric year. Eugene Debs, the Socialist candidate for the presidency, received nearly a million votes, while among the major candidates the one genuine conservative, William Howard Taft, ran a poor third, behind Woodrow Wilson and Theodore Roosevelt. In 1912 more than a thousand Socialists across the country held public office, and Socialists—tending to be the more respectable members of the movement, but nevertheless formally affiliated, self-proclaiming Socialists —ran the governments of numbers of middle-sized American cities, including Milwaukee, Berkeley, Butte, Schenectady, and Flint. In 1912 the Socialist party was, besides what else it was, a very large publishing enterprise: it published 5 English and 8 foreign-language daily newspapers, 262 English and 36 foreign-language weeklies, and 10 English and 2 foreign-language monthlies. The AFL under Samuel Gompers was deliberately nonideological and Samuel Gompers was unbeatable, but at the union's convention in 1912 he was opposed by a Socialist who secured an approximate one-third of the vote. Further to the syndicalist left, meanwhile, in the same year the IWW secured the most substantial victory and the most conspicuous standing it was ever to have, when it led the strike of twenty-five thousand textile workers at Lawrence, Massachusetts. The strike, moreover, assumed large symbolic significance. It was violent, and it seemed to prove the current actuality of the class struggle. The twenty-five thousand strikers were semiskilled immigrants of twenty-eight different nationalities.[25] These immigrants were an American mass, undeniable now as fact and force in American life. In 1912 and for a few years thereafter, that is to say, the movement leftward in popular, practical, quotidian American politics might seem to be so real and socialism could seem, at least to Socialists, to be so imminent that one might relax within its inertia and, in the words of Eastman's injunction, "Enjoy the Revolution."[26]

The kind and amount of presence registered by socialism meanwhile had its equivalent in the high arts, specifically writing and painting, in realism. Realism circa the early 1910s was at least as much a cause or a movement as was modernism. This realism was perforce nativist. It was also harsh and fervid (as distinct from the tonalities which had been proposed thirty and forty years before by William Dean Howells), and it suggested that truth and hence aesthetic standard was a function of the discovery and exposé of the low, ugly ordinary in contemporary American life. It was in 1911–12, with the third publication of *Sister Carrie*, that Theodore Dreiser finally, suddenly, had reputation as a writer of the vanguard. The time was also the moment of the great fame of Jack London, entered upon his realization of class warfare. It had been just a few years before, in 1906, that Upton Sinclair had published *The Jungle*, proposing thereby not precisely an aesthetic standard, but something akin, a substantial and vivid social pertinence for fiction. It was in a brief period from about 1908 to about 1916 that such poets as Edgar Lee Masters, Vachel Lindsay, and Carl Sandburg came into their prominence, purchased by the authority of their nativist realism. They, in turn, had associations with the so-called Chicago Renaissance in which, in a way to complete the circle, Floyd Dell had been a prime mover.[27] (The mix contained in that episode, of radical politics, Bohemianism, and populist poetics, also nourished Harriet Monroe, who established *Poetry* in Chicago in 1912, and Margaret Anderson, who was to move to New York in 1914 to found *Little Review*.)

In painting, this was a moment of decisive rebellion in behalf of—in John Sloan's words—"everyday subject matter."[28] In fact the rebels who came into prominence and notoriety in the years approximately 1907–1913, and who seemed to compose a collective, were quite various in their individual talents and preferences. Painters including Sloan, Robert Henri, Maurice and Charles Prendergast, George Luks, William Glackens, and others, happened to know each other. They were united chiefly, to speak of ideology, in their opposition to an especially heavy-handed officialdom in American art. Nevertheless, it was as realists—and as the "apostles of ugliness" and as the Revolutionary Black Gang—that they were known, celebrated, and derided.[29] And, quite on the basis of their subject-matters—nonideal nudes, street scenes, alleyways, theater scenes, saloon life, dance halls, docks, gutters, night courts, pigs—they made news. The exhibition of the Eight (Sloan, Henri, Maurice Prendergast, Luks, Glackens, Ernest Lawson, Arthur Davies, and Everett Shinn) in 1908 in New York drew crowds at the rate of three hundred an hour. In 1910 the exhibition of the Independent Artists, an extension of the Eight, required summoning of the riot squad to control the two thousand people who jammed into the street in front of the warehouse in which the exhibition was held. It was, then, largely the same group that sponsored the Armory Show in 1913, where it happened that it was the European modernists, who had been included somewhat as an afterthought, who dominated the exhibition. Afterward it was not possible to say that "realism" was the appropriate term of generic description for the American rebels, but even so, the change was in styles and forms and not in the more important fact of the rebellion's spirit of happy abrasiveness. There was irony but, after all, explicable irony in the fact that the artists who together with some of their immediate disciples were to be known, in the mid-thirties, as the Ashcan School brought Cézanne, van Gogh, Matisse, Brancusi, Picasso, Picabia, and others, to America. The intention, like that of the *Masses* itself, was impertinence, antagonism to rigidity and dogma, arrogance on the part of the lowly.

Not surprisingly, most of the realists, among both writers and painters, associated themselves with the political left, to one degree of extremity or another and to one degree of formality and enthusiasm or another. For one instance: John Sloan in 1908 ran for New York assemblyman on the Socialist ticket. This art and this politics were concordant in their assault upon contemporary civilization, seen in both cases to have become static, closed, institutionalized, and decadent.

And not so ironically, the assault in both cases was carried forward with the implicit, sometimes explicit, sanction of schoolbook lessons in democracy. American socialism and American realism, circa 1912, were very American, and only in part because of the happenstance that America was the inevitable subject of their endeavorings. Their license was an American tradition of dissent, in turn the consequence of the uniquely American idealization of the rabble. Their appeal was to folk Americanism. Quite reasonably, the "Apostles of Ugliness" in their 1910 exhibition chose the pine tree to be their emblem, thereby connecting their cause with that of the American Revolution. Quite reasonably, the Socialist party, multifactional from its beginnings, found almost its only symbol of unity in the figure of Eugene V. Debs, that long, angular, sincere, authentically midwestern radical, a poor boy, self-taught, deeply compassionate, nondoctrinaire, keen in his sense of injustice—for whom the only single appropriate term of description was Lincolnesque.[30] Among the realists and the socialists, the celebration of the low, the outcasts, and the despised might have served any number of specific functions for the individual celebrants—might have satisfied a need for charity or for vengeance or for relief from proprieties or a need just for fun, not to discount a vision of the ideal—but whatever the particularities of function and expression, the celebration was authorized by the folktale of American democracy.

The time was propitious for a magazine called the *Masses*. It happened that Max Eastman and Floyd Dell were, in the moment in time, themselves singularly appropriate to the ambition of a venture called the *Masses*. They were dedicated to socialism, of course, but—within this moment, at least—belonged to no faction. They were as latitudinarian as they were dedicated, implicitly defining socialism so as to include many kinds of popular revolt. Eastman was initially recommended to the board of contributors of the

Masses on the basis of two achievements: that he had been dismissed from Columbia for his outspokenness, and that he had written a charming, humorous account of his having organized the first Men's League for Woman's Suffrage in New York.[31] Realism was not an immediate issue for either Eastman or Dell. Eastman later confessed that at the time he assumed editorship of the magazine he had not been interested in literary realism and had not heard of the realistic movement in painting, despite the fact that John Sloan was one of the more active members of the editorial board; he had learned quickly, however, and eventually was proud to say that the *Masses* under his leadership did become the primary journal of the movement.[32] But more than anything else, Eastman and Dell, although quite different from each other in personality and background, were rebels in a recognizably and therefore authoritatively American mode. Their presence was a benediction.

They were not provincials, exactly, nor, of course, were they patriots in any usual sense of the word. They were receptive to all manner of intellectual news from abroad. The very tone and format of the *Masses* were derived, deliberately, from European models: the German *Simplicissimus*, particularly, with inspiration taken also from *Jugend*, *Gil Blas*, and *Assiette au Beurre*.[33] But it would have been unthinkable for either Eastman or Dell to become an exile after the style of Pound and Eliot. (When Dell later on, in May of 1925, made his one trip to Europe, his observations were those of an innocent abroad: he found that London "reeked . . . of a hateful past"; he liked Paris little better; and he was happy to return home the following September.)[34] Eastman and Dell, in their different ways, simply incorporated an American tradition of principled dissent within themselves. It came so easily that the obligation to dissent could be known with grace and humor, as a normal portion of American citizenship and perhaps its glory.

Dell, who had been born to a poor family in a small town in Illinois, had been a socialist and freethinker almost from the moment he had first had letters. In his early teens he was reading Edward Bellamy, William Morris, and Robert Ingersoll. At the age of sixteen in Quincy, Illinois, he heard a street sweeper talking about socialism, joined the local branch of the party, and read *The Communist Manifesto*. A year later, in Davenport, Iowa, a mail carrier became his socialist mentor.[35] The time was just after the turn of the century. His education in a kind of generalized impiousness was, as indeed his example proved, a normal possibility of town life in America. In his novels Dell was to make much of the restrictiveness of the small town, but it must have been the case that there were in the time and place opportunities for learning and rebellion which might be, as it were, picked up from the streets, with little of any concordant necessities for fine discriminations and dogmatic fierceness. Art, atheism, socialism (and sexual impiety, too)—they had a sameness of high purpose and constituted a quite available happiness for boys and girls. In Dell's first novel, *Moon-Calf,* published in 1920, the poetical young hero, Felix Fay, coming of age in the Middle West, is wonderfully delighted to learn that he has been a Socialist for a long time without knowing it. His first girl friend tells him so, her information based on the fact that Felix celebrates the birthday of the atheist Bob Ingersoll:

> Her look was of mischievous pride in the sharing of a pleasant secret, while his was a burning flash of wonder and gratitude. . . .
> "Why," she said, "I was brought up on Bob Ingersoll. My father's a Socialist and freethinker."
> "And you never told me!" he said.
> "Why should I tell you? You never asked me. But I always knew you were a Socialist, too."
> "Am I?" he said.
> "Of course!"
> It came out that he didn't know there was such a thing as the Socialist party. She clapped her hands. "It will be fun to take you to the Socialist local," she said.[36]

The conviction of the passage is that socialism is, more than anything else, wholesome. Socialism is something that nice young people do together in America. The novel focuses on Dell's memories of his own life in Davenport, where in fact he had had a large number of friends—a large number of kindred spirits who encouraged him, sustained him, and, most of all, did exist as a datum of his cultural experience. The fact is recorded in the dedication of *Moon-Calf:* to a certain "Daughter of the Middle West," Dell wrote, "Is Affectionately Dedicated This Tale of That Strange Region—This Record of Its Grim Yet Generous Hospitality to the Fantastic Beauty of Young American Life."

Eastman had traveled a higher road. He was of old family. The first American Eastman had arrived in Massachusetts in 1638. Daniel Webster was somewhere in the genealogy. Both his father and his mother were Congregationalist ministers in Elmira, New York. The family was comfortable, if not wealthy. Eastman had been sent to a prep school and then to Williams, and then had studied philosophy at Columbia under John Dewey. His formal commitment to the particularity of socialism had come comparatively late—compared with Dell's—but in his case, too, the commitment was more in the nature of a discovery of what he had always known rather than a conversion. A girl friend, as he was to record the matter later, had told him about the Marxist class struggle and the eventual victory of the proletariat, and he had been delighted. "Ida," he said that he had said, "that's a perfectly wonderful idea!" That conversation was, he said, "a turning point in my mental life." Moreover, he had married the girl. In 1920 Eastman was to be described by the *New York World* as being "the most influential radical in the United States," and he was, reasonably, neither pleased nor displeased but simply bewildered. He was not a ferocious man, nor doctrinaire, nor narrowly militant, nor whatever the most influential radical in the United States might most properly be. He was indeed very influential, however, in all likelihood for the reason that he did not wear a beard or throw any bombs. He was influential by the fact that his radicalism was charming rather than perfervid, and it was presumptive. Radicalism as expressed in the personality of Eastman was an orthodoxy, its tone determined most of all, as he was to say, by the teachings of his Congregationalist mother and father. He had been bred to revolution by their humane, upright, innocent, and very American idealism. "If there was anything in my childhood," he was to write in one of his volumes of autobiography, "to account for my leaning toward revolution, it lay rather in the good than the bad luck of my birth. I grew up in a family where kindness and fair-dealing and sound logic prevailed to such a degree that, when I got out into the public world, it looked excessively unjust, irrational, a subject for indignation and extreme action." Ida's good news perhaps provided him with a fresh formulation, but otherwise it was not news at all. "From childhood I had despised valuations based on wealth, social position, race, color, caste, or class. I took very seriously the American ideals of freedom for all, justice and equal opportunity for all. They were axioms of my emotional nature." In the instance of this reflection, written some fifty years after his choosing to stand up for Karl Marx, Eastman was looking back on himself with some irony, wondering about the complexities to which his ideals had led him, but there is no need to doubt his memory of a quite noble early family life that had provided him with his radicalism.[37]

It was in good part the narrowness of their experience that allowed Dell and Eastman to be so hospitable to so many various currents of rebellion, just as the cosmopolitanism of Pound and Eliot had something to do with their exclusiveness, and it was in good part the narrowness of their experience that made them pertinent to the creation of a literary left. Dell and Eastman expressed little real fury in their radicalism. They were not heroic sufferers, nor were they driven men. They were not compelling, charismatic figures. They had no commerce with and were on the whole rather suspicious of grandeurs. Indeed, they were not very exciting. Rather, they were good Americans in their somewhat different ways—progressive by every inclination of the spirit, innocent on principle, sassy, and democratic. Radicalism was for them the expression of a known heritage, to which they were absolutely loyal. The time would come, very quickly, when the kind of their experience would be challenged and the kind of their poise would prove to be inadequate to events, but meanwhile they implied a tradition—American democracy as a cultural propriety—which would offer accommodation, coherence, and sanction to many varieties of modern rebels.

How precarious was the particular poise which Eastman and Dell had charmed into being was to be indicated by the defeat of the *Masses*—glorious, in a way, and a fine demonstration of high principle, but a defeat nonetheless because what had been a joyous eclecticism of revolt was reduced to principle.

The *Masses* ran afoul of the law. It was 1917, there was a war going on, and one of the magazine's causes, inevitably, was pacifism. The *Masses* was banned from the mails under terms of the Espionage Act. Eastman and Dell and a number of their associates on the magazine were indicted by a grand jury, charged with "conspiracy to obstruct the recruiting and enlistment service of the United States." There were to be two trials, eventually. Both of the trials ended in hung juries and thus in qualified victory, and meanwhile the trials did more to make the *Masses* group famous than anything the group had ever done for itself. There were also moments of high-spirited irony during the course of the trials, as on a morning when a military band playing on the street beneath the courthouse windows struck up "The Star-Spangled Banner," and everyone in the court, including defendants and judge, solemnly rose. But the indictments nevertheless constituted a most sober matter. Given the temper of the time and the outcome of some similar cases, the possibility of conviction was quite real. The defendants faced maximum sentences of twenty years in jail and fines of ten thousand dollars. In these circumstances there could be at best a forlornness in the cause of "a Magazine," as Eastman and Reed had advertised it, "whose final policy is to do as it Pleases and Conciliate Nobody."

Eastman and Dell, in particular, were put to the necessity of defending their rights under the lesser principle of the First Amendment, and it was the general purpose of the defense, necessarily, to prove that the accused were not conspirators but men of good character who loved their country. Necessarily, the technical victory of the editors of the *Masses* was the result, to some certain if undeterminable extent, of their being separated from the basic meaning of their enterprise: acknowledgment of the fact of the "masses". At the end of the second trial one of the holdout jurors told them as much. "It was a good thing for you boys," he said, "that you were all American born; otherwise it might have gone pretty hard with you."[38]

Even so, the fact that the *Masses* was a casualty of war hysteria was perhaps more of a lucky eventuality than not. The government of the United States manifest in its judicial system was at least a palpable enemy. At the same time the peculiar coherence that was the *Masses* was being sabotaged by socialism itself. The socialist movement in the United States after 1917 was subject to rigidities of sectarianism as never before, following the Bolshevik Revolution, and as a whole allowed to those who called themselves socialists, including Eastman and Dell, much less vagueness and much less latitude. The time would come very soon when Eastman—who was, after all, a professional philosopher and not unused to rigor—would be denounced for his softness, and worse.

And even Floyd Dell, the most fluent of rebels, apparently found himself to be insufficient to the new moment. In a series of essays, published as *Intellectual Vagabondage* in 1926, he issued a call upon what he now conceived to be his own older generation of radicals to a greater sense of stringency, but in fact the essays constituted a kind of left-wing *Education of Henry Adams,* a proud and melancholy tale of irrelevance. Dell recited the steps in the typical education of his contemporaries. There had been a seduction, first, of *The Rubáiyát of Omar Khayyám*, then the impact of *A Doll's House,* then *Looking Backward* and utopian socialism, then the Free Woman movement, then the influence of the *Songs of Vagabondia* of Bliss Carman and Richard Hovey, and so forth, through the postwar disillusion. The result of all of this, he said, was that the "intelligentsia"—in a word newly borrowed from the Russian—had abandoned all sense of duty. "Meanwhile, an actual social relation, however ignored and repudiated by ourselves in our helplessness, does persist between ourselves as a class and the masses, which in its most striking aspect may be described in an old phrase: the hungry sheep look up and are not fed." But then finally, desperately, after the elegant diagnosis, he had nothing much to offer. In his final pages Dell abandoned the intention of his little book altogether, turning hopefully to rally not his own generation but the younger one, and then presenting to it a conception of duty so vague and so general as almost to prove the validity of his claim to miseducation. He cited "the mere familiar duty of interpreting life, as conditions change, for those who are too busy with more material tasks to do it as well for themselves: the duty of explaining life in terms of the arts ... so as to make living more comprehensible and more enjoyable in its widest sense."[39] One could have known what he meant, but still the message lacked polemical edge.

Most of the reflections in *Intellectual Vagabondage* were published first in 1919, by which time—just a year after he had barely escaped a twenty-year prison sentence—Dell was not mistaken in thinking himself to be somewhat passé as a revolutionary. A more militant literary left was discovering Dell to be something of an embarrassment, and would shortly, given some further political complications, discover that Eastman was a traitor. On its side, this new literary left, confronted by new historical severities, was chary of gratitude, but nonetheless it had been—and knew itself to be—shaped and defined in an idealism and a tonality anterior to its own polemics, by the heritage which it mocked or condemned. The newer literary left spoke and condemned with a pretense to cultural authority, which it possessed in the first place because Eastman and Dell, allowing them their primacy, had created the *Masses*.

The fact that the *Masses*, in all of its eclectic and attractive rebelliousness, had managed to exist for five years was in itself an eventuality of great practical value. More than that, the subject-matter of the *Masses*—described by Dell as "fun, truth, beauty, realism, freedom, peace, feminism, revolution"[40]—had in the most absolute and direct way created this succeeding generation of literary radicals. The *Masses* had been hospitable to and had encouraged new writers who on the basis of class, race, and politics revealed in their writing a matter which would have been excluded elsewhere.

In terms of a similar prominence on the literary left, the likely generational successors to Eastman and Dell were Michael Gold and Joseph Freeman. Both of them eventually, by the 1930s, were to be so closely identified with their careers in the Communist party that their literary intentions were either indiscernible or forgotten, but they had begun with the conviction—nay, the proof—that literature and politics were twin expressions of one impulse. Gold's first national publication, a poem, had appeared in the *Masses* in 1914, and thereafter until the end of the magazine he was a regular contributor and a member of the circle. Eastman and Dell may not finally have been proud of what they had wrought, but in any event, according to Gold's own later testimony, they were his teachers.[41]

Gold was twenty-one when he came to the *Masses*. Freeman was

a sixteen-year-old socialist when he discovered the magazine, and he
found in it suddenly, as he was to say in his autobiography, a response
to all of his incohate longings:

> One rainy afternoon, in the socialist local on Graham Avenue,
> the sixteen-year-old boy in search of heaven on earth found the
> Thing Itself. It was Just, Beautiful and American. Marx and
> Byron, Debs and Michelangelo, politics and poetry, the unity I
> was seeking. Somewhere in that mysterious Greenwich Vil-
> lage . . . there were native Americans who had integrated the
> conflicting values of the world. These men did not share each
> other's views. But they were frank about that too. The magazine
> they published, the *Masses,* which lay in a neat pile on the
> shelves of the socialist headquarters, had no dividends to pay
> and nobody was trying to make money out of it. . . . The lectures
> at the socialist local often bored me, but I went there every
> month to read this wonderful magazine. Its editors could write,
> and they were not crudely materialistic like the socialist soap-
> boxers. We looked upon them as not only poets but scientists.
> That made their integration of conflicting values appear even
> stronger: politics, poetry *and* science; justice, beauty *and*
> knowledge. And they were revolutionary too.[42]

The *Liberator*

The *Masses* died, but still there was manifest life in the allure, if
only that, of the peculiar integration it had wrought. Despite new
exacerbations of political events and despite the bluntness of new
political demands, much of the venturing of the literary left through the
1920s and into the 1930s was to consist, quite explicitly, of an attempt to
rediscover or reinvent what was now remembered to have been a moment of easy, buoyant unity.

The attempt was tentatively successful at best. The couple of
magazines which claimed direct descent from the *Masses*—the
Liberator and then *New Masses*—did finally succumb to ideological
purity; both magazines, one officially and the other unofficially, ended
by becoming journals of the Communist party. There were many difficulties. In the years following the First World War it was not necessarily the case that the hungry sheep were looking up to be fed, but,
rather—so it was thought—that they had to be told what was good for
them. Opportunities for certain kinds of expression were diminished;
what had been sassiness edged toward fulmination. Bohemianism,
which for a while in its sportiveness had had serious implications for
freedom, was more glamourous and less provocative than it had been,
and thus was diminished as a possibility for radical expression; Floyd

Dell, for one, seemingly in his desperation, in 1923 wrote a series of polemical essays in behalf of legal matrimony. More pointedly, those who ventured most ambitiously to establish an organized literary left were in most instances persons who did not have easy access to an acknowledged America, and were not necessarily geniuses, either, and were forced to extremities—sillinesses, often, and sentimentalities and raging exhortations and ideological rigidities—by way of establishing their cultural authority. It had been something of a source of embarrassment to Max Eastman, but then also a matter of good fortune for his radicalism, that Woodrow Wilson happened to be one of his personal acquaintances. These others did not have such connections.

Given the many difficulties, it was the more meaningful, then, that the *Masses,* with its nativism, its fervor, its eclecticism, and its fun, did remain a vital ideal for the shaping of a literary left. Given the circumstances, the ambition required an embracing of social militance *and* an equal resisting of narrow dogmatisms, at the cost of many tortured consciences. It happened finally that there was impossible discrepancy in that ambition, but meanwhile the ideal defined strategies for cultural citizenship.

In fact the *Masses* itself was reborn almost before the corpse was cold. The final issue of the magazine, in November of 1917, had promised a forthcoming eyewitness account of the Russian Revolution by John Reed. In February of 1918—on Lincoln's birthday, as its manifesto pointed out—the *Liberator* appeared, with Max Eastman as editor and Floyd Dell as associate editor, and with Reed's reports constituting the important part of its contents. Reed had the materials which were to become *Ten Days That Shook the World.* They were important property. Reed was a famous correspondent. No other substantial reports were coming through from Russia. Eastman founded the new magazine particularly in order not to lose the opportunity which had been frustrated by the fate of the *Masses.* He had a scoop.[43]

The news from Russia dominated the magazine, especially in the first months when Reed was sending in his articles, but thereafter as well, until the end, in 1924. It remained the case that the *Liberator* was in large part defined by the fact that it was the only magazine of national importance that had direct and constant access to Russian information. It was the *Liberator,* in natural consequence, that published Lenin's "A Letter to American Workingmen" in January of 1919. In natural consequence the *Liberator* had additional definition thrust upon it by the formation in 1919 of the American Communist party. When it was not celebrating the achievements of the Soviet Union, it was a magazine necessarily engaged in exposés, because the country as a whole was moving toward "normalcy," which would have been to say moving toward the right, and exposé was a duty of the left-wing press. It was the *Liberator* that first publicized the arrest of Sacco and Vanzetti, in 1920. Finally, just before the end, the *Liberator* became frankly a Party journal, but throughout its career it was confronted by political pressures of a degree of forcefulness which discouraged the freedoms—and the evasions—which had been managed by the *Masses*. Furthermore, the intricate, often fantastic maneuverings of the post-Revolutionary American left were to constitute a continuous murmurous bass to the magazine's existence.

A new and much more stringent political context was now imposed on that high-spirited rebellion which had once delighted in conciliating nobody, with the result that what had been the miraculous impertinence of the *Masses* was transformed very frequently into a kind of jollity of bravado. Floyd Dell, the moon-calf, in this moment agonizing and groping for an adequate militance, summarized not the situation but the tone of the *Liberator* when, in his editorial address for the issue of January 1919, he raised his head above the barricades to sing out, "This magazine goes to two classes of readers: those who are in jail, and those who are not."

Even so, the magazine did manage from the beginning and almost to the end to resist utter reification of its principles and did manage to maintain its own separate identity, separate from all segments of the organized political left, and the whole history of the magazine, through successive editors and successive causes, was an attempt to reconcile the clear demands of left militance with aspirations for broad cultural authority. In the beginning the personnel of the *Liberator* was nearly identical with that of the *Masses*, and as in the old days just a couple of months past the magazine was still conceived to be a group activity, with room for all sorts of variegations. The happenstance of the intersecting of John Reed and the Russian Revolution certainly was not intended to be a limitation. According to the announcement in the first issue, the *Liberator* was to be a magazine of art and poetry, and it was to devote itself to a breadth of revolutions, including progressive education, progressive penology, birth control, and feminism. And even at the very end, in 1924, when the principal writers for the magazine were such Communist party regulars and leaders as C. E. Ruthenberg, Jay Lovestone, and Max Bedacht, some measure of independence was still being asserted, and asserted apparently, significantly, *not* in clear opposition to the demands of the Party. In June of 1924, in the time of its maximum politicization, the *Liberator* was a magazine in which a twenty-year-old Max Shachtman, in this moment still a Party leader, could review a scholarly-critical book on James Joyce, with no apologies and without, in all seeming, any sense of anomaly.[44]

Despite everything, for a period of a half-dozen years the *Liberator* sustained its discrepancies, and therefore the plausibility of a literary left. The magazine had manifest authority deriving in good part from the fact that even its editors seemed never, at least until the very end, to have had a clear, comfortable, and definite idea of the purpose of the magazine. Eastman, who in 1920 was being described as the most influential radical in the United States, was forced out of his editorship of the magazine in 1921 for the reason that he was not so sufficiently or exclusively proletarian in his sympathies as to meet the wishes of the other members of the group. There was indication of Eastman's own uncertainty of purpose, meanwhile, in the fact that he allowed himself to be forced out. He and his sister were the major stockholders in the magazine. He was succeeded by two executive editors, Michael Gold and Claude McKay, who had nothing in common except their attachment to the *Liberator,* and who were directed to act conjointly. Mike Gold was perhaps the most zealous proletarian in the United States. McKay, as a black and an immigrant from Jamaica, was proletarian by definition but not at all by taste: as a poet he was deft and subtle and quite elegant. Within a few months these two were threatening each other with bodily harm and McKay resigned.[45] In succeeding installments, Joseph Freeman, who had contributed some occasional poems to the magazine, became Gold's associate editor; then Gold went to California, and Dell once again took over, along with Freeman; then at the end of 1922 the executive editors were Freeman and Robert Minor.

It was under the editorship of Minor, who had been a cartoonist for both the *Masses* and the *Liberator,* that the magazine most distinctly moved toward granting itself to the Communist—in 1922, the Workers'—party. Minor himself was now a Party official. The number for December 1922 announced, "We expect to direct our attention more than we have for some months past to political issues, and to direct attention more deliberately than heretofore to the Workers' Party, the organized political movement which ... best represents the revolutionary interests of the American workers." (The statement of ownership in the same number was notorized, perhaps ominously, by one "Augusta Moskow.") In the next months dual "Political" and "Art" boards of editors were established, with the former being clearly dominant, and finally the *Liberator* was merged with some other odd and marginal publications to become the *Communist Monthly,* edited by Earl Browder.

But even Minor, despite his leadership position in the Party, in bringing the magazine to the Party was acting under a conviction which hurt him, and which also was very recent. He had considered himself to be an artist, and he was now giving up art for the cause. Moreover, in the matter of organized politics, until sometime in 1921 he had been identifying himself as being on the other side of one of the many fences: he had been an anarchist—as late as 1921 Eastman was worrying about Minor's influence, fearing on the one hand that he was too much identified with Greenwich Village and on the other hand that as an anarchist he was dangerous to Marxist socialism.[46]

Writing in the mid-thirties (when he was still a Party member), Joseph Freeman was to say that the old *Liberator* had died because of the growing prosperity of the middle classes around 1922, and because of the disillusionment of intellectuals with the social revolution; the old base was gone.[47] It was patently the case, however, that the *success* of the Revolution and the consequent transformations wrought upon American socialism had had fully as much to do with this death. A new stringency of commitment was demanded, and demanded by people involved in enterprises to which the writing of humane letters was pretty clearly irrelevant. It was the case that the editors and writers of the *Liberator* had been engaged in making a revolution which was more than its politics, a matter not easily accessible to formulation either from within or outside the engagement, but much more important, finally, than the adventures of the Communist party. The matter had to do, precisely, with the humanization of politics and the politicization of art, both at the same time. It had to do with art and politics as equal—indeed, identical—assertions of citizenship in this country.

Freeman himself was exemplary both of the *Liberator's* revolution and of its vulnerability. He was an absolutely dedicated socialist, of course, and as a member of the Communist party he was most loyal. He was also a poet—not a propagandizing or polemical or even satirical poet, but a lyrical poet and lover of Keats. The poetry he wrote tended to be of the order of his lines called "At a Concert":

O Love, the flute faints in the dark,
The music melts, the cadence dies,
And beauty stumbles—hark! O hark!
Its heart is breaking and it cries.

Beauty is perishing in pain,
Fallen from its astonished flight
Like a bird haunted and half-slain
Fluttering in the wounded night.

—which lines he published, of course, in the *Liberator*.[48] He lacked talent, perhaps, for being either a great social revolutionary or a good

poet, but his refusing to abandon either kind of assertion in behalf of
the other was in itself a precision. The example of Robert Minor, who
had abandoned his "art" in behalf of a full commitment to politics,
troubled him greatly. "What restrained me," he was to say, "was the
conviction that I had no capacity for practical action. I could never be
an organizer. I looked upon myself as a poet; . . . a 'creative' writer was
of no use to the movement."[49] He gratefully received testimonies to
the contrary from Party leaders. He learned that C. E. Ruthenberg
appreciated good prose and had himself written moving letters from
Sing Sing. No less a one than the Comintern leader Karl Radek had
praised the social usefulness of Jack London's *The Iron Heel*. But
then, luckily, Freeman was evasive and self-excusing, knowing undoubtedly but at a level below articulation that the Ruthenbergs and
Radeks implied a definition of "literature" quite different from his
own.

Neither Freeman nor Gold had any talents for tractarian narrative. Neither of them could have been the Jack London whom they
both ritually acknowledged to be their master. Gold was not only the
most zealous of proletarians, but also the most sentimental. There was
forthcoming irony in the circumstance that by the mid-thirties both
Freeman and Mike Gold—Gold the more especially—would have fame
chiefly for their being Party hacks and hitmen, for within the Party and
at the expense of some confusion of conscience, they had struggled for
a relative freedom for art. In his *Liberator* days Gold had absolutely
and explicitly opposed the capitulation of art to the stringencies of his
own politics.[50] Both Freeman and Gold, whether by means of vacilla-
tion or in a bravado of high principle, and given some opportunity for
free expression, had in actuality been loyal to their own contrary kind
of revolution.

No matter that they might later be seen to be inflexibly, indeed
vulgarly doctrinaire, they—even they—in the episode of their joint
editorship of the *Liberator* did provide and maintain a broad context of
possibilities for new writers. They provided enough liberty, enough
knockabout, enough openness that, for instance, along with appeals for
volunteers to go to Siberia, the *Liberator* would print an unsolicited
manuscript by a young Stuart Chase defending nudism at Harvard;
along with news from the strike fronts, their magazine would print
some Stevensesque poetry by Eugene Jolas; along with attacks on
Bohemianism, they would print the poems of Maxwell Bodenheim and
Louis Ginsberg. Until the very end, indeed, and under Robert Minor's
editorship as well, the *Liberator's* operating definition of the left was
only not so broad as that of the *Masses* had been, but it was still large

enough to provide the idea of a culture rather than an ideology, and one which was hospitable.

Besides and beneath everything else, all of the editors of the magazine subsequent to Eastman and Dell shared an essential adventure: they were outsiders to any putative mainstream of American cultural tradition, and consequently they were engaged in making an American tradition in which they would have a place. It did follow that the *Liberator*, despite all of its schisms and despite the creeping sectarianism, was ready to distinguish new social data of American culture and to afford welcome to those many who either by fate or by choice were sensitive to the new data. The magazine published plays and poems and stories and reportage and reviews (including, significantly, movie reviews) and cartoons by such various contributors, some old and many brand new to print, as Elmer Reizenstein (later Elmer Rice), S. N. Behrman, John Dos Passos, James Weldon Johnson, Jean Toomer, Ruth Suckow, Mary Heaton Vorse, Edmund Wilson, Witter Bynner, Louis Untermeyer, E. E. Cummings, Carl Sandburg, Boardman Robinson, William Gropper, and scores of others, many of whom, of course, were never heard from again. A contributor named Bertha Fenberg might publish a whimsical—and quite charming— genre anecdote of Yiddish life in the Bronx. Mary Heaton Vorse continued to publish, as she had in the *Masses*, reportage on the lives of the immigrant industrial proletariat. Roger Baldwin, not now nor later a poet, could publish poetry (consisting of generalized tribute to the hordes of the downtrodden). Dos Passos reported on farm strikes in Spain. Edmund Wilson inveighed in sarcastic couplets against an action by the New York State Assembly "to thoroughly Americanize all war veterans, then to utilize them in the work of making good citizens of the foreign born of the State":

> Yet stay! it never shall be said
> We cannot still redeem the dead!
> Strike out from any epitaph
> The kind of name that makes us laugh:
> The Ivans, Isadores and Fritzes,
> The Rosenburgs and Meyrowitzes,
> The Kellys, Kovalskys and Krauses,
> Schapellis, Swensons, Stanislauses—
> And give us graves with every man
> A simon-pure American![51]

The unifying element in all of this was certainly not politics in any narrow sense, but rather a feeling for the engagement of the social actualities not recognized by official politics or official literature. The same principle applied seemingly even to the numbers of strivings for pure poesy published in the magazine, concerning such subjects as the night and love and music and the hummingbird. If not the poems themselves, then the writers themselves, in their personal situations, were conceived to have particular authority because they were outsiders.

And the *Liberator's* inevitable Russophilia was, in the same way, something more than a celebration of vanguard socialism. It was also, subtly but pervasively, a lesson in the triumph of the barbarians as Americans. Russia itself, which had been a cultural designation simply outside the normal range of reference for official Americans, was now suddenly a presence in the world, a place to be known. It followed, suddenly, that all of those Russian-Polish Jews with the laughable names, who had been Americans at best only technically, could now believe that at least they were no longer so foreign as they had been, and hence the more American. It could now be conceived, at a greater reach of enthusiasm, now that the masses had risen, that Russian-Polish-Jewish immigrants were emissaries of true democracy. They were pioneers, ahead of the rest in bringing true civilization to America. As for so long the truest and bluest of Americans had been transported Britons, now the best could be conceived to be these Russians. It behooved Americans to celebrate their Russians. The point was implicit, for instance, in Robert Minor's cartoon on Trotsky which bore the caption, "The East Side Jew Who Conquered the World"— Trotsky's few months of exile in New York's Lower East Side constituted sufficient technical qualification; more to the point, Trotsky certainly looked like many other contemporary Americans, and spoke the same language.

The same point was implicit, finally, in the *Liberator's* peculiar nativism, which coexisted quite comfortably with the appeals to the Soviet Union. At issue, once again and continuously, was the matter of the true cultural identity of the true Americans. So in the few instances when the *Liberator* acknowledged the existence of Ezra Pound, T. S. Eliot, and their circle, the magazine attacked them particularly on the grounds of their expatriation, meaning their contemptuous noninvolvement with basic Americans. On the one occasion when a book of poems by Pound was actually reviewed in the *Liberator,* it was compared—unfavorably, of course—with the poetry of a real proletarian, the Wobbly organizer and songwriter Ralph Chaplin, and the comparison was offered not in literary terms nor strictly in political terms, either:

> since Pound foreswore all moral and artistic allegiance to his country, he has seemed international in a sadly fugitive way.... Ralph Chaplin, a poet serving twenty years in the

United States penitentiary at Leavenworth for being a member of the Industrial Workers of the World, does not like the United States any more than this leading and devoted champion of James Joyce, Brancusi, and T. S. Eliot. But he remained on its soil and among its shops to alter it in proportion to his greatness.... When Pound in England thumbs his nose westward he includes Ralph Chaplin among the objects of his gesture of scorn. For Chaplin, too, is an American.

The case of Pound grows more complicated as the American scene thus widens.[52]

There was something in this almost like patriotism, derived from prior distinction as to who were the real Americans.

There was a dilemma here, too, which went to the heart of the *Liberator*'s difficulties, and which in its generalization was so sufficiently pressing as to secure the best energies of Ezra Pound himself, and, for that matter, of serious American writers at large and for all of the years to follow. The particular reviewer seemed indeed to have been having some trouble in working up a proper enthusiasm for the poems of Ralph Chaplin, but he certainly had no doubt that Chaplin *should* be the better poet. At issue was that "common center of energy" from which both politics and the arts might be expected to derive their power—the phrase and the sentiment originating, it happened, not with any writer on the left but with Allen Tate in his most bumptiously reactionary mood.[53] Ralph Chaplin was manifestly in touch with contemporary American facts, his poetry being not only shaped but necessitated by American facts, while Pound had drifted away into a remoteness. The poetry of Ralph Chaplin had, or should have had, importance, while the obverse of such a poetry as his would have been trivial.

The particular reviewer did not say so much nor did he attempt to analyze his own momentary difficulties, but he was nonetheless speaking from within a problem intrinsic to the literary left. Gold and Freeman, so soon as they were addressed by the narrow demands of active political commitment, took up the cause of art, as against politics for politics' sake. On the other hand, they knew that art needed politics in order to be serious, and when confronted with the idea or practice of the primacy of art, took up the cause of politics. Writing from California, Gold cautioned Freeman against allowing the *Liberator* to be taken over by Party politicians. At the very same time, however, he was critical of what he took to be the indulgence of Bohemian aestheticism by the literary left in San Francisco and urged the primacy of political dedication. Freeman's immediate editorial difficulties were to come to an end fortuitously when in 1924 the Party moved the magazine to Chicago, but meanwhile and afterward the dilemma was insistent. "For my generation," he was to write, "the problem of art and revolution was to remain a thorny one. Even on the level on which we worked, to break trails meant to struggle with the most elementary questions."[54] By the time of this writing, he had settled the matter temporarily by accepting the somewhat patronizing advices of the leaders and becoming a literary functionary within the Party. But the problem did not disappear in this ending, either.

The problem was indeed deeper than the postulated conflict between art and the particular revolution. If it had been merely that, then the authority of Trotsky might have been sufficient, as it was to be for numbers of ex-radicals of a later generation. The "proletarian art" associated with the revolution, Trotsky had said in *Literature and Revolution,* was only passing through an apprenticeship. Proletarian art would never actually exist, furthermore, because the proletarian regime itself was only transient and a step toward a culture above all classes.[55] But the difficulty aside that after 1924 it would have been a questionable matter for a Party loyalist to cite Trotsky in any connection, there was more at stake, truly, than the question of an art which might be serviceable to the class conflict. Both "proletarianism" and "revolution" were local names which contained the basic social experience of such writers as Mike Gold and Joseph Freeman. Their problem had to do with art and culture, not merely art and revolution. It happened as a likelihood of their education in the formalities of literature and the arts that Gold and Freeman, like most of the members of their immigrant literary generation, tended to conceive of "art," basically, in the most conventional and romantic terms— although Gold did have some broader apprehensions—and by that fact they were further barred from any middle ground where art and culture might have easy correspondence. A non-autotelic art required an extreme adjustment. Freeman's initial inspiration to poetry had been Keats. Therefore, in the first place and prior to the imposition of Party demands, his integrity as a poet would have stipulated his continued adherence, not to nightingales, but indeed to that which in the moment was called "revolution." T. S. Eliot quite to the contrary, poetry was an expression of emotion and personality; and personality and emotion, in the case of Freeman and his like, were things most definitely qualified by social determinants. To write out of the knowledge of the innermost self, after the manner of Keats, required of Freeman, or should have required, an accounting of the experience of urban immigrants, so that to begin with a lyric meant engaging social polemic.

Keats and the urban immigrant experience were not readily reconcilable, however, as, given another turn of the political screw, it was obviously impossible to reconcile the twin inspirations of Keats and Stalin.

The tensions within the problem were in every way authentic, involving, just as Freeman was to say, a "struggle with the most elementary questions." These included, among much else, the root question of literary form, seen not as a matter of rejecting and replacing exhausted literary modes but as a matter of personal integrity. Mike Gold, who was to become famous for the narrowness of his aesthetic principles, actually experimented widely, in forms ranging from Futuristic drama to narratives based on techniques of collage. Freeman himself, deliberately and in search of a formal appropriateness, turned to literary criticism. He did not like the writing of criticism, he was to say, but "there was no longer a choice. When you are deeply rooted in one world, you can create poems and stories out of emotion, out of unquestioned presupposition. When you are in the No Man's Land between two worlds, you must analyze, weigh, compare, question, test, hypothesize."[56]

Literary criticism as a genre, as a literary form equal to but independent of fiction, poetry, and drama, was in fact to turn out to be the major mode for expression of the literary left, to the point where to be a critic was to invoke the highest possible literary status. Eventually, a critic associated with *Partisan Review* would dismiss the work of a poet on the ground that the latter was merely a poet. To be a literary critic, meanwhile, allowed one to be at once an artist and a revolutionary—perhaps neither with any purity, but something might well have been expected to happen when the dichotomies were allowed to inform each other. Perfectly silly things sometimes happened within the terms of the same rationale, as when, in the mid-thirties, the critic F. W. Dupee wrote of the book called *The New Soviet Constitution*, by Joseph Stalin, that this "short work breathes the dignity of the man himself . . . this is a document which for charm, frankness, and simplicity can have few counterparts among the state papers of history. And just as it confirms socialism in the field of law, so it exemplifies the new regime in the character of leadership."[57] The occasional excesses and gaffes aside, however, literary criticism as a genre was a necessary invention of the literary left—not a brand new one, of course—and it did succeed in maintaining conversation between art and politics. In the particular case of the *Liberator,* the politics finally silenced the art. Ultimately, on the other hand, literary criticism was the chief means by which politics was humanized for literary intellectuals.

New Masses

The problem, meanwhile, was art *and* revolution; it was not art *for* revolution. When the *Liberator* collapsed into politicization, that event signified a frustration. Gold and Freeman were now the most likely spokesmen for the literary left, but they were not Communist party spokesmen. When in 1926 they undertook the establishment of a new organ for writing on the left, the journal to be called *New Masses*, it was explicitly with the intention of recouping some of the breadth, freedom, and incidentally the native bias of the old *Masses*. If no one in this moment or ever again could invite the world simply to "Enjoy the Revolution," still Freeman, in the prospectus he wrote in behalf of the editorial board, did stress the apparently mutual feeling that the new magazine "must never take itself too seriously." *New Masses* was to be "interesting above everything else; fresh, vivid, youthful, satirical, brave and gay" while at the same time it was to be "sympathetic to any crudeness which is the expression of something young, vital and as yet groping and undeveloped."[58] Like the old *Masses*, the magazine was to be the work of a group of writers and artists organized by concordant sympathies but not by programmatic allegiance. And like the *Masses*, it was to be conscientious in its alertness to varieties of current change and native rebellions. "This country is fast becoming the greatest empire in the world," Freeman said in his prospectus, "and with this development are appearing modes of life which have no precedent in history or art." The premise had two implications, one political and one aesthetic. *New Masses*, it was suggested, would pursue both. There were "potential riches" for American artists within this new American standing. "The stockyards of Chicago, the steel mills of Pittsburgh, the mines of West Virginia, the lumber camps of Washington and California, the lynching of Negroes in the South, the clothing industries in the East, the Klan, tabloid newspapers, automobiles"— and so forth, the startling juxtapositions of subject-matters being deliberate, certainly—"these have still to find expression in imaginative, essential and permanent forms."

New Masses appeared in May of 1926, promising resurrection of the broad left despite the fact that, like the *Liberator* before it, it might have seemed at its beginning to have been endangered by the auspices of political event. The event was the textile strike in Passaic, New Jersey—nothing so urgent as the Bolshevik Revolution, but pressing nonetheless. The strike was bloody, large, and nearby. Moreover, it had a political definiteness. It was the first American strike to be led entirely by Communists, with the enemy being the AFL as much as the employers. The Passaic strike was the Communist party's major activity for the year, and the Party's best efforts were given to popularizing the strike and raising relief funds.[59] The new *New Masses* inevitably became an instrument for the promotion of what was advertised as a "united front." The first number had a report on the strike by Mary Heaton Vorse. A large part of the second number was given over to "A Passaic Symposium," in which all of the participants—including John Dos Passos, Grace Lumpkin, Arthur Garfield Hays, and Norman Thomas, among others—agreed with each other. The featured piece of the next number was a dithyrambic "mass recitation" by Michael Gold, called "Strike."

But the editors of *New Masses* chose not to be overwhelmed. It happened that the strike was over, and lost, by September, but even from the beginning and while it was alive, the strike was apparently regarded as being an opportunity rather than a fatality. It was, said Freeman, "our first issue to fight for,"[60] and the magazine itself demonstrated that it was not much more than that. The kind of the ambition of *New Masses* was indicated more directly in Babette Deutsch's "Dialogue in Limbo" between the ghosts of Lenin and Anatole France, which was the lead piece of the first number. Lenin of course has the best of the dialogue, saying that "beauty and wisdom" must be "in life itself, in the existence of those who do the work of the world,"[61] but if Lenin, as against the notoriously vacillating France, is given the superior authority, still it is a problem in humanism that he is authorized to answer. Or not even to answer, in any probative way. The shade of Lenin was being called upon to provide a benediction which might be appropriate to the aspirations of Michael Gold, Joseph Freeman, Babette Deutsch, et alia. The cause in its fundamental terms, was the discovery of beauty and wisdom within the structures of *real*—current, quotidian, and experienced—life.

New Masses began with a grouping of fifty-six writers and artists including just two members of the Communist party, the others ranging in their ideological commitments from the vague socialism of Van Wyck Brooks to the afflated goodwill of Waldo Frank (who at first had been named editor of the magazine), to the Bohemian radicalism of the California poet George Sterling. The various editors and executives and contributing editors included, as well, Max Eastman and Floyd Dell, John Sloan, Claude McKay, Arturo Giovannitti, Lewis Mumford, Upton Sinclair, Jean Toomer, Elmer Rice, John Dos Passos, Louis Untermeyer, Sherwood Anderson, Carl Sandburg, Art Young, and Edmund Wilson. They constituted altogether not only a significant breadth within the left, but also a momentarily manifest evidence of its durability. The assemblage of these, and the others, made credible the fact that since about 1908, through the war and through prosperity, through persecutions, through the episodes of gradual rigidification of the political left, and through the gradual rigidification of the literary right, this party dedicated to art and revolution had maintained a kind of coherence. At least in the beginning the fifty-odd writers and artists did meet together to make policies. They also quarreled, although on common ground. In any event they did not constitute the kind of propaganda "front" or ad hoc committee organization of friendly intellectuals which now and later the Communist party was able to fabricate. *New Masses* soon enough succumbed to new rigidities, but in its beginning it offered a proof, again, that the left was more than its politics.

The judgment of Lenin through Babette Deutsch, on the nature of beauty and wisdom, had plausibility in the first months of the magazine. The report on Passaic by Mary Heaton Vorse, in the first issue, did recruitment work, but not merely that. Her special subject since the time of the old *Masses,* of which she had been a founder, had been the lives of eastern European immigrants. She had been something of a left-wing Willa Cather, finding drama in the confrontation between the richnesses of the past of her immigrants and the industrial poverty of their present. The Passaic strike offered new instances, new opportunities to repeat foreign-sounding names and to point to the humanity and the nobility of those who bore them. And the same editorial policy which, in this first issue, found aptness in a report from Passaic apparently found equal aptness in, on the one hand, an exposé of a labor spy (Robert Dunn, "John Sherman's Progress") and, on the other hand, Robinson Jeffers's "Apology for Bad Dreams," a poem which had nothing whatsoever to do with the organized political left but which betrayed a nice sense of the experiential harshnesses in which wisdom and beauty have being:

> "for what are we,
> The beast that walks upright, with speaking lips
> And little hair, to think we should always be fed,
> Sheltered, intact, and self-controlled? We sooner
> more liable
> Than the other animals. Pain and terror,
> the insanities of desire; not accidents
> but essential,
> And crowd up from the core:" I imagined
> victims for those wolves, I made
> them phantoms to follow,
> They have hunted the phantoms and missed
> the house. It is not good to

    forget over what gulfs the spirit
Of the beauty of humanity, the petal of a
    lost flower blown seaward by the
    night-wind, floats to its quietness.

That realization, in that form, was also of the left. As was a story by William Carlos Williams, "The Five Dollar Guy," which told an anecdote of life among the lower classes, but for the stated reason that therein was the source of an aesthetic. The story begins:

> All the forenoon I had been thinking, returning to it and hav-
> ing it submerged again as more pressing matters were thrown
> over it by the tide: To put down, to find and to put down some
> small, primary thing, to begin low down so that all the color and
> the smell should be in it—plainly seen and sensed,—solidly
> stated—with this we should begin to have a literature; but we
> must begin low.

In the narrative which follows, a pediatrician on his rounds—Williams himself, by implication—[62] has a mild and indeterminate flirtation with one of the young mothers. The scene is a tenement, put perceived emphatically in its ordinariness and not as a degradation. The mother tells him about the old guy at the Gas and Oil Company down at the end of the street who had offered her five dollars for her favors, and she has a good laugh. And that is all, the meaning of the anecdote coming to reside in the narrator's realization "that here it was, the inexplicable, exquisite, vulgar thing—rarest of the rare in the imagination, the trod-den and defeated atmosphere of perfection." The narrative elaborates "lowness" so that the word will mean at once recognition of the com-mon object and of fleeting emotion in the moment of touching the ordinary, and strives, explicitly, to know a context of commonality beyond the expressive range of, merely, "a fascinating tissue of words."

This distinction of the propriety of narrative was not editorial policy, of course—the story was something Williams had written pre-viously and had filed away—but neither was it extraneous. Williams's reflections touched aesthetic principle which was fundamental to the literary left, and his reflections were somewhat exceptional only be-cause they expressed conscious, deliberate adjustment of literary form to plain fact. Given similar sensibility and less reflection, the more obvious manner of dealing with form was to dismiss it while assuming the simple transparency of words. In any event, plain fact was the touchstone of literary accomplishment. Plain fact did not even neces-sarily have a class origin, although most likely it did. What was impor-tant was that it be recognized as that which *was,* as a matter of ordinary experience—and if ordinary experience, the "some small, primary thing," was associated usually with socially-defined lowness, therein was an assumption which really did not need to be examined.

The aesthetic principle as actually practiced by *New Masses* did not enjoin special value in the social utility of literary forms, although it made inherent the possibility that propaganda, too, was literature, simply as a consequence of the interchange between words and the given kind of experience. The principle accommodated a range of expression, extending all the way from the fiction of D. H. Lawrence ("Smile," which appeared in the second issue of *New Masses*) to battering fulminations against supposed esoterics—"the farcical literateur," in the words of Herman Spector, and "the psychotic dilettante [who] is received with so much applause and reverence by the 'enlightened' sophisticates of modern bourgeois society" in this "age of the freak in matters esthetic."[63] Literary work was bad not when it failed to achieve form but when it failed to correspond to plain fact and was therefore trivial.

The distinction was submitted to particular challenge and illumination by the case of Ernest Hemingway, now and hereafter to be a worrisome presence to the literary left. The kind of crisp actuality of Hemingway's prose should have been, and was, demandingly attractive. On the other hand, Hemingway's fiction was inappropriate—*not* on the grounds of direct political implication even though such grounds might have been quite available to discovery, but on the grounds that the prose lacked the credentials of ordinary experience. Dos Passos reviewed *The Sun Also Rises* for *New Masses*. He said that he liked the book because it was so "extraordinarily wellwritten.... The people are so vividly put down you could recognize their faces on a passport photo." But then, on the whole, he did not like the book, because its subject was exotic and Hemingway had indulged his exoticism: "This novel strikes me as being a cock and bull story about a lot of summer tourists getting drunk and making fools of themselves at a picturesque Iberian folk-festival—write now to Thomas Cook for special rate and full descriptive leaflet." The novel was not even really faithful to its setting because the vision was that of an expatriate; falsity was inherent in the vision: "There's a lot of truth in the old saying that Paris is where good Americans go when they die. When a superbly written description of the fiesta of San Firmin in Pamplona, one of the grandest events in the civilized uncivilized world, reminds you of a travelbook by the Williamsons, it's time to call an inquest."[64] In the particular instance there might have been an unacknowledged rivalry. Spain was John Dos Passos's special subject. But even that rivalry would have been pertinent because, so Dos Passos might have thought, his own intention was to achieve the real, the low, and the ordinary facts.

As a more usual but not uncomplicated matter, it was manifestly assumed by the editors of *New Masses,* as it had been assumed by their predecessors on the left, that the proper subject-matter for American writers was American experience. The complication occurred because everyone now also subscribed in some measure to the idea of an *international* working class as a fundamental unit of society, and the matter was the further complicated because everyone acknowledged, although in some varying measure, that the international working class had a national headquarters, in the Soviet Union. Provisional resolution of the dilemma was to be forthcoming with the imposition of the Popular Front in the mid-1930s, but meanwhile there was real and obvious question as to how foreign-seeking sentiment was to be made conformable to an aesthetic of vulgate realities. Dos Passos, the expert on Spain, argued for a deliberated and exclusive, 100 percent Americanism:

> Particularly I don't think there should be any more phrases, badges, opinions, banners, imported from Russia or anywhere else. Ever since Columbus, imported systems have been the curse of this country. Why not develop our own brand? What we need [for *New Masses*] is a highly flexible receiving station that will find out what's in the air in the country anyhow.

Mike Gold argued that "Soviet Russia and its revolutionary culture form the spiritual core around which thousands of the younger writers in every land are building their creative lives." There were direct political implications in this literary debate, and indeed there were direct echoes in it of the continuous divisions within the American Communist party between the nativists and the internationalists. At the moment of this utterance, Gold had but recently returned from his first trip to Russia and was filled with new enthusiasms. But even Gold, in the same moment and in the same argument, finally supported the native bias:

> What I deny is that I, or anyone else, demands of young American writers that they take their "spiritual" commands from Moscow. No one demands that, for it is not necessary. . . . Moscow would not have created John Reed, Upton Sinclair, Jack London . . . American life created them. It will create others like them and better.[65]

Later reviewing Trotsky's *Literature and Revolution*—a book which might have posed great difficulties because it was so parochial in its own way, so much devoted to Russian schools and untranslated writers—Gold for the moment solved the problem of Russian inspiration for an American writing by discovering the similarities of culture in Russia and America. Neither of these countries was France:

> intellectual France has ended in Dada. Young America can learn nothing from the 200-year old boulevardiers, except to sit at sidewalk cafes and sip aperitifs, literariously. . . .
>   We who turn to Soviet Russia for help in self-understanding are luckier. There we find a new dynamism akin to our own American spirit. There we find titan artists who are grappling with the Machine Age. There we find a world seething with experiment, a huge fascinating art laboratory.[66]

The aesthetic presumed expression which would be minimally fictive, and exciting because of its unmediated engagement with common, current fact. There was within it no necessary preference for anti-intellectualism, but the aesthetic was based upon hard, self-evident, extrinsic fact, implying in turn a distrust of unfettered high-browism. So Edmund Wilson, a certified man of letters, in a piece of doggerel called "Representative Americans," established an equation between Henry James and Woodrow Wilson, finding both of them to be comically remote, comically ill at ease when faced with honest vulgarity—James who "Having ever vainly fingered ladies' lace / But never slept with Lison nor Lisette," and Woodrow Wilson who "could neither bully, trick, nor win / The old whores at Versailles."[67] The aesthetic also suggested a value in youthful perception, and in sincerity, with beauty attached to the credentials of the author, the more unliterary the better. A political credential combined with all of the rest would be better still, wherefore the biographical note attached to a story by a certain David Gordon was virtually a lyric in itself: "Dave is seventeen years old, and a member of the Young Workers' League. His father works in a paper plate factory, and his three brothers are workers. All of them, and his mother, too, are members of the Workers' Communist Party." Dave was a Western Union boy, and the title of his story was "Call Western Union."[68] Whittaker Chambers contributed a poem to the first issue of *New Masses*. He was not a worker and he was not credited with political affiliations, but he earned distinction as a young poet who had "recently left Columbia in protest against the censorship of the undergraduate literary magazine."
  The total tendency of this aesthetic was perhaps most perfectly realized, or literalized—which is not to say most fully exploited—in the appearance of James (Slim) Martin, who contributed stories and re-

portage with some regularity. With apparent conscientiousness, he wrote in the untutored American lingo. His subject was the pride—the skills, the concrete achievements, the masculinity, and the comradship—of the American proletariat, all episodes of verification being taken from his own life. According to the author's note accompanying his first appearance in *New Masses,* Martin had been a migratory worker for a number of years, a harvest hand, a lumberjack, and a member of the IWW. For thirteen years he had been a structural ironworker. Perhaps unfortunately, he had also been an actor, but "in some of Eugene O'Neill's proletarian dramas." In this first instance, an item of reportage called "It's a Hell of a Game," he wrote about himself as a construction laborer:

> Well, I'm an ironworker. I build skyscrapers and walk steel beams sixth of a mile up in air. Sure it's dangerous. A hell of a game. If a man had any sense he wouldn't be at it. But guess a guy just has to follow out his natural bent. Some folks aspire to reach the top of Everest; or find Cathay. Most young janes have their heads full of a trip to Paris, or a hitch-hike thru New England. All looking for a kick, a thrill. That's what attracts men to this savage pastime and invaribly keeps them there for a lifetime at hard labor.[69]

This was, as Lewis Mumford said in a letter to the editors, "not only what a steel worker might write: it is what he *ought* to write." "Slim Martin's stuff," said Mumford, was "almost too good to be true."[70] (The remark might have provoked a suspicion, but in fact there really was a Slim Martin. He was one of the regulars among the Providencetown Players and one of O'Neill's preferred drinking companions. Undoubtedly he would have been known to many of the persons connected with *New Masses,* probably including Mumford.)[71]

Slim Martin's stuff may or may not have been too good to be true, in Mumford's sense, but of course it was its seeming truth that made it good. the stuff was so conventionalized as to be schematic, and was therefore exemplary. Martin touched upon all of the appropriate attitudes: the superiority of blue-collar to white-collar workers, the superiority of builders to owners, the moral brotherhood of workers united in their craft and in the dangers they accepted and in their achievement, all in an artifice of folk language. The stuff was further validated, moreover, by the hard materiality of the subject-matter—life in a candy factory would not have conveyed the same implications. "This is a specimen of the kind of worker's art the *New Masses* is mining for," said the editors. "Sit down, you bricklayers, miners, dishwashers, clothing workers, harvest hands, cooks, brakemen, and stone-cutters. . . . Write us the truth—it is more interesting than most fiction."[72]

Come to the point of being literalized, this aesthetic was terribly restrictive, as many associated with *New Masses* in its earliest days came to know. Proletarian credentials would come to count more and more heavily, and there was the inherent embarrassment that despite the fact that some of the writers and artists responsible for the magazine had indeed held some varieties of part-time jobs, and despite the fact that many of them did indeed have proletarian parents, they were primarily writers and artists. The value in the aesthetic depended on its remaining an ideal tendency. Just in the moment, for instance, that Lewis Mumford was writing congratulations to Slim Martin, he was publishing his tribute to the American transcendentalists, in *The Golden Day*. It would certainly be exaggeration to say that he was patronizing Slim Martin. No doubt that Mumford even felt that he had something to learn. But Slim Martin could have been no model nor true mentor for him. The calculations within that aesthetic implicitly shared by all of the *New Masses* group would merely have aspired toward Slim Martin.

The aesthetic, although it was never really defined, did become absolute and was to be imposed. The whole of the discussion of "proletarian literature," which had had some currency since the early part of the decade, was by the late 1920s condensed into dogma—or not even that, but just a slogan. Earlier in the decade V. F. Calverton had been able to say that "the proletarian motif has introduced a new psychological element into art," which would mean new opportunities for art. "Artistic substance becomes imbued with a freshness and a universality that classical art could never attain. The interwoven dependence of one form of life upon another, the collective unity of the human race, become realities pregnant with esthetic as well as social significance." Moreover, he had said, greater freedom for art would be achieved through proletarianism, as the problem of sex was unfettered from bourgeois prejudice, as crime came to be seen as a product of social conditions, and so forth.[73] By 1930 Newton Arvin, a literary critic who was then fully convinced of the need for building the consciousness of the proletariat, was writing to the editors, "What I do not like about the *New Masses* is the affectation of idealized proletarianism, the monotonous strumming on the hard-boiled string, the hostility to ideas on other levels than one, the contempt for modulated writing and criticism, the evasion of discussion."[74] And shortly thereafter, into the mid-1930s, critics would argue the contradictions of what had become an accepted orthodoxy. "Proletarian literature" was to be a subject for scholiasts.

No one, in the earlier time, had been more orthodox than Michael Gold, and it was largely his doing that so early as 1928 a literalized proletarianism was becoming predominant in *New Masses*. And there was irony in that, because the inspiration of his earlier orthodoxy had been not necessarily, had in fact in only small part, been political in any narrow and sectarian sense. A conspicuous proletarianism had been his style, literary and otherwise—he had costumed himself, even in the *Liberator* days, in dirty shirts and "a big, black, uncleaned Stetson with the brim of a sombrero," had smoked Italian three-cent cigars or chewed tobacco which stained his teeth, and frequently had spat on the floor.[75] "Comrade Mike," Floyd Dell had said back in the *Liberator* days, was "for some obscure reason ashamed of not being a workingman. . . . And so he is in awe of the workingman when he meets him, and says extravagant things in praise of him." If there were validity in Gold's preference for Strength and Steam and Steel and Noise and Dirt, said Dell, then "why abolish capitalism?"[76] On the occasion in 1921 when H. G. Wells had come to New York, he had argued to the *Liberator* group that revolutionary socialism was impossible in America because the conditions of class struggle were not present. "We have classes in England, but you have none in America. Here anyone may become a gentleman." To which the seemingly inevitable retort, by one of the group, was, "You don't know Mike Gold."[77]

Beneath the costuming, however, there had been a purpose which might have been anomalous within the literary left only, if at all, by being so intense. In 1921 in the *Liberator* Gold had argued for what he called a "Proletarian Art" on grounds anyone on the literary left might have accepted, namely, that such an art was a natural extension in modern times of a true humanism. The issue was the choice of Man rather than Eternity, and the choice of the former demanded acknowledgment of certain kinds of modern lives and the hope for a new kind of human solidarity. What alone might have disturbed anyone within the literary left was Gold's insistence on bringing a certain kind of authority to this argument, namely, his own Lower East Side tenement background and information.[78]

As the political context changed, however, so did everyone's conception of what was implied by a proletarian art. Gold himself, having been an engaging and probably tonic presence within the left, found himself to be a power. He survived an attempt in 1927 to remove him from the editorial board of *New Masses*. He was charged with inefficiency, but his allies saw the attempt to remove him in terms of a struggle between opportunistic liberals and dedicated revolutionaries. By 1928, Gold, as the captain of the latter party, was largely in control of the magazine, which he deliberately and candidly turned toward a hard proletarian bias. In the earlier time, as when Calverton had encouraged the coming of a proletarian literature, the essential definition had been a matter of dramatic protagonists: the working man was to replace the noble, the merchant, the *magister,* and so on.[79] Now the essential definition of proletarian literature was in the credentials of the writer; "the working men, women, and children of America," said Gold in his editorial for the issue of July 1928, would hopefully "do most of the writing in the *New Masses.*"

There was still the theoretical difficulty which had been advanced by Trotsky, that because the proletariat was but a transitory class in history, a proletarian literature did not and could not exist. "Our policy in art, during a transitional period," Trotsky had said, "can and must be to help the various groups and schools of art which have come over to the Revolution to grasp correctly the historic meaning of the Revolution, *and to allow them complete freedom of self-determination in the field of art, after putting before them the categorical standard of being for or against the Revolution.*"[80] Here might have been a dilemma, but Gold had already resolved it in his essay on *Literature and Revolution* in 1926, and had resolved it in fact with better historical prescience than Trotsky's. "Even if," he had said, "for only fifty years the proletariat remains in subjection to capitalist society, will there not be some art growing out of this mass of intense, tragic, active human beings? . . . it is a fact that a proletarian style is emerging in art. It will be as transitory as other styles; but it will have its day."[81] And in any event, Gold was now in a position to command the coming of the day.

New and unlikely names began to appear in the magazine: A. B. Magil (a poet by primary ambition, but from the Yiddish-speaking ghetto of Philadelphia), Joseph Kalar (a lumber worker from Minnesota, of Slovenian family), Martin Russak (a textile worker from Paterson), and others.[82] Some of the elders, meanwhile, looked upon the new dispensation and retired.

Max Eastman, who had been in Russia for the years 1922–27, had returned with a new glamour which the new *New Masses* could not, in the event, abide. Eastman was now the spokesman to the West for the Trotskyist opposition within the Soviet Union. He was Trotsky's English translator. He had possession of Lenin's Testament, that mysterious document which purportedly denied the succession of Party leadership to Stalin. He had been expelled from the International. Now in some essays in *New Masses,* which were to become chapters of his

Marx and Lenin, he set forth to explain the questions at issue between the opposition and the ruling group in Russia, and he was denounced, as was to be expected by the American Party. In the moment—the summer of 1927—Eastman was a member of the Executive Board of *New Masses,* having received titular promotion from the rank of "contributing editor." *New Masses* still advertised its independence from the Workers' (that is, Communist) party, but by late 1927 that independence was vulnerable. Eastman's theoretical speculations were no longer welcomed by his fellow executives. He resigned from the magazine in January of 1928.

In the following year Floyd Dell resigned, for reasons having to do with the new stringencies of literary expression in the magazine and therefore implicitly for political reasons. He had been associated with the magazine in the first place, he said in his letter of resignation, "because it represented a partly Communist and at any rate rebellious literary tendency." Now, however, it had come to represent "a neurotic literary and pictorial aestheticism." Dell's vocabulary was odd, but it was also ironical and a little bit vicious. A mere aestheticism was the consequence of any dogma, right or left. And the word "neurotic" had a more particular and personal bearing. Some years earlier Gold had suffered a neurotic breakdown, well advertised by his friends on the *Liberator.* They had conducted a fund-raising campaign in his behalf. One of Gold's more violent episodes had occurred in Dell's bedroom. Dell would have used the word on this occasion perhaps with a feeling for fierce exactitude—the trouble with *New Masses* under Gold's dominance was that it indulged a monotonously sentimental proletarianism to the point of neurotic obsession. In any event, Gold's lengthy, bitter, freewheeling, and sarcastic response implied an extraordinary necessity. Gold could not allow it to be said that an aesthetic which justified itself as *truth*—hence the stress on biographical verification—was really a neurosis. He called Dell a careerist and a dilettante and several other things, but the main part of his response was an attack on Dell's credentials. Dell discovered neurosis everywhere because Dell himself had no fundamental reserves of experience. He could not be "sincere emotionally." He had nothing inside of himself. He was "a skimmer of surfaces." He was not related to anything. "At no time was Floyd Dell a real revolutionist. At all times he had a distaste for reality, for the storng smells and sounds and confusions of the class struggle. He had none of the contacts with workingmen and strikes and battles that John Reed made. He was a Greenwich Village playboy." Again, "Mr. Dell, the 'revolutionist,' has not had a moment's time in the past five years to walk on the picket line of a strike, or to write a single article for a revolutionary paper, or to lecture to a group of workers. . . . He has been busy 'authoring.'"[83]

Meanwhile, the Communist party was issuing orders. Although *New Masses* was never to be a Party journal by official designation, by 1930 it was accepting editorial policy from the International Bureau of Revolutionary Literature, which was to say the Comintern. At the Congress of the International in Kharkov in November of 1930, a "Program of Action" was voted for the United States, which stipulated that *New Masses* was to be "in every respect the cultural organ of the class-conscious workers and revolutionary intellectuals of this country"—which elevation need not have compromised the magazine in any way, but duties, obligations, and instructions went along with the honor.[84]

The "Program," as it happened and as might have been foreseen, simply led to new confusions. *New Masses* was obligated, among other things, "to enlist all friendly intellectuals into the ranks of the revolution." Neither as a practical matter nor as a matter of temperamental bias was it easy to conjoin "class-conscious workers," provided that they could be located, with revolutionary intellectuals, provided that they had not already been antagonized, in a magazine which, as someone must have remembered, was to have been "interesting above everything else; fresh, vivid, youthful, satirical, brave and gay." Gold, with his bias, had indeed been on his way toward forestalling the dilemma, by humbling the intellectuals and then replacing them with real proletarians who were to learn how to write proletarian literature. A year before, in the latter part of 1929, *New Masses* had established the John Reed Club of New York, which was to be a workshop. According to Gold's suggestions, club members were to attach themselves, individually, to single industries in which they would then become expert and they were to write publicity for strikes. The effect would be that *New Masses* would have a "staff of industrial correspondents" and would therefore be in a position to be the cultural representative of the American working class.

The John Reed Club did in fact flourish for a while, although only after rejecting Gold's assumption of advisory status. Other chapters were established in other places. The Chicago club was to be immensely helpful to a young, lonely, and groping Richard Wright, a dishwasher, insurance agent, and postal clerk by occupation. The clubs, too, however—after rejecting Gold's advisory status—finally found difficulty in uniting intellectuals with genuine proletarians. Members of the parent New York club eventually found their own rival journal, *Partisan Review*, which did not long remain a haven for the workers.[85]

Gold's initial definitions—reductive and fanciful, to be sure—had had at least the advantage of their forthrightness. He was with the proletariat and against all intellectuals who refused to look, smell, and speak like proletarians. But no matter. Now he, *New Masses,* and the John Reed Clubs as well were in effect instructed to screen literary eminences who might prove to be of value to the Russian-dominated Party. Gold did not feel himself to have been betrayed. He had been present at the drafting of the "Program of Action," and he was enthusiastic. He tried. But try as it might, *New Masses* could not meet the expectations of the Russians. In 1932 the editors were conscientiously confessing their sins to the International Union of Revolutionary Writers; they would hereafter, they said, do better in the fight against "social fascism" (a term which defined any deviation from Soviet policy), attend more to the achievements of the USSR, try harder to rid the magazine of "mild and harmless" bourgeois humor, "petty bourgeois passiveness," and "pacifist humanism," make more strenuous attempts to define proletarian literary theory, and so on.[86]

There were other American journals at the end of the 1920s which might have been seen to be sustaining of a revolutionary literary left, but *New Masses* had special claims. Whatever its more recent special biases or lapses or dogmatisms or follies, it still was engaged more noticeably than other journals in an attempt to locate the energies of an imaginative literature within the main line of radical politics. It made more noise. It was predominant, and therefore perforce it defined the situation of the literary left.

And the definition it implied was finally not discontinuous with earlier visions. No matter how erratically, *New Masses* did carry forth the genealogy of the old *Masses.* In point of fact, Mike Gold's singular and personal influence on the magazine was soon to decline,[87] and the newer writers whom he had particularly sponsored were in the 1930s to become for the most part, in terms of literary presence, Party regulars on the cultural front. But in point of fact also, Gold's own influence, at its maximum extent, occurred within a context of qualifications. In mid-1929 the list of contributing editors to *New Masses* still included Sherwood Anderson, Van Wyck Brooks, John Dos Passos, Waldo Frank, Arturo Giovannitti, Claude McKay, Lewis Mumford, Upton Sinclair, Mary Heaton Vorse, Edumnd Wilson, and Art Young, along with Joseph Kalar and Samuel Ornitz and Herman Spector. This was prior to Kharkov. Even if, as was the case, few of these contributing editors did much contributing, still Gold must have found inspiration in naming them; they comprised the large tradition of the left, to which, so he must have felt, he was still loyal. (There was nothing moderate about Gold, but he was neither a buffoon nor simply the Stalinist hired gun some later literary radicals have made him out to be.) On the other hand, these old boys did have their nominal presence in the magazine, signifying at the least some amount of concurrence in the magazine's practice. And indeed, Mike Gold's enthusiasm for writing-by-real-workers was not an idiosyncracy; it was a reasonable extension of that preference for the vulgate realities of American life which Van Wyck Brooks had been urging some twenty years before.

Certainly the more *New Masses* submitted to extrinsic political demands, the less it allowed for an imaginative buoyancy in a properly left-wing literature, but there was no necessary betrayal in that. The times after all were making stringent demands of a sort to which writers on the left would have had to be sensitive virtually as a matter of aesthetic principle. The left was the party which engaged literature in contemporary history, and also, emphatically, so engaged the writer of literature. Therein—in the credibility and honor and purposiveness of the author—was the justification of literature. Literature was serious not for the reason of being intricate or learned or literary or because it strove for transcendences, but because it addressed the circumstantiality of the world.

Therein, to speak of principle rather than circumstances, was and had been the difference between the left and the right. The technical achievements of the modernists could be acknowledged, and sometimes were, but the trouble with modernism finally was that it was trivial. If T. S. Eliot was "Modern Literature incarnate"—in Karl Shapiro's later phrase—then the case was made. When Max Eastman, belatedly, came upon *The Waste Land,* he was envious but baffled. (He had been in Russia when the poem was published. In France, on his way back, he stopped for a visit with Scott Fitzgerald, who read it to him one afternoon.) He was to recall that there were passages in the poem which seemed to appeal strongly to understanding, but which did not really make any sense. Eastman, it is to be remembered, was a poet and a professional philosopher. He concluded by thinking, "Perhaps I am too intellectual... and the old boyhood sense of American shame about having brains came over me."[88] And there were grounds for judging that *The Waste Land* was an intellectual nullity. For all of its hugenesses and showiness of learning, the poem, of course, neither achieved nor attached itself to any precise system of thought, and it moved through its own perceptions only to the point of murmuring its "Shantih, shantih, shantih." The message was irrelevant to the problems of the working classes, but much more than that, it was also beyond all contingency and factuality. It was soft. It was inapplicable to the standing and development of men as they lived among events and in places. Thus, even for one who, like William Carlos Williams, was more particularly engaged in making a poetics for contemporary poetry, Eliot was retrograde. Williams was to say in his *Autobiography* that the publication of *The Waste Land* had been a "catastrophe."

> To me especially "The Waste Land" struck like a sardonic bul-
> let. I felt at once that it had set me back twenty years, and I'm
> sure it did. Critically Eliot returned us to the classroom just at
> the moment when I felt that we were on the point of an escape
> to matters much closer to the essence of a new art form—*rooted
> in the locality which should give it fruit*. . . . to have the man run
> out that way drove me mad.[89]

Lacking engagement, modernism was decadent, and therefore it was to be regarded—although it took someone of Mike Gold's crudeness to say so—not as an invention in literature but as another of the amusements of the decadent classes. Our day, he was saying in early 1929 in an editorial essay titled "Go Left, Young Writers!" "is dominated by a hard, successful, ignorant jazzy bourgeois of about thirty-five, and his leech-like young wife."[90] It was they who were the consumers of those things made by F. Scott Fitzgerald and Ernest Hemingway.

> Just as European tours, night clubs, Florida beaches and
> stream line cars have been invented for this class, just so litera-
> ture is being produced for them. They have begun to have time,
> and now read books occasionally to fill in the idle moments be-
> tween cocktail parties.
> They need novels that will take the place of the old-fashioned
> etiquette books to teach them how to spend their money
> smartly.

It was not the case, of course, that Mike Gold thought that Fitzgerald and Hemingway were missing out on something more spiritual. Such gestures as they made toward transcendences implicated them the more in their triviality. Gold knew that literature was neither divine nor its own discourse, but "is one of the products of a civilization like steel or textiles. It is not a child of eternity, but of time." The pretense to eternities merely disguised class bias.

Gold was, as always, hyperbolic, but he was not imperceptive in thinking, as apparently he did, that there was something unconscionably arrogant in that which was being generally accepted as the best in modern writing, nor was he mistaken in saying that "the

great mass of America is not 'prosperous' and it is not being represented in the current politics or literature. There are at least 40 million
people who are the real America. They are Negroes, immigrants, poor
farmers and city proletarians and they live in the same holes they did
ten years ago." (As it happened, he was not, either, so very far from
wrong when he went on to say that "upon their shoulders the whole
gaudy show-palace rests. When they stir it will and must fall." The
date of the prediction is January 1929. There was to be no such rising of
the masses as might have been set forth in a Robert Minor cartoon, but
within a few months the era of prosperity did, almost officially, come to
an end.)

On the other hand, predictably, here was opportunity for young
writers: revolutionists of the left wing had been presented by default
"with a monopoly on the basic American mass." Gold had in mind an
exemplary author:

> a wild youth of about twenty-two, the son of working class par-
> ents, who himself works in the lumber camps, coal mines, steel
> mills, harvest fields and mountain camps of America. He is sen-
> sitive and impatient. He writes in jets of exasperated feeling and
> has no time to polish his work. He is violent and sentimental by
> turns. He lacks self confidence but writes because he must.

The portrait was simplistic and derivative—a cartoon precipitated from
a tradition, like John Bunyan's Christian—and at the same time it was
excessive, but, once again, Gold had a prescience to offer and he spoke
with authority. Very few of the younger writers who were to have their
day in the succeeding decade did in fact work in steel mills or coal
mines, and of course they came in all sorts of personalities. Their
particular opportunity for literature, however, was the basic American
mass, just as had been promised.

History cooperating, that meant plainly and as a most practical
matter that, just as had been promised in a tradition of left-wing writing, to be *of* the masses, whether by genealogy or as a matter of preference, was to have a literary credential.

Part Two

who owns america?

...the forgotten man....

Franklin Delano Roosevelt et alia

Franklin Delano Roosevelt, of Hyde Park, New York, and also president of the United States, said to the convention of the Daughters of the American Revolution in 1938, "Remember, remember always that all of us, and you and I especially, are descended from immigrants and revolutionists." He could afford to sermonize on this "text," he said, although in fact he did not, "because it so happens, through no fault of my own, that I am descended from a number of people who came over in the *Mayflower*. More than that, every one of my ancestors on both sides . . . every single one of them, without exception, was in this land in 1776. And there was only one Tory among them."[1] It was true, but of course he was joshing, or kidding on the square, and no doubt he intended to fluster the ladies a little bit. He was not on good terms with their organization. He was punning. The words "immigrant" and "revolutionist," especially conjoined, in recognized common usage referred obviously to persons of quite another genealogy and politics, and temperament and habits and manners and dress. But in Roosevelt's punning there was also an acknowledgment and a curious presumption of status, to the effect that immigrants and revolutionists in the common meaning really were Americans and perhaps the true inheritors of the essential American tradition. Here was a particularly patrician president of the United States claiming credentials by saying that, properly or charitably judged, he had just as good a family connection with American history as any Wop or Hunky or Mick or Polak or Sheeney-Jew. The country had changed since the time when Woodrow Wilson had interpreted its history.

On the other hand, the Communist party of the United States, having known a history of embarrassment in the fact that so few of its members wrote or spoke English,[2] had entered upon its People's Front period and was creating antecedents which might make it indistinguishable from the Liberty League. If it frequently invoked the spirits of Tom Paine and Abraham Lincoln, that was not surprising, but it also claimed an equal inheritance from George Washington, Benjamin Franklin, and Thomas Jefferson. According to some Party plans, the Lincoln Brigade in Spain was to be supplemented by a George Washington Brigade. The Party declared its readiness to defend, and its privileged understanding of, the Constitution of the United States. The slogan of the People's Front was "Communism is Twentieth Century Americanism." Historical scholarship was produced by way of confirmation.[3] Earl Browder himself, throughout the 1930s the most powerful leader in the Party, was made to be a document and a testimony. Surprisingly, not only was he himself not an immigrant, but his American roots did indeed extend back to the seventeenth century; his ancestors, impeccably Anglo-Saxon in their own descent, had been in this land for more than a hundred years prior to 1776. Party hagiographers exploited the happy circumstance. Robert Minor wrote the tale of Littleberry Browder, who had served Washington and country in the Continental Army. A leader among Yiddish-speaking Party members pointed out that "the Browders have a right to say that they are among the founders of America."[4]

The People's Front was a political tactic, of course, which had been invented by the Comintern in its own interest and which for the ten years of its life, 1935–45, was administered with considerable crudeness and apparent cynicism. It was not a cultural flowering. As a tactic, nevertheless, it was remarkably successful in securing for the Party an amount of acceptance in American life which certainly it had not enjoyed before, and also an amount of political power. And that it had any effect whatsoever was after all astonishing. Here was a clan of weird malcontents, un-American by definition, in popular thought and for that matter largely in point of fact outrageous in their basic cultural affiliations, who were asserting a presumption of, in the antique words of a specialist in democratic distinction, a certain Professor Giddings, their "equality of estate."[5] There was very little genius in the strategies of the People's Front. The Party's acquisition of the royal blood and of the accoutrements and symbols of 100 percent Americanism was so blatant as to advertise itself as a lie, but within the lie and within the hyperbole there was a beckoning truth. Even into the time of the People's Front, not to speak of its brief prior history, the Communist party had been preponderantly an organization of immigrants.[6] These latter were now saying, credibly and whatever the ulteriority of the Party's aims, that some of their best friends were Americans.

Apparently at a reach deeper than politics, the Communist party of the United States and Franklin Delano Roosevelt really did share a common interest. Everything at once—the Depression, Nazism in Europe, the pressure of the fact of the sheer numbers of new-stock Americans and therefore the transformation of the citizenry—all of these forced a remythicizing of American society, ideals, and tradition. The matter was urgent and practical. The country was perforce in process of being unified, and perforce along new lines. Bolsheviks enjoyed sudden pertinence in being radical democrats in coonskins. On the other side, whatever Roosevelt did or did not accomplish, he created a government which acknowledged the actual population of the country. There was testimony in the fact that so many of Roosevelt's major appointees were not statesmen at all, in any sense which, say,

Henry Adams might have understood the term, but were social workers recruited from settlement houses; if they were not exactly of the
people, at least they had met the people. There was testimony further
down the line in the cases of judgeships and bureau heads and such,
that so many of his appointees did have urban ethnic identities. The
whole style of Roosevelt's government was accessibility. This government in effect gave some new authority to the myth that America
was essentially a democracy.

That myth was important now virtually for everybody, and was
being revitalized into folk simplicity. So recently as the time of the turn
of the century, "democracy" had been primarily a matter of "liberty"
and therefore had been an argument and a property of laissez-faire
conservatism. More recently still, although posthumously, in the
teachings of Henry Adams, "democracy" had been the special
achievement of an elite, lacking whom democracy disintegrated into
greed. The beginning of democracy, said Adams, "as well as the form
it took and the standard which must serve as the measure of its advance
or recession in intellectual power, is to be computed according to the
personality of George Washington, who, without doubt, stands at the
apex of democratic civilization. . . . Hardly had Washington gone to his
grave when the levelling work of the system of averages, on which
democracy rests, began." So recently as the late 1920s, the mild, rather
cheerful humanist W. C. Brownell had written his book *Democratic
Distinction in America*, in which he discovered that while "'Jeffersonian democracy,' inevitably, as developed by 'Old Hickory,' had direct
results, both political and social, that lovers of all kinds of distinction
have no doubt legitimately deplored," nevertheless "distinction" quite
in a European and aristocratic sense was a realizable ideal for Americans and was the true task for democracy.[7] But democracy now was,
precisely, a leveling toward the average (if it could be found, for that
was a basic problem) and an assault on aristocratic distinction, with
appropriate villains and heroes.

The villains were easier. Roosevelt himself seemed sometimes to
be fighting in the ranks of the radical democratic revolutions of the
eighteenth century. Everyone, including Herbert Hoover, knew that
Business was the enemy, but Roosevelt attacked the "Bourbons" and
the "economic royalists." He was a leveler. When real royalty came to
visit, in all cheeky good humor the Roosevelts served hot dogs. In the
rhetoric of the Communist party, perhaps the most favored term in a
rich vocabulary of contempt was the word "imperial," as applied to
Morgans, Rockefellers, Du Ponts, and William Randolph Hearst. "Imperial Hearst," according to the advertisement for a book of that title in

1936, was "America's public enemy No. 1."[8] And meanwhile, even over on the political right, it was being said of Roosevelt as part of the standard, popular repertoire of abuse that he was not a champion of the people but a rich man's son who had never done a day's work in his life and that he was setting up a "dynasty," with son James as the crown prince.[9]

The hero of the democratic drama, on the other hand, was the "forgotten man," who was the authentically American democratic everybody but who was finally very indistinct, ambiguous, and variable. The particular phrase was Roosevelt's or that of one of his speechwriters, and was associated with Roosevelt. There was a probable if not necessarily calculated shrewdness in it because it suggested an inevitable victor in a warfare among the classes without naming any classes. The figure nonetheless, and no matter how indeterminate, was most significant. Whoever he was, the forgotten man was the true heir of America, and therefore was its aristocracy.[10]

The indeterminacy of the forgotten man indeed created a large measure of the literary, popular, and political culture of the 1930s. The proposed role was in many ways wonderful because anybody could play it; its potentiality for definition was almost infinite. The forgotten man was, at random, one-third of a nation; a sharecropper in Alabama or Georgia or Mississippi; Charlie Chaplin's Little Tramp; Edward G. Robinson's Little Caesar (in 1929, actually), whose imperial pretensions were wistfully unrealistic; a lumpen-proletarian from Texas; a son of the pioneers; a dime-store beauty; a hash-house waitress; John Dillinger and Bonnie and Clyde; the huge, stylized worker of WPA murals, hammer in hand; and Okies and little Jews and large Slavs and chain-gang convicts mostly black but including Paul Muni. The forgotten man was in temperament sweet, dignified, reticent, racy, hardbitten, militant, aggressive, shy, and broadly comical. Whatever else he was, he was seldom subtle, as might have been anticipated because he was a figure in a national epic. He could be almost anything, but most of all the forgotten man was an opportunity for appropriation of a consequential identity, in a time when such appropriation had peculiarly urgent social and cultural importance.

three

Lost Causes

Some figurations of the forgotten man, however, were more available for exploitation than others, for some forgotten men had been famous almost continuously in the mythical history of the United States and therefore, being more traditional, were the more pertinent to current use. Their legendary estate was in itself virtually a political authority. True Americans with folk credentials were to be found especially in the South and the West, where in contemporary circumstances they did not flourish but, glamorously fighting in a lost cause, under assault by the forces of deracination, did manage at least and provisionally to assert their significant identities.

WHISTLING DIXIE

White southerners had a clear advantage. The region was in fact poorer than others. The predominantly agricultural economy of the South had been foundering throughout the 1920s. The price of cotton, the mainstay of the economy, had collapsed almost utterly with the coming of the official Depression of 1929. Small farmers were affected particularly. In 1929 a half million southern farm families had marketed crops each worth less than four hundred dollars. Throughout the 1920s farming in the South had been in process of being consolidated and industrialized. With the ruinous fall in the price of the cash crop, the pace of industrialization increased, with the effect that marginal farmers, both landowners and tenants—the tenants typically being recently displaced landowners—were at increasing rate forced from their traditional livelihoods into towns and factories, becoming then a population of cheap and unskilled labor.

Here was an instance of genuine dispossession, the more available to imagination because the population was so credibly—if one overlooked the black portion—of the fine old stock. These were the sons and daughters of the dream of Thomas Jefferson. If anyone had lineal claims to America, these did. They composed, indeed, a remarkably homogeneous population. They were a people, bonded—if, again, one overlooked the blacks—by manners, speech, religion, place of national origin, deprivation, and their provincialism. Especially, for the purposes of cultural figuration, by their provincialism. There were differences in manners and speech and economy and so forth between Upper South and the Lower South and between East and West, but the South as a whole, if it had not been entirely exempted from the influences of the past half century of Big Business and Big Industry and urbanization and political radicalization and immigration, had been far removed from the main action. In terms of high culture, the South had been seen to be not only provincial but ridiculously so. As long before as 1917, H. L. Mencken, with his persuasive city sophistication, had dismissed the whole of the South as "the Sahara of the Bozart." "In all that gargantuan paradise of the fourth-rate there is not a single picture gallery worth going into, or a single orchestra capable of playing the nine symphonies of Beethoven, or a single opera-house, or a single theater devoted to decent plays, or a single public monument that is worth looking at, or a single workshop devoted to the making of beautiful things. Once you have counted James Branch Cabell . . . you will not find a single Southern prose writer who can actually write. . . . In all these fields the South is an awe-inspiring blank." That was a point of view, moreover, to which numbers of young literate southerners in the 1920s had assented.[1]

Mencken had said: "The picture gives one the creeps. It is as if the Civil War stamped out every last bearer of the torch, and left only a mob of peasants in the field."[2] But if so, then by the same measure the South did have its uniqueness: it was the one region of the United States which might be considered to own an authentic peasantry. In that happenstance there was the stuff of new myth, exploitable by northerners as well as southerners and by radicals of the left as well as radicals of the right.

For the left there was particular opportunity in the series of textile strikes in 1929–1930. The families who worked the mills in Elizabethton, Gastonia, Marion, and Danville were mountain people and white tenants, in both cases old-stock natives recently removed from the land. Among them there were virtually no migrants from other regions or immigrants. Less than 3 percent of this work force was black. The sense of shared and stable culture among these mill hands might in fact have seemed from one point of view—northern and liberal—to be forbidding. The strike in Danville was supported by the local Ku Klux Klan, among other civic groups. But of course the Piedmont strikes, which had begun (in Elizabethon, Tennessee) as unorganized and spontaneous demonstrations, constituted open invitation for various factions of the trade union movement and for the

Communist party. The Party concentrated on Gastonia, which became its chief political activity in 1929.

The Gastonia strike, as led by the Party, was singularly brutal and, as class drama, wonderfully simple. The police and militia were without doubt owned by the employers, and acted with criminal obtuseness. Communist leaders were without doubt framed. Martyrs were created—particularly, Fred Beal, the Party's chief organizer, who was framed, and Ella May Wiggins, who sang mountain ballads to the strikers and was shot. Without doubt also, the Party not only led the strike but manipulated it to its own advantage, but it did have extraordinary social as well as economic materials with which to work. When sometime earlier a manager in one of the South Carolina mill towns had said, "We govern like the Czar of Russia," the drama had already been fully conceived.[3] The class divisions in Gastonia were so clear that, for once, there was utter credence in the idea of an American proletariat, and at the same time, because the mill hands were *not* lineal proletarians but sons and daughters of the native soil, it could be known that there were serfs in America.

In both conceptions these laborers were unimpeachably American, and for once—years prior to the People's Front—the left could fully arrogate nativism to itself. In all unlikelihood, in May 1929, a month after the first actions in Gastonia, *New Masses* was lecturing the employers on the subject of the virtues of white Anglo-Saxon Protestants:

> The mill bosses forget that the 100% Anglo-Saxon has produced several loud detonations upon history. There was Wat Tyler and the peasants' revolts, the Chartist movement, the American revolution, to mention the most resounding explosions. These southern mill workers are an explosive people, hot-headed, handy with a trigger. Especially when they come from the hills. . . . Undoubtedly the southern worker gives the appearance, not so much of meekness, as lack of physical vigor. His eye is lack-lustre, his shoulders stooped, his attitude dejected. The terrible devastation of the Civil War, a rotten caste government, lack of leadership, a frightful diet of grease have combined to deplete his vigor. But the eyes light up, defiance springs from mind to the trigger finger. And as for courage, remember it was a Tennessee mountaineer who was acclaimed the outstanding U. S. warrior in France.[4]

At which point Sergeant York entered the Pantheon of the class struggle.

In another, related aspect, the proffered vision was Blakean,

with regional emphasis. Frederic Cover, a poet, published a poem
called "Carolina" in the July 1929 issue of *New Masses:*

. . . .

Here was a village town
Surrounded by a fringe of lazy hills,
Serenely passive to the march of time.
But the mill came down,
Or the factory, or mine,
Filling the valley with the smoke that kills
And drives away the laurel and the pine,
Beating them down
From the hills.

. . . .

The women frown
At childbirth with its customary ills
Because it must exact a certain fine
Of wages from the mills.
And they go down
Beneath the load of industry in town,
As went the pine
And as their men go down.[5]

The Party's literary task consisted, in effect, in discovering that
southern mountain people were latent Communists and that Communists, at least at some reach of imaginative capability, were just like
mountain people. Although Party analysts insisted on talking about
"the economic and political hegemony of the textile barons" and "the
black forces of capital," the task was not very difficult. It was, indeed,
providential. Mike Gold, for one, was ready. He had been soliciting the
stories of bricklayers, miners, dishwashers, clothing workers, and so
forth. Writing by these new folk had the greater advantage that it was
already perfectly conventionalized; one could know what the writing
should sound like, that it be as simple and dour and dignified, though
smoldering, as the folk themselves. It would not have been improbable
that there were literate mountaineers who also knew what they should
sound like, but in any event Gold, as editor of *New Masses,* was quick
to recognize a credible authenticity of rhetoric.

A point of maximum realization was attained in the lead article for
the issue of *New Masses* for August 1929. A certain Ella Ford wrote a
piece called "We Are Mill People." She was, said Gold in his editorial
comment, a Gastonia striker and a mountain woman, and no attempt
had been made to improve the literary quality of her story. The latter

assertion was perhaps not quite to be believed—particularly because the story ended so very gracefully, from the Party's point of view, with declarations of friendship for Fred Beal and expressions of gratitude for the Party's various interventions; but the writing otherwise had just exactly the untutored eloquence it should have had. The kind of the compassion evoked by the writing, moreover, had very little to do with Fred Beal. The point was the dispossession of a nobility.

> I am one of the strikers in the Gastonia textile strike. It was the first strike I ever was in. I was raised in the mountains of the western part of North Carolina. It was near the Balsam mountains. My parents died when I was small and I was raised by my grandparents. They rented land and raised corn, beans and such things, and had chickens, cows and hogs to make meat for the winter.
>
> Then I was married at an early age. My husband and I took up some land in the mountains but it was hard living. You can get enough to eat, but not enough for clothes. That's why we went down to the cotton mill one winter. Many of the mountain folks did that. They worked in the mills winter to get their clothes and shoes then went back to the farm for the summers. Sometimes the mills sent men up to the mountain towns and farms. They would go around and make all kinds of promises and ship off a whole trainload of farmers and their families to work in the mills. They said it was free transportation, but when we got there they took the fare out of our first weeks wages.
>
> They liked to ship off big families, because then there'd be lots of children for the mills. At first none of the farmers would go down to the mills. They didn't like to leave the farms. They called the people who went the "poor trash." But as times got hard everyone started going to the mills.
>
> Once people were down in the city they got into the habit of living there. They liked the movie shows and the radios, and being surrounded by people. And they got to buying dresses and things on the installment plan, and that kept them working, too. So fewer and fewer mill people went back to the mountains.[6]

There was needed only the addition of a motif of slow, innocent, and reluctant awakening to militance, which Ella Ford also supplied, and the story was not merely more interesting than any fiction, as Mike Gold would have said, but it *was* fiction.

As the story of Gastonia was told in such novels as Fielding Burke's *Call Home the Heart* and Grace Lumpkin's *To Make My Bread*, both published in 1932, the emphases of the tale and its grounding in mythopoesis and the strategies of language were those of Ella Ford. Although in both novels there were clear allusions to the major episodes and personnel of the strike, the strike itself was in neither instance really the main thing.

The emphasis was, rather, on the heroically conservative traditionalism of the mountain people. The Lumpkin novel begins in 1900, with a scene at a village store on Choah Mountain, where some farmers, in this stolen moment leisurely and neighborly, discuss the weather and the neighbors; what is revealed, in addition to some necessary exposition, is that in 1900 the ways and talk of these farmers are entirely pleasant and already thoroughly ritualized:

> "Still snowing?" Fraser McDonald asked Sam.
> "Yes," Sam answered, and being reminded of the snow, felt his shoulders to see if the wet had come through.
> "Think it'll come up hard?" Jim Hawkins asked the company. No one answered. But presently Fraser McDonald said, "No danger of it coming up hard."
> "If it was winter," Jim Hawkins said, "and it a-snowing, I'd be making tracks for my cabin."
> The men sat bent over, close to the stove. They puffed at their pipes and occasionally one of them spoke.[7]

The Burke novel begins with the childhood of her heroine, on Lame Goat Ridge. Ishmalee Waycaster has been born into a house built by her great grandfather, Frady Starkweather, ninety years before. Even in earliest childhood her life is very hard, but the woods and waters just a little ways off provide her with a continual refreshment. "Fer the land's sake, Ishmalee," her mother says to her, "the strength ort to be dreened out o' ye, cruisin' so fur, but you look like you could heave a hoss."[8] And what follows in both novels is a tale of several overlapping generations of a family, the moral and even the realized, if not intended, political message being that generational continuity is to be preserved and that the old ways are best.

The intended political message in both novels has to do with the potential for revolutionary solidarity which these mountain women—these are women's novels—offer to the revolution. The mountain women are to be regarded as genuine instances of the international working class, needing, both for their own sakes and for the sake of the reader, only some knowledge that they are such, but in both novels the point is broached only belatedly and tangentially, and is obscured by actions which take the novels in other thematic directions. In *To Make My Bread* the necessary conjunction occurs only at the end and after Lumpkin's heroine has died. The heroine's daughter, who has not prior to this been a major figure in the novel, now—although, as we are told, after a passage of four years—takes up the part of Ella May Wiggins, and then in fact it is left to her brother, who has been less consequential in the novel, to become the revolutionary explicitly. In *Call Home the Heart* this elevation to exemplification is less a matter of a final tag line, but is still more discrepant. Ishmalee is a large, capable, strong-willed woman, but the terms of the characterization will not permit her to be an intellectual visionary as well, and so there is something plainly aberrant in her ascribed enjoyment of the works of Henry George (for openers) and Karl Marx, the gift of the local doctor, as also in the excitement of her learning about her comrades in Russia and China.

Nor is it even so vividly clear in these novels as it might be that it is the mill owners who are the villains. The novels have the significant structural similarity that in each instance the first half of the book is given over to genre description of life on the farm and the second half to life in town. In both instances the accounts of the rounds of the days in the mountains do resist sentimentality. Work is unrelenting and frustrating. Random accidents are fatalities. The mountain folk are illiberal in their views, and constricted, and are sometimes mean and not infrequently violent. But it is the town, of course, that is corrupting, and it rather than the bosses is the real enemy. In town, houses are not homes. The promised joys of town living are not necessarily vicious, but they are inessential and therefore unsatisfying. The installment plan is a particular vindictiveness. Not only do the mill owners enslave these folk, but, what is really worse, they and their minions— preachers, politicians—tell lies and confuse them, with the effect of corrupting their basic social assumptions. It is in these areas of evil that the heroines are made to call forth their nobility.

The purpose is restoration, proved as much in the language of the texts as by any overt actions. The language in both novels is remarkably formal and elegant; it is spare and abbreviated by silences, and not efficient for conveying new information but, rather, suggestive of a complete and static community. The message of the language, as in the case of Hemingway's peasant Spanish, is that all necessary things have already been said, that all utterance is but a courteous acknowledgment of the wisdom of the tribe. Both novels break down when the northern organizer arrives, standing in for Fred Beal, and not only because the propaganda becomes temporarily more overt, not only because the character fails to sprinkle his speech with "yores" and "reckons" and "taints," but because this goodwilled outsider must be so expatiating.

What is to be known is already known, and finally it is not at all clear that the heroines of these frankly ideological, propagandizing novels learn anything much beyond that. The Burke novel supplies the appropriate ending for both books. Ishmalee returns to the mountains, her heart having been called home. To her slightly teched old mother she says, "I don't doubt that I've forgotten a good many things that you know, mother."[9] The tone of her saying so is, by ascription, hard and superior, but nonetheless the brief coda to the novel brings her back to her old life and explicitly to a realization of the contentment that is in it, although a bit qualified.

The thematic concern of Sherwood Anderson's Gastonia novel was, first of all, sex, and then the passional life in general. *Beyond Desire*, published like the Burke and Lumpkin novels in 1932,[10] ruminates most protractedly, and, at the same time, as narrative it is peculiarly disjointed. Anderson had in fact shifted direction as he was composing the novel. He had begun by writing a novel about, in his own words, "the ordinary problem of middle-class people in love," and then had determined to deal with "working people in the mills . . . the poor whites, in the mills in the South."[11] The thematic unity which finally he willed upon the text might have constituted, with the accents of a different kind of shrewdness, a not unreasonable judgment on some of the covertnesses of emotion in organized communism in the United States, particularly for the young and the middle class. The book he actually wrote, however, ambulates hither and thither, seemingly in search of an action which will prove the thesis that communism is the next step after fornication. Anderson's hero, significantly named "Red," manages the first step just in time before he is killed in the strike and the novel ends.

But even in this novel, for all of its brooding extravagances, there was apparently something like a regional imperative at work. The communism to which Red is made to aspire—blunderingly, wonderingly—has no ideological content whatsoever, but is a matter of communal feeling with a subcommunity, namely, the poor whites in his native Georgia. Red is a doctor's son and a college boy. He has little knowledge of the poor whites in his town. Anderson's main attempt to present him with appropriate information is contained in the short section of the novel called "Mill Girls," and what is emphasized in that section is not, as might have been anticipated, the sensual vitality of low-life, but its provincialism, the provincialism of both its frustrations and its joys. There is a sex motif in this section too, as everywhere in the novel, but it is not sexuality that is the allurement of the mill girls. Anderson's own knowledge of the mill girls seems after all to have been as conventionalized as had been his knowledge of Negroes when he had written *Dark Laughter*, but this convention carried him toward sweet mildnesses and simplicities. The major episode within the section is a visit to the country fair by a number of the girls. They watch a comic trapeze performer, and they are delighted. And that is all, but that moment of naive integrity is, lacking better, the centerpiece of the novel. In the beginning of the novel an avowed Communist has exhorted in behalf of the "big little people," and these are they.

If, on the other hand, this conservative southern folk, this dispossessed nobility, was iconographic for communism in the United States, it was equally available and useful for explicit anticommunism.

In the decades immediately following the Depression, the study of literature in the United States, if not quite the making of it, was virtually to be dominated by a handful of southerners: John Crowe Ransom, Allen Tate, Robert Penn Warren, and Cleanth Brooks, among the most prominent. That loose system of literary attitudes they represented, which, after the title of one of Ransom's books, came generally to be called the "New Criticism," would particularly encourage the reading of the poem as "autotelic" object. "Autotelic," like "tension" and "ambiguity," was to be one of the catchwords of the New Criticism. But the word itself was not a little ambiguous, because in practice it was most applicable to a kind of poetry which in its turn suggested certain and quite specific social assumptions. The New Criticism in practice preferred a poetry—significantly, it was not much interested in prose—which was grounded in a felt antiquity of manners and beliefs. The good poem might well make a gesture of rebellion, particularly in behalf of private feelings—most particularly, lust—but the good poem did so never with any revolutionary, antinomian fervor, but rather with the effect of accepting the provenience of the ancient wisdom. "Form" in poetry was a matter of paramount concern, and "form" did not mean merely the matters of metrical schemes and stanzaic arrangements and so forth, nor was it something that existed independently of a cultural context. It was a vision and a message. It was a reconciliation of the urgencies of the bumptious individual with the enduring knowledge of the tribe. Form was an expression of *amor fati*. "Form," said Brooks and Warren in their preface to *Understanding Poetry*, that most influential literary textbook of modern times, "is the recognition of fate made joyful, because made comprehensible."[12]

The New Criticism for all of its autotelicism did have an underlying social and indeed political meaning, which the southerners who were its primary inventors had in their earlier years addressed quite directly and as a self-conscious, spokesmanly, somewhat organized political movement. (Cleanth Brooks came to the movement belatedly, not having been in the right place at the right time, but he, too, participated in it.) These particular southerners, excepting Brooks, first of all had been associated with each other in the Fugitive group at Vanderbilt University in the 1920s. That was a happenstance, without ideological content. The Fugitives were some literary people in Nashville, of various ages, who met together for literary and philosophical discussions and who for a period of three years, 1922–25, published a magazine, the *Fugitive*. In retrospect the Fugitives could be seen to have been, in Tate's words, "an intensive and historical group," who were, again in Tate's words, "supported by the prejudices, feelings, values" into which they had been born, but in the time of their being a historical group they seem not to have been very conscious of their regional bonds.[13] The had such consciousness shortly afterward, however, as, separately and variously, and defensively, they discovered that their regionalism, their provincialism, was within contemporary American circumstances the cultural authority which they uniquely had. The cause they invented, which they called "Agrarianism," was, it followed, a defense of the politics, economy, and social history of southern life, the enemy being industrialism, urbanization, immigration, and, quite specifically, the radicalism of the American left. The manifesto of Agrarianism, published in 1930, was the anthology, composed by Twelve Southerners, *I'll Take My Stand,* which Tate and Warren had wanted to call *A Tract against Communism.*

Tate and Ransom, along with Donald Davidson, were the principal begetters of *I'll Take My Stand.* Tate had been the first to introduce the idea of a "Southern Symposium," as long before as early 1927. Warren had been one of the first of the contributors to be solicited for the enterprise.

These men were themselves not provincial southerners except by the technicality that they had all of them been born in small towns in the Upper South—Ransom and Davidson in Tennessee, Tate and Warren in Kentucky. In the Fugitive days the one certain thing that they had shared had been their sense of cosmopolitan superiority, and only Davidson had been something of a southern apologist. Ransom, in his editorial statement for the first issue of the *Fugitive,* in trying to justify the name of the magazine had said that it was the object of the contributors to flee "from nothing faster than the high-caste Brahmins of the Old South." When the magazine appeared, H. L. Mencken himself had taken pains to exempt the Fugitive poets from his general dismissal of the retrograde South, which was fitting because on their side they had held Mencken in very high esteem.[14] At the time when Agrarianism was being conceived, Davidson and Ransom were still at Vanderbilt, although Ransom was to leave soon afterward, but Tate was living in New York, having recently returned from Paris, and

Warren in the years 1927–30 was doing graduate work at Berkeley, then Yale, and then Oxford as a Rhodes Scholar.

In making Agrarianism, these men, Davidson perhaps excepted, were not really or with any necessity justifying their own lives, or rationalizing any continuous, abiding love for the South. They were, rather, like so many others, engaged in appropriating an identity for themselves, to be created from an available myth of dispossession.

And it was not the contours of high tragedy that they sought. Faulkner, who was much more authentically southern than any of the southern Agrarians, could exploit the more naive and romantic elements of the southern myth—the fall of great houses, the sheer glamour of individual daring, cavaliers and defeat and the sin of slavery—thus to produce, of course, a fiction of singular imaginative complexity. The Agrarians were less enraptured by the myth but more shrewd in estimating its current usefulness. In their role as regional southerners, they in effect laid claim to being the forgotten but peculiarly essential Americans, whose legends might propose the idea of true and reasonable community defined as the continuum of identity in private and family and public life. The antebellum South to which, necessarily, they turned for ideal confirmation, had actually not, in their accounting, had any really great houses. The old southern society had been organized, said Ransom with an effort toward strenuous distinction, on the order of a "squirearchy" rather than an aristocracy: "And even the squires, and the other classes, too, did not define themselves very strictly. They were loosely graduated social orders, not fixed as in Europe. Their relations were personal and friendly. It was a kindly society, yet a realistic one; for it was a failure if it could not be said that people were for the most part in their right places."[15]

Repeatedly in the writings of the southern Agrarians the truly emblematic figure of the South, both ante- and post-bellum, was the "yeoman." The yeoman, said George Marion O'Donnell, was the potential salvation of a southern economy which had become overly committed to cotton, and not only for reasons having strictly to do with economics. "Yeoman," he said, "is a good, healthy, Anglo-Saxon word for the sort of farmer who lives within the [alternative] tradition; yeoman means a lesser freeholder who cultivates his own land. The word is strong, and it has connotations of independence, character, and bravery."[16] The Roman Gracchi, said Frank Lawrence Owsley, had always particularly appealed to southerners "because the Gracchi were lovers of the soil and died in the attempt to restore the yeomanry to the land." And since in the old time there had been little difference of quality in the lives of yeomen and planters, yeomanry—Owsley did not quite say so much but he clearly implied it—was the nation's authentic patrimony; George Washington, father of our country, had "inhaled the smell of ripe corn after a rain, nursed his bluegrass sod and shade trees with his own hands, and, when in the field as a soldier or in the city as President of the United States, was homesick at the smell of fresh-plowed earth. He kept vigil with his sick horses and dogs.[17] "The farming South, the yeoman South, that great body of freemen," said Andrew Lytle, had been great and contented in its self-sufficiency, and he urged a deliberate return not only to the economics of yeomanry but to its customs and language, and also entertainments: "Do what we did after the war and the Reconstruction: return to our looms, our handcrafts, our reproducing stock. Throw out the radio and take down the fiddle from the wall."[18]

When they said "yeomen," the southern Agrarians seem to have been referring to farmers who owned and cultivated anywhere from fifty to two hundred acres, whom they converted into a folk. This folk was heroic in the folk manner; its heroism was its endurance as a community and the preservation of its ways. There were indeed current signs of a weakening, as real farmers were seen to be succumbing to the allurements and false promises of industry, business, and commerce—but that was not entirely a misfortune; it provided the southern Agrarians with a job to do beyond lyricizing. The folk tradition was to be revitalized from within and defended from without. The southern Agrarians had for their uses, therefore, both a plausible myth and a cause, an adventure. The world, in Ransom's words, was to be "made safe for farmers."[19] This was not the stuff of tragedy in the high Faulknerian mode, but it was the stuff of betrayal, and therefore the more immediately relevant to contemporary circumstances in America.

An ancient mode of communal stability was to be reconstructed, which is to say invented. That meant that history was to be rewritten, and, in the particular nature of the case, it meant that the Confederacy was to be made to live again. The northern victory had abidingly despoiled an economy, had robbed a people of its birthright, and, by way of further insult, had in the years since Reconstruction almost succeeded in convincing the South that virtue had triumphed. Herbert C. Nixon, who in matters of economics was the most-informed of the contributors to *I'll Take My Stand* and also the most progressive, proved that the northern invasion had abrogated what had been the South's normal, reasonable movement and development. The old South, he said, "was working toward a balanced industry, a reformed agriculture, and a free school system for the yeomen, when the war upset the orderly process of evolution.'' The old agricultural South, said Lytle, perhaps less knowledgeably but with more vigor, would never have accepted any portion of the economy of industrialism had it not been for the imperial North. The view to the contrary ''strangely argues that the victorious planter and the small yeoman farmer would have abandoned what they had waged a desperate war to preserve from others; and what, in spite of defeat, survived in its essential features until the second decade of the twentieth century; and what still possesses sufficient strength to make a desperate fight for its inherited way of life.'' And generations of innocent schoolchildren, Owsley pointed out, had been subjected to Yankee deceptions, until now the great-grandchildren of proud rebels themselves joined in singing songs about ''John Brown's Body'' and the hanging of Jeff Davis on a sour-apple tree:

> Thus the North defeated the South in war, crushed and
> humiliated it in peace, and waged against it a war of intellectual
> and spiritual conquest. In this conquest the North fixed upon the
> South the stigma of war guilt, of slave guilt, of treason, and
> thereby shook the faith of its people in their way of living and in
> their philosophy of life.[20]

Slavery was a problem, recognized as such by at least some of the Agrarians. (But it was not the main issue. Industrialism, said Lytle in an unfortunate turn of phrase, was the real ''nigger in the woodpile.'')[21] The one essay in *I'll Take My Stand* which set about to confront the matter directly was Robert Penn Warren's ''The Briar Patch.'' Warren did recognize, and feelingly, that the black population of the South had been oppressed for centuries. As was to be anticipated, he attached particular historical blame to the carpetbaggers and scalawags of the years 1865–80, but he was more concerned with what was now to be done. Warren, in this company, was emphatically, even sternly, liberal. The Negro in the South, he said, must receive justice from the law. More generally, he said that it was the duty of the southern white man, if only for the sake of his own preservation, to see to it that the Negro achieved equality of economic status. That was the message of the essay, but the essay was after all, in this company, not entirely discordant. It contained at least interlinear implication to the effect that the harmonious, hierarchical society was already essentially in place, having only to be protected from northern industrialism. Warren thought that the radical Negro aim for social equality—which, however, he did bother to consider—was impractical. He liked the ideas of

Brooker T. Washington. Most of all he thought that the status-quo-ante of Agrarianism was the proper solution to the Negro problem:

> In the past the southern negro has always been a creature of the small town and farm. That is where he still chiefly belongs, by temperament and capacity; there he has less the character of a "problem" and more the status of a human being who is likely to find in agricultural and domestic pursuits the happiness that his good nature and easy ways incline him to as an ordinary function of his being.[22]

For the larger part, insofar as the history of the black population of the South was touched upon at all, it was seen that slavery had been a most unfortunate imposition upon the southern way of life, to which the South had responded and was continuing to respond with a good deal of grace. It had been William Lloyd Garrison, Owsley argued, who had been most singly responsible for transforming slavery into an abstract moral issue. Prior to the 1830s slavery had been a recognized dilemma in the South, with which the South had struggled in a practical way; the slaves could not be sent back and they were too dangerous to be set free, and so, deplorably but understandably, they were kept in bondage. After William Lloyd Garrison, the fervency of southern race feeling was more reactive than anything else. And then came the war and then Reconstruction, when the South "was turned over to the three millions of former slaves, some of whom could still remember the taste of human flesh and the bulk of them hardly three generations removed from cannibalism." Slavery, said Ransom, had been "monstrous" in theory "but, more often than not, humane in practice." As for the present, education was one answer, but not in white schools and universities. Southerners would do well, said John Gould Fletcher, to support "such institutions for training the negro as Tuskegee and the Hampton Institute, which are adapted to the capacity of that race and produce far healthier and happier specimens of it than all the institutions for 'higher learning' that we can ever give them."[23]

The race issue was an impudent actuality, not to be ignored but not, either, to be allowed to disconcert the cause, which had to do with providing a historical reference for the myth of the organic community.

No one made a more painstaking or informative effort toward creating the usable past than did Allen Tate. He had been the chief instigator of southern Agrarianism. If the writings of any single person defined the movement, at least in its mythical if not its political dimension, his did. Soon after his removal to New York Tate had begun contemplating his own relationship to southern history. The evidence of his poem "Ode to the Confederate Dead," the first version of which he composed in 1926, suggests that he discovered initially that the kind of relationship he could claim was in fact very ambiguous, but that an effort of inheritance was therefore the more imperative. In the poem he had asked the question—not quite a rhetorical one, as it turned out— "What shall we say who have knowledge / Carried to the heart?" What he did immediately thereafter was to write his biographies of Stonewall Jackson, published in 1928, and Jefferson Davis, published in 1929.[24] (He next began, but then abandoned, a biography of Robert E. Lee.) Certainly it was to be assumed that the meaning of the southern patrimony, of the memories that "grow / From the inexhaustible bodies that are not / Dead," was to be found in the lives of these authentic, or in any event acknowledged, heroes.

What Tate in both instances discovered, either by reason of the factual nature of the material or by reason of the bias of his interpretation, was a heroism which had little to do with individual achievement. Much of the Jackson book was given over to military problems. A very large portion of the Davis book had to do with the history of the Confederacy as a government, and left Davis the man out of account altogether. The quality of heroism Tate was able to accord these heroes was nothing, or nothing much, in personal terms. He discovered, rather, the authority of his heroes' exemplification. In *Stonewall Jackson,* indeed, Tate would seem at first to have intended a kind of deliberately naive mythicization of the sort appropriate to boys' books:

> One summer day Tom Jackson climbed up from the river bank into the road that ran by his uncle's mill. He was barefooted; he wore ill-fitting homespun pants held up by striped bed-ticking galluses. Over his shoulder, on a forked twig, hung a big pike he had caught in the mill-pond. As he came to the road, Colonel Talbott, a gentleman of the county, stopped him.
> "That's a nice fish you got there, Tom. What'll you take for him?"

And what follows is a bit of narrative which proves that young Tom was a sturdy and honest lad.[25] That tone of address to the subject was abandoned fairly soon, as Tate moved the narrative toward Fort Sumter, but his portrait of Jackson did not become any the more subtle or complex. Tate's Jackson was the "Good Soldier." He was a Virginian, of "yeoman" stock; he was a devout, albeit reasonable, Protestant; he was a humorless man; except in matters of military strategy, he was a man really unequipped with any ideas of his own making; he had no politics, but he did have pride and deep loyalties. His country—that is, Virginia—was his kin, and when his country had called him, he had served without question or any need of question.

Tate's Jefferson Davis was more problematic, and try though he did, Tate apparently could not discover firm reason for approving the man. Numerous things were to be scored against Davis. His prominence and election to leadership, both early in his career and later, had been matters of accident and not the result of demonstrated ability. In a time demanding concrete actions, he had been too much devoted to abstract political principles. Although "Jefferson Davis's character, his honor, his integrity, were almost saintly," and although "in political philosophy he was superior to Lincoln," he had failed in the simple matter of soliciting and maintaining the trust of the people. During the sixties, said Tate in a rare moment of petulance, Davis had been a "chronic neurotic."[26] Nevertheless, the book did discover a mode of heroism for Davis, which if it was not so available as Jackson's was just as conventional. The Jefferson Davis who emerges from the biography is a synthesis of some royal Greeks upon whom fortune did not shine—brooding Agamemnon, baffled Oedipus, sulky Achilles—with all of their faults, true leaders of their people because emblematic of their people. The War between the States was, finally, not history, but drama, and "there was Davis, the protagonist, suffering the consequences of his mistakes, but equally the victim of circumstances and fate; never faltering; never admitting defeat; but always, in his austere gray cape and wide hat, walking along Clay Street, the very image of unbending pride, of that vice of the mighty which the Greeks called Hybris."[27]

Tate's personal relationship to the southern heritage was in fact not uncomplicated, and more than others among the Agrarians he seems to have known that that heritage was itself quite heterogeneous. One of the difficulties he had with Jefferson Davis derived apparently from the fact that Davis had been a man of the Lower South, where cotton was king, and Tate, as he probed Davis's background, did not find it to be totally agreeable. Tate had been born in Kentucky and had been raised not at all in the agrarian South, but in Nashville and Louisville. Moreover, it was his mother who seems principally to have provided him with an idea of ancestry, and the place she thought of as home was Fairfax County, Virginia. There was a family estate there, Pleasant Hill, which was in ruins having been burned by the invading Yankees.

In his most persevering reconstruction of the heritage—his novel *The Fathers*, published in 1938—Tate turned to Fairfax County. The title of the first of the three sections of the novel is "Pleasant Hill." He was not writing fictive autobiography, exactly. The time of the novel is circa the turn of the century, and the narrator is a sixty-five year old

man engaged in recollecting events of forty and fifty years before. But
there can be no doubt that Tate was searching for the terms by which
he might acquire a traditional past for himself. He incorporated into the
beginning of the novel a nonfictional work, *Ancestors of Exile,* which
he had started in 1932 and abandoned the following year, in which he
had tried to deal explicitly with the private significance of his southern
history.[28]

In its plot *The Fathers* is a family novel with historical resonances. The narrator, Lacy Buchan, as a small boy had been caught
between opposing influences: on the one side there had been his father,
the Major, owner of a small plantation, a man of great honor, a gentleman who lived in the old way by the old codes; on the other side there
had been a brother-in-law, who was not a gentleman in the same way
but who brought new energies and practicalities to the family. At issue
are the old traditions, which the Major represents but cannot protect
and which the brother-in-law salvages even though he is scornful of
them. Lacy inherits them, at least in some degree.[29] The achievement
of the novel, however, was not in the plot, in the plausibly characteristic actions by which southern values were rescued—although that
was obviously important to Tate—but in the mannered Tidewater
society which Tate constructed and which was to be made available
for rescuing.

The Fathers is a remarkably dense novel without being very intricate thematically. The society of the novel is one in which everyone
is kin, or at the most remote a country neighbor. When war comes, that
is credibly a family and neighborhood matter; Washington was after all
a southern town, made by Virginians who felt that the government of
the United States was theirs and that its crises were at once as distant
and as near as their own family affairs. Men, says Lacy, had that way
of seeing themselves at that time:

> as in all highly developed societies the line marking off the
> domestic from the public life was indistinct. Our domestic man-
> ners and satisfactions were as impersonal as the United States
> Navy, and the belief widely held today, that men may live apart
> from the political order, that indeed the only humane and honor-
> able satisfactions must be gained in spite of the public order,
> would have astonished most men of that time as a remote fan-
> tasy, impossible of realization.[30]

The society is one whose enjoyments have a perhaps foolish but
nonetheless satisfying implication of custom and antiquity. The
brother-in-law wins his bride at the annual jousting tournament, appearing caparisoned as a masked rider. The society is one in which

both gestures and rhetoric are so ritualized that the slightest deviation will signify ominousness. The attained if not the intended theme of the novel is, indeed, the ability of this society to compel sensibility. The brother-in-law, who is the new man and who is brash and rather cynical, not only is able partially to salvage what the Major represents, but does so.

Tate's novel, which powerfully adumbrated a conservative social attachment but not a politics in any narrow sense, was the success of southern Agrarianism. It was its appropriate success because Agrarianism had not ever been a discrete, well-defined program for action, despite some hyperbolic statements to the contrary. The approximately ten years during which it had had a kind of institutional presence had seen its ranks change, and the detailing of just what, really, was meant by Agrarianism had always been largely a matter of the personal vagaries of its quite various personnel. Southern Agrarianism was a partisanship of political sentiment, not a party.

But that is not to say that it was quaint and dreamy and, in the narrowest sense, merely literary. Certainly it inferred a claim to special social and cultural privilege. Tate in 1936, with Herbert Agar,[31] published a second (and final, as it turned out) Agrarian symposium under the title *Who Owns America?* and that title with all of its accusatory social, cultural, and economic implications accurately enough suggested the quality, the integrity, and the scope of the Agrarian ambition, as, plainly enough, it suggested that the proper owners of America had been or were in process of being displaced. Indeed, despite the lack of a program for action and despite discrepancies in the ranks, the southern Agrarians did very clearly define the kind of their partisanship.

They were against Big Business (that being the primary emphasis of the second symposium), Big Industry, communism, urbanization, the presumptuousness of the urban North, and social heterogeneity. Southern Agrarianism was inherently, logically, xenophobic. Writing in 1934, Donald Davidson would say, reasonably, that it was New York that had seceded from the Union, in the 1920s:

> What the regions of the hinterland did not see at the time was that New York was beginning a spiritual secession from the America of which it had been an organic part. In its population it was already a foreign city, with an amazing preponderance of heterogeneous new racial stocks.... Thus it happened that New York transmitted, to the one people on earth who were freest of class-consciousness, the Marxian theory of the war of the classes. To the least neurotic and most energetic of races it offered the Freudian doctrine of repressions and complexes. To a

people the greater part of whom were schooled in Protestant religion and morality New York presented, with a knowing leer, under the guise of literary classics, the works of voluptuaries and perverts. . . . Through a like consideration one can begin to understand books that are otherwise meaningless: the laboured attempts of Waldo Frank, Granville Hicks, Ludwig Lewisohn, V. F. Calverton to camouflage American traditions with their own peculiar obsessions about sex, Zionism, and the downtrodden proletariat.[32]

On the other hand, the southern Agrarians believed in private ownership of real property (that being a moral imperative, an instigation to responsibility), subsistence farming as an economics, the farm as the primary locale of civilization, nonprogressive Protestantism (the subject of the essay by Cleanth Brooks in *Who Owns America?*), the intactness of the South, the organic society, kinship, rootedness, stability, and, of course, tradition.

No doubt Tate in his essay in *I'll Take My Stand* had been to an extent carried away by the progress of his own rhetoric when he claimed that the "method" of southern Agrarianism was to be "political, active, and, in the nature of the case, violent and revolutionary."[33] Or perhaps he was being ironical for the sake of some of his friends in New York. The Agrarian point of view was nonetheless so distinct as to bring its conceivers to the point of consideration of practical means and methods of political action. "Just what must the Southern leaders do to defend the traditional Southern life?" Ransom asked, by way of introducing *I'll Take My Stand,* and he proposed a series of at least more refined and more leading questions, if not answers:

> Should the agrarian forces [in conjunction with western Agrarians] try to capture the Democratic party, which historically is so closely affiliated with the defense of individualism, the small community, the state, the South? Or must the agrarians . . . abandon the Democratic party to its fate and try a new one? What legislation could most profitably be championed by the powerful agrarians in the Senate of the United States? What anti-industrial measures might promise to stop the advances of industrialism, or even undo some of them, with the least harm to those concerned? What policy whould be pursued by the educators who have a tradition at heart?[44]

Ransom himself took a year off, on a Guggenheim fellowship, to study economics. He wrote a book on the subject. The book was not published, but he stated some of the particularities of his views in later essays. He sounded not unlike Ezra Pound:

Is it necessary to persuade Americans to guard the right to administer their own property? We are singularly enfeebled if we now resent the thought of such a bother. Yet our economic 'progress' brings the steady increase of a class of persons who might be defined as economic geldings; they are the *rentiers*, or the investors. The bad repute which once attached to the usurers when usury was nothing but interest was born of the plain man's notion that the lender of money, dissociating himself from the pains and pleasures of capital production, was dodging his responsibilities, and really was too deficient to relish the taste of them.[35]

The southern Agrarians, that is to say, were, although variously and for varied periods of time, engaged in making something more specific than social myth. It was the myth, on the other hand, which provided coherence to their ambitions for a cultural appropriation. Midst the chaotic circumstances, they had an identity. They were an American folk.

As, in not dissimilar terms, were dogmatists of the Communist party.

As were, for that matter, some number of eastern European immigrants, engaged necessarily in seeking out available terms of an American identity. The Odessan Jew named L. Wolfe Gilbert as long before as 1912 had presented his yearning, certainly not unmixed with irony, in the lyrics of "Waitin' for the Robert E. Lee." Sammy Lerner, a Jew from Rumania, had a nicer sense of the South as a folk place. In 1936 he wrote, "Is It True What They Say about Dixie?" Surely it was an eager, impish ignorance bordering on genius which inspired him as he composed the lines, "The sweet magnolia blossoms at everybody's door / The folks keep eatin' possom 'till they cain't eat no more."[36] But why not? If the habitudes of the southerners were somewhat grotesque, still they were traditional, and that was what mattered.

PUNKS AND PIONEERS

In James M. Cain's *The Postman Always Rings Twice*, published in 1934, Frank Chambers, a drifter, drifts into a roadside lunchroom somewhere near Los Angeles, and there he meets Cora Papadakis, nee Smith and late of Des Moines, Iowa. Her lips stick out in a way that makes him want to mash them in for her. She on her side is not unwilling, and they are in bed together within the space of something less than four thousand words. Subsequently, after two attempts, Frank and Cora together murder her husband, a happy, gracious, naive, and melodious Greek, inefficiently but brutally. At the scene of the crime the two make violent and delightful love. When the crafty district attorney closes in on them, they turn on each other. Their own lawyer is more crafty and they do get away with the murder, but the rancor of their seeming readiness to betray each other has been established. At that point Cora says to her lover and accomplice, "We're just two punks, Frank."[37]

Something which might be mistaken for justice finally does catch up with them. The postman, banal figure of retribution, rings a second time. Cora dies in an automobile accident as Frank is rushing her to the hospital in order to save her life, and he is convicted of killing both her and her husband. But justice has a relevancy in the novel not at all for its own sake but rather only as another confirmation of doom. *Postman* is a tale, precisely, of two punks, meaning feckless rogues or waifs who by definition are society's victims. No matter what terrible things they do, their innocence is absolute and unmitigable. Frank and Cora are just a couple of literary-mythical conventions, and the novel is not ethically preposterous. It is the case, merely, that a different kind of ethics applies.

The proper criminal is the City of Los Angeles and the much that it represents: money, the social order, and law. Recalling the night of the murder and the great lovemaking, Cora says, "God kissed us on the brow.... He gave us all that two people can ever have."[38] Unfortunately, however, investigation reveals that they are to receive something additional and unanticipated, namely, ten thousand dollars in life insurance monies. Such fortune is bound to undo them, as is any kind of material riches. Cora, submitting to entrepreneurial allurements, recapitalizes the lunchroom; she wants, now, to *be* something, to amount to something, and not to be a bum. Frank senses the danger in ambition of that sort, but he is helpless. There is a suggestion in the novel that the husband, Nick, had himself been undone by the fact of his proprietorship, of a lunchroom and a wife; he had had a fine singing voice, and therefore it is to be known that he had been in touch with the superior mysteries. (Cain, himself, had in his youth wanted to be an opera singer, and in all of his novels music is a signal of transcendence, beyond good and evil.) Cora had come to Los Angeles in the first place because she had had the bad luck to win a high school beauty contest, the prize for which had been a trip to Hollywood and the end of which had been, of course, a job in a hash house. Hollywood beckons, betrays, and corrupts. There is irony but also inevitability in the happenstance that Frank is caught when, at the cost of some considerable effort and danger, he is for once attempting to do something good. The law has neither subtlety nor accuracy, and is in fact absurd.

And it is to the point of the novel that its locale is a place some twenty miles outside of Los Angeles, for if Frank and Cora were inside the city, then there would be no dilemma, or there would be in any event a less unencumbered conflict. Los Angeles signifies imprisonment and, finally, death. Whenever Frank and Cora go to Los Angeles, they are in one way and another entangled by the law. Los Angeles is, in a word, civilization, and therefore it is the antagonist of freedom. Being in a middle place between Los Angeles and freedom, Frank has his choices. He does, explicitly, want to be a tramp. "It's fun," he says.[39] But he also wants Cora, who, if she is a self-described hellcat, nevertheless inherently has attachments to civilization. She is a woman. She represents home and family and all that follows therefrom. Indeed, at the time when Cora is killed, Frank has married the girl and she is going to have a baby, and they are driving toward the city.

Postman, which made Cain rich and famous, is nothing if not schematic, but therein was its achievement. Cain was dealing in conventions which were immediately apprehensible and which would resist imagination only as they were explained. Nor was *Postman* unique in either the general kind or the manner of its exploitation. Like such of his contemporaries as Horace McCoy and, more notably, Dashiell Hammett, and like the younger Nelson Algren, Cain was composing a final melancholy episode in that most authentic of American myths, the myth of westering. Algren was to move on, or back, geographically, but in any event his first novel was placed mostly in Texas. For the others among these writers, the typical setting was the West, and more particularly, California. With whatever degree of realization—for the most part, probably, very little—these writers were using a material they had inherited from James Fenimore Cooper and Walt Whitman and Mark Twain, to speak of higher literature, and from the whole of the folk fiction of the mountain man and the trapper and the pioneer and the cowboy and the hobo, and apprehending it at the point of its termination.

Edmund Wilson, in his one essay on Cain and the people he associated with him, "The Boys in the Back Room" (1940), was finally at a loss to account for what he perceived to be a lack of "weight" in the writings of these California novelists, as also incidentally in the poems of Robinson Jeffers. He was moved to a perverse poetry of his own. It was, he said,

> partly no doubt a matter of climate: the empty sun and the incessant rains; and of landscape: the dry mountains and the voids of the vast Pacific; of the hypnotic rhythms of day and night that revolve with unblurred uniformity, and of the surf that rolls

up the beach with a beat that seems expressionless and
purposeless after the moody assaults of the Atlantic. Add to this
the remoteness from the East and the farther remoteness
from Europe.[40]

But that which Wilson found wanting, seemingly a Balzacian texture of
social reference, would have been entirely contrary to the tale being
told by these novelists. In their sense of society there was no demand
for discretions and distinctions. Society just in itself and as a whole was
a bad thing. It was not even necessary to test the idea in cogent dramatic actions, for the pertinent knowledge had been established long
ago. The essential adventure of the westerer had always been not the
discovery of society but escape from society.

The adventure had always, also, been foredoomed. This most
authentic of American myths has its essential promptings in hopelessness. Try to light out for the Territory ahead of the rest, but the others
are not far behind. For every cowboy there is a schoolmarm. Nevertheless, these novelists were in a position to refresh the old tale with
new despair. They were indeed in the place at the very end of the
open road, and there they found: Los Angeles and Glendale and Malibu
and Santa Barbara and, what was no better a piece of luck, San Francisco. Their misfortune and opportunity, Edmund Wilson to the contrary, was exactly in the circumstance that the West was now obviously not remote from the East, not that the presence of large conglomerates of humanity was required in order to prove the matter.
Lesser numbers would also do. The setting of Dashiell Hammett's *Red
Harvest* is a small smelting and mining city in Colorado, population
forty thousand, called Personville. We know within the first half-dozen
words of the novel that the more appropriate name for the place is
Poisonville. Persons in community are, per se, poison. That, within a
half-dozen words, is the whole of the premise of the novel. And the
realization that the West now was the East, although with a little room
for abatement, licensed and directed everything: the episodic plots, the
casualness and repetition of instances of sex and violence, the ironic
detachment from orthodox values and the affectlessness of the telling
(authorial modes which might have been learned from Hemingway, but
were not Hemingway's; the problematics and the resulting tension in
Hemingway had been eliminated), the stylized argot, and the abbreviated, coded characterizations.

The plots had to be episodic because the essential conflict was
already and anciently established. Any attempt to revise the essential
conflict would have been not only impious but contrary to common
sense. It could not be maintained that Los Angeles was a beneficence.

The task of the novelist was serial illustration of the folk wisdom. And the same with the sex and violence, which are remarkable in their instances, at least usually, for being so lacking in lust or horror. Frank Chambers is not a womanizer, not—in the appropriate old term—a chippy chaser. Lust would entail some sense of inhibition and the *frisson* of encounter with the forbidden and therefore an acknowledgment of social law, but Frank is by definition beyond the law. The moral implication in Frank's sexual adventuring points away from Frank and toward the civilized idea that sex has become something which is regulated by the power of the state. Cora, on the other hand, is guilty, although we sympathize, because as a woman she is already involved in the state and because she does not want to be a bum. Likewise, whatever burden of guilt there is in the violence rests in the law itself. For people entrapped in civilization, murder is the obvious and ordinary mode of solving social problems. In *Postman*, the murder of Nick is Cora's idea, of course. She cannot simply take to the road, despite Frank's urging that she do just that, because she cannot be a bum.

On the other hand, the contemporary western setting, while it represented the final end of the open road, also revitalized the tale of the westerer. Something could be salvaged, or, better, reasserted, by means of attitude and style. Frank Chambers—like Dashiell Hammett's Sam Spade and the anonymous Continental Op and the Ned Beaumont of *The Glass Key*, and like Robert Syverton, the protagonist of Horace McCoy's *They Shoot Horses, Don't They?* and like Cass McKay, the poor jerk who is the hero of Nelson Algren's *Somebody in Boots*, and like the cowboy before them, and like the cowboy's own antecedents back to Natty Bumppo—is a character who, while not necessarily inarticulate, achieves eloquence by saying as little as possible and that little as tangentially as possible. These characters do not inhabit their places. Dialogue would be an abrogation of their integrity. In the later time they are situated in a West which has been fatally urbanized, or which at the minimum is about to be, and they are conscientiously, explicitly not involved, even though, in instances, the state may kill them. They are lonely men, for whom cynicism in their relationship with organized society has typically become so customary as to be expressible in the merest gestures, the merest fragments of conversation. And they are not only forgotten men but self-effacing men, who nevertheless are powerful by the amount that they appropriate an available American folk identity. Though they may be killed, their loneliness is the signal of their endurance, even dominance, in the urbanized West. These characters do seem to stand for some vague positive values—freedom, honesty, honor—but the values are only derivative from an idealism which in earlier versions of the tale of the westerer might have had some specific content, and does not and need not now. It is the suggestion of a last stand in their appropriation of the stock hero of the tale that gives these characters their special style.

That style had a force of implication beyond, apparently, the ambitions of even its creators. James M. Cain in particular certainly inclined toward a higher seriousness, but what at best he attained subsequently to *Postman,* in such of his novels as *Serenade* (1937) and *Mildred Pierce* (1941), was what could be deduced from the initial construction. These latter are novels with a message, and they are also inflated, uncertain, rather directionless novels, but salvaged by an idea from which Cain could not free himself despite his seeming efforts to do so.

Serenade probes the mystery of the inspiration of music. John Howard Sharp, a great opera singer, has lost his voice. He finds it again when he is put in touch with primitive religion and heterosexuality, combined in Juana Montes, a Mexican girl not distantly descended from the Aztecs; but then he again loses his voice when the influence of Juana is removed. The contention in the novel that homosexuality is vocally deleterious—that is where the plot thickens—was something that Cain had cleared with a physician, and Cain was afterward pleased to hear that *Serenade* was prescribed reading in psychiatry courses.[41] But the theme, a mix of D. H. Lawrence with Krafft-Ebing, was not what provided the novel with its sheen and its movement. John Howard Sharp, opera singer that he may and may not be, is a tramp, for whom Music is an abstract figuration of the last and, as of course it turns out, impossible frontier. In the approximate first third of the novel, as again at the end of the novel, he is a tramp by designation, down and out in Mexico. All of the conflicts by which he is engaged in the middle part of the novel are of a kind appropriate to a tramp. He goes to Hollywood, and, what is worse, he goes to Hollywood parties. He goes to New York. He signs contracts. He makes money. He becomes involved with a homosexual dilettante. The homosexual entrapper is in fact supererogatory, for clearly it is to be understood that the singer is doomed as soon as he abandons his solitude, and the homosexual villain summarizes that doom not indeed because his lust goes in the one direction rather than the other, but because he is very rich and, in the way of the very rich, able to manipulate the law, and because he is hypercivilized. Among other things that he owns, he virtually owns music. He has a private orchestra and arranges performances. And John Howard Sharp, despite his being entrapped and serially beset by all that society has to offer, never really wavers. Opera singer or not, his voice throughout is that of Frank Chambers: laconic, wearily cynical, simple to the point of being deliberately simplistic, even or especially in moments of attributed excitement:

> It was about nine o'clock at night, and the place was pretty full, with bullfight managers, agents, newspaper men, pimps, cops and almost everybody you can think of, except somebody you would trust with your watch. She [Juana] went to the bar and ordered a drink, then went to a table and sat down, and I had a stifled feeling that I had had before, from the thin air up there, but that wasn't it this time. There hadn't been any women in my life for quite some while, and I knew what this meant.[42]

It goes without saying that Juana, his quondam salvation, is a prostitute. This hero cannot be in love with domesticity.

Mildred Pierce is a woman's book, and as such must have seemed to Cain to present a peculiar challenge. In the event, however, there was no necessity for straining after new perspectives. The protagonist of the essential tale had been a man alone. Mildred is a woman alone, who might as well be a man. (And it was entirely appropriate that in the movie version of the novel, in 1945, the role of Mildred should have been played by Joan Crawford.) The starting point is a little different. Mildred has a husband and two daughters, and she lives in a development tract in Glendale. It is also the case that this is a Depression novel, and at least in the beginning there is a deliberate attempt to make of Mildred a typical, middling case. But having established these premises of action, Cain quickly pared away the differences. Mildred's husband leaves her, in the first chapter. Not long thereafter one of the daughters dies, quite without fictive logic except that in the first place the character had been an encumbrance on the tale. The second daughter remains and is functional, but not as an intrusion on Mildred's integrity. She is an ungrateful child who becomes an unscrupulous, amoral woman, and a singer, and therefore Mildred's own further adumbration. Mildred herself is designated to be a very strong woman who by dint of hard and honest labor will make a great deal of money and thereby triumph over her humdrum circumstances. But in fact the conflict in the novel is elsewhere because what might be the unmitigability of circumstance is resolved almost as soon as she begins and for the rest, like Cain's other protagonists before her, she is engaged in exemplary adventures in which self-sufficient isolation will be rescued from social conquest.

The money itself is not a good thing for Mildred, and in the end she will be rescued from it, too. Money—both making it and having it—unfortunately introduces her to civilization, which in this novel is chiefly figured forth in the playboy who becomes Mildred's lover. There is no ambiguity whatsoever in this conflict. The playboy is directly related to the homosexual villain of *Serenade*. He is an idler, he is very rich, he is the scion of an old family, he has impeccable tastes, he is a manipulator, he is as mannered as he can possibly be. He is a polo player. He refers to the lower classes as "varlets." But on the other side, Mildred, like Cain's other protagonists, although she is lured to self-betrayal, is never really in danger. Because this is a woman's book, much of the testing of Mildred's identity will occur in her responses to men. Given the time of the novel and, more pertinently, given the genre of the female romance novel, it is a little bit shocking that Mildred has love affairs outside of marriage, but it is more shocking and much more to the particular point that the love affairs entail no loving. Everything in the novel, however, is directed toward proving Mildred's ability to remove herself from dependencies. At the very end of the novel she will free herself even from loving her daughter. In her penultimate line of dialogue, addressed to her first husband and the father of the child, she says, "O.K., Bert. To hell with her!" And that is a triumph. Then she says, "Let's get stinko," for Mildred is a good man.

Cain was already in his forties when he published *Postman*, which was his first novel. He was at this point a screenwriter. No doubt, and despite whatever intentions he might have had toward a higher seriousness, the daily job of work he had and for which he was being paid affected his composing of fiction. Among some other things, his plots, like his characters, were defined within common assumptions, requiring little when not actually forbidding exposition. His characters were sometimes caricatures. and even at the very best they were almost entirely lacking in interiority. The mythic qualities of the fiction were also filmic techniques in the standard Hollywood practice of the 1930s. Those techniques were, as the event proved, transferable between genres, and in fiction, too, were appealing to a mass audience. Not without knowledge and not without some pride, Cain did deliberately strive to write popular novels,[43] and if that single simple hero he created had resonances, that was perhaps partly fortuitous.

But Cain was also and even primarily a journalist, with particular specialties in politics and economics. His immediate mentors in journalism for some dozen years prior to his coming to Hollywood had been Mencken and Walter Lippmann. Cain had been a reporter, an editorial writer, and a columnist. He was not a political ideologue, but some of the product of his journalism, notably a collection of

Menckenesque dramatic sketches called *Our Government,* published in 1930, suggests that he had at least a very vigorous idea about what was wrong with our government, from top to bottom, from the presidency down to the local school board. In the sketch in *Our Government* called "The President," the president is revealed to be only a barnstorming politician who can and does fool the people, and a plagiarist besides. In a sketch on state government, the governor is a drunk. In a sketch about the administration of justice, jurymen are shown to be hypocrites and cowards. Commissioners of public education are illiterate. An exemplary sheriff is afraid of ghosts. Even your local fireman is a gallumphing roughneck and practical joker, when he should be a noble fighter of fires. What is wrong with our government, in a word, is the people who run it. They are at once dishonorable, stupid, and dangerous. The indictment was total and therefore, of course, comic, and not amenable to particularized partisan response.

Another kind of response, however, was implicit. "As for our government," Cain might well have said, "to hell with it! Let's get stinko." That would have been to say that it was best not to be civic-minded, given contemporary social reality in America. The authorial attitude in turn defined, although no more than implicitly, a certain and familiar kind of heroism. To be non-civic-minded was to be a hero of American democracy in the old and ideal way, in the tradition of those who had always been on the run, on the road, strenuous and stylized in the adventures of disengagement. Hence Frank Chambers, who if not an inevitable development in the imagination of James M. Cain, was quite inferable. No less than in the case of, for instance, Allen Tate, who was Cain's opposite in every other way, a political attitude in effect attached itself to an available myth.

The same kind of politics attached to the same myth was present even more clearly in at least some of the novels of Dashiell Hammett, notably *Red Harvest* (1929) and *The Glass Key* (1931), although for Hammett the politics seemingly did not come first. In *Red Harvest,* which was his first novel, there is indeed a hint, but certainly not much more than that, of left-wing sympathies. The one person in Personville who is excused from the general folly and corruption is an ex-Wobbly union organizer. The novel was written serially. The organizer figures prominently in the first few pages, but then, rapidly, less and less, and Hammett seems not to have known what to do with him other than finally to excuse him. Hammett himself did move toward political affiliation, on the left, as Cain never did. He joined the Communist party and was to some extent an activist. But that happened in the late 1930s, some years after he had ended what was actually his very brief career as a novelist—all of his novels appeared in the years 1929 to 1934.

As a novelist Hammett created a hero rather than a politics, but a hero whose moral qualities might be especially discernible when his field for action was our government, perceived and accepted in its shoddy and brutal actuality. Personville, in *Red Harvest,* is a town in Colorado—Colorado with its spaces and great mountains and sparkling freedom—which was founded by bad taste and has quickly degenerated into feculence.

> The city wasn't pretty. Most of its builders had gone in for gaudiness. Maybe they had been successful at first. Since then the smelters whose brick stacks stuck up tall against a gloomy mountain in the south had yellow-smoked everything into a uniform dinginess. The result was an ugly city of forty thousand people, set in an ugly notch between two ugly mountains that had been all dirtied up by mining. Spread over this was a grimy sky that looked as if it had come out of the smelters' stacks.

And as with the place, so with community virtue: "The first policeman I saw needed a shave."[44] This is detective fiction, composed initially for the pulps, and there is a crime to be solved, but in fact the sequence of crime and detection is almost immaterial to the novel and is in any event terminated within the first few chapters. The novel then draws new breath and addresses itself to other plot-lines. The real organization and the real action of the novel are based, meanwhile, on the single fact that the hero, the anonymous Continental Op, is in this town for the duration of the novel, and the climax consists of his being able, at the very end, to get away.

Hammett created a most unlikely, but then also a most pertinent hero. The Continental Op is forty years old and rather short and fat—he is five-foot-six and weighs one hundred ninety pounds not all of which is muscle. This dumpy middle-aged man has only one passion, although indeed Personville will threaten him: he wants to go to sleep. He is neither glamorous nor morally excellent. His honor is reduced to the lonely principle that he will do the job for which he gets paid, the job itself being a fatality which clearly he does not enjoy. "'If you've got a fairly honest piece of work to be done in my line,'" he says, "'and you want to pay a decent price, maybe I'll take it on.'"[45] As he says in the final line of *The Dain Curse,* published in the same year as *Red Harvest,* he is not a "refining influence."[46] But he is nonetheless authoritative, and in a conventionalized way. The very fact that he is neither dashing nor noble—it is the negatives that count—testifies to his knowledge. Whatever else this man may not be, he is also not foolish. He has seen it all, and particularly, being the walking irony that he is, he has seen the other side of things. Nothing should surprise such a man, and *almost* nothing does.

Finally, the plot of *Red Harvest,* such as it is, is a matter of the Op's discovering that the town in its every function is run by crooks and then his subsequent cleaning-up of the town by turning all of the crooks against each other. He manipulates them so that they will all kill each other. And therein is the politics of Personville: everyone is a potential murderer, needing only the slightest provocation to become an actual murderer. The Op knows, and should know, because the very name of the place tells him so much. "Personville" lends itself to the pun which makes it "Poisonville," but the town is also, simply, "Personville," a designation of weightily neutral significance: it is The City, an aggregate of persons. Persons in community do, necessarily, kill each other, and for some small variety of motives which, however, are less various because they have in common a human contrariness to regulation. Sometimes people are in love. Often they are greedy. The crooked sheriff is moved to murder by feelings of family loyalty. The only distinction of value between the various persons who commit the murders is in the frankness of their acknowledgment of their motives, but no matter what they know of themselves, people will kill each other. The Op performs a job of purgation, providing welcome but temporary relief, but peace can be imposed on Personville after all only by brute force—and at the end of the novel, as the Op leaves, the state militia comes in, wherefore "Personville, under martial law, was developing into a sweet-smelling thornless bed of roses."[47]

There are no villains in this fiction, which begins with the idea that persons in community are inherently harmful. The hero nonetheless is endangered—not by any person, but rather by the skill with which he himself is able to enter into and manipulate the politics of Personville. He will say to his client, expressly, at the beginning of his residency, that he will not "play politics" for the man, but the job he takes on involves his doing just that, and the more so the more he succeeds in the job. His moral low point occurs when he begins to feel pleased with his performance and thereby to become a part of the community's essential politics, although of course only relatively because his irony protects him:

> As I reached the hotel, a battered black touring car went down the street, hitting fifty at least, crammed to the curtains with men.
>
> I grinned after it. Poisonville was beginning to boil out under

the lid, and I felt so much like a native that even the memory of my very un-nice part in the boiling didn't keep me from getting twelve solid end-to-end hours of sleep.

His moral high point occurs, on the other hand, when he correctly diagnoses the contamination inherent in the town:

> "This damned burg's getting me. If I don't get away soon I'll be going blood-simple like the natives. . . .
> "I've arranged a killing or two in my time, when they were necessary. But this is the first time I've ever got the fever. It's this damned burg. You can't go straight here. I got myself tangled at the beginning"[48]

And then having discovered to his surprise that he is susceptible, he can once again assume his customary aloof integrity.

The Glass Key is less schematic and more furnished with circumstances and particularized motivations. The scene now is a real city, presumably San Francisco, rather than an emblem of The City, and the hero's field for action is city-style boss politics, in its details of patronage and organization. The hero himself is not, either, so distinctly and essentially remote from the action, but is a credible youngish man who does, precisely, play politics. He describes himself as "a gambler and a politician's hanger-on," and in fact it is never clear just what he is by ambition and social determination, but for the duration of the novel, in any event, he is by occupation a political strategist. Moreover, the premise of the conflict in the novel is a typifying American version of the class struggle. The political boss for whom the hero does strategy has a foreign-sounding surname—Madvig. Boss-style, he has been an honest crook, practical and efficient in his warfare with rival crooks but a bearer of responsibilities, protective of the weak, loyal to his friends, and a man of strong family feeling. His troubles begin when he becomes involved romantically and politically with the WASP aristocracy, who will be found out to be using him for their own willful and arrogant ends. It will be the hero's plot function to return Madvig to his proper sphere of crookedness by revealing how much more grossly immoral is the politics of gentlemen. Almost fatally, Madvig, the political boss, had allowed himself to be enticed into society.

The hero of the novel is less legendary than was the Continental Op—for one thing, he has a name. The address of the novel is toward a more analytic realism—for one thing, this novel is told in the third person. But the tale being told is based upon those same tensions and realizations which inform *Red Harvest,* and the moral in the tale is the more defined, although not more definite, only because seemingly a greater amount of credible social detail has been engaged. Just like the Continental Op, Ned Beaumont begins at a level of social cynicism which should allow no possibility of surprises. He is not a weary detective, but, although youngish, he is already a hardened, dispassionate gambler, and in the matter of privileged knowledge of the human community, that amounts to the same thing: he has seen society at its naked and exemplary worst and knows what to expect. It follows that he has wonderful instincts for political mechination. Like the Op, Beaumont is an outsider, both in fact—he is from New York, where presumably he has learned a great deal about San Francisco—and on principle. And like the Op he is endangered finally only by his own skill. He is, again, a virtuoso of social corruption. As the plot of the novel is worked out, the city's fine old aristocracy present instances of greater iniquity than even he is used to, but his knowledge is equal to the necessary task of exposé and he is able to return the city to its proper thieves. His ability, however, entails risks: of gratitude, of friendship, of fortune, of power, even of romance, and, in sum, of involvement. The plot of the novel might in itself, indeed, allow Beaumont to introduce good government to our government, with just one more turn of event, but then the plot would contradict the character because his heroism is in the fact that, like the Op, he is fundamentally and from the beginning aloof from all social engagements. He has risked himself, but at the end of the novel he packs his bags and lights out—for New York, as it happens, but that, too, is a mode of westering given the fact that there is no more West.

Robert Syverton, in Horace McCoy's novel of 1935, *They Shoot Horses, Don't They?* says, "I try to do somebody a favor and I wind up getting killed myself." There are many ironies here, not the least of them being that throughout the main action of the novel he has been performing a very close approximation of a *danse macabre;* he has been dead for a long time, albeit without full realization. At the moment of the utterance he is being sentenced to die because he has murdered his girl friend. That is the favor he had tendered. But the girl, Gloria, had indeed begged him to kill her as an act of friendship, and as a friend, her only friend, he had complied. ("'Ain't he an obliging bastard?'" says one of the policemen who arrest him.)[49] Moreover, she had taught him something and so he had owed her a favor. What in particular she had taught him was that it was better to be dead, wherefore it is to be understood that in his own forthcoming execution there will be an ironic graciousness.

The novel is compact, swift, reductive, and unremittingly deathly. The whole of the action takes place in flashback as the judge is pronouncing sentence. The whole of the point of the dance marathon which is the scene of the main action is degradation leading to utter exhaustion of the body and the spirit. Robert himself prior to his enlightenment is a passive, accommodative, moderately sanguine kind of fellow, but throughout the marathon he holds death in his arms. Gloria is absolutely, naggingly suicidal. She speaks death virtually in every instance in which she is given voice. "'It's peculiar to me,'" she says to Robert at the time of their first, implicitly romantic meeting, "'that everybody pays so much attention to living and so little to dying. Why are these high-powered scientists always screwing around trying to prolong life instead of finding pleasant ways to end it?'" Encountering a pregnant woman in the dance contest, she advises abortion. "'I'd be better off dead,'" she says, "'and so would everybody else.'" She is unremittingly propaedeutic. "'Before I met you,'" Robert will say to her, "'I didn't know what it was to be around gloomy people'"[50] *They Shoot Horses, Don't They?* had great success in France in the 1940s and was praised by Camus, Sartre, and Simone de Beauvoir on the ground that it was the first existentialist novel to have appeared in America.[51]

But the death theme in the novel is not so philosophically pretentious, nor, peculiarly, is the novel itself finally so somber as the message it so persistently propounds. The question of suicide is not really a question at all; it is not argued, appraised, considered. While Robert does undergo some process of being converted to Gloria's view of things, the amount of the process is very modest; he is ripe for hopelessness and is not a deep thinker, and, moreover, he is from the beginning in general agreement with Gloria. On that occasion of their first meeting, she says, "'I'll tell you what I would do if I had the guts: I'd walk out of a window or throw myself in front of a street car or something,'" and he says, "'I know how you feel... I know exactly how you feel.'"[52] His education, such as it is, consists not in his being convinced by, but rather in his being attracted to, Gloria. And she, for all her morbidity, provides him not with an idea about death but with an exemplum of glamour.

They Shoot Horses, Don't They? is another of the California novels of the 1930s. It is a Hollywood novel, more particularly, which, in a Hollywood way, is consistently, determinedly superficial. Gloria and Robert are a couple of punks. At the beginning of the novel they have already for some time been trying to get their break in pictures and are already almost totally disenchanted, but insofar as they are not, the dance marathon is Hollywood-in-small and completes the lesson. There should be lovely promise in the dance, something as alluring as whatever it was in the movie magazines which had brought Gloria to Hollywood in the first place, but of course the reality of the marathon is its hucksterism and politics and greed and brutality. And Gloria, being one step ahead of Robert in her knowledge of sordidness, creates style out of her knowledge, which, if it is one-dimensional, is also unmitigable and therefore extraordinary, larger than life. Gloria's morbidity is mythologized. McCoy seems to have taken some trouble, in fact, to excise specific causes and justifications from the novel. In an original draft there had been references to bread lines and other data of the Depression and to the current plight of the poor.[53] At least in this instance (if not in his one other, subsequent Hollywood novel, *I Should Have Stayed Home*) apparently he knew that such allusions were beside the point or, at best, betrayed the character into bathos, because Gloria's achievement of style has little to do with common, credible, topical motivations.[54] She is pure. She is, indeed, a star, and is the equal and the ironic counterpart of Sue Carol, Alice Faye, Anita Louise, and others among the known stars who come to visit the marathon. These latter are in the gallery, and Gloria is in the pit; Gloria, that is to say, is as far down as they are far up, and in this case the way down and the way up are the same way. And Robert, it is to be noted, has had ambitions to be a director and therefore is the more likely to recognize a star when he sees one.

As the novel is structured, Robert tells the tale of Gloria, but he is nonetheless himself the protagonist of the novel, his action being his appreciation of Gloria. Prior to the marathon, Robert has liked to visit a certain park where, by sitting and gazing fixedly at the surrounding apartment buildings, through the palm trees, he could make them seem to recede. "That way you could drive them as far into the distance as you wanted to." The dance hall is located on an old amusement pier, and throughout the dancing Robert feels the continuous throbbing of the Pacific Ocean beneath his feet. He is, says Gloria, " 'hipped on the subject of waves.' "[55] The dance hall is enclosed but there is a window to the west, and Robert spends every afternoon dancing in the light of the setting sun. All of these suggestions, then, converge in Gloria. She is not misnamed. In a most conventionalized way, she represents rejection, intransigent disengagement, and transcendence, in the midst of the marathon. She is fundamentally innocent, fundamentally untouchable. She gives her name to a heroism Robert—and, presumably, Horace McCoy—can recognize, that heroism being once again that of the westerer come to the extremity of a last stand.

In Nelson Algren's first novel, *Somebody in Boots*, also published in 1935, the hero is utterly one of our lumpen. Cass McKay is one of the

"Homeless Boys of America" to whom the novel is dedicated. He is utterly a social victim. He is, besides, a weakling and a sniveler and a cowardly thief and an ethical moron and an intellectual nullity, who nonetheless is to have something to tell us.

The novel is uneven, as Algren himself said in a preface to a later edition,[56] and more particularly it suffers from a dedacticism which the tale will not justify. The novel has specifically Marxist ambitions. Cass leaves his home in West Texas at the age of sixteen and takes to the rails, and wherever he goes, from one city to another, he is exposed to implicit and often explicit homiletics. While still at home he learns from the hoboes camped in the local jungle that the world is divided between "we" and "them," the latter being "people who lived ample lives, who always stayed in one place, who always had a roof over their head. . . . In judging a man, Cass learned, the larger question was not whether the man was black, white, or brown—it was whether he was a transient or 'One of them "inside" folks.'" The time now is 1926. In 1930 he learns about "'the big trouble.'"

> Wherever he walked that winter, whether in New Orleans along the icy docks or on the Railroad Street in Baton Rouge, he saw the vast army of America's homeless ones; the boys and old women, the old men and young girls, a ragged parade of dull grey faces, begging, thieving, hawking, selling and whoring. Faces haggard, and hungry, and cold, and afraid; as they passed, booted men followed and watched.

Shortly thereafter, in San Antonio, he meets a displaced Litvak, from Memel, who in the manner of medieval romance tells him his exemplary story: "'For one year I am scab,' he said, 'I get reech. Not unnerstan'. Then unnerstan': I am scab. I join oonion. I strike. I am fire. No *joo*stice. I am poor once more.'" In Chicago, at the site of the World's Fair, Algren himself intervenes to speculate in rolling sarcasms on the subjects of war, private ownership, and the *Chicago Tribune*. Still in Chicago, Cass is brought to a Communist party rally, by a black, and he listens to an elderly black speaker who says that the bosses, black and white, have stripped him of all he has earned in a lifetime of toil, whereupon "fists shot upward into light-black fists, white, and brown—and everyone was standing up and singing." He also hears about the Scottsboro Boys.[57] And if at the end Cass fails to awaken but rather relapses into all of his old characterological and ideological faults, as he does, that is because, according to the moral of the novel as derived directly from *The Communist Manifesto*, the conditions of life of the lumpen-proletariat prepare it far more for the part of a bribed tool of reactionary intrigue than for proletarian revolution.

But in fact Cass, the *Lumpazivagabundus,* is all the while engaged in quite another version of the class struggle, which is more
befitting to him and much more inspirational. It is very important that
he comes from somewhere on the prairies of West Texas. The image of
the "somebody in boots" is continuous in the novel and signifies brutal
authority, but it is important that the image is of boots: Texas boots,
cowboy boots. Cass is by definition rootless, but he has an antecedence
of rootlessness which is in itself a distinction of identity. The first
section of the novel is called "The Native Son," and Algren's original
title for the whole of the novel was *Native Son.* The McKays—a father,
a brother, a sister, and Cass, a sorry lot altogether—are "Texas-
American descendants of pioneer woodsmen. . . . Unclaimed now they
lived, the years of conquest long past, no longer accessory to hill and
plain, no longer possessing place in the world."[58] The hyphenation in
"Texas-American"—as in "Polish-American" or "Italian-American"
—at once raises and resolves a question of identity: just prior to and
intricate with the current circumstances of displacement, there is
heritage, which in this case, as in the case of the myth of the South,
is more perspicuous because it has been popularly acknowledged.
According to Algren's later preface to the novel, Cass was intended to be "a Final Descendant,"[59] and for all of the propaganda
through which he is moved, he is animate and stylish in terms—no
matter how meretricious or merely fictive those terms may be—of his
loyalty to his lost heritage.

Cass is defined in some large part by the dialect he speaks, even
to the end and after some period of residence in Chicago: "'Ah'm the
big shot here,' he said, waving the hat toward the Little Rialto. 'This is
where ah work, Blondie, an' that there is mah boss. Ah work here.
This's Mist' Hauser.'" That drawling, incrementally repetitive, evasive kind of speaking is indeed the major achievement of the novel:
"'Ah guess if we was down South *now*' he finally said, 'Y'all'd find out
somethin' 'bout guts and whose got 'em. Y'all wouldn't talk so high an'
mighty 'bout niggers down *there*. Not where ah come from, no sir yo'
wouldn't. We'd whip somethin' out o' yo' fo' talkin' thataway in mah
home town.'"[60] In this uneven novel Algren also provided his character with the soul of a poet: Cass is curiously moved by, among some
other things, the sight of lilacs in the dooryard blooming. But that is
concordant in effect because Cass is made to move through episodes of
most gruesome violence and can be fundamentally untouched. In his
soul he is related to neither his circumstances nor his actions. Cass is
also defined in large part by the fact that he is really incapable of
learning anything; he is equipped with a capacity only for slow won-

derment, but by the same token he is wonderfully stubborn in his retention of the truths of his patrimony. And Cass lives within informative dreams of glory. He commits armed robbery and is a legend in his own mind; he is "Texas McKay" and "Bad-Hat McKay" and "Two-Gun McKay," and in his last words in the novel he is looking forward to having the name "Hell-Blazer" tattooed on his chest.

There is dignity in this dreaming, moreover, which is the more vivid for all of the discounting ironies. The class struggle in which Cass is involved has little to do with *The Communist Manifesto* and certainly has nothing to do with the case of the Scottsboro Boys. Cass is, exactly, a Final Descendant. He is a cowboy come desperately, ironically, hopelessly to Chicago. He has been dispossessed and forgotten, and is nevertheless the bearer of the mythical history of his westering forefathers. No matter that the particular metaphors of his ambition are the inventions, as he cannot know, of Owen Wister and Zane Gray, this forgotten man is engaged in asserting his claim to his birthright, and if he is also so much less than he wants to be and pretends to be, that testifies to Algren's imaginative, as opposed to ideological, apprehension of the plight of the forgotten man. If Cass is a weasel, conditions have made him so. Were he not such a weasel, his dreaming would not be so tawdry in its particulars. But he is on the right track, appropriating an identity from his privileged folk heritage.

four

Field Full of Folk

The 1920s, said Roosevelt, had been "a decade of debauch"—
which was to say, after all paradoxically, that this time, of the big
trouble, was a better time, with better values and truer perspectives.
Malcolm Cowley, now a radical, meanwhile discovered a large symbol
in the suicide, in 1930, of Harry Crosby, his exemplary poetical exile of
the 1920s: "The religion of art had failed when it tried to become a
system of ethics, a way of life." Now, however, "a new conception of
art was replacing the idea that it was something purposeless, useless,
wholly individual and forever opposed to a stupid world. The artist and
his art had once more become a part of the world." And others, including politicians and poets, were saying the same thing. The Depression
had brought an end not only to the season of "the putrid pestilence of
financial debauchery"—that phrase was the invention of the vice president, Alben Barkley—but also to a period when morality itself had
somehow disappeared into hedonism and self-indulgence and into private and frivolous mysteries.[1]

Given this attitude toward the immediate past, current experience,
with its component of necessary recognition of the lowly masses, was
chastening and, moreover, refreshing, and given this attitude, it was obvious that the excitement—not merely the duty—of the literary enterprise in particular was to be found in modes which might most directly
render the experience of lowness. Therein were to be discovered the
basic and tonic values, a new loveliness after the season of decadence.

The invitation of the 1930s was not to "proletarian literature" as
such, except in the cases of some few and strict ideologues. The at-
traction to direct experience of the lowly did not necessarily implicate
any political commitment at all except in the most extended sense.
What was at issue really was an aesthetic, founded upon and warranted
by a recognition, under the impress of current circumstances, of a
sustaining, even joyous, vitality in the lower depths, down there where
the social actuality of America was—the lower depths, given the
American social situation, being variously the ghetto and the proletariat and the peasantry and habitats in between. So—to take widely

disparate examples—Thomas Wolfe, who was at best an ambivalent friend of the left, participated in the moment as much as did Michael Gold; and Henry Miller, in his fashion, as much as, say, so certified a friend of the left as Ruth McKenney; and Archibald MacLeish (although not without urbane and skillful doubting) as much as, say, a novelist so approved by the left as Clara Weatherwax.

Wolfe, for instance, like many another writer—and for that matter like many self-consciously "proletarian" writers—wrote his one tale about the special sensibility of the artist, but, as an artist and as a man and as the hero of a saga and as a book made flesh, he verified himself by being the natural man extravagantly exemplified. What was chiefly remarkable about Wolfe was that in every respect he was so big. He had his special hungry sensibility because unlike, say, Jake Barnes, he had *not* been wounded and he was not overly refined. He was an authentic country boy, a hillbilly—and not surprisingly he did appear in the pages of *New Masses* in the late 1930s.[2] And while Henry Miller in the 1930s was the last of the Bohemian expatriates and while his political predilections (he had some) were little more than accidental, he, too, in a manner not uncomplicated, justified his aesthetical, even rather effete, literary ambitions[3] by being down and out among the lowest of the low. He justified sensibility by hitting bottom.

Again, no one in his time agonized more than MacLeish about the proper role of the poet. He resisted the politicization of art, and, perhaps even more plainly, he resisted being commandeered. That was the message of his "Invocation to the Social Muse," in 1932, a poem which was notorious in its time and which provoked much debate, commentary, and contumely.

> Does Madame recall our responsibilities? We are
> Whores Fräulein; poets Fräulein are persons of
>
> Known vocation following troops: they must sleep with
> Stragglers from either prince and of both views:
> The rules permit them to further the business of neither:
>
> It is also strictly forbidden to mix in maneuvers:
> Those that infringe are inflated with praise on the plazas—
> Their bones are resultantly afterwards found under newspapers:
>
> . . . .
>
> Is it just to demand of us also to bear arms?

But then almost immediately afterward in his defense of his position, in prose now rather than in the elegantly ironic terza rima of the poem, in an essay called "The Social Cant," MacLeish argued in effect that, while work per se ought not to be glorified in America as it was in the Soviet Union, in fact he, MacLeish, the poet, was just as much a worker as those Americans who sowed and reaped the American wheat.[4] And in any event, even as he agonized and queried, however urbanely, the clear direction of his major work in the 1930s, as in *Public Speech* in 1936 and *Land of the Free* in 1938, was toward an evocation of an America defined by its lowly and ordinary phenomena. As for politics and the question of the bearing of arms and the matter in general of social engagement, by 1940 he was inveighing sarcastically against the recent tendency, as he saw it, of both scholars and writers to take refuge in their professional seclusions, thereby removing themselves not only from society but from their own most private fulfillments as well:

> Both subjected themselves to inconceivable restraints, endless disciplines to reach these ends. And both succeeded, Both writers and scholars freed themselves of the subjective passions, the emotional preconceptions which color conviction and judgment. Both writers and scholars freed themselves of the personal responsibility associated with personal choice. They emerged free, pure and single into the antiseptic air of objectivity. And by that submission of the mind they prepared the mind's disaster.[5]

The case of MacLeish was indeed singularly illustrative of the impress of the moment. He was a man of an earlier generation—born in 1892—whose time of flourishing should have been the 1920s. He had been born into a well-to-do family of impeccable New England ancestry. He had attended Yale and Harvard and had then gone off to the war, where, unlike many others among his postwar American literary contemporaries, he had actually been engaged in battle and had seen his comrades die. He had returned to Cambridge to be a teacher at Harvard Law, and in the 1920s he had in fact been a very successful lawyer in Boston. Such a man, turned poet, had every reason, so it must have seemed to him, to question the local social muse and the social cant and to be a little acerbic in his estimate of those who currently used the word "comrade" (as in his poem "Speech to Those Who Say Comrade"). The testimony of his poetry altogether is that he was the most decent and the most just of men, whose instincts demanded that on the one hand he fend off all pretensions to aristocracy and power but that on the other hand he resist not only dogma but, even more than that and more deeply, the forces of cultural deracination—the local symbol for him for both dogma and cultural abrogation being as often as not the Communist party. With good and easy conscience he attacked the Harrimans and Vanderbilts and Morgans and Mellons. On the other hand he found discomfort and cause for derision in the spectacle, as in "Frescoes for Mr. Rockefeller's City," of "Comrade Devine"—"Comrade Levine" in the first version of the poem—

> who writes of America
> Most instructively having in 'Seventy-four
> Crossed to the Hoboken side on the Barclay Street Ferry

and cause for derision as well in the sepctacle of the authentic American who had lost his way:

> Comrade Edward Remington Ridge
> Who has prayed God since April of 'Seventeen
> To replace in his life his lost (M.E.) religion.

There was a dilemma here which might have been resolved in any number of ways.[6] Wallace Stevens, who in the 1930s in some degree encountered the same dilemma, posited Imagination as a principle. Stevens, however, was not only of but was also committed to an earlier scheme of things and did subscribe to the religion of art. MacLeish, too, made a principle of Poetry, but poetry was for him a thing which after all was verified by its involvement in social actuality. The language of his poems was often wonderfully modulated but was essentially vulgate, precisely down-to-earth, and the same with his rhythms, and what he did most typically in his thematics was to appeal to the low ordinariness of American life on high, lyrical ground:

> *She's a tough land under the corn mister:*
> *She had changed the bone in the cheeks of many races:*
> *She has winced the eyes of the soft Slavs with her sun on them:*
> *She has tried the fat from the round rumps of Italians:*
> *Even the voice of the English has gone dry*
> *And hard on the tongue and alive in the throat speaking. . . .*
>
> *It may be that the earth and the men remain. . . .*

The sheer presentness of current public history did make poetry vulnerable to an ethical and/or political accounting and revived ancient questions about the social function of poetry, but the same presentness also created an opportunity for a refreshment of poetry. For MacLeish, as for Henry Miller and Thomas Wolfe and countless disparate others, the big trouble after the decade of debauch was also a dispensation. The social base—variously determined, to be sure—was the locale of a new literary authenticity.

PROLETARIAN LITERATURE IN THE UNITED STATES

The question of accomplishment quite aside, it was so even for the most doctrinaire of the proletarian writers. Even in the most confined definition of the phrase "proletarian literature," as the phrase indicated not really a body of literature but only a polemical activity and a slogan of the Communist party (used by the Party for a period, actually, of only about five years), "proletarian literature" was also an aesthetic. In its sense merely as political statement, indeed, the phrase proved, notoriously, to be most vague and was subject to constant, cunning, scholiastic glossing and quarreling—could a bourgeois write proletarian literature? was the material to be revolutionary or could it be only descriptive? what in American terms was the proletariat? if the author was proletarian, did the subject of the writing have to be proletarian? and on and on. Despite all of that, those writers, and critical theoreticians, too, who were engaged in the thing did have something definite in mind, to which the dogma was almost an addendum.

Lacking better, the most nearly official statement of the meaning of proletarian literature was the anthology *Proletarian Literature in the United States* published in 1935—ironically, at the moment of the proclamation of the United Front, when the phrase "proletarian literature" was being withdrawn from the Party vocabulary.[7] The six editors of the anthology were all stalwarts, unimpeachably dedicated to the idea that the poet was a bearer of arms: Granville Hicks, Michael Gold, Isidor Schneider, Joseph North, Paul Peters [Harbor Allen], and Alan Calmer, and the introduction to the volume was written by Joseph Freeman. That the volume had a content of sectarian propaganda was to be expected. The anthology achieves what is in one way its essential moment in a reprinted scene from the play *They Shall Not Die*, by John Wexley, about the Scottsboro Boys, when a Black Mammy of a character is made to sing out, "Yes, pray . . . chile. Pray fo' yo' life an' fo' the blessed N.L.D."[8] But the anthology also had a different kind of a bearing. The editors especially were most self-congratulatory, most assertive in claiming and proving that there was such a thing as a proletarian literature in the United States and that it was a new thing. They were passionate and bumptious, and tortuous in their uses and dismissals of literary history—which is to say that they spoke in the voice of any self-proclaiming literary avant-garde. And what they said was that at the base of the social structure, they had discovered not just a politics—that did go without saying—but also a literary inspiration. "What we are seeing today," said Hicks, "is the emergence of a galaxy of young novelists who happen to be artists, even by the admission of the enemy, and who have discovered what the bourgeois critics never saw . . . that art is more than a parlor game to amuse soulful parasites, that the American workers, farmers, and professionals are the true nation, and that the only major theme of our time is the fate of these people." Said Freeman, "We have here the beginnings of an American literature, one which will grow in insight and power with the growth of the American working class now beginning to tread its historic path toward the new world."⁹

Freeman, who was himself of an older generation and who in fact possessed a good literary education, having been now set to the task of defining an avant-garde of which he had been a precursor, addressed the matter professorially:

> American writers of the present generation have passed through three general stages in their attempts to relate art to the contemporary environment. Employing the term *poetry* in the German sense of *Dichtung,* creative writing in any form, we may roughly designate the three stages as follows: Poetry and Time, Poetry and Class, Poetry and Party.
>
> From the poetic renaissance of 1912 until the economic crisis of 1929, literary discussions outside of revolutionary circles centered on the problem of Time and Eternity.

And so forth, to the point where he could say that "in the past five years many writers have fought their way to a clearer conception of their role in the contemporary world." It was the truth that "the teachings of communism correspond to the realities of the contemporary world," but that was a truth really in the nature of a minor premise. What was important about this new time of Poetry and Party was that writers could have direct contact with the proletariat. "The workers and their middle-class allies, in their struggles against capitalist exploitation, against fascism, against the menace of a new world war, furnish the themes of the new literature" and, he added, sagely and as a veteran of many years of writing for radical journals, they also provided an audience.¹⁰

Freeman was an elder and spoke befittingly. William Phillips and Philip Rahv were members of the younger generation and spoke befittingly in their own way, but to the same point. Now at the beginning of their joint careers in spokesmanship, they were particularly authoritative and severe. In a joint editorial originally published in *Partisan Review,* they recognized "Recent Problems of Revolutionary Literature." (It was their duty, as critics, to do so. "The critic is the ideologist of the literary movement," they said, "and any ideologist, as Lenin pointed out, 'is worthy of that name only when he marches ahead of the spontaneous movement, points out the real road, and

when he is able, ahead of all others, to solve all the theoretical, political, and tactical questions which the "material elements" of the
movement, spontaneously encounter' "—the "material elements" in
this instance presumably being poets, playwrights, and novelists.) On
the one hand, they said, the revolutionary writer was prone to the
danger of "leftism," meaning in this case politicization of his art at the
expense of spontaneously sensed specificities; on the other hand, the
revolutionary writer faced the equal and opposite danger of the
"right-wing tendency," in left-wing literature, toward political fence-
straddling and disinterest in Marxism. Nor, for good measure, were
those revolutionary writers who had succumbed neither to the errors of
"leftism" nor to the errors of the "right-wing tendency" in good order,
because they lacked sufficient consciousness of the fact that they had
problems. As critical ideologues marching ahead of the rest, Phillips
and Rahv might indeed have seemed to be marching the movement
toward a sad impasse—the revolutionary writer could not go left, right,
or down the middle—but in fact the premise of their essay, prior to the
mannered dialecticism, was once again that proletarian literature had
arrived and that it was a new and vivifying thing in literature, especially
as measured against the practices of the recent past:

> This new literature is unified not only by its themes but also
> by its perspectives. Even a casual reading of it will impress one
> with the conviction that here is a new way of looking at life—the
> bone and flesh of a revolutionary sensibility taking on literary
> form. The proletarian writer, in sharing the moods and expecta-
> tions of his audience, gains that creative confidence and har-
> monious functioning within his class which gives him a
> sense of responsibility and discipline totally unknown in the pre-
> ceding decade. Lacking this solidarity with his readers, the
> writer, as has been the case with the aesthetes of the twenties
> and those who desperately carry on their traditions today, ulti-
> mately becomes skeptical of the meaning of literature as a
> whole, sinking into the Nirvana of peaceful cohabitation with the
> Universe.

And in fact the emphasis and conclusion of the essay had to do particularly with the error of "leftism": "literature," they said, "is a
medium steeped in sensory experience, and does not lend itself to the
conceptual form that the social-political content of the class struggle
takes most easily. Hence the translation of this content into images of
physical life determines—in the aesthetic sense—the extent of the
writer's achievement"—which, in effect, was an advice to writers to
experience ever more profoundly the discrete actualities of lower-class
life.[11]

What constituted proletarian literature in the United States for the editors of the anthology was defined ostensively by the contents of the anthology, and except perhaps in the section devoted to literary criticism, those contents were much less restrictively "leftist" than might have been anticipated. (The critics tended, although not exclusively, to practice criticism by picking political targets of opportunity, usually liberals or renegades, and then leaping. Obed Brooks [Robert Gorham Davis] went after Archibald MacLeish; Malcolm Cowley chose Paul Engle; Joshua Kunitz took on Max Eastman, on the issue of the latter's calumny on the state of the arts in the Soviet Union; the anthology reprinted Mike Gold's notorious attack on Thornton Wilder; Bernard Smith realized that the triviality of the bourgeois 1920s was traceable back to the example of the substanceless James Huneker.) In the *Dichtung* there was a latitude, and if the subjects of the writing were often topically revolutionary, the writing nonetheless comprehended quite variously personal sensibilities and experiences and literary learning, ranging from the sardonic urban elegance of Kenneth Fearing to the ballad simplicities of Ella May Wiggins and Aunt Molly Jackson, from the straight-out agitprop of John Wexley to the practiced ironies of Dos Passos to the Gothic horrors of Erskine Caldwell to the controlled neutrality of James T. Farrell.

Virtually every piece of writing in the anthology did make some reference to the political struggle. Therein undoubtedly was a principle by which the pieces had been selected. And the result sometimes was a grotesque and distorting parochialism—an extreme example was an elegy for Hart Crane, by David Wolff, which began as a rhetorical imitation of Crane and ended, some twenty lines later, by promising that the Party would be the true bridge and a fit memorial:

O Party of one weld, O living steel,
arc whose first pier destroys the tenements![13]

But the anthology did have a plausibility and a definition after all more subtle than its dogma. A story by Albert Halper, "Scab!" moralized on the theme of the guilt and conversion of a scabbing taxi-driver, but it was also a story about the quotidian life—and language—of a New York City taxi-driver. A story by Tillie Lerner, "The Iron Throat," rendered exposé of the criminal economies of the mining industry, but more emphatically it attempted to evoke a feeling of a special sensitivity in the ordinary family life of the mining towns; considering the opportunity for sensational exposé, it was singularly understated. A story by Ben Field, "Cow," posited the case of a Jewish radical come for a season to work as a farm laborer. He does an amount of pamphlet distributing, and the teller of the tale, a would-be writer who admires Chekhov, professes having learned something, but not from the pamphlets. The protagonist, who calls himself "Cow," is, by ascription, charismatic, and is so chiefly because he is a bull of a man. He is very large and very strong. It follows therefrom that he is very earthy. Although previously inexperienced, he is prodigious in haying and milking. And the plotting of the story is much more Chekhovian than it is Leninist. The protagonist is killed as a result of an accident which in its turn is the result of a muted constancy of petty spites and jealousies and adulteries, such as might well be customary to life on the farm.

Throughout the volume the theme of conversion to Party was much less remarkable than the theme of conversion to a myth and a consequent poetics. The locales for exploitation were (with a few exceptions) those American places where the real people were: the street and the road and the farm, and mine and mill and picket line, and with remarkable frequency the chief message of the writing was that here was the material which would renew writing. The teller of the story by Ben Field is to learn how to get some grit into his Chekhov. The plotting of the story by Tillie Lerner has to do with the discovery by a little girl of a complex poetical image, the tongues of fire emanating from the mine culm, the discovery coming pointedly after her ascribed failure to find words for the complex of her emotions. One of the sections of the anthology was given over to reportage, a genre of obvious literary significance to self-consciously proletarian writers, as well as to a great many others writing in the 1930s. Reportage was of course not the same thing as journalism, but fiction authenticated first of all by fact and then by a certain kind of fact, the exemplary data of the life of the masses. In a way not represented by John Wexley, the anthology achieved its essential moment in the reportage account of a strike (carefully, cunningly unidentified) by Meridel LeSueur, "I Was Marching." She had participated, as an anonymous observer, and had even been wounded by a blast of buckshot. The issue of the writing was, however, only implicitly political. It was her having managed to participate, no questions asked, that was important, and more important still was the meaning of that eventuality for the writing:

> I have never been in a strike before. It is like looking at something that is happening for the first time and there are no thoughts and no words yet accrued to it. If you come from the middle class, words are likely to mean more than an event. You are likely to think about a thing, and the happening will be the size of a pin point and the words around the happening very large, distorting it queerly. It's a case of "Remembrance of things past." When you are in the event, you are likely to have a

distinctly individualistic attitude, to be only partly there, and to
care more for the happening afterwards than when it is happening. That is why it is hard for a person like myself and others to
be in a strike. . . . Now in a crisis the word falls away and the
skeleton of that action shows in terrific movement.[13]

Just as there were never to be any firm perimeters to the definition
of "proletarian literature," so there was never any firm consensus on
the boundaries of the canon of proletarian writers. In this respect, too,
the movement was akin to most other literary avant-gardes, although in
this instance the peculiar demands of Party policy, personnel, and
certification intervened. James T. Farrell for prominent example,
having been licensed by his inclusion in the 1935 anthology, was in 1936
a class enemy—in part because he took the Trotskyist side on the issue
of the Moscow Trials but in part also as a more purely literary matter.

The matters and the manners of the literary quarreling became
complicated. In 1936 Farrell published *A Note on Literary Criticism,* in
which first he exposed the errors of aesthetes of the camp of Joel
Spingarn and of Humanists of the camp of Irving Babbitt and Paul
Elmer More, but then argued much more pointedly against doctrinaire
"leftism" and the practice of the exclusively political evaluation of
literature. He sought to regard art not as propaganda but as "an instrument of social influence." This commonsensical and even potentially winsome argument reached, however, to a level of ad hominem
scurrility which in every respect at least matched the capacities for
invective of those whom he named, particularly Isidor Schneider, Malcolm Cowley, Mike Gold (representing the "school of revolutionary
sentimentality . . . crying for songs of 'stench and sweat'"), and, most
particularly, Granville Hicks.[14] And there were further ironies. The
circumstantial data of his life and letters indicate that Farrell had been
very close to the Party at least since his arrival in New York, from
Paris, in 1932. He had been publishing regularly in *New Masses,* of
which Hicks was literary editor, and in the *Daily Worker.* He had lived
for a while in the home of the business manager of *New Masses.* He
knew those people. Hicks, on the other hand, seems to have been a
genuinely reluctant convert, and had joined the party only in 1935.[15]

Nonetheless, certain writers were unquestionably of the canon,
including—at random, for there were many, and many of the names
have become indistinct—Benjamin Appel, Thomas Bell, Robert
Cantwell, Jack Conroy, Mike Gold, Albert Halper, Josephine Herbst,
Josephine Johnson, A. B. Magil, Albert Maltz, Clifford Odets, Myra
Page, Isidor Schneider, Herman Spector, Clara Weatherwax, and
Leane Zugsmith.[16] But even these, while what they wrote usually had a

direct Party bearing, were also manifestly engaged in attempting—the question of achievement aside—to exploit a new and vivifying experimental basis for art.

No single novel, to take a not quite random instance, could have been more acknowledgedly orthodox than Clara Weatherwax's *Marching! Marching!* It won the *New Masses*–John Day Company contest of 1934–35—the only year there was such a contest—for the best American novel on a proletarian theme. Certainly it did a good job of anthologizing major doctrinal positions. Its subject was a strike at a sawmill (in Aberdeen, Washington, which had been the locale for two other proletarian novels: *Lumber,* by Louis Colman, in 1931, and *The Land of Plenty,* by Robert Cantwell, in 1934). It pointed to the necessity, and joy, of rank-and-file unionization. This being 1935, it repeated the phrase "united front," in several contexts. It made reference to the League against War and Fascism. It stressed the internationalism of the community of the working class. At the same time, this being 1935, it challenged the bosses' accusations that foreign agitators were at the bottom of all the trouble, saying "Communism is Americanism! That's what! Americanism!" And at the same time it awarded the due praise to the Soviet Union. ("'They howl about The Red Flag of Moscow!'" says one of the sawyers, "'when all the time the Soviet Union's the only nation really pulling for peace!'") At the end the organized rank-and-file masses march up a street, en masse, toward the bayonets and machine guns of the militia.[17]

As a matter of politics, as Walter Rideout has pointed out, this ending, like that of many of the strike novels of the 1930s, indicated a degree of uncertainty about the ultimate victory of the proletariat, which uncertainty indeed was not extorted by historical fact. In most of the novels the strikes ended in failure. Had there been a next page to Clara Weatherwax's novel, those marching masses would have had little chance against the machine guns. In point of fact, however, the labor movement did secure large victories during the decade, and in point of particular fact, as Robert Cantwell himself said in his review of Weatherwax's novel, a general lumber strike did occur in Aberdeen in 1935, which labor won "hands down."[18]

But the novel's ambition for accuracy had a different dimension, beyond its eager, perhaps self-doubting militance and its dissemination of exclamation points. The novel told the story, among other things, of the contemporary conflict of the generations. The protagonist is the son of the owner of the sawmill and is engaged in rejecting his past, which consists not only of capitalist exploitation of labor but of an unconscionable frivolity and triflingness. (But this protagonist is not really the son of the owner. He has the authentic royal blood. In appropriate reversal of the tale of the lost dauphin, it turns out that his father actually had been Big Mel, one of the mill hands.) The protagonist has been to college and therefore has had a 1920s kind of experience which he must reject:

> The young men smoking squat pipes, swarms of them spending what other hands had earned. Youngsters calling themselves poets and writers—fellows in love with mellow words, words once generous with meaning, but now confined, identified with this or that class of mourners—these pap-suckers with their yearning for the "lost years." College talkers swash-buckling up to large ideas; young squirts whoring after the good old days—not men enough to take their pants down healthily to a working world.

Our hero would be man enough, and the novel tells the story of his exposure to and engagement with the ascribed actuality of the working world. Therein is a matter of aesthetic health, which as a matter of aesthetics occasionally becomes explicit in the novel. The only fellow whom our hero had liked at college had been a piano player, who near the end of the novel captivates an audience of workers by his techniques of dissonance and volume:

> He repeated the slow fall; the piano responded, the volume increasing, swelling like a storm, louder, louder every time he leaned on the keys. They saw that he was playing with his whole left forearm, beginning at the elbow and rolling gradually wavelike to his wrist, sounding half the keys of the piano at a time. Now his right hand began playing chords and a melody while the left forearm kept up the rich surging background. A few of the young children started giggling . . . but the grown workers were leaning tensely forward, some beginning to stand to see better how he did it, while the music, moving faster, louder, flooded to tremendous climax. Steve was using both forearms now, and occasionally a fist alone. Low excited whispers flew about: "The best I ever heard!" "It's like a battlefield!"

And the novel altogether attempts to create a folk, the while it seeks to enable the revolution. The setting itself has the value that it is at once the site of a proletariat and is not New York City. The Northwest is America. There are Indians here—we are told in the first paragraphs of the novel that our hero has recently, after leaving college, spent some time among them, discovering incidentally that the Indians, too, on their reservation, are suffering dispossession from their authentic folk past, meanwhile offering a model of the harmonious, equable, peaceable culture. Other enclaves offer the same, notably the local Finnish community, "welcoming non-Finnish workers, but by the ease of their native language remaining a clan. . . . On certain nights they gave Finnish proletarian plays, eating and dancing afterwards, dancing especially the schottish to fiddle and accordion, their feet stamping heartily through the robust two-four measures."[19] Quite to the same point, in an instance, at eventide when the loggers and gandy dancers have returned to camp from the day's work, a number of them swap stories about Paul Bunyan. To the same point, again, a considerable amount of the novel's effort is given to technical description of the operation of a sawmill, an operation in which the workers are easefully, cooperatively prideful, responsible, and capable, and the owners not. Altogether, the novel redefines the proletariat so as to make it a folk, awarding to it feelings for tradition and custom, separateness, practicality, honor, and community allegiance. Much of the novel is told in dialogue, that dialogue consisting in large part of a rhetoric of gasps and unfinished sentences, having a function of making for a feeling of immediacy but more subtly and pervasively being a method for conveying an idea of a closed and fixed language. The workers speak for the most part in clichés, which they can do because they share, not, indeed, a common language, because they are variously Indians and Finns and Filipinos and Chinese and Hungarians and English-speaking Americans, and so on, but a common wisdom. They can speak in clichés because words are for them, refreshingly, less than the knowledge in their experience.

The political ambition of the novel was after all not clearly distinct from its effort to find a literary vision, a kind of writing in which the experience of lowness would be more eloquent than words. The politics was perhaps inaccurate by the test of history. The political attitude in this novel, as in many others like it, was also undoubtedly vitiated by an amount of guilt, and condescension, and romantic—not to say erotic—middle-class rebelliousness which would have been inherent in the attempt to achieve unity, healthily with pants down, with the real workers of the world. Clara Weatherwax, in particular, was in fact the granddaughter of an Aberdeen mill owner, and she had had a couple of years at Stanford during the 1920s. But all of the qualifications of political purity testify merely to the point that there was a considerable presence of literary ambition in that avant-garde which was called "proletarian literature," and that the ambition *included* a politics as much as, if not more than, it obeyed a politics.

And so throughout the accepted canon. The doctrinal portion of the politics is always present to some degree and is sometimes blatant, but that portion is everywhere included within a manifest effort to create a new and refreshing literature, which might, in the apt words of T. S. Eliot, "express new objects, new groups of objects, new feelings, new aspects." And certain techniques were virtually mandated by the nature of the ambition. Proletarian literature made use of a supposedly common, supposedly exemplary language. It relied greatly on folk references, as often as not in the practice becoming a celebrational Americanism. It was a genre literature, and consequently rather static. As a literature about workers it tended toward exact—and lengthy—descriptions of jobs of work: how steel is made, how roadways are laid, how tires are fabricated.

Albert Halper, in his novel of 1937, *The Chute*, reached a pinnacle of a sort. The scene of the major action is the fifth floor of a Chicago mail-order warehouse, and the "chute" of the title is the circular ramp down which the order-pickers dispatch their orders. There are disciplines and dangers involved, and Halper was fully informative. One of the new hands bungles the discipline and falls down the chute, breaking both his legs. The protagonist of the novel, also a new hand, is singular in his adeptness, thus being able to fit right in with the older hands: "Although not so fast as Killer Howard, Paul had a sense of neatness, and when he piled the trucks, they did not fall over on their sides. Big Stella helped him at each loading and, though the schedule of the floor was still lagging, it did not fall further behind."[20]

Robert Cantwell's Aberdeen novel, *The Land of Plenty*, was told in a series of workers' vignettes—"Hagen," "Winters," "Marie," "Johnny," and so on—all of these clearly meant to be distinguished by their typicality, and the language of the novel is, once again, a fragmented, abbreviated vernacular. The foreman and efficiency expert in the sawmill does not know how to run a sawmill, and therefore he also does not know how to talk, but the others do know and therefore understand each other.

No novel within the canon was or could have been more explicit in its political expression than Myra Page's *Moscow Yankee*, published in 1935. As had been the case in her Gastonia novel of a few years before, *Gathering Storm*, Myra Page was engaging herself with complete deliberation in writing propaganda. In this instance she told a story of a young fellow come from a Detroit assembly line to take a job in a truck factory in Moscow. Things are of course better in the Soviet Union, where it is really the workers who run things, and at the end Andy marries the Russian girl and decides to stay on. But the claim for the superiority of the Soviet system required no considerable effort toward fictive proof, and the novel was in fact much more emphatic in its attempt, once again, to create the experience, not of an international proletariat, but of an American folk. In very great part it is the effort even of this novel to create the low, authentic American language, and thus to be in touch with social fact. The English-speaking Russians whom Andy meets are anxious to learn his lingo. They want to know about such words as "kidder" and "okay" and "attaboy." And we are to appreciate the fact that Andy's crudeness of speech constitutes a high eloquence. By way of a farewell letter to his girlfriend back in Detroit, he writes: "One thing, Elsie. When you get a closeup on it, everyday, you'll find working stiffs like me count here. No kidding. Office girls, too. You won't have to sling the dog to make a splash. I'm starting in to train as an engineer. Honest, no kidding."[21]

Others were more subtle, more muted, in both language and political statement, and were therefore perhaps more persuasive in their makings of typical instances of American lowliness. Catherine Brody's *Nobody Starves*, published in 1932, told the tale of a working girl. The tale does end in melodrama: married too young, without money and without a job and with a baby on the way, she is killed by her husband, who tries, but fails, to kill himself as well. But prior to that ending, the real purpose of the novel is to discover the detail of the life of a contemporary working girl in all of its representative ordinariness. Molly has a series of factory jobs, and once again the jobs of work are described at length. More intimately, the novel recreates at length the supposedly typical gossip of the working girls, consisting for the most part of talk about their boyfriends or husbands, and the novel attempts to make fiction from such matters as buying clothing and buying furniture and the economics of "boarding." There is a presence of union activity in the novel, but Molly is carefully prevented, by the author, from knowing about it. Thomas Bell's *All Brides Are Beautiful*, published in 1936, told a tale of a politically aware young fellow. Peter is an artist and a skilled machinist and, by way of making him a proletarian triple threat, a reader of the *Daily Worker*, and on occasion he is made to think thoughts "of workers jailed and beaten; of strikers killed, of union organizers murdered, of Negroes lynched; of the businessmen's protective associations and California vigilantes and manufacturers' associations, and Southern klansmen and chambers of commerce and civic leagues and leagues for the preservation of liberty—all the scabby growths on the sores of a sick capitalism," and so forth.[22] Peter marries Susan, who is the proper wife for him. By way of honoring their third-week anniversary, she presents him with a copy of John Strachey's "Nature of Capitalist Crisis," for she knows how to please her man. But indeed, and despite the exactnesses of political reference here and there throughout the novel, Bell's manifest intention was a somewhat wry, bittersweet, and typifying story of young love and marriage, specifically in the Bronx and specifically in the time of hard times. Certainly according to design, nothing of any great moment happens in this novel. The adventures of Peter and Susan consist very largely of their very ordinary relationships with family and neighbors. When Peter loses his job, the event entails an account of domestic economies and also a lesson in the deferral of modest dreams, but at the end Peter does have another job, which promises no security but which has the effect of bringing the novel back approximately to where it began. The ambition of this novel, too, was not a linear development but an exemplification. It took the Bronx and insisted on its inherent value as a literary material—and with some success at least by the measure of the fact that the novel went through several printings and was popular.

With significant frequency, proletarian literature in the United States consisted in fact of stories of artists and writers finding their way to the revivifying plausibility of an American folk. In Dos Passos's *U. S. A.* (which may or may not have been a proletarian novel but which was indisputably a very large fact for proletarian novelists), there was the centrality of the autobiographical "Camera Eye," that sensitive young man who moves outward from Proustian introspection to all of *U. S. A.* In Edward Dahlberg's *Bottom Dogs*, published in 1930, Lorry Lewis wishes that "he knew enough to be a writer"[23]—that statement containing a passing irony because Lorry Lewis was Dahlberg himself, a most self-conscious and ambitious writer whose special access to a new voice, at least in this early time, was the bottom-dog experience which he had lived and which he was engaged in recounting. In Josephine Johnson's novel of 1937, *Jordanstown*, a compulsively lyrical novel, a sensitive young aristocrat and writer discovers his singular occasion for responsive sensibility in social activism among the real people. In *Rope of Gold*, in 1939, the final volume of Josephine Herbst's trilogy in the 1930s, the male protagonist, Jonathan Chance, is expressly a New York intellectual and writer who seeks, expressly, to improve his writing by organizing the farmers in the region of Pennsylvania where he has a home. He wants, he says, to "touch actual people." Herbst herself had come of literary age as an expatriate in the 1920s and had had her learning in all of that which had been called "modernism." Now, in *Rope of Gold*, her writer-hero invokes the spirits of John Reed and Jack London—criticizing them, however, in an access of purity, for their failure to stay in touch with actual people

persistently enough and citing them as examples of what happens
to good writers who distance themselves from the sources of their
beliefs.

Nor for any of these writers, as writers, and no matter what the
degree of their political commitment, was the jargon of the Communist
party the credible source of literary beliefs. Kenneth Burke in his
address to the Party-inspired American Writers' Congress in 1935
suggested that the very vocabulary of the Party was a detriment and
needed revision for the purposes of propaganda. He wanted to eliminate such terms as "the masses" and "proletarian" itself, substituting
the word "people." The suggestion was in fact not well received. His
theories, as he said in his report on the congress, "even called down
upon him the wrath of the party's most demonic orators."[24] But no
matter what might have been said against him in this instance of direct
engagement with the problem of propaganda, and no matter that by and
large his audience might well not have understood what he was
saying—for Burke, as always, was somewhat quirky, somewhat
abstruse, holding many things in mind at once—it must have been the
case that he touched upon a shared sentiment. A great amount of the
technical effort of proletarian literature went into, not precisely the
translation of Party jargon into a supposed Americanese, but an attempt to elicit from the American "folkways" (Burke's word) the true
language which would be, inevitably, hopefully, concordant with the
Party's jargon.

There was indeed a paradox inherent in the whole enterprise of
proletarian literature, of a kind which was likely to become pressing,
particularly in the many reflexive stories of artists and writers. By the
amount that the unlettered Americans of the folkways constituted the
source of belief and therefore of literary vigor, proletarian literature
erred as soon as it became a distinct and specialized job of work in
itself, which is to say as soon as it became literature. The artist-hero
had to despise artists—except perhaps (but even then, tenuously) when
art could be seen to have a direct propaganda function. Josephine
Johnson's protagonist took the easy and obvious way out by giving up
writing entirely, for social action. Others, like Herbst, tried to come to
rest right in the middle of the paradox.

Perhaps the fullest statement of the paradox—fullest although still
unresolved—is to be found in Albert Halper's *Union Square*. The
novel was published in 1933, when apparently Halper was still troubled
by both the social and the literary implications of proletarian literature,
and prior to his settling down to such straightforward tasks as his
novels *The Foundry* (1934) and *The Chute* (1937). *Union Square* was

ambitious, sophisticated, and not unconfused in design. It has many characters. A number of discrete and separate stories are told simultaneously. The tone of the novel is so unremittingly ironic as almost to prohibit any kind of an assertion. Nevertheless it managed to intimate a continuous theme, to the effect that there is a social actuality out there which is not being apprehended—not by anybody and especially not by Communist literary people.

The trouble with Party propaganda, says one of the protagonists, in premature echo of Kenneth Burke, and of the Popular Front, is that it is so intransigently foreign: "Do you really think," he asks of an artist friend, "that a movement appealing to the American masses can be successful as long as the agitators of the movement are not Americanized themselves and have not de-Russianized the propaganda they're trying to hammer into the heads of American labor?" But on the other hand, de-Russianization will not, either, be sufficient. In a long set speech on the subject of proletarian art, the same protagonist advises a roomful of aspirants that first of all they must be good artists but that then, anyway, they will probably not be useful to the class struggle because the proletariat does not need art:

> "Comrades, if you will allow me to say so, all of us here are
> nothing more or less than parasites, we're barnacles on the bot-
> tom of a boat. The Revolution doesn't need us at all, what it
> needs is militant workers, militant intelligent workers. . . . What I
> say, and I say it for the last time, is, that, if you want to help the
> movement, you must first be capable in your craft. The Party
> doesn't want bad posters, in fact, the movement really doesn't
> need you at all. Two or three intelligent, articulate workers
> could do more good than a whole hall full of "class-conscious"
> painters or writers."[25]

And it should have followed therefrom that proletarian art was by definition hopeless, but clearly Halper wanted to save the cause from slackness and derivativeness, and to bring it somehow to an engagement with the social actuality.

The novel has two major protagonists, both of them artists. The one, a painter, is a faithful and helpful member of the Party, but he is a pip-squeak. He is atremble with excitements but does not know the score about some basic things, and obviously he is not going to make the revolution. The other is an ex-Communist and ex-poet, and also tubercular, who has fallen into the purlieus of cynicism. He has taken to writing sexy potboilers which are parodies of sexy potboilers. Behind these protagonists the novel develops a number of stories of individual lives of Union Square in the year 1931, and it is one of the very many ironies of the novel that neither of the artists knows anything about any of these lives at their doorstep. Moreover, each of the other characters suffers some variety of inability to encounter life. There is a businessman who is a widower, who has taken a vulgar little tart into his home and knows that he is being cuckolded and otherwise demeaned, and can do nothing. There is a dapper little barber who is called upon to rescue a childhood sweetheart. Conscience and love demand, but he has syphilis, and he commits suicide. More pointedly, there is an honest laborer, wholesomely named Hank Austin, who is fired from his job and refuses to believe that he is one among a potentially powerful many; he is the proper object of the concern of the Communists, but they do not know him and cannot inform him, and he goes along believing in Herbert Hoover. Pointedly in a slightly other way, there are a Mr. and Mrs. Otto Drollinger, who have found in the revolution a new opportunity for chic. They surround themselves with Russian knickknacks, they call each other Vanya and Natasha, and they converse in the manner of a translation of Gorki.

In this constancy of ineffectuality, virtually of somnambulism, the real proletariat, if it could be located and rendered, would be an aesthetic relief. A janitress of Union Square is made to say, pertinently, "'Artists. . . . There was a time . . . when this neighborhood had only working people, now it's lousy with phony folk. Artists, phony people, I calls them.'" And the continuousness of the irony in the novel is interrupted in just one instance, by the introduction of some folk who in Halper's thinking are apparently the real thing and not phony. The Party has arranged a mass meeting to aid the Kentucky coal miners. Some of the writers who have been down to Harlan County address the meeting, and the audience is bored. The miners themselves, however, as artists precisely, are, by ascription, electrifying. The "Kentucky miners' orchestra" plays some selections:

> From the wings came seven or eight men, dressed in overalls and old overcoats, wearing miners' caps with small lamps at their foreheads. All of them were tall and gaunt, the old mountaineer stock, men of the long blue rifles and the days of Dan'l Boone; they looked out upon the massed heads with dead, dull stares. They came shuffling across the stage, sat down, shifted into good positions with their instruments, then one of the men slapped his foot against the floor and all swung into action.
>
> Such bleak, homespun music the hall had never heard before—hill tunes and barn-dance numbers, the whining twang of steel guitar string. . . .

When the music stopped, the hall shouted and cheered. There was a stamping of feet. Here was the genuine stuff.[26]

When one of the miners speaks (in transcription of dialect, using such words as "sa-ay" and "you-all"), the audience again stamps and shouts, being genuinely enthusiastic.

It is just after this episode that the ex-Communist, ex-poet, cynical protagonist tells the young artists that they are barnacles, and we know that his bitter wisdom has been previously, partially, qualified. We have had at least an indication of what would constitute a true aesthetic standard. The "genuine stuff" exists—but it exists far away from Union Square and is a function of American folkways of sorts which are not likely to be available to the residents of the Square. Nor does Halper, in this instance, offer any good advice to artists on how to get any of that genuine stuff.

One ought to have been born to it, thus to be in a position to make convincing pretense to authorized use of it.

Some were. It was in good part because of the author's manifest authority that Jack Conroy's novel, *The Disinherited*, also published in 1933, was one of the more celebrated items in the canon of proletarian literature. The novel was closely autobiographical, and Conroy had exceptional credentials. Like his protagonist, Larry Donovan, he was a coal miner's son, from Missouri, and he had actually himself worked at a variety of jobs of hard labor which are described in the novel. Conroy was Larry Donovan, who was in turn, as defined by one of the Soviet critics of the novel, a typical "unheroic" proletarian,[27] and therefore unquestionably reliable in his representing the consciousness of the American proletariat. Conroy was not one of those New York Bohemians who had turned modishly pink.

Nevertheless, the relationship between himself and Larry Donovan, as also between himself and the materials of his experience, was not uncomplicated. The novel tells the story of, first, Larry's growing up in a mining camp, and then, with the death of his father and the onset of hard times, his going forth to a series of jobs and periods of unemployment, and then his briefly returning home before setting forth again, now to be an organizer. His adventures have brought him to the point of explicit, desirable realization: "I knew that the only way for me to rise to something approximating the grandiose ambitions of my youth would be to rise with my class, with the disinherited: the bricksetters, the flivver tramps, boomers, and outcasts pounding their ears in flophouses." The novel tells the story of a typical unheroic proletarian as a young man. The novel also, however, in the same telling, presents a portrait of the artist as a young man: Larry's conversion is as much, and explicitly, poetical as it is political. Larry has had a taste for letters. At the end he is impressed by the advice of an old German revolutionary, which is to say a wise man, who says to him: "Here's living poetry for you—an epic as vast as the earth. Feet in broken and worn-out shoes beating the streets of cities like a drum; clenched fists storming toward the sky! I can take you and show you poetry with a rhythm that shakes the earth!"[28]

And in fact the merging of the politics with the poetics, insofar as it really occurs in the novel, is achieved much less forthrightly. Conroy was a writer and was equipped, by the time he came to write this novel, with something more than merely a taste for letters. He had edited little magazines. He had been particularly encouraged by H. L. Mencken, who had no proletarian sympathies but who had published some of the sketches which went into *The Disinherited,* in the *American Mercury.* He had literary education and seems by later testimony to have been studiously engaged in learning from and evaluating certain useful masters, for instance moving away from Hemingway and toward Thomas Wolfe.[29] In 1933 he was editor of the *Anvil,* which later, with pride, he was to describe as "the pioneer of proletarian magazines devoted solely to creative work—fiction and verse."[30] Like Larry Donovan, he had spent some time working in a plant which manufactured rubber heels, but the plant was located in Hannibal, Missouri, and apparently the locale spoke to him. Sometime just prior to writing *The Disinherited,* and as a matter with some implication for the novel, he had begun to write a biography of Mark Twain. He was all the while a miner's son and a laborer at manly jobs and as authentically proletarian as could be desired—meaning, however, that as a writer he had possession of a certain experience which promised a literary vitality.

And that experience demanded a working and a transformation in order that it might be something more than stridency. Like any other writer, Conroy was engaged in creating value from the materials of his own life, and what in fact he wrote in *The Disinherited,* as a matter of movement and emphases, was in large part a series of adventures in folk identity. Larry Donovan is made to move through midwestern America but not really to the point of any realization other than recognition of what he has known from the beginning. The novel begins and ends with scenes of Larry at home, in the mining camp. At the end the mine has closed down and only a few rotting shacks remain, but there is a memory in those timbers which is fetching and which has been written into the novel at length. The first approximate one-third of the novel is an account of the camp in its earlier phase, when Larry was a boy, and although there are cruelties and terrors here, of a kind to invite a political awakening, there is much of something else, also—a kind of glowing of nostalgia even in the current life of the camp. The time of this portion of the novel is pre–World War I. The house in which Larry grows up is a simple one, but we are made to know that it is neat and that it is indeed rather superior to the other houses in the neighborhood. Larry, very much like his predecessor Tom Sawyer, who had lived nearby, plays with his playmates at games which have a literary folk character and are suggestive of stability and identity and ritual rather than revolution: "Diamond Dick rode valorously to rescue his sweetheart Nell from scalping at the hands of the redskins just in the nick of time; while Handsome Harry, the old sarpint of Siiskiyou, proclaimed to the world that he was an extremely pisen rattler possessing sixteen rattles and a button; moreover, he was not a bit averse to biting viciously if he were provoked sufficiently."[31] There are woods nearby, where Larry, the future organizer, hunts for birds' nests. The older fellows repair to those woods to play their accordians and flutes. A girl comes into Larry's young life, and although later in the novel she is to be a bearer of ideological information—and at that point will be ridiculed just a little bit for allowing her academic learning and vocabulary to be more important than her experience—in the beginning she is a girl possessed of all the flouncing and charming righteousness of a Becky Thatcher, and her name is Bonny Fern.

Larry Donovan, the typical unheroic proletarian and future organizer, is equipped chiefly, by Conroy's working of these materials, to be an American bard. The novel is dedicated to "the disinherited and dispossessed of the world," but the subject of the novel is somewhat more lean than is implied by that rotund sentiment, and more limited. Larry has been disinherited and dispossessed not, certainly, from any material wealth and not from any rights in civil governance, but from the presumption of a certain modest, satisfying, plausible, and seemingly antique culture wherein, by Conroy's literary presumption, was the genuine stuff. His political authority is consequent upon his cultural authority, which comes first and which entails by far the greater part of the effort of the novel. Conroy, too, like so many others, was engaged in creating a folk which might provide him with a new literary authenticity.

By the end of the 1930s "proletarian literature" was collecting death notices, and, ironically, it was only in its obituaries that for the first time it achieved a firm, if also simplistic and trivializing, definition. It was seen, chiefly by literary Trotskyists, to have been a Stalinist vulgarity and a thing written to an order which had been dutifully, stupidly, and brutally enforced by the official powers in the Communist party in America, and which in its effect, if any, had demeaned both literature and revolution. That case for the matter was presented very forcefully by Philip Rahv, in an essay in 1939 called "Proletarian Literature: A Political Autopsy," which appeared in the friendly pages of the *Southern Review*. Rahv pointed out that proletarian literature had never been truly class-conscious nor had it even had true Marxist credentials, but had been directed and controlled strictly by opportunistic party directive. "It is clear," he said, "that proletarian literature is the literature of a party disguised as the literature of a class," and it had been, he said, not a literary event, but "an episode in the history of totalitarian communism."[32] And that judgment persisted and took root. With perhaps a couple of exceptions—chiefly Henry Roth—those writers who in the first place had been vaguely accepted into the vague canon of proletarian literature—and almost never, it may be noted, without challenge by reviewers for *New Masses* and the *Daily Worker*, for enconiums were not inherent to the Party vocabulary—were sent to literary exile or were, at best, recalled briefly in order to be exiled again. Conroy, in later estimation, was a servile lackey of Moscow with little talent and less artistic integrity, and also a hopeless drunk.[33] Clara Weatherwax was remembered for having written a pastiche of "proletarian" clichés.[34] For almost anyone who had occasion to speculate on proletarian literature, Michael Gold was the constant symbol of bullying combined with sheer vulgarity. Such other writers as had in fact held some kind of position in the Communist party, including, for instance, A. B. Magil and Isidor Schneider, were dismissed as hacks and functionaries or, at best, pitied for the error by which they had betrayed such small talent as they had had.[35]

And in truth the proletarian movement of the 1930s did not produce very much of such a literature as might survive its immediate context. (In 1930 Michael Gold had promised that the movement would create its Shakespeare within ten years, nay "a hundred Shakespeares,"[36] and, as usual, he had erred greatly on the side of enthusiasm.) But in the instances which constituted by far the greater part of the actual canon of proletarian literature, the movement had not been, first of all, utterly and crassly lacking in literary intelligence, and not, second, a mere mechanical repetition of doctrinal directives.

A. B. Magil, to take the case of one of those minor writers who had been indisputably close to the workings of power in the Party in America, did turn after a while to doing political writing almost exclusively, but for a period of about ten years at the beginning of his career he had been a poet primarily and had considered himself to be engaged in a cultural enterprise which in fact the Party did not encourage. Along with others, as he was to recall, he had "sought to express the struggles and aspirations of a large number of Americans who had previously been largely faceless and voiceless in American literature."[37] And he had written poems which, taking the faceless and voiceless for their subject matter and by that much being political in nature, were nevertheless far from being Party screeds, and were more remarkable for their generalized sweet intention to compassionate than for any narrow strategies of militance.[38]

Isidor Schneider, to take a similar case, had done literary work for the Party, and perhaps by assignment. It was he who wrote the response to James T. Farrell's *A Note on Literary Criticism* for *New Masses*. He was adept, moreover, at a kind of innuendo which people on Farrell's side of the issue must have found to be outrageous— "Certainly," wrote Schneider, "the fact that the Catholic Book Club recommends *A Note on Literary Criticism* illuminates the nature of its Marxism."[39] But Schneider, in particular, was first of all not unsophisticated in his making of literary assessments. There had been, for instance, a delightful moment of incongruity, which he appreciated, when on assignment from *New Masses* he had gone to interview Gertrude Stein. He had been charmed by her poise and by her sheer friendliness, and what finally he had to say against her—inevitably and as a Marxist but not necessarily as a Communist—had a shrewdness and an accuracy. Stein had genuine importance for her direct and personal—and beneficial—influence on a number of writers, but that in itself did not make her own work to be serious. "She has been, in a fantastic version, the bourgeois housewife, living on the labor of others and keeping a stylish house." For all her seeming reasonableness, in conversation, Stein was imprisoned in the habit of speaking in metaphors, which bred submetaphors, which ended in evasions.[40] On the other hand, Schneider had been among the first to recognize and respect the completeness of the artistic dedication of Hart Crane, and by Crane's own testimony he had been one of the few to show evidence, in his review of *The Bridge*, of a "recognition of practically all the aspirations implicit in the poem."[41] And Schneider, second, at the same time that he had been doing the Party's work, had been a poet, usually a lyric poet, engaged in the positive act of making a literature for and of those many who had previously had no voice in literature, including, of course, himself. The polemical part of his intention as a poet was the retrieval of literature from *them* and the delivering of it to *us:*

> For them were written
> the books; the heroes
> and Edens were theirs;

the love like long play,
and war like adventure.

. . . .

In their books
We were summed with
the acres and crops,
the cattle, the fish,
the ores and the lumber,
their richest resource, "an
industrious population."

There comes
a revision of life;
the books are rewritten.[42]

Philip Rahv to the contrary, the quite heterogeneous writings
which went by the name of proletarian literature did have a class basis,
if not necessarily a "proletarian" one (for lack of firm definition of that
latter term in American experience). The previous American literary
generation had in all of its glamorous instances left a large portion of
the American population out of account, and therefore was to be accused of arrogance or frivolity or both. Vitality—literary vitality—now
demanded the rewriting of the books.

THE PEOPLE TALK

Gertrude Stein said to Isidor Schneider that she was a better
communist than the Communists, and Schneider knew that she was
joking—although, quite conceivably, Stein herself might not have
known that she was joking. She was, had been, and always would be one
of *them,* despite the fact that in her own village she often talked with
tradesmen and other plain citizens. Likewise Wallace Stevens, who
confused matters in several ways—by being responsive to the facts of
the Depression, by being a reader of *New Masses,* and by being a
declared friend of the left. For all of his goodwill toward "those who
suffered in the depression," however, and despite the superb grasping-
ness of his imagination, there was a large amount of contemporary
experience and feeling which he did not comprehend—manifestly so,
because in poems of the 1930s, notably *Owl's Clover,* he did strive for
comprehension, but succeeded at his strenuous, ruminative best in
creating an aesthetic perspective in which all merely contemporary
experience and issues tended to vanish away. The "gaudium of
being"—in one of Stevens's many tentative definitions of his own
practice—truly had had pertinence in a time different from this time.[43]

Being interviewed by Isidor Schneider of *New Masses,* Stein no doubt had readied herself for a political kind of conversation, and Wallace Stevens, reading the newspapers or actuarial tables or whatever, no doubt had considered that he was being confronted by a demand upon his conscience, and if so, they were largely mistaken. Underlying both the political and even the moral issues of this moment, there was the matter of the sheer, huge being of that other American population—not the matter of its neediness, although that was relevant, but its actuality, which was not to be approached easily by anyone who, like Wallace Stevens, discovered in a destitute old woman, "black by thought that could not understand," a "symbol of those who suffered during the depression." The way of this time's avant-garde was in knowing that old lady, and beyond her the forgotten masses of the people, and not at all in symbolizing.

There were some problems; where were the masses to be found? and being found how was conventionalized response to be avoided, and how, outside of the practices of dead conventions, were the masses to be rendered recognizable? and what would constitute authentic instances of a thing which was infinitely multiform whatever else it was? and what did *knowing* consist of? and so forth. On the other hand, the problems themselves proposed technical and thematic opportunities for a new and relevant literature.

One kind of opportunity seemed to be promised by fieldwork.

As in perhaps no other time since the flourishing of the goliardic poets, writers went on the road, for it could be assumed that the real people were not in the books but were somewhere out there, having actual being. "The place to study the present crisis and its causes and probable consequences," said Edmund Wilson in 1932, having just finished his study of symbolism in *Axel's Castle,* "is not in the charts of the compilers of statistics, but in one's self and in the people one sees."[44] Wherefore he had gone forth upon the road to see some people and to write *The American Jitters.* He began with some observations on the state of things, particularly political affairs, in the East, and then by way of contrastive elucidation, moved out to the Midwest, particularly Detroit, and then to California, and then back through the South, for the purposes of observing and listening and recording. The authority of *The American Jitters* was in the fact that "this book is made up almost entirely"—there were a few necessary alterations—"of straight reporting of actual happenings," and the accomplishment of the book as has been acknowledged, was its plausible transcriptions of the voices of the people:

"It's not human—I could just bust when I talk about it—break the spirit of an elephant, it 'ud. I'd starve before I'd go back! They don't give ye no warnin'. Pick up your tools and get a clearance, the boss says—then they inspect your toolbox to see you're not takin' any of the company's tools—then ye report to the employment office with your time card and they give ye a clearance that says they 'cahn't use ye to further advahntage'—then ye're done."[45]

And Sherwood Anderson was saying, in 1935:

I am in the position of most writers nowadays. Formerly, for a good many years, I was a writer of tales. It may be that I should have remained just that, but there is a difficulty. There are, everywhere in America, these people now out of work.... People want to tell their stories, are glad to tell. I blame myself that I do not get more of these stories, do not often enough get the real feeling of the people to whom I talk.[46]

Wherefore he had gone on the road—first South, then to the Middle West—to listen to stories by real people and to write *Puzzled America*. And Erskine Caldwell in the same year was advising:

What is worth traveling thousands of miles to see and know are people and their activity. Each geographical division, practically each state, in America has its own peculiar and arresting background. The majesty of nature is a trivial sight when it is not viewed in relation to man and his activity. Merely to see things is not enough; only the understanding of man's activity is satisfying.... During such a trip the contact with people is the one and all-important matter.[47]

Wherefore he went across the country, West to East, and made a couple of special investigations of Detroit and of the farm-tenant South, and wrote *Some American People*.

And so forth, and indeed at increasing rate during the latter part of the 1930s. In 1937 Nathan Asch published *The Road: In Search of America*, based on four months of travel by bus and equipped with the longest ticket that the clerk, in New York, had said he had ever sold. Louis Adamic's *My America*, in 1938, was not a road book in precisely the same way. Adamic had not gone traveling for the specific purpose of writing this book, but aside from that difference the intention of the book was the same as that of all of the others. "Since 1931," he said, "I have traveled perhaps 100,000 miles in America, by train, by automobile, by plane, as well as afoot, pausing here and there to look and listen, to ask questions, to get 'the feel of things'"[48]—and thus he had his authority, and the book he wrote was, like the others, a collection of seemingly random sketches and records geographically distributed. Louise Armstrong's *We Too Are the People,* also published in 1938, was, again, not precisely a road book. Armstrong had been administrator of relief in a rural county of northern Michigan for a period of three years and she was writing about her experiences on the job and in the place, but, again she was nonetheless writing in the genre of the road books. Her subject was the look and the being and the sound of the people out there, as transcribed by one who had actually been there to look and to listen.

It was perhaps inevitable that the very titles of all of these books and dozens like them should have been virtually identical and certainly interchangeable, the ambitions and techniques of all of them being so closely similar. Perhaps the single most exemplary title for the whole of the genre was Benjamin Appel's *The People Talk,* published in 1940. There was a content of news—abrasive news—in both noun and verb. The single most important datum of American culture was that "the people" *were.* Moreover, and as had not been at all sufficiently appreciated heretofore, and especially not by literary people, "the people" had an articulate—which would be to say, a cultural—existence.

Appel, in his book, began by going on the road in New York City, interviewing a grocery delivery boy and a street cleaner and a musician encountered by happenstance on the street and a fruit vendor, and so on, then proceeded to the Midwest and then the Far West, and then circled back through the South, and in that traveling provided, also, the exemplary itinerary of the road books. Almost all of them began in New York and then moved out from there, and whether or not they took precisely that direction they all of them anyway implied by the form of their itineraries that the news they bore was addressed especially to the readers back in parochial New York. New York was of course the literary capital, as also the political capital, and therefore was prone to sophisticated abstractions. Because most of the writers of the road books were themselves literary people residing in New York, they were well acquainted with error. And the tone of almost all of these books was the same—deliberately naive, deliberately flat, and seemingly unmediated—implying that the usual kind of literary and political thinking needed an awakening to simplicities. There were real people out there.

For all of their seeming, moreover, to make a narrative principle of meandering, the road books composed and attempted to give significant shape to the idea of "the people," as they went along. "The people," in fact, were first of all not to be found just anywhere. Certain locales were favored, notably Detroit and, still more particularly, the rural South. If there were such a thing as an industrial proletariat in the United States, then obviously Detroit was where it was most likely to be found, and if there were a dispossessed peasantry, it was to be discovered in the South. The routings of the road books, that is to say, were not likely to be so lacking in predetermining biases as they appeared to be. And they were books which had a political bearing—always, and most often explicitly, they made a record of how bad things really were in America, and, beyond that, they said that the existence of "the people," now entered into the record, constituted a threat to arrogance and ignorance. Very frequently they divined revolution. Edmund Wilson ended his book with a brief sketch of "A Man in the Street," who was a specter come from the people to be a foreboding to New York:

> He is a tall man with square shoulders—looks able-bodied and self-dependent. A pure Nordic type, he has straight brows and a long straight nose. But his color is pale and he seems soiled, as if his quarters and food were poor; and though there is no demoralization in his face, he looks dazed as if he were not a part of the world in which he is walking. . . . His dark brown overcoat is old; his flat-topped straight-brimmed hat is too small for him. You can't tell whether he is a skilled mechanic or a former auto dealer or a bank cashier or a department store manager—he might even have been a provincial lawyer. But he wanders incongruously along West Fifty-eighth Street past the restaurants with smart French names and the half-empty apartment houses where liveried doormen guard the doors.[49]

And Appel ended his book still more explicitly and on a note of more particular sectarianism, quoting Representative Vito Marcantonio of New York (of the American Labor party and the lone usual spokesman in the United States Congress for the Communist party), addressing his colleagues in the House: "Gentlemen, but the people are talking. Can't you hear them?"[50]

Nevertheless, and despite the recorded instances of suffering and despite the threats, the road books also suggested an optimism, and of a kind which verged on coziness. To discover "the people" was at the same time, once again, to discover a folk, in their sturdy traditionalism and in their quaintnesses. When the people were heard, they were heard to speak usually in the regional dialects—although not by Louis Adamic, peculiarly, although he had a special concern for the preservation of cultural pluralism. And what "the people" had to say with surprising frequency had to do not with the current crisis but with the way things had been in the old time. An antique Tidewater oyster fisherman appearing at the end of Appel's frankly polemical book looks like "George Washington come to life again, a plainer George, an older George, but of the same Virginian stock," and the fisherman says, "'They can't understand my language over in Europe and I can't understand their language'" and goes on to recall memories, several times removed, of the Revolutionary War. The people of Louise Armstrong's polemical, programmatic *We Too Are the People* were inhabitants of Paul Bunyan country. "Perhaps Paul himself and Hels Helsen and Babe, the Blue Ox, had known these very woods. To the modern generation here, they are merely characters in a book, if they are known at all. To the old-timers they are tradition. The Indians know them and have told us many stories of them we never knew before, and the old woodsmen remember them too." Nathan Asch's *The Road* ended, like so many of the other books in the genre, with an image of impending apocalypse, but nonetheless Asch asserted, in his prefatory statement, that his time on the road had been an inspiring time. There was something about America that "makes it possible to travel in this country, looking at places where not the fortunate ones live, but those dispossessed, and see much want and hear of many troubles, and still feel there is hope, there is a chance, there is a future. It's what makes it possible to be happy while traveling in America"—that something being, specifically, a fundamental and pervasive feeling of equality, despite many abuses. And Sherwood Anderson's principal discovery about "puzzled America" was that at bottom there was among the people a fundament of belief, specifically in democracy.[51]

For all of the traveling, what was to be discovered were images of stillness and a continuous (if imperiled) antiquity. Many of the road books were largely or even primarily picture books, photographs and photographers being supplied usually by the Farm Security Administration, and what was recorded in the photographs tended, again, to be souvenirs of a supposed American traditionalism. Certainly there were differences of technique and attitude between such of the photographers as Walker Evans and Ben Shahn and Margaret Bourke-White and Dorothea Lange and Carl Mydans—they were hard-edged or soft-edged, or dramatically aggressive or passive and formal[52]—but their subjects, at least for the purpose of these books, had a sameness. The "documentaries" documented sharecroppers or tenant farmers, typically lean, with high cheekbones, and gazing steadily, and old-timers, and quaint monuments in town squares, and the facades of weathered buildings, and furrowed fields—not news events, but icons of abidingness, all carefully fixed and centered in their frames and rendered static even when, as rarely, figures were caught in a moment of action or high emotion.

The most celebrated of the photo-documentary books during the 1930s was *You Have Seen Their Faces,* with photographs by Margaret Bourke-White and text by Erskine Caldwell, published in 1937, and it was an examination of faces at best only in part. The faces themselves, first of all, of white tenant farmers and of black tenant farmers, were very similar to each other; the favored look was of a burdened stoicism, signifying that these folk had been and would be in their place forever. But then the faces were not necessarily so prominent as the appurtenances and decor—the artifacts—of the civilization of the southern folk. In the first photograph of the book, of a boy with a plow, shot at an angle and from below, it is the plow that occupies the most of the space while the boy's face is partially shadowed. A photograph of children in a black schoolhouse is dominated by the stove at the front of the room. Other photographs in which human figures are present are dominated by fireplaces and quilts and interior walls papered with advertisements and calendars and magazine covers.

Sherwood Anderson's *Home Town,* published in 1940, was a selection of photographs, by various hands, from the files of the Historical Section of the Farm Security Administration, with an obliquely relevant, rambling text supplied by Anderson. The purpose of the book, according to the editor, Edwin Rosskam, was functional, sociological, and historical in nature. In a period of five years the FSA had accumulated some thirty-five thousand original negatives, now neatly arranged in rows of filing cabinets and waiting for today's planner and tomorrow's historian. "The Small Town, focal point of rural life, place of exchange, forum of ideas, is a necessary part of such a coverage." But historical "coverage" was manifestly not the point of the book as it was actually composed. Anderson, indeed, had a shrewder idea of what the book really wanted to be about: much of his narrative emphasized the idea, first, that the hometown, and not the city with its big thinkers and abstracters, was the true site and emblem of American tradition, and the idea, second, that the hometown was just now engaged in a struggle to preserve itself—which struggle, by the way, it was likely to win. Immigration had come to the towns, and, what was more disturbing, radio communications:

> The market place come into the sitting rooms of small frame houses in the towns, tooth paste, hair restorers, trade with

South America, fascism, communism, the Yanks have beaten the White Sox, the old quiet sleepiness at evenings in the towns quite gone.

Still babies being born, lads with their lassies in cars parked under trees, hopes and dreams, the life in the towns still more leisurely, the same faces on the streets day after day, the problem of living with others a little closer, more persistently present. The real test of democracy may come in the towns.[53]

And what was at stake—what democracy looked like—was in the pictures, which, once again, tended to be very still still-lifes, with emphasis on buildings and street scenes and signs and town-square monuments and handicraft tools and other such artifacts, and with people rigidified into typical postures and gestures.

The manifest purpose of *Home Town* was to celebrate the virtues of the American hometown, which virtues were found to be surviving despite everything. One of the photographs offered as evidence was of a street in Moundville, Alabama, by Walker Evans. There are a few people on the street, but they are rendered very diminutive by the camera angle. It seems to be a Main Street. There are parked automobiles and there are stores, and the little people are shopping. The tale told by the photograph is one of typifying, stable, homey ordinariness, seen in long perspective. The particular photograph had been taken in 1936 when Evans, on loan from the FSA, had gone to Alabama with James Agee in order to do the study which eventually became *Let Us Now Praise Famous Men*—and it appeared, again, in that book. The photograph served equally well, that is to say, to support the contention that America was essentially, virtuously, a hometown and to document the lives—by all report, the terrible lives—of the tenant farmers in the South. And that was reasonable because what Evans and Agee in fact documented—Agee more strenuously than anybody else—was, again, the being of a folk.

Let Us Now Praise Famous Men, published, belatedly, in 1941 and then again in 1960, came, belatedly, to be regarded as a piece of work much greater than the genre from which it had sprung. It was a documentary which transcended the documentary. And it was indeed much more agonizing in its approach to its materials than had been, say, *You Have Seen Their Faces*, and was much more self-conscious and self-doubting, with the incidental result that the text had as much to do with the spiritual adventure of James Agee, the artist trying to be a nonartist and engaged in writing this book, as it had to do with the three tenant-farmer families who were to be the subject of the book. The book was nothing if not reflexive, and was therefore to become very appealing to a kind of literary-academic taste which was to flourish in years subsequent to 1960. Agee throughout the book challenged the artifice of a thing which was a "book," and he challenged his own motives and methods, and he also apologized time and again for his own inevitable intruding on the lives which constituted his ostensible subject. The subject which he found to be underlying the ostensible subject had to do with the problem of *knowing*. "The nominal subject," Agee himself said, "is North American cotton tenantry as examined in the daily living of three representative white tenant families."

> Actually, the effort is to recognize the stature of a portion of unimagined existence, and to contrive techniques proper to its recording, communication, analysis, and defense. More essentially, this is an independent inquiry into certain normal predicaments of human divinity.
> The immediate instruments are two: the motionless camera, and the printed word. The governing instrument—which is also one of the centers of the subject—is individual, anti-authoritative human understanding. . . .
> This is a *book* only by necessity. More seriously, it is an effort in human actuality, in which the reader is no less centrally involved than the authors and those of whom they tell.

And throughout the book Agee said the same thing again and again, in the same or slightly other words. He regretted the fact that his readers would be picking up the living he was attempting to present "as casually as if it were a book." He regretted his own act of writing, preferring that the book be made of photographs and, for the rest, of "fragments of cloth, bits of cotton, lumps of earth, records of speech, pieces of wood and iron, phials of odors, plates of food and of excrement."

Let Us Now Praise Famous Men was indeed much less polemical than, say, *You Have Seen Their Faces*—a fact which in the time of the writing need not have been considered an attribute of virtue—and it devoted a proportionately much lesser amount of text to the actualities of tenant farming in the South in their economic and political aspects. In other respects, however, the book was not the transcendence of a genre but was rather something closer to being the ultimate statement of the road-writers, with or without photographs. For all of his tormented acknowledgment of the relativity of perception—for all of the epistemological *Angst*—Agee in fact went further than anyone else in creating an idea, from a limited number of instances, of a fixed, ancient, and wholesomely organic culture pocketed somewhere out there. The whole of the book turned, finally, on a single irony, concerning which Agee was infinitely apologetic and infinitely explanatory: that in the meanness of the lives of the families whom he called the Gudgers and the Woodses and the Ricketts, he had found beauty. His truly singular talent was his ability to draw implications of large and radiant harmonies from very small discretenesses of detail:

> that a house of simple people which stands empty and silent in the vast Southern country morning sunlight, and everything which on this morning in eternal space it by chance contains, all thus left open and defenseless to a reverent and cold-laboring spy, shines quietly forth such grandeur, such sorrowful holiness of its exactitudes in existence, as no human consciousness shall ever rightly perceive, far less impart to another: that there can be more beauty and more deep wonder in the standings and spacings of mute furnishings on a bare floor between the squaring bourns of walls than in any music ever made: that this square home, as it stands in unshadowed earth between the winding years of heaven, is, not to me but of itself, one among the serene and final, uncapturable beauties of existence: that this beauty is made between hurt but invincible nature and the plainest cruelties and needs of human existence in this uncured time, and is inextricable among these, and as impossible without them as a saint born in paradise.

The informing irony, that there was beauty in this particular kind of poverty, was not at all the unique discovery of Agee and Evans. Agee, however, by wresting from the journalism he was doing an interpretation which was explicitly aesthetic, verging on theological, went further than did any of the others. Throughout the book he appealed to analogies in music, particularly Beethoven. The lives of the Gudgers, Woodses, and Ricketts had the absoluteness and the integrity of a Beethoven composition: "The Beethoven piano concerto # 4 IS importantly, among other things, a 'blind' work of 'nature,' of the world and of the human race; and the partition wall of the Gudgers' front bedroom IS importantly, among other things. a great tragic poem."[54] As he was writing the book, said Agee in one of his letters to his friend and counselor Father Flye, he found himself confronting "the whole problem and nature of existence."[55] The problem, that is to say, and despite Agee's many assertions to the contrary, was less a matter of the techniques of perception and, more and more directly, the matter of finding a large meaning—a theme, merely—in what was perceived.

The Gudgers, Woodses, and Ricketts have a large amount of meaning because they are *there*, as indisputably as a plate of food or a plate of excrement or the Red Wheelbarrow of William Carlos Williams. Like many others, Agee as writer was engaged in making a raid on the suspect amplitudes and abstractions of high literature, albeit in a style of high lyricism. Beyond that, and as a matter finally of greater importance for the achieved theme of the book, these lives are beautiful because they have a fixity and a harmony and an appropriateness in their place which is folksy to the point virtually of being vegetative. Agee allowed very little dialogue into the book, and thereby frustrated what might have been suggestion of an adversariness, or simply a difference, between people and people or between people and environment. In an instance George Gudger is allowed to say, "'You never can tell what's in a cloud,'" the utterance putting him in the position of a postulant to nature, but that is one of the very few instances in which he is allowed to say anything at all. For by far the larger part, Agee's technique consisted in observing typical actions and, more than these, typical things, and, more often than not, finding the integration of actions and things within nature. The Gudgers eat breakfast,

> and breakfast is too serious a meal for speaking; and it is difficult and revolting to eat heavily before one is awake; but it is necessary, for on this food must be climbed the ardent and steep hill of the morning, steadily hotter, up to noon, and for Fred and George then a cold lunch only, and resumption, and hours more of work; so that your two halves are held together and erect by this food as by a huge tight buckle as big as the belly, giving no ease but chunk, stone, fund, of strength: endurance in it, or leverage on the day, like a stiff stone: this slowly thaws and is absorbed more evenly throughout the body, and the strength becomes easy leather.

The siding of the Gudgers' house is another, similar, opportunity for speculation:

> each of these boards was once of the living flesh of a pine tree; it was cut next the earth, and was taken between the shrieking of saws into strict ribbons; and now, which was vertical, is horizontal to the earth . . . and the sun makes close horizontal parallels along the edges of these weather-boards, of sharp light and shade, the parallels strengthened here in slight straight-line lapse from level, in the subtle knife-edged curve of warping loose in another place: another irregular 'pattern' is made in the endings and piecings-out of boards.

Which is to say that what was once a living thing in nature is again a portion of the pattern of nature. The area of earth under the front porch of the house is by chance and temporarily different in its look from the rest of the earth, but eventually the house "shall have passed soft and casually as a snowflake fallen on black spring ground" and the land will be as once it was, for the Gudgers are nothing if not organic, in the cultural sense hyperbolized into the biological sense of the word.[56]

And Agee's essential interpretation of his folk, far from being unique, was institutionalized in the 1930s.

In July of 1935 there was born, in Washington, the Federal Writers' Project. In the authoritative opinion of Harry Hopkins—who was the administrator of the Works Project Administration of which the Writers' Project was a unit—the Project was created for the purpose, merely, of providing employment for a certain class of the unemployed. It was buffeted by difficulties and confusions from the beginning until its end seven and a half years later. There was the problem of deciding who was and who was not a writer, and further problems were created by the fact that decisions concerning the first of these problems were often very latitudinarian. There were, infinitely, bureaucratic difficulties. There were difficulties of jurisdiction, as between and within the national office and the various regional offices. There were political difficulties, right and left. And there was the problem, among so many others, of what all of these writers—more than six thousand of them in the seven and a half years—were to do by way of justifying the making of literature into a collective and putting it on government salary.[57]

Indeed, it could not be argued, finally, that the federal government really was engaged in sponsoring imaginative literature, except in a few odd and special instances, or in nourishing genius. The chief production of the Project, eventually, was the fifty-one major volumes of what was called the "American Guide Series," along with some of the one hundred fifty volumes of the similar "Life in America" series, and the kind of appropriateness of this production was first of all practical and, in the small sense of the word, political. According at least to the original intention, the Guides were to constitute a kind of American Baedeker. It was quite possible that there would be some potential small practical usefulness in such an undertaking. Moreover, it was not likely to offend anyone. Still more to the point, such an undertaking necessitated a great deal of research in the field and in the library, and thereby created opportunity for several thousands of actual, verifiable, if often trivial, jobs of work. Young Saul Bellow was assigned to copying lists of magazines in a library, and envied his friend Isaac Rosenfeld, who had been presented with the more creative task of writing an account of pigeon racing in Chicago. The Project, like the WPA itself, and despite some grandeurs of vision, was one of the New Deal's makeshift, make-work responses to the Depression, and was only that. And the real writers who were employed by the Project tended— although not universally—to be properly cynical.

Thus engendered, and managed and directed as it was, it might have been surprising that the Project should have produced anything at all or that it should have subsidized any writers of genuine talent and ambition. In fact, however, some three hundred volumes were completed and published, plus several hundred pamphlets, and the Project employed a very large number of writers who either had or within the next couple of decades were to have literary prominence.[58] More surprisingly still, although explicably, the major productions of the Project, no matter that the Project was so miscellaneously organized, did have a distinctive character as literary invention.

The major books, as also the major tendency of the Project as a whole, abandoned strict Baedeker, and what was emphasized was regional history and the abidingness of regional diversity in the culture of the United States, particularly as discovered in firsthand encounters in the field. Much of the effort of the Project was devoted to the gathering of authentic folklore, particularly black folklore, under the direction of John Lomax and then Benjamin Botkin. Much effort was devoted to ethnic studies, with emphasis on the preservation of ethnic traditions—"living lore"—within American culture. The studies of individual cities and states and towns emphasized local lore of a kind to be found residing only in local archives or in the memories of old-timers. The various books were frequently quaint, and they made a style from suggestion of unmediated factuality, and they were often irreverent regarding both an official and a pompous kind of American idealism and also the pretensions of high literature, and occasionally they had a polemical edge, as especially in the collections of ex-slave tales. In their apparent general ambition, that is to say, the books were not finally very different from the road books, and, not surprisingly, numbers of the writers of the road books were employees of the Writers' Project. Like the road books, the Guides and the other major publications of the Project created an American folk.

The ambition to do so was manifest everywhere: right, left, in the middle, and even among such employees of the Project as became disenchanted and wrote exposés.

There was, for convenient summary instance, the case of the Massachusetts Guide, published in 1937. Conrad Aiken had been briefly employed by the Project and wrote some of the essays for the Guide. Aiken was at least relatively conservative in matters of philosophy and politics. He wrote the essay "Literature," which offended the left-wing members of the state editorial staff because it stressed the heritage of individualism in Massachusetts, come to its flowering, as Aiken maintained, in the years of the nineteenth-century renaissance. The left wing insisted that another, parallel essay be included in the volume. The latter essay, "Literary Groups and Movements," first of all stressed the *collective* nature of writing in Massachusetts in the past, and second brought history forward to the prediction of a new literary renaissance set to begin just now, in 1937, "unless war again intervened to blast it at the roots." (Aiken had said that "EmilyDickinson was the last of her line, the last of the great Massachusetts frontiersmen")[59] No matter that Aiken's essay was peculiarly eloquent, and that the essay written (collectively) by the left wing was neither deep nor eloquent nor, as scholarship, impeccable, the two, printed back to back, represented true and equal ideological division. Aiken disliked the "Commies," and they liked him no better.

But despite the discrepancy in sheer critical talent and despite the obviously significant difference in historical emphasis, the two essays did nevertheless share certain discrete assumptions and did after all have a sameness of implication. Both of the essays began with the presumption of the cultural independence of early Massachusetts. New England was not Olde England, some ironies of appearance to the contrary. Aiken pointed to the fact that Boston in its remotest beginnings as a civilization was an English city, but with a population of exactly one cranky, curious, solitary, and reclusive Englishman, William Blackstone, or Blaxton. For the left the premise of literature in Massachusetts was the radically dissenting congregation at Plymouth. And in both accountings what followed, necessarily, was a narrative of the regional distinctiveness, if not quite isolation, of Massachusetts thought and literature. For Aiken the informing motif was the tradition engendered by William Blackstone, or Blaxton: proud, independent, and frontier-oriented. For the left the dominant motif was the progress toward democratic plainness, with Hamlin Garland and William Dean Howells, oddly enough, becoming the greatest of all literary Bostonians because, in effect, they had rescued Boston from betraying its own best principles of secularism, simplicity, realism, and nativism. And in both accountings literary Massachusetts was made to be a small place, redolent of a peculiar past which was at once charming and noble; both of the essays, moreover, while they acknowledged heroes, managed also to reduce them to the stature of plain folks.

And in the very middle there was Harry Hopkins himself, who in his brief preface to the Massachusetts Guide noted that the Guide

Series as a whole, beginning as a public-employment measure, had "gradually developed the ambitious objectives of presenting to the American people a portrait of America,—its history, folklore, scenery," and so on, which was to suggest at a minimum that America did have some kind of composite, democratic identity such as might be discovered by adequate research in the field.

In the Missouri Project, one of the editors was a short-story writer named J. S. Balch. The Missouri Project had some special problems of a jurisdictional and political nature. The most talented and experienced of the members of the editorial and writing staffs went on strike, and Balch, after refusing reinstatement, wrote a novel, *Lamps at High Noon,* in which he exposed corruption, bias, and incompetence in the Project. Norman MacLeod, a poet, was attached first to the New York City Project and then to the New Mexico Project. He wrote a novel, *You Get What You Ask For,* in which he exposed, among some other number of things, the interference of politicians and bureaucrats in the work of the Project and the dissensions between internal sectarian political factions, nowhere more exacerbated than in New York City. Balch and MacLeod, like many others, were very much disillusioned. On the other hand, and while tracing the adventures of their disillusions, they—even they—asserted emphatically their abiding adherence to the great cause itself, which was, in Balch's words, "to produce The Story of America":

> the land, the wide wonderful land, with the illimitable
> continent-wide farms on it, the cities, the big cities and the little
> cities, the cities with the Dutch names, the English names, the
> Indian names and the French, the factories, the mills, the adobe
> huts of the craftsmen, the fishing villas on bamboo legs of the
> creoles, the skyscrapers that looked at each other across the
> telegraph wires between New York and Chicago, San Francisco
> and St. Louis; and under all these, under the earth, the dead, the
> fragrant dead of the Americans of all races, intangibly rising
> through the wheat-roots and the unmined coal, the uncollected
> songs, the mystic and mighty traditions. . . .
>   Yes, the mystic and the mighty traditions.

Miraculously, said Balch, in the midst of Depression, here was an opportunity—or here, at least, had been the promise of an opportunity—for Americans to present themselves with a riches which heretofore they had never been able to afford, namely, the possession of a culture.[60] And MacLeod, who had been a *New Masses* editor, apparently found in the Federal Writers' Project something tonic even to his own revolutionary politics. His protagonist says:

But dogmatism—no matter of what sort—will not win in
America. Progress here must have something of the prairies in
it, something of the Rocky Mountains and the Eastern Seaboard.
It must be flavored with Indian speech and the smell of pine
forests, earthy and rugged as the gnarled hands of American
farmers watching the wind blow their lives away in the dust
bowls of neglect.

America must have something of the South in it—the Negroes
must be given a voice in our destiny—as the Jews should have a
word in the phrasing of this land, the Scot descended, the workers, and the refugees from Fascism recently arrived.[61]

As in the case of the road books, the manifest general ambition in
the major productions of the Writers' Project was to create a new,
grand, and unified vision of America, which vision was to be determined by the recovery of static smallnesses and discretenesses and
simplicities of actual and ingenuous lives in America.[62] Therefore, of
course, a considerable amount of disingenuous editing and selectivity
went into the making of those major productions. There was much
emphasis on the distinctiveness of supposedly real native American
language. In Balch's *Lamps at High Noon* the fictive national director
of the Project (based on the real Henry G. Alsberg, a man who knew a
great deal about foreign places and cultures) is presented as being
fascinated by specimens of American slang. The emphasis on language
in turn commanded an emphasis on dialect. One of the most successful
of the Project's productions, in terms of both popularity and critical
reception, was *These Are Our Lives,* a collection of thirty-five autobiographical tales of plain and exemplary folks in North Carolina,
Tennessee, and Georgia, as told to Project field-workers. The tellers of
the tales are for the most part farmers and mill people and small-town
types, and, as in the case of the road books, much of what they say has
to do with the way things used to be, although there is some special
attention to the effects of current New Deal programs, but the salient
part of what they have to say is the language of their telling—which no
doubt, lacking recording equipment, had been edited so as to be made
to seem to be authentic and native:

> "I like to read the paper and listen to the radio right well, but
> I don't care a thing about the moving picture show. Why I
> reckon I ain't been to see one—let's see, hit's been five year or
> more now. The State Theatre give me three annual passes for
> fixing some machines for them and I could a'gone to the show,
> without paying a cent, any time I took a notion to for three
> years, but I never did use them passes a single time; I wore 'em
> out jist carrying 'em around in my pocket."

And again, this time a black voice:

> "I was bo'n in '89. I'm what they calls a off-child—my mother
> wasn't ma'ied to my father. She give me to her daddy to raise,
> then she took off up Nawth. I ain't heerd of her since. I don'
> know if she's livin' or dead. The man who was my father got
> ma'ied. We didn't have nothin' to do wid each other. He jus'
> died about a yeah ago and lef a three-hoss farm to his chillun.
> My gran'daddy went by the name of Allen Doyle; my name's
> Thomas Doyle, but everybody calls me Tom."[63]

Withal, if the Federal Writers' Project did not really sponsor the
making of literature in America, except in a few special instances, it did
at the least subsidize the idea that demotic American culture—
whatever it might finally turn out to be after all the data had been
gathered—was the likely source of an appropriate, current American
literature.

And this was true even in the few instances when the Project did
publish Literature. The notable instance was an anthology called
American Stuff, published in 1937. It was the intention of that anthology to provide print for some of the literary work (judged and selected
according to literary merit) being done by Project writers on their own
time. The contents included a technical study by Dorothy Van Ghent of
patterns of imagery in the writing of Gertrude Stein, one of the more
elegantly attenuated poems of Claude McKay, some intricately compact satirical poems by Lionel Abel, some other poems, by other poets,
which strongly suggested the diverse influences of T. S. Eliot, Edwin
Arlington Robinson, and Wilfred Owen, and Richard Wright's "The
Ethics of Living Jim Crow." Henry G. Alsberg, as national director of
the Writers' Project, wrote a preface to the anthology which was
curiously—subversively, so any of the contributors might have
thought—apologetic. Many of the Project's best writers, he said, had
not responded to the call for manuscripts: some of the contents of the
anthology were crude in style and inexpert or diffuse in technique.

On the other hand, it must have been the case that at some level
of editorial responsibility seeming crudeness and inexpertness constituted positive criteria. The very title of the anthology suggested as
much—what was to be published had the value that it was distinctively
American (no old-world effeteness here) and that it was *stuff* (not literature). Moreover, an approximate one-third of the contents, inter-
spersed between the imaginative works, consisted of folklore collected
and prepared by Project researchers, so that a particularly complex
poem by Dorothy Van Ghent, for instance, was followed by and in

some manner authenticated or justified by a recovered Gullah narrative, and a collection of sonnets about youth and bitterness by a certain Aaron T. Rosen was followed by some square dance calls which had been recorded in Arkansas, and so forth. And Alsberg himself half-converted his half-apology into a positive assertion along the same lines. The best of the Project writers had not submitted manuscripts, but the general quality of what had been submitted was surprisingly high, "and, what was even more interesting," he said, "we found that the average unemployed writer was concerned not with the remote aspects of far islands of existence, but with the realities of the American here-and-now." The style of the contributions was sometimes crude and the techniques often inexpert, "but," said Alsberg in words which might well have been uttered by Mike Gold, "there is sincerity in it, a solid passionate feeling for the life of the less prosperous millions." "In this book," he said, "the reader will find comparatively little to remind him of the classics, little echo of the higher aestheticism or the delicate attenuations of emotion. This is the American scene to the life, very often as it appears from the roadside ditch, the poverty-stricken tenement or shack, the relief station."[64] "American stuff" was in effect a name for an aesthetic, and it was the name for an apology for poetry based on an appeal to folk tradition. It was right at least to hope that there was a concordance between the poetry of Dorothy Van Ghent and an authentic Gullah story.

And as in the various cases of proletarian literature as a movement, and the road books, and the Guides, the making of an avant-garde literature during the Depression years encumbered, generally, the recovery and invention of a plain and lowly and democratic American cultural tradition.

In the writing of American literary history, there were, at the outposts, the frankly parti pris, which is to say frankly Marxist studies, notably Granville Hicks's *The Great Tradition*, published in 1933 and revised in 1935, which frankly, systematically, and rather querulously evaluated American writers according to the degree of their sympathy for the proletariat—and thus, for instance, awarded beatitude to John Dos Passos and dismissed Henry James—and Bernard Smith's *Forces in American Criticism*, published in 1939, which traced the decline of religioaristocratic biases in American critical thought, from Cotton Mather to T. S. Eliot, and the inevitable forcefulness of the force of Marxist thinking:

> To whom does the future belong? In January 1939 Eliot announced that the *Criterion*, the literary journal he had edited

since 1922, would no longer be published. His Europe had crumbled; the culture in which he had put his faith was dying. . . . Eliot had arrived at a mood of detachment. There was nothing he could hopefully fight for now. But those who believe in scientific methods, in realism, in social equality and democracy, are hopeful and are fighting.[65]

The major critical-historical studies of the 1930s (allowing a small amount of latitude in dates) were undoubtedly Vernon L. Parrington's *Main Currents in American Thought,* the final volume of which was published in 1930, and F. O. Matthiessen's *American Renaissance,* published in 1941. These books were not committed to ideology in any such strict way as were the writings of Hicks and Smith, but their biases of interpretation were nonetheless distinctly, candidly populist and democratic. Later, in an influential revisionist essay, "Reality in America," Lionel Trilling was to suggest that Parrington's essential weakness as a historian of letters had been implied by the very title of his great work: the culture of a nation, said Trilling, could not be figured in the image of a current, as in a river, but had the form of a struggle, a debate, a dialectic. And indeed Parrington had had difficulty with certain writers whom he had not been able to place in his currents, notably Poe, but on the other hand, first of all, his currents were quite broad, and they were plural and they were remarkably accommodative—he was dealing after all and in considerable detail with a history extending from 1620 to 1920—and, second, his ambition to discern and clarify some continuities in a length of history was neither eccentric nor frivolous, although it might have been hopeless. Hegel himself, to speak of dialectics, had attempted the same. What was distinctive about *Main Currents* was its engagement itself, as a partisan study of American Literature, in a cultural dialectic. Parrington's assertion was the opposite of that of, say, T. S. Eliot. He frankly preferred one tradition over others, namely American equalitarianism and democracy as expressed particularly by Jefferson and then by Emerson, whom Parrington read as a transcendentalized Jefferson. Parrington's method, moreover, consisted in discovering not monuments but the "germinal ideas" of American letters, as they were to be found by following "the broad path of our political, economic, and social development, rather than the narrower belletristic." He did not live to complete the final volume of his study but he wrote approximately half of that volume and left notes for the remainder, and clearly his idea of the present task of American literature in the harshnesses and the antiequalitarianism of the present time was the recovery, by the exercise of a critical realism, of the equalitarian past.

"Jefferson," he wrote at the end of his introduction to the third volume, "was not as foolish as many of his disciples have been, and Jeffersonian democracy still offers hope."[66]

F. O. Matthiessen's first important book had been his study of T. S. Eliot, published in 1935, which had been written precisely, so he said, in order "to emphasize certain of the fundamental elements in the nature of poetry which are in danger of being obscured by the increasing tendency to treat poetry as a social document and to forget that it is an art." (He retreated from this position, to an extent, in later editions of the book.)[67] And in *American Renaissance*, too, he was much more, and more explicitly "belletristic" than Parrington had been, but at the same time, and explicitly, and in the actual writing of the book he proceeded at least as emphatically from the assumption that the common denominator between Emerson, Thoreau, Hawthorne, Melville, and Whitman had been "their devotion to the possibilities of democracy." These writers, who constituted the inheritance of American culture if any did, had shared as their major desire the ambition "that there should be no split between art and the other functions of the community, that there would be an organic union between labor and culture." Of a particular importance to all of them had been Emerson's idea of the "central man," and Matthiessen in fact ended his exhaustive study by locating Emerson's idea in a folk context; its true implication was to be discovered in that "myth of the common man," which included the tales, factual and fictive, about Davy Crockett and Sut Lovingood and Mike Fink and Johnny Appleseed, and so on, all of these figures being, in Emerson's phrase, "Representative Men" rather than being, in Carlyle's term, "Heroes" deserving of "Hero-Worship." For Emerson even Socrates, so Matthiessen pointed out, was a "plain old uncle...with his great ears, an immense talker," "what our country-people call *an old one*."[68]

And as in the writing of literary history, so in the recovery of the great American leaders. They were the plain folk, great for their exemplary plainness. Carl Van Doren's *Benjamin Franklin*, published in 1938, was not only a good book but also, as the historian Carl Becker pointed out in the moment, a "timely" book. Andrew Jackson, in the guise of Old Hickory, was recalled to the present particularly in two popular volumes of biography by Marquis James: *Andrew Jackson: The Border Captain,* in 1933, and *Andrew Jackson: Portrait of a President,* in 1937. And above all, of course there was Lincoln, in poems and plays and movies, and conjoined, appropriately, with Carl Sandburg. The Lincoln of Sandburg's creation, extending from *The Prairie Years*, published in 1926, to the four volumes of *The War Years*, published in 1939, was the ultimate exemplar of the moral imperative which was in democratic plainness. Lincoln was a true American because he was a folk hero.[69]

Perhaps no single person more thoroughly or persuasively documented the idea that America was essentially a folk nation than did Constance Rourke, whose influence on American writing and cultural thinking generally in the 1930s—often acknowledged and often not—was absolutely pervasive. She was a collector of folklore and a historian of popular culture and an art historian and a literary critic and an anthropologist and incidentally a director of the WPA Art Project, parallel to the Federal Writers' Project, and thereby in charge of the work of the approximately one thousand artists she sent out into the field to discover and copy specimens of American folk art. She had been influenced by cultural theorists extending in a line, which she herself traced, from Montaigne (specifically his conception, in the essay "Of Cannibals," of a "poesie populaire") to Vico to Rousseau to Herder[70]—but very little of what she wrote was itself theoretical, and that little was by way of introduction to particular subject-matters. As Stanley Edgar Hyman was to point out, she was not so forcefully learned as numbers of her immediate folklorist English predecessors and contemporaries: Sir James G. Frazer, Andrew Lang, Gilbert Murray, F. M. Cornford, Jane Harrison, Jessie Weston, Lord Raglan.[71] Therefore she seldom speculated far beyond the data at hand, of American culture. Nor, of course, was she a pioneer—even in her own generation, not to mention the documents which had been piling up for three centuries prior to her generation—in discovering a distinctness of American culture. Rourke's first book, *Trumpets of Jubilee,* appeared in 1927. William Carlos Williams, for one, had preceded her in speculating at some length on popular American myths and heroes; *In the American Grain* had been published in 1925.

But *In the American Grain* was very impressionistic, and the fragments of the native past which it collected had been moralized in such a way as to suit Williams's own particular uses—the American past was found to be largely a history of oppressions.[72] And the transcultural, or Ur-cultural, discoveries of which, say, a Lord Raglan was capable were not immediately relevant to a nation which as matter of political as well as cultural necessity was engaged in trying to define itself. Nor was the theory what was needed, with its potential excess and schematization—Herder's folk theories were in the moment being more logically elaborated in Nazi Germany than by Constance Rourke. What was wanted now more than ever before was a usable democratic past such as might suggest a plausiblity of coherence to a nation which was in fact multinational and which was also in numbers of other ways currently susceptible to chaos.

Rourke collected data. In *Trumpets of Jubilee* she had given a different kind of accounting of the Golden Day and/or the American Renaissance of the mid–nineteenth century, and in this instance somewhat at the expense of the figures of the canon—Emerson, Whitman, Melville, Thoreau, and even Abraham Lincoln. Her subject was the popular, which was to say the successful, public spokesmen of the day, namely, the major figures of the Beecher clan (Lyman, Henry Ward, and Harriet Beecher Stowe), Horace Greeley, and P. T. Barnum. They were the true representatives of the cultural moment of the Renaissance, as proved by the size and enthusiasm of the audience which together they had commanded. And it was with some explicable irony that Rourke discovered that these figures for all of their tendency to bombast and for all of their marvelous magnitude had also been seekers, often baffled, after a national coherence.

Trumpets of Jubilee was followed by *Troupers of the Gold Coast, or The Rise of Lotta Crabtree,* published in 1928, in which Rourke recovered still another version of the origins of tradition in nineteenth-century America, namely, the popular stage particularly as it became institutionalized in culture-hungry San Francisco in the latter part of the century. In 1934 she published *Davy Crockett,* which for all that it read something like a child's biography contained ambition to discover the American method of mythopoesis. In 1936 she published her *Audubon,* which was a biography of the man, as Rourke said, partly by accident: she had concerned herself originally with a study of American frontiers and had therefore been drawn to Audubon's writings. But the Audubon she created indeed was a frontiersman, not unrelated to the Davy Crockett whom she had created. There had been an element of tall-tale-telling in Audubon's (nongraphic) reports on the American wilderness, while the heart of his painting had been its utter simplicity. Like Davy Crockett, Audubon had been at once a naive truth-teller and an artful exaggerator. There was certain anecdotal material which Rourke found to be especially suggestive, as in an instance when, being visited at his home in Kentucky by a touring naturalist, Samuel Constantine Rafinesque, Audubon "began to try out his visitor in a mild way, as western hunters and trappers invariably tried out the stranger or greenhorn, to see how much they would believe," for "it was not for nothing that [Audubon] had consorted with western hunters who could pull the long bow and spin the tall tale."[73] And then as the administrator and editor of the Federal Art Project's Index of American Design, Rourke was directly responsible for thousands of graphic transcriptions of American artifacts; anitque quilts and weather vanes and Shaker furniture and barn ornaments, and so on.

Rourke collected the data, and she did more. Her book on *Charles Sheeler*, published in 1938, was subtitled "Artist in the American Tradition." Sheeler, both as a painter and, significantly, as a photographer, was seen to be important because he had created a work which was generally acknowledged to be high art and he had done so not only and not necessarily by using American subjects, but also by the use of clean, solid, architectural forms of the type which, according to Rourke, were peculiarly and traditionally American. The French influences which had come to America after the Armory Show had been either antagonistic or, as in the special case of cubism, unnecessary because Sheeler had had no need to rid himself of the kinds of softness which had been inherited by French artists. The work of Sheeler demonstrated, altogether, the facts both that a distinctive American folk past did exist and that it was *usable* in the making of contemporary, schooled American art.

It was implicitly the same kind of revelation that had been the principal accomplishment of her most celebrated book, *American Humor*, which Rourke had published in 1931. That book, subtitled "A Study of the National Character," had been first of all an adumbration of some American folk archetypes: the Yankee, particularly the Yankee peddler, and the braggart backwoodsman and the black minstrel and some American kinds of mountebanks (evangelical and theatrical). Rourke's research was deep and wide. Given her perspective, there was in the book an implied praise of those popular artists of the past—bards, in effect—who had originally been able to grasp and define the American archetypes. (Given the perspective, Rourke could award honor to, for instance, the probable inventor of blackface minstrelsy, the white theatrical producer Jim Crow Rice—now forgotten except as an epithet but in his time, by Rourke's measure, an authentic and imaginative maker of tradition.) By such accounting she hugely expanded and democratized the canon of American art. But then the truly stunning part of her achievement was her reading of the accepted canon of the nineteenth century in such a way as to discover the folk rudiments—the folk inspiration—of it. Mark Twain was easy, as was Whitman, and Emerson and Thoreau were not difficult, but Rourke also found American folk bias and basis in Hawthorne, Melville, Poe, and Henry James and Emily Dickinson.

In the case of Poe, to take one seemingly intractable instance, Rourke could point to the probable impact of popular comic storytelling. The patterns of Poe's tales, if not their substance, were those of

a native western type. "plumbing horror, yet turning also to a wild
contrived comedy." The kind of his laughter was inhuman and mixed
with hysteria and was intended as a triumph over his readers, but such
in Poe's time was "the familiar objective of popular comedy." Again,
Hawthorne—at his finest—had adapted the devices of western storytelling in order to reveal, not the abstractions of the Puritan system, but
the earthy, grotesque workings of the inner mind, and he was, for all
the delicacy of his style, "close to the rude fantasy-making of the
pioneer." And it was Henry James who, after all, had written the novel
The American, a novel which completed the early and already
established American fable of American innocence: "Even the title
was a fulfillment. Who ever heard of a significant English novel called
The Englishman or an excellent French novel called *Le Français*? The
simple and aggressive stress belonged to an imagination perennially
engaged by the problem of national type." The particular novel was of
course singularly relevant to Rourke's thesis, but in fact Rourke read
James at length and subtly and appreciatively, and although she regretted what she called the "gentility" of James's late style, she was
persuasive in arguing that there was a style and a vigor in the work as a
whole which had origins in folk sources. James's taste for the fabulous,
for one thing, was akin to that of the backwoodsman—as, again, Emily
Dickinson's air of improvisation owed a debt to the American sense of
comedy with its deep divisions between the outer and inner worlds.
"Emily Dickinson was not only a lyric poet; she was in a profound
sense a comic poet in the American tradition."[74]

Rourke's reading of the archetypes perhaps provided no serious
writer of the 1930s with explicit models to be copied, but her work did
give authority to that kind of imaginative creation which, in one way or
another, made an appeal to American folk tradition. And that kind of
appeal was ubiquitous in the 1930s, making for a consensus among
otherwise quite discrepant writers and works. John Steinbeck's Okies
and the poor whites of Erskine Caldwell's rural Georgia, for instance,
were attractive not only because they were sufferers and not only
because they might have been portrayed (as in the case of the Joads) as
a simple people who really were noble, but also because they were an
articulation of a known folklore, and in this respect they were the
equivalent of, say, the great American author whom Bernard De Voto
had created, in 1932, in his book called *Mark Twain's America*. Even
Wallace Stevens, in *Owl's Clover*, amidst his strenuous ruminations
and elegant sarcasms and gorgeous images, paused momentarily to
encourage an appreciation of the folk inheritance, addressing an apostrophe to "O buckskin, O crosser of snowy divides" as a possible

salvation—although it is to be said that in Stevens's difficult poem the moment of this reaching would seem to have been especially difficult and awkward for the poet.

And there were hoboes everywhere—in fact, of course, but also in fancy—who were not the Bohemian free spirits of the *Songs from Vagabondia* of the 1890s and who were not either, precisely, lineal descendents of Walt Whitman's equable traveler on the open road; these hoboes had their own unique glamour, composed of the two facts that they had touched bottom in a time of bottoming and that they were the true, loyal sons of the pioneers. They were themselves proof, and they were in a position to record proofs, that a legendary America still survived.

Such record was tendered by Nelson Algren's Cass McKay, who was the "Native Son" by explicit ascription, and not less (although somewhat less explicitly) by Edward Dahlberg's wanderer, Lorry Lewis. The stuff of naive American legend was intricate in the vocabulary and in the kind of allusions from which Dahlberg made prose. Lorry's mother, the lady barber of Kansas City, is visited by aspiring beaux: "When a big leather-skinned cattlerancher from Wyoming or the corn-state, Nebraska, would come in . . . she was gleeful for the whole day." One of the young Lorry's pals disappears from the orphanage in Cleveland: "As time went on Herman Mush Tate became a legendary hero and several stories were told of him. One that he had drifted into an Oklahoma Indian reservation and had won an argument from an Injun chief and that now he was living in the happy hunting grounds where there is always Indian summer."[75] And of such (both mother and Mush Tate) are the kingdom of heaven for an American boy, by clear implication. Lorry himself, who was Dahlberg himself, is in one salient aspect of character a teller of tall tales of the Middle West and the Far West, which is to say the frontier. Indeed, there is a great deal of comic buoyancy in this bottom dog.

And there was an amount of such buoyancy even in so very bottom a dog as the character named Tom Kromer in the novel *Waiting for Nothing,* by the mysterious author named Tom Kromer. That novel, published in 1935, plunged swiftly and efficiently to the desolation of the life of the "Stiff." It was, seemingly, authentic—Kromer said in an introduction that, save for four or five incidents, the novel was autobiographical. Some of what was recounted was so revolting that it had to have been authentic. But the novel was also—as Kromer also said—a study of idiom, and by its very language the novel in fact converted the adventuring of the one Stiff into a tale of a folk. The language was not merely antiliterary and it was not merely distinct from standard English and it was not merely slangy—although it was that, and it relied to great extent on racy synecdoches. (The Stiff's ambition is "three hots and a flop.") The language was curiously formal, and stilted in its rhythms, and formulaic, and repetitive:

> It rains. It will rain all night, but I cannot stand here in the wet all night. I shiver in this doorway and watch this peroxide blonde. . . .
> "Think it'll rain, sweetheart?" she says.
> "If it don't rain tonight, it will tomorrow," I say. "You can't never tell about rain."
> "Got another cigarette, deary?" she says. "I'm dyin' for a cigarette."[76]

This language mocks itself and dispenses with itself. These are merely sounds, which, however, have the positive connotation of a static, timeless community. And although there are no overt, oracular appeals here to a specifically American folk, the community which is invoked cannot be anything other than American, given this language.

The great epic in poetry of the 1930s—although in fact it had been composed almost entirely during the late 1920s—was without doubt Hart Crane's *The Bridge*. By explicit intention it was a national epic which was "to enunciate," as Crane said, "a new cultural synthesis of values in terms of our America."[77] The envisioned scope of the poem was enormous, and perhaps impossible of realization. The poem was to be affirmative, in direct response to T. S. Eliot. On the other hand, Crane was not capable of simply litanizing "the people, yes." The cultural synthesizing he sought demanded images and emblems which would convey, among other things, an equal commingling of the American past and the American present, and the hobo was one of the more prominent figures by which he attempted to make his reconciliations. Crane's particular hoboes were again, like their other literary compatriots, modern-day pioneers who could recollect the past, and Crane's hoboes were, besides, so situated—presumably because they were outside of standard society—that they could also recollect the present, in a series of puns:

> So the 20th Century—so
> whizzed the Limited—roared by and left
> three men, still hungry on the tracks, ploddingly
> watching the tail lights wizen and converge, slip-
> ping gimleted and neatly out of sight.

The hobo is the major figure in the section of the poem called "The River," and what Crane wanted to do in that section he himself defined in a letter to his Aunt Sally Simpson, who appears in the poem. He was trying, he said, to chart the pioneer experience of our forefathers—and to tell the story backwards, as it were, on the "backs" of hobos. These hobos are simply "psychological ponies" to carry the reader across the country and back to the Mississippi, which you will notice is described as a great River of Time. I also unlatch the door to the pure Indian world which opens out in "The Dance" section, so the reader is gradually led back in time to the pure savage world, while existing at the same time in the present.[78]

These hoboes, as such, appear only in the one section of the poem, but in their figuration as wanderers in time and space with privileged purview of both, and in their figuration also as the vernacular part of the American civilization, they are recapitulated again and again in the poem, as sailors and as Indians and as Walt Whitman, and even as the hero of the poem—the epic poet who is doing the wandering and observing and imagining. That poet is in fact quite indistinct in the poem, but some characterization does attach itself to him, and he is much more a hobo than he is Virgil.

The great prose epic of the 1930s was without doubt Dos Passos's *U. S. A.*, which for all of its breadth and its multiple ambitions, and its multiplicity of tales, did have a single identifiable protagonist and then also a single identifiable hero. The protagonist is that Proustian "Camera Eye," who certainly is to be regarded as a figuration of Dos Passos himself, particularly as he had once been a youngster and had been sheltered and had been raised in quite elegant circumstances. The "Camera Eye" is the sensitive, naive Dos Passos engaged in observing the exemplary fates of a number of exemplary little people in the modern generation (1900–1929) of the U.S.A. What in general he is made to observe throughout the enormous length of the novel is that all of these little people—the McCrearys and the Janey Williamses and the J. Ward Moorehouses and the rest—are in one way and another gradually dispossessed from the true heritage of their U.S.A.

What the "Camera Eye" is made ultimately to observe, however, is another and superior observer, the character named Vag. This Vag occupies only a few pages in the enormous length of the novel, but those pages constitute the preface and the epilogue to the novel, and being there at the beginning and at the end, he has unique authority to moralize everything that is in the book. Moreover, as hobo he is himself the ultimate emblem of all of the little people who have been dispossessed. U.S.A. is mostly, he says at the end of the brief preface, "the speech of the people," and all of the voices which follow are in effect his own various voices. Moreover, and at the same time, he is a figure beyond dispossession and therefore, perpetually, ready for new hope. After all of the compromise and the utter failures, he remains a seeker after the true America. He has been from the beginning a lonely wanderer but not all a purposeless wanderer. "It was not in the long walks through jostling crowds at night that he was less alone," we are informed, "or in the training camp at Allentown, or in the day on the docks at Seattle, or in the empty reek of Washington City," and so forth through a catalog of episodes and places, "but in his mother's words telling about long ago, in his father's telling about when I was a boy, in the kidding stories of uncles, in the lies kids told at school, the hired man's yarns, the tall tales the doughboys told after taps; it was the speech that clung to the ears, the link that tingled in the blood; U.S.A." In the final scene of the novel we find the Vag still traveling, and specifically and appropriately traveling westward. There are ironies in the scene. An airliner passes overhead, also traveling westward, and the conjectured route of its travel elicits a lyric addressed to the spaces of America;

> Omaha. Great cumulus clouds, from coppery churning to creamy to silvery white, trail brown skirts of rain over the hot plains. Red and yellow badlands, tiny horned shapes of cattle. Cheyenne. The cool high air smells of sweetgrass.[79]

And so forth. The irony in this is that the well-to-do passengers in the airliner know nothing of these lyrical possibilities. But the Vag down below, hitchhiking, does know. And for all of these reasons—because he is an emblem of all of the little people and because he is in touch with the national past and because he knows the beauties of the American spaces and because he remains a seeker—this hobo is a hero.

The concomitant implication of all of this seeking for the low and ordinary exemplifications of American life—in the poetry of Archibald MacLeish no less than the proletarianism of Clara Weatherwax, in the frequent quaintnesses of the American Guide Series no less than in the strenuous lyrics of Hart Crane—was democratization of the idea of authorship in America. Paradoxically but explicably, the discovery of a folk essentiality meant that new Americans, too, might assert cultural citizenship. In a word, this American past was just as available to the sons and daughters of the Great Migration and of the New Immigration as it was to the natives. For that matter, it was more available as also more necessary for such persons than it was for the sons and daughters of America's aristocracy.

five

Tales from the Ghetto

Back at headquarters, in Washington, a young man named Joseph Gaer was one of the field supervisors for the Federal Writers' Project in its early, organizational days. The field supervisors were few in number and they were important personnel. They made forays into the field, they got things done, and they had an influence. According to Jerre Mangione, the Project's coordinating Editor, Gaer in particular had a singificant influence in shaping the early development of the Project. "A small and intense Russian immigrant who had come to the United States at the age of twenty, and spoke with a pronounced accent," he was very good at his job. He was efficient and had had good experience: he had written extensively about folklore. His activities in behalf of the Project had to be subjected to some restrictions, however, because "his Russian-Jewish accent could mislead strangers into thinking he might be a dangerous radical." For the most part he was kept out of the Midwest and South, but he did do extensive work in the New England area.

Gaer's immediate superior was the national director of the Project, Henry G. Alsberg. Alsberg would perhaps have been especially sensitive to the requirements of diplomacy within this federal bureaucracy, which was dedicated, nominally, to the explication of America. He was himself an ex-radical and had been a friend of Emma Goldman. He was, also, the American son of German-Jewish parents, and he had to some extent in his previous, varied, and colorful career claimed and used the fact of his antecedence. He had at one time been a courier for the (Jewish) American Joint Distribution Committee, in charge of distributing money to needy Jews in Russian villages after the revolution. He had been a journalist more than anything else, but his major literary success had been an English adaptation of the Yiddish play *The Dybbuk*. The play had had a run in New York of almost two years.[1]

And in fact a suggestively large number of the researchers and writers who were engaged (with whatever varying degrees of seriousness and enthusiasm) in the creating of the enterprise called the American Guide Series were immigrants or were the children of immigrants, or were black. This federally sponsored discovery of the American mainstream, that is to say, was conducted to large extent, and throughout the ranks, by explorers who from any conventional point of view were quite outside the American mainstream.

The road-writers, meanwhile, being sponsored only by their own initiative, undoubtedly were serious in their endeavoring to find essential America, and their numbers included many real Americans—Edmund Wilson, among them, and Eleanor Roosevelt, who wrote a documentary book called *This Is America*—who might have been presumed to have a special access to the material, but their numbers also included Louis Adamic and Benjamin Appel and Nathan Asch, and others, who, when they showed up in all of those folk places in the United States, must often have provoked some astonishment and amusement among the natives.

Among those writers of the 1930s who considered themselves to be subscribed to the "proletarian" movement, the most prominent (if prominent only momentarily) tended to be American mainstreamers, as in the case of Clara Weatherwax. Perhaps the Communist party in the United States, which was sensitive about the matter of the predominance of foreigners in its ranks and which, especially in the period after 1935, was committed to the Americanization of communism, was influential in creating a good press for its friends among the natives. But literary proletarianism in the United States, along with its deliberate and explicit nativist bias, had been invented, first of all, by Mike Gold, with gloss supplied by George Goetz (who became V. F. Calverton), and as a movement had then been continuously defined and advertised and sustained by barbarians. The lust of Clara Weatherwax for the American vernacular had everything to do with the sweaty provocations of Mike Gold.

Nor was it unlikely that the business of interpreting American culture should have been conducted so largely by, and under the influence of, marginal Americans. By 1930 an approximate one-half of the population of the United States did in fact consist of marginal Americans, who necessarily were put to the task of discovering a native land from which they might claim rights of nativity. Nor was it unlikely that the version of America which would be preferred by marginal Americans would be that one in which a folk tradition was the determinant part of culture. By definition, the American folk past was nonexclusionary.

The folk past was of course created in order to authorize a version of American civilization in the present moment. Now, as a folk-place, the nation also sanctioned and even encouraged assertions of newer typicalities in American life. It was not odd that a Russian-Jewish immigrant with a heavy accent should have supervised a large endeavor in the collecting and recording of the history of New England. Such a man might well have been especially interested in such an enterprise. And it was not odd that other aliens, whether or not so conspicuously alien, should in some similar ways have engaged themselves in recording their own equal participation in American life. If America was really the culture of its low and ordinary folk, then they really were latter-day Americans. And it was also the case, given the special circumstances of the Depression, that the hard times such aliens were likely to have known in the times of their own youth gave them additional special license to claim that they were exemplary Americans.

The ghetto—Irish, Italian, black, Jewish, and so on—thus could be presented for consideration as a kind of Home Town. It could be celebrated not only in spite of but also because of all of its deprivations and confusions and strangeness. The urban ghetto—chiefly in New York and Chicago—was not the only place in which the new American folk had been created, but it was in fact the usual place. Moreover, to tell the tale of one's youth in the ghetto was to secure several benefits at once. One could pay one's filial respects and thereby assuage guilt. By mythicizing the ghetto, one could further emigrate from it. In addition, one could make a statement and teach a lesson to all of those official Americans who persisted in thinking that they owned the country. And altogether one could say that here, too, was a genuine and informative typicality of the true America.

GROWING UP IN NEW YORK

In 1930 Michael Gold published his *Jews without Money,* a book which in its time was very much esteemed and which earned its author a great deal of money. It was published beautifully, with woodcut illustrations, in several languages. On the strength of his royalties from the book, Gold did the authorly thing and bought a farmhouse in Bucks County. Fictionalized memoirs of the ghetto had been published before, but the success of *Jews without Money* in effect established a contemporary genre.

By 1930 Gold had already had a long and formal association with the political left, but he was not quite yet the spokesman (and literary hatchet man) for the Communist party which later he was to be, and as which he was to become notorious. Indeed, his political usefulness to the Party was to derive directly from the large commercial success of the book. He had written the series of sketches of which the book was composed all through the years of the previous decade, addressing

himself not to revolutionaries but to readers—of *American Mercury,* in
which some of the sketches had appeared, and *Menorah Journal,* as
well as *New Masses.* He was by 1930 a recognized spokesman for and a
power only within the literary left, in which, at the age of thirty-seven,
he was in fact something of an elder. As long before as 1921 he had
been urging the deliberate creation of what he had called a "Proletarian
Art." On the other hand, his definition of "proletarian art" had been
almost as lacking in strictness as it had been rapturous. And there was
irony in the fact that when the book was published, it was attacked
from the left for not being proletarian enough. It was said that Gold had
written "without reference to the mass," that his characters were
"merely poor people," and that he had singularly failed to mention
episodes of clear political implication, such as the shirtwaist-makers'
strike and the Triangle fire, which would have been within the scope of
the book—for which deviations Gold did apologize.[2]

No doubt he had intended at some point in the writing, and
perhaps continuously, to discover a story of inevitable revolutionary
conversion in this somewhat randomly recalled, somewhat fictive story
of his own childhood on the Lower East Side of New York. There,
certainly, amidst the physical horrors of that ghetto, was the breeding
place of the revolutionary idealism which was now his profession. In
the last scene of the book the young Michael Gold listens to a man on
an East Side soapbox and hears tell of the world movement, born out of
"the despair, melancholy and helpless rage of millions," which will
abolish poverty, and the Michael Gold of the present moment says:

> O workers' Revolution, you brought hope to me, a lonely
> suicidal boy. You are the true Messiah. You will destroy the
> East Side when you come, and build there a garden for the
> human spirit.
> O Revolution, that forced me to think, to struggle and to live.
> O great Beginning![3]

No matter that the event upon which the recollection was based—a
Union Square rally—had in fact occurred in the spring of 1914,[4] by
which time young Michael Gold had been, although young, a little too
long-in-the-tooth to be considered "a lonely suicidal boy," and no
matter that in fact he had already had a good amount of exposure to
radical teaching, which was not included in this memoir. (And no
matter, either, that the man on the soapbox was in fact Elizabeth
Gurley Flynn, that siren of the left whose appeal to young men must
have been more than political.)[5] If the actual event had been a little
different in both time and implication from what Gold now

memorialized, the event as he recorded it should have been accurate
as fiction. That "great Beginning" should have been the natural and
anticipated climax of this autobiography which was really a novel.

But it was not. The scene has a duration of exactly six sentences
and is remarkable chiefly for being so abrupt as it is, and so actually
discordant with what has gone before. In a previous episode the
young Michael's young aunt has had a discussion about the union
movement with the doctor who is courting her, but that, prior to the
ending, is the total of the book's dealing with the specifics of political
education. Nor is it the poverty of the East Side ghetto that is the
distinguishing subject of *Jews without Money*. The characters who are
moved through the novel are indeed poor Jews, at least for the most
part, but what they have to offer to the tale is something more than,
and other than, the dynamics of poverty. (In the time of his childhood
as recorded in the book, the real Michael Gold had really been raised
in circumstances somewhat better than those of his neighbors.) It was
perhaps a frustration to Michael Gold that he was not Maxim Gorki,
but so it was, and *Jews without Money* is not *The Lower Depths*. Nor
is class antagonism in any strict Marxist sense the ground from which
the novel's adventures are drawn.

The novel begins with the words, "I can never forget the East
Side street where I lived as a boy," and therein was the novel's not
uncomplicated subject. What follows from this beginning is a catalog
of some awful circumstantialities—the first and second chapters deal
with the prevalence of prostitutes in the neighborhood, and thereafter
there is information about the gangsters in the neighborhood, about
the noise and the filth and the cockroaches, and about the constant
harassments by the *goyim*—but in fact, and obviously despite Gold's
intentions, these things are not so awful as by all rights they should
be. A peculiarly disproportionate amount of the whole of the novel is
given over to accounts of prostitution, and the subject might well
have—should have, given Gold's special ideological learning—led to
pointed speculation on the social and economic determinants of prostitution, or it might have led to observations on the matter of the
sociopsychological motivations of prostitutes, or even to a study of
the trade as an instance of bourgeois capitalist venture; but first of all,
all of Gold's prostitutes are emotionally healthy (although one of them
is dim-witted) and have hearts of gold, and, second, Gold's reiterated
theme throughout all of the accounts is the corruption of innocence: that of the prostitutes and, much more pointedly, that of the
little impressionable boy, himself, who cannot help but be witness.
All of the instances of all of the horrors, moreover, are moralized in

such a way that the sheer ugliness which should be in them gives way to a constant implication of betrayal. Those persons in the neighborhood who do wicked things are not to be blamed, for wickedness has been forced upon them. Essentially, they are very nice people. Harry the Pimp has a wife and two children, of whom he is very proud. He does not seduce any of his employees; to the contrary, he protects them and teaches them manners and sobriety, and he is proud of the fact that many of his girls have saved enough money to bring their parents over from the old country. He is in a dirty business, but he is a benign man. And there is Louis One Eye, who is a young gangster and a dangerous fellow—he has killed people—but he is also a mother's son. He has a feeble old mother who insists, after all not implausibly in the general milieu of the novel, that "my Louis is a good boy, he doesn't hurt any one." (99) And besides, as we are informed, it was the state reformatory in which he had been raised that had made him into a criminal. And similarly, the vermin and the filth and the noise are not endemic to the East Side, but are encroachments.

For all of the horrors, this Lower East Side has an essential loveliness, made the more lovely because it is so fragile and so subject to arbitrary encroachments and fatalities. For all of the tough-guy stance of the author, the novel is very sentimental, to the point not infrequently of being maudlin. The basic lesson in the drama of this ghetto is that goodness and innocence are imperiled—and not even necessarily by any particularized villainy. Among the many sentimentalities of the novel, the most purely bathetic is the brief story of the child named Joey Cohen who was run over by a horsecar. The story of Joey Cohen is totally irrelevant to whatever little there is of a plot or a narrative in this novel, but it does encapsulate a basic attitude. Joey is one of the kids in the neighborhood gang. He is, we are told, rather a dreamy young boy, but he is otherwise virtually an anonymous character. At the end of a chapter devoted to telling of the typical activities of the "gang of little yids," Joey hitches a ride on the horsecar and, in jumping off, suffers his fatal accident. The next chapter begins with expostulation by Gold: "Joey Cohen! you who were sacrificed under the wheels of a horse car, I see you again, Joey! I see your pale face, so sensitive despite its childish grime and bruises. You are precocious in the Jewish way, full of a strange kindness and understanding. There are dark rings under your eyes, as under mine." (32) There has been nothing in the novel to motivate such grief, and the observation that Joey had been "sacrificed" is patently absurd—there is an important lesson here for little boys, but not so grandiose a one. Nonetheless, much of the meaning of the novel is compressed in this putative sacrifice. Joey had been ripe for sacrifice because he was a little Jewish boy, with pale face, on the Lower East Side, and therefore defined by a fated, lamblike innocence. The fact that he was killed testifies—sufficiently—to his value. The sacrifice of Joey does not occur in behalf of anything. We are to know, rather, that Joey, like all the other emblems of the East Side, had valuable existence because he was so easily crushed.

The same is true of the honor of Harry the Pimp, and of the religious mores of the older Jews, and of the social and economic safety of these Jews. The mode of the whole of the writing is elegiac rather than polemical.

And, appropriately, this elegy reaches backward, behind the moment which is being memorialized, in order to find a source of meaning. The Jews of the Lower East Side, children as well as elders, do have a past of which they have been deprived, and which therefore is available to be idealized. They are old-country people. They are peasants. And the remembrance of that lost identity constitutes almost the total of what they know of joy. Even Louis One Eye is a keeper of pigeons. All of the boys in the tenements had a "hunger for country things," says Gold. "Once Jake Gottlieb and I discovered grass struggling between the sidewalk cracks near the livery stable. We were amazed by this miracle. We guarded this treasure, allowed no one to step on it. Every hour the gang studied 'our' grass, to try to catch it growing. It died, of course, after a few days; only children are hardy enough to grow on the East Side." (25–26) And when, at the end, Gold addresses his apostrophe to "O workers' Revolution" and says that "you will destroy the East Side when you come, and build there a garden for the human spirit," the pastoral figure he uses is not quite so lax or merely conventional as it might seem to be. Quite probably despite Gold's conscious intentions, the novel does properly, logically, culminate in an idea of revolution in behalf not of progress but of redemption. The truth in the yearning of Gold's Jews who are without money is not that they want a redistribution of the wealth, but that they want the garden from which they have been dispossessed. The yearning, moreover, is not quite so merely conventional or merely literary as it might seem to be. This garden is not the Eden of the King James Version; it is—absurdly, pertinently, assertively—Eden in a Hungarian version.

Insofar as the novel has a plot or a narrative, the climax occurs right in the middle, in a chapter called "Mushrooms in Bronx Park." This chapter does in any event provide the novel with its moment of maximum intensity. On a Sunday Michael's family goes to Bronx Park for an outing. The occasion is one of adventure because this immigrant family never goes anywhere. The mother in particular has not hereto-fore dared to breach the perimeter of her American *stetl*. Now when she does, she is wonderfully delighted to discover, not America, but Hungary, a bit of the old sod. "Ach," she says of Bronx Park, "it's like Hungary!...One can breathe here." (107) She removes her shoes and takes the children into the woods to hunt for mushrooms, and little Michael's idea of his mother is transformed by sudden knowledge—this is the single instance of genuine epiphany in the novel. His mother is an expert in the matter of finding mushrooms. Moreover, she knows a great deal of lore concerning birds and snakes and other eventualities of the woods. She becomes purposeful and lithe. She is a peasant, radiantly. And the episode ends explicitly:

> Suddenly my mother flung her arms around each of us, and kissed Esther and me.
> "Ach, Gott!" she said, "I'm so happy in a forest! You Ameri-can children don't know what it means! I am happy!" (110)

And the chapter, if it is climactic because it provides a summary emblem of the yearning of the Jews of the Lower East Side, also suggests the lineaments, and the problematics, of Gold's revolution. The outing on this Sunday is only a picnic and Bronx Park is not America, but the adventure has happened and has been known, and has indicated the shape of a reasonable salvation. The basic truth of the mother, as of all the other Jews, is that, of course, she is an immi-grant, which is to say that she has no home at all, neither in the Old World nor in the New World. The Lower East Side has no stability: it is, precisely, the place in which things and values and lives are wit-nessed in their movement toward disappearance. When the mother goes to Bronx Park, reluctantly, she is engaged in an act of explora-tion, a movement forward into the future of her coming to America—and, miraculously, she discovers that the future offers a possible recapitulation of her peasant past.

For all of the seeming randomness of selectivity and emphasis in *Jews without Money*, there is an inevitable basic arrangement of forces in the novel, namely, between the Old and the New. The con-flict between the two is in fact very complicated. The protagonist of the novel in his guise as the author is engaged quite plainly in honor-ing and mourning the Old. The Jews of his childhood, including him-self, are engaged, however, both in reprobating and approving the New. "A curse on Columbus," say the elders in this novel, as do the

elders in virtually all of the memoirs of the Yiddish-speaking ghetto.
"Ein klug tsu Columbus"—it was, and vestigially remains, a
Yiddish-American folk expression. America is the destroyer. If some
of the "gang of little yids" become gangsters, that is America's fault.
"There never were any Jewish gangsters in Europe. The Jews there
were a timid bookish lot. The Jews have done no killing since
Jerusalem fell. That's why the Christians have called us the 'peculiar
people.' But it is America that has taught the sons of tubercular
Jewish tailors how to kill." (23) If spiritual belief was not successfully
transmitted from the old to the young, that, too, is America's fault.
One of the circumstances of the ghetto in America is bedbugs, and the
young Michael who is being initiated into the beliefs of the elders
asks, "Did God make bedbugs?" A young rabbi with good orthodox
credentials is imported into the Lower East Side in order to stave off
the American corruption, but he is himself soon corrupted; he quickly
learns the American way and moves to a wealthier congregation.

But there is another America out there, which not only might
provide a homeland to its new Jews but which, miraculously, is
itself a plausible version of the old homeland. To know America in,
first of all, its formal, official traditionalism is—ambiguously but
certainly—to be a good Jew. Little Michael's official Americanism is,
of course, largely school-begotten, but it is not inappropriate to the
spirit of the ghetto. In a quite tender scene in the novel, Michael is
asked to perform for his elders. His father and his father's cronies are
having one of their evenings at Moscowitz's wine cellar, where Moscowitz himself plays the Rumanian gypsy cymbalon.

> A hundred Jews in a basement blue as sea-fog with tobacco
> smoke. The men wore their derby hats. Some were bearded,
> some loud, sporty and young, some brown as nuts. The women
> were fat and sweated happily, and smacked their children. Mos-
> cowitz played. The waiters buzzed like crazy bees.... The
> whole room sang....
> Then talk, talk, talk again. Jewish talk. Hot, sweaty, winey
> talk. A sweatshop holiday.

The subject of the talk is learning and the Talmud. Michael's father is
a pretender to knowledge, and he impresses the others by alluding to
obscure text in which it is said that it takes the Angel Gabriel six flaps
of his wings to come down to earth. "The Talmud," says the father,
"is the greatest book in the world.... From the Talmud one can
learn anything." Then Michael is placed on a table and made to recite
the poem he has learned in school. He intones text:

I love the name of Washington,
I love my country, too,
I love the flag, the dear, old flag,
The red, white and blue. (80–84)

This is, plainly, a scene of initiation into the tribe, and the elders do
applaud Michael's performance. Michael is a scholar, in the Jewish
way, and is a memorizer of antique wisdom, and the learning he ex-
hibits is after all not more quaint, irrelevant, and therefore pure than
is that of the sacred book.

And the America which is the inevitable future of these immigrants offers another kind of past which, because it is still more
mythical, is the more usable—precisely, a folk past. In school
Michael learns about Washington and the flag, but he is also especially advised of the example of the supreme American folk figure, the
young Abe Lincoln. Outside school, he learns more. His private and
persistent image of the Messiah is Buffalo Bill. (He was an unsophisticated lad. The first recorded words of Ernest Hemingway,
who was raised in different circumstances, were "I don't know Buffalo Bill ")[6] One of the great tutelary figures of the East Side is Jake
Wolf, the saloonkeeper. Jake Wolf knows English and he has a pull
with Tammany Hall, but the most fascinating thing about him is his
substantiation of American myth: "The great man is kind to boys,
generous with free lunch pretzels, and full of fine stories. He spent a
year in the west in Chicago, and saw the Indians. They looked like
Jews, he said, but were not as smart or as brave. One Jew could kill a
hundred Indians." (34) Wherefore little Jewish boys with their pale
faces were cowboys—and/or Indians—and are insinuated into
America. Incredibly enough, the Lower East Side is, moreover, a
kind of cultural palimpsest. The backyard of Michael's tenement had
once been a graveyard. "Some of the old American headstones,"
says Gold, with inscriptions dating back a hundred years, "had been
used to pave our Jewish yard." (41) The boys had once dug up one of
the gravestones and had found human bones.

The "workers' Revolution" whom Gold so abruptly personified
and apostrophized at the end of *Jews without Money* is as indistinct as
it is abrupt, and is the merest formality of an ending for a book which
should have been about revolution but was not. But the book did
manage to make an assertion, and that assertion did indicate at least
the lineaments of some kind of grand and synthesizing and perhaps
grotesque but nonetheless necessary hero. Finally, the novel had
said nothing more than "I can never forget the East Side where

I lived as a boy,'' but after all there was an aggression in that statement as one might say that the East Side was as good a place to come from as any other place in this country and maybe better. It had been an alien place, which, if viewed properly, was an authentic American place, the propriety consisting in the fact that the Jews without money were a folk whose traditions, transported from the old country, were surprisingly concordant with the true past of the new country. Only the names were changed. Lurking within that polemic at the end there was an avenging socialistic Messiah who looked like Buffalo Bill and who when he came would compound Hungary with Bronx Park.

There was not much less of such aggression in Henry Roth's *Call It Sleep*, published a few years later, in 1934, despite the fact that as a work of literature it was so much more deliberate, subtle, artful, and learned. This fictive memoir of early childhood on—mostly—the Lower East Side was written after all not by a child but by a real Henry Roth whose place in the world in 1930 to 1934, when he was writing the novel, was that of an unpublished, would-be writer situated in circumstances—particular but exemplary—such as would virtually have necessitated that the act of making literature would be an assertion of cultural rights.[7]

He was twenty-four years old when he began to write the novel. (The time was the summer of 1930. *Jews without Money* had been published just a few months before, in March. Perhaps the success of that book had something to do with Roth's perception of a licensing of his subject-matter.) The novel itself says plainly, to the point of an urgency suggesting obsession, that Roth, too, was unable to forget the East Side where he had lived as a boy, actually only from the age of two to age six. He was, technically, an immigrant, having been born in a *stetl* in Galicia, although he had been transported to America while he was still an infant. On the other hand, at the age of twenty-four he was quite removed from the milieu of his childhood, as also from his parents and from Judaism and from all of the cultural habitudes of the East Side, and had been so removed or at least in process of removing himself for at least a half-dozen years. He had graduated from City College, where he had had some encouragement toward literary ambition. More pertinently for him, he was living with a lady, Eda Lou Walton, to whom he was to dedicate *Call It Sleep* and who was not just any lady. She was in herself a milieu, and she was his particular visa to the New World.

He was to live with her for ten years, before, during, and after

Call It Sleep, and there can be no doubting her importance to Roth's thinking about his place in the world. For one thing, she was, comfortably and successfully, both a Real American and a New Woman—born and raised in New Mexico, having a doctorate in anthropology from Berkeley. She must have represented to Henry Roth a life which was at once alien and fascinating. And, moreover, she had quite special credentials as a representative of contemporary literature in America. She was twelve years older than Roth. When he first met her, in 1924, she was a professor at NYU and she was a poet and she taught courses in contemporary poetry, when others did not do so. Roth moved in with her in 1928. In the later 1920s and throughout the 1930s she was an acknowledged expert in and a spokesman for the modern moment. Her essays about modern poetry and her reviews appeared in the *Nation* and the *Saturday Review of Literature.* Her circle of friends—and Roth's, too, therefore, but certainly at a significant remove, for they were *her* friends—included people who certifiably were creating the contemporary cultural moment: Hart Crane, among others, whom Walton particularly praised to her students and her readers, and other poets, and Margaret Mead and Ruth Benedict and Constance Rourke. The literary influences of prime importance to Roth, according to Roth himself many years later, were Joyce and Eliot, and Walton had introduced him to the works of Joyce and Eliot.[8]

The novel he was to write was in one of its major aspects to be a lyric to the Oedipal conflict, and there can be no doubt that in the time he was composing the novel Eda Lou Walton was a mother figure for Roth. By his own testimony, he had exchanged "a Jewish Mama for a native American Mama."[9] There can be no doubt, either, that in her demands and her promises Eda Lou Walton was absolutely discrepant from Leah Roth, the real mother, but at least equally imperative for him in the shaping of his childhood. She must have had an active influence upon the shaping of his childhood for the reason, among many others, that she could read the novel he was writing, while Leah Roth, to whom this very candid love letter of a novel would seem to have been addressed, did not know English. This is to say that even at the basic, sexual level of his address to his subject, Roth, as he was composing the novel, was engaged in making a statement concerning his social and cultural identity. He had two mothers, two lovers, two nativities, from which circumstance, confirmed in many and less metaphorical ways, it followed that the job of the novel had to be a resolution of his life into a single significant idea or image.

He would have wanted a knowledge of certainty in his social existence, and perhaps for that reason, although certainly there were others, he joined the Communist party. The Party was a large thing with which to identify, as he himself was to say: "We [Jews] were all seeking for a re-entry into the people as a whole. And for a while we thought we could do it irrespective of Judaism. It was a much larger re-integration"[10] And it was not only larger but, perhaps, also a much more definite route of "re-entry into the people as a whole" than either the Judaism with which he was struggling in the novel he was writing, or the novel itself. The time of his joining the Party was 1933, when he was coming to the end of his long novel. The ending which in fact he accomplished was very literary and it was ambiguous—it did not concretely resolve anything at all, and Roth seemingly very much wanted concreteness and absolutes. He had written a book so complex and so rich in its realization of conflict that it could not be brought to an end by any simple summary statement—and Roth was, seemingly, a most unquestioning member of the Party, eager for its simple summary statements and quite willing both to disregard malign revelations and to abide the serial contradictions of the Party's line. He stayed with the Party until the 1950s,[11] through the episodes of the Trials and the Nazi-Soviet Pact, and thereafter through the war. He spoke to the issue of the Moscow Trials, and as naively and as winsomely as the Party could possibly have wished. "Probably in common with a good many writers," he said in an article in *New Masses*, "my political development has not reached as high a level as it might—many of my beliefs seem the product more of intuition than of analysis." It was not intuition, however, so he said, which convinced him of the guilt of the accused Trotskyists, but evidence. These accused were not in the situation of Dimitroff in Germany, as was being contended by the Committee for the Defense of Trotsky.

> In what way were the principals in the recent Soviet trials similar? None maintained his innocence there, none became the accuser; no matter how brilliant, none was backed by a principle, all confessed their guilt. Some wept at the loathsome company and the bleakness and obscurity of the pass their historical steps had led them to, some bragged and some jeered, but they all stood convicted, their sentences sustained by the demonstrations of Russian workers. I do not believe together with the Hearst press that these men were under the influence of mesmerism or mysterious narcotics; therefore, I believe them to be, as they themselves acknowledged, guilty.[12]

One might not have expected such reductiveness from the author of *Call It Sleep*.

Irrespective of Roth's known loyalty to the Party and despite the fact that he had written a novel about suffering among the lower classes, the novel, when it was published, was of course immediately attacked from the left—"of course" because the left seldom commended and also because the novel failed to be prescriptively Marxist—although in fact there was a subsequent revision of critical opinion on the left. The initial, anonymous reviewer for *New Masses* was angered by "the sex phobias" of Roth's protagonist, "this six-year old Proust," and he said, "It is a pity that so many young writers drawn from the proletariat can make no better use of their working class experience than as material for introspective and febrile novels." The novel nonetheless had a critical success, and even, to an extent, a commercial success, and *New Masses* admitted revaluations, but on political grounds. Kenneth Burke wrote a friendly letter to the editor in which he said that Roth had very nicely, " with considerable sympathy and humor," caught "the 'pre-political' thinking of childhood." In a lengthy article in *New Masses,* Edwin Seaver defended the novel against the infantile disorder of leftism among the critics on the left, and he said that, moreover, the novel spoke political truth: "What better use could Roth have made of his working-class experience as a child than to have shown honestly and greatly exactly what that experience consisted of? . . . When we close the book we honestly feel that such a childhood can mature into a revolutionary manhood."[13]

Circa 1960, when the novel was rediscovered and turned out to be everybody's favorite forgotten novel,[14] the matter of the amount of its proletarian-revolutionary truth was known to be a false lead and a bum steer at best, and also evidence of the vulgar obtuseness of Stalinist literary criticism. But Roth himself was a Stalinist as he was writing the book, and while evidently he thought that he was not a propagandist but an aspiring novelist—he was to say, later, that he never accepted the idea that art was a weapon[15]—the matter of the political implication of the book he was writing must have been present to his own thinking. He would himself have been, most likely, eager to believe that such a childhood as he was shaping into a book could and would indicate maturity "into a revolutionary manhood," albeit he had not written about that childhood according to Party formula. He in particular, with his contemporaneous education in literary modernism, must have felt that there was a social aggression in what he had written: he had asserted the actuality, and the density and the piteousness and the beauty and also the ugliness, of a life in America which Americans of the other classes—not quite the *goyim* because he himself, currently, was not quite a Jew—either overlooked or despised. Joyce's *Ulysses,* he was to say later, had shown him that "literature can be created out of junk,"[16] from which paradox it would have followed that he did regard the materials of his own life as being a kind of junk and not the anticipated stuff of literature—no Hyacinth Girls in his childhood, but, rather, crippled Annie with her talk of putting the petzel in the knish—but which nonetheless might be stated as the stuff of literature and maybe a better stuff. That, in the circumstances, was a political assertion.

He wrote a novel about the discordancies of his own identity, discovered primarily, as a matter of plotting, in terms of an elaborated Oedipal conflict. The little boy David Schearl knows his parents both in their parental and in their sexual meanings. Father is brutal and rejecting, although also, finally, quite vulnerable, as according to formula, and, as also according to formula, little David is allowed to suspect, continuously, that the father is not his real father. Mother is serene, loving, and protective, and at the same time she intimates, almost continuously, a kind of being which is more than motherly. David is allowed to know that she has had a girlhood past which in its implications is doubly, alluringly nonkosher. Back in the old country there had been some kind of a liaison with a church organist, who might be David's real father. In the present time there is a possible liaison with the boarder. David learns that some of the boys in the neighborhood have seen his mother naked. Throughout the novel David is engaged and terrified by the confusions of sexuality, both directly and at various symbolic removes. Insofar as this plotting is actually resolved, the resolution is accomplished by transformation of the Oedipal conflict into a religious conflict between Judaism and Christianity. Chiefly by means of an abrupt, dreamlike concatenation of symbols near the end of the novel, David achieves a tenuous and ambiguous but plausible moment of transcendence. He has run away from home. In his running he overhears random and suggestive fragments of conversation—of a shape and a rhythm and a kind of suggestiveness very reminiscent of parts of Hart Crane's The Bridge. He picks up a milk ladle (signifying mother). He uses the milk ladle as a sword (signifying father). He plunges the sword into the live third rail of a trolley track, that rail having been previously associated with humiliation and ecstasy, purification and apocalypse, mystical Judaism and the Church. David is shocked, electrically, orgasmically, and redemptively. The image which, then, is offered for holding all of his implicit realizations together—postcoital and postlapsarian—is "sleep," by which figure Roth was probably indicating suprarational art and imagination, which would be to say the novel itself.

But the novel was more than its plotting. It was a recollection of childhood created in a present moment by a writer for whom the recollection of that childhood as the generative past time of this totally different present time involved a statement of doubts overcome, if not really settled, and a statement, precisely, of reintegration. Roth's task, not unlike that of Michael Gold before him, was resolution of his life into a single idea, meaning that he had to prove that he had a native place in this place. And while Roth was not likely to discover Buffalo Bill, dealing as he was in alternately erotic and theological metaphors, and while all of the narrative of the novel testified to the disequilibrium of this immigrant childhood, he did, like Gold, make the ghetto itself to be a place of contingent memories of an alluring previous past. The ghetto had been entirely confusing for a young boy, but it had been so in large part because it bespoke a mysterious earlier time which had been harmonious and stable and lovely. The ghetto by that much had been a place in touch with a tradition, and a tradition which was as eloquent as could be claimed by anybody else, and maybe more so. It followed that the American author Henry Roth had become himself by having been born from a traditional past.

According to his later testimony, Roth had been tremendously influenced by *The Waste Land*. ("I realized there was this anti-Semitism," he said "but I was willing to accept it.")[17] He would seem paramountly to have learned two technical lessons from Eliot: the contemporary dramatic possibilities in the story of spiritual redemption, and the device of juxtaposed rhetorics, high formal against low vernacular. *Call It Sleep* is a story of redemption, and it is made of its languages, namely, high formal and low vernacular. The particular social implications of Eliot's usage are, however, exactly reversed, so as to say, further, that two could play at that game. The vernacular is the street English of the ghetto as spoken by the children who are in the process of being Americanized, which is to say that it is a figure of America herself, the wicked mother who is robbing the children of their inheritance, and it is an unmelodious thing:

> "Didja ask yuh modder fuh a nickel fuh de Xmas poddy in school?"
> "No. I fuhgod."
> "My ticher calls id Xmas, bod de kids call id Chrizmas. Id's a goyish holiday anyways. Wunst I hanged op a stockin' in Brooklyn. Bod mine fodder pud in a eggshells wid terlit paper an' a piece f'om a ol'kendle. So he leffed w'en he seen me. Id ain' no Sendy Klaws, didja know?"[18]

The high formal, on the other hand, is Yiddish, as translated and transmuted and invented by Roth, and it is fluent and sinuous and richly metaphorical. It is lofty even as a language of cursing. The father says: "They look at me crookedly, with mockery in their eyes! How much can a man endure? May the fire of God consume them!" (22) And it is daintily adaptable as a language of memories. Speaking of her own grandmother in the old country, the mother says: "She was very small, my grandmother, very frail and delicate. The light came through her hands like the light through a fan." (65)

This translated Yiddish is the basic language of the narrator's own thinking, and hence it is the basic language of the novel. It is, clearly, the proper language of literature—and to say so, as Roth would have known, was to assert a most impertinent claim to cultural citizenship.

Just a few years prior to Henry Roth's and David Schearl's growing up in the ghetto, Henry James had visited the Lower East Side and had been frightened in some complex ways. Particularly, he had said,

> It was the incurable man of letters under the skin of one of the party who gasped, I confess; for it was in the light of letters, that is in the light of our language as literature has hitherto known it, that one stared at this all-unconscious impudence of the agency of future ravage. . . . That was where one's "lettered" anguish came in—in the turn of one's eye from face to face for some betrayal of a prehensile hook for the linguistic tradition as one had known it. . . . Just so the East side cafes . . . showed to my inner sense, beneath their bedizenment, as torture-rooms of the living idiom; the piteous gasp of which at the portent of lacerations to come could reach me in any drop of the surrounding Accent of the Future.

And, presciently enough, James had found evidence in this episode to predict the death of English in the United States "in any sense for which there is an existing literary measure."[19] James in 1904–5, when he made his visit, was reflecting a general idea, which if it was not so general as it had been was nonetheless quite evident in what still constituted literature in the time when Henry Roth was learning how to be an author. It was in the face of that idea that Roth wrote his memoir of childhood in a translation of the language of his childhood.

In the same year, 1934, Daniel Fuchs published *Summer in Williamsburg*, the first of the three novels which were to compose the trilogy of his ghetto. The second volume, *Homage to Blenholt*, appeared in 1936, and the third, *Low Company*, appeared in 1937.

The books became a trilogy only, in fact, by Fuchs's later designation.[20] They are not related to each other by plot or in being organized around repeated characters or by any explicit single thematic design or even, entirely, by locale: *Low Company* goes southwest from Williamsburg in Brooklyn, to Coney Island. At the time he was writing *Summer in Williamsburg,* Fuchs obviously did not know that two more volumes were to follow. The books were part-time work. He had graduated from City College. He was a grammar-school teacher by profession, and he was writing fiction during his summer vacations. For that reason, most likely, all three novels take place during the summer. As anyone might have anticipated, the story he began to write in his first novel took for its main concern the adventures in sensibility of the artist as a young man. Even that first novel, however, did not end exactly within the confines of the subject it had broached at the beginning, and the novels which came afterward demonstrated a lesson in sensibility which at most had been the merest implication of the beginning.

In *Summer in Williamsburg* Philip Hayman, an intellectual young man approximately twenty years of age, is set to the task, at the beginning, of discovering the reasons for the suicide of Meyer Sussman, butcher to the fat housewives of Ripple Street. Although a butcher, Sussman had been a sweet man. No one knows why he had put a basketball bladder over his head and turned on the gas. There is a general air of victimization hanging over Williamsburg, but that is something which Fuchs knows, and not Philip. Near the beginning Philip is given instructions by Old Miller, who earns his bread as a professional mourner and is also, in the structuring of the novel, an Old Nestor for a Young Daedalus, equipped with the wisdom of Balzac, Dostoevski, James Joyce, and Emile Zola. He says to Philip:

> "To find out properly you must first understand Meyer Sussman, and this, of course, is the most difficult thing to do. Even if I were God, I am afraid I might not be able to do this, there are so many persons. But even when you know Sussman you are only at the beginning of the problem, for then you must make a laboratory out of Williamsburg to find out what touched him here, why these details affected him and in what manner. This is a tremendous task, but you insist, young gentleman. If you would really discover the reason, you must pick Williamsburg to pieces until you have them all spread out on your table before you, a dictionary of Williamsburg. And then select. Pick and discard. Take, with intelligence you have not and with a patience that would consume a number of lifetimes, the different aspects that are pertinent. Collect and then analyze to understand the quality of each detail. Perhaps then you might

know why Sussman died, but granting everything I do not
guarantee the process.

Certain men are the sum of a million infinitesimal phenomena
and experiences. . . . The atoms are no physical substance but
psychical, and, further, they do not belong to any one type but
are variously commingled. The ultimate product, man, therefore
moves mysteriously, but he is a scientific outcome of cause and
effect."[21]

These are, of course, literary instructions, and Philip recognizes them
as such. He will improve upon them by the end of the novel to the
extent of realizing that the methods of Thackeray—he has been reading *Pendennis*—are inherently falsifying.

But Philip never does learn just why Meyer Sussman committed
suicide. As the novel progresses Philip himself, indeed, drifts somewhat away from being its central, informing consciousness. Fuchs,
however, having provided himself with a broad opportunity for the
human comedy, gradually does discover a pointed conflict of values.
The chief antagonists of the novel are, finally, Philip's father on one
side and his Uncle Papravel on the other. Nor is Philip caught between them. Another character, his brother Harry, is brought in to
serve that dramatic purpose.

The father is a man who has suffered defeat in America with great
dignity, having managed to protect his integrity if not much else. He
sells newspapers from a concession in a building in Manhattan and is
gone from early morning until late at night while time withers him.
Despite evidence of degradations on all sides of him, he is true to and is
a transmitter of his old-country ideals. He believes in feeling and pity
and charity and courtesy and honesty, and gentleness and conscientiousness. The father's way of living, says Philip, is "beautiful and
heroic." (245) Uncle Papravel, on the other hand, runs a strong-arm
operation and, in the particular action of the novel, sells protection to a
small excursion-bus company, which—for his prices are high and his
ways of business, although regretted, are ungentle—he comes to own.
He says to Harry:

"Harry, you went to school, I don't know anything about fancy
things, what I know only is, a man's got to make money. Everybody who makes money hurts people. Sometimes you can't see
the people you are hurting, but you can be sure all the time there
is always somebody who gets squeezed if he is not ruined.
That's the kind of world it is, and who am I to change it? Only,
in my business you can see the people you hurt. . . . But remember this, Harry, no matter where you go, no matter what

business you'll be in, remember there will always be people who
will live in rotten houses, who will have no money for a good
time and who will die ten years earlier on account of you." (253)

From which statement there might follow a powerful indictment
of the whole rotten capitalistic system, but nothing of that sort does
follow. One of Philip's friends does become a Communist, transiently,
but he is a pitiful fool of a character and not a source of instruction,
and anyway he works for the Party really and unbeknownst to himself
only in order to find liberated women. The located conflict of the
novel—as in *Jews without Money* and *Call It Sleep,* and perhaps
inevitably—is between the old-country Jewish ideals and powerful,
disinheriting America. And consequently the task of the novel is
finally, and once again as in the other novels of the genre, a discovery
of some idea or figure of reconciliation. But in the case of Fuchs, in
this novel and in the ones to follow, that reconciliation occurs very
much on the side of those who beat the system, however regretfully
or contingently. In *Summer in Williamsburg* the father is rather an
isolated, encapsulated character, and is thematically appropriate, but
he is also, comparatively, rather a colorless character. All of the
glamour goes to Uncle Papravel. The wickedness he does is explained
and virtually explained away by his competent understanding of his
situation as an immigrant: this is America and a man's got to make
money. He has his troubles because there is always another, bigger
operation, but nonetheless he does very well in his chosen field.

He becomes a native American, and more. In the final scene of
the novel he is in place in the fabled Catskills, fabulously called
"Aligerville." He and the hoodlums in his employ are at rest, having
beaten out the rival bus company. They are staying in the home of
Mrs. Van Curen. Outside, the full-starred sky resembles "a huge
ceiling in a Brooklyn burlesque house." Inside, Papravel counts his
blessings. "And just this morning the railroad company sent out an
announcement they take no more passengers, only freight," he says.
"And it is only a beginning, because, remember, there is still a God
over America." "America," he says, "is a wonderful country. Seriously, seriously, I mean it. Look at me, look how I worked myself up
in four short years. In America everyone has an equal chance. I don't
know how things are in Russia now, even God Himself don't know
what's going on there these days, but even so, where, I want to know,
where in the world could a Jew make such a man of himself as right
here in America?" Hearing Papravel say so, Mrs. Van Curen weeps,
as well she might, but for the reason that Papravel is such a fine man

and yet will not go to heaven when he dies, because he has not been baptized. Papravel thinks that perhaps she is joking, but in any event he is quite equal to any such inconvenience. He smiles happily and says, "Just you leave this to me, Mrs. Van Curen, and everything will be all right." (379–80)

 Homage to Blenholt is related to the previous novel by the amount that the protagonist is again a young man who is a dreamer and a searcher, but the goal of his searching is now candidly comic and pretentious, and he is himself, as a dreamer, now patently a schlemiel. The "Blenholt" of the title is the late commissioner of sewers. Our protagonist, Max Balkan, goes to his funeral. That is the major part of the narrative of the novel. Blenholt, insofar as he has been known at all to anyone else, has been known to be a common gangster, but Balkan insists that truly he was a hero in a flat age. He says:

> "Let other people call him a gangster, but to me Blenholt was no racketeer, no politician, no sewers man, living on the money he forced from the storekeepers. He was a kind of king, like the ancient Romans and Greeks, like the glorious Renaissance tyrants, powerful and crushing, exacting tribute from those who were obliged to bow before him. That is what makes a hero in any time and any land, power, but in return a hero relieves his followers of responsibility for he is authority in all things and sets their poorer minds at rest. As it says in Carlyle! Do you know anything about Spengler and T. S. Eliot?[22]

Equipped with an imagination for heroism and royalty, like T. S. Eliot before him, Balkan wants to be a hero. Tamburlaine had once been but a lowly shepherd boy, having an estate not much different from that of Max Balkan in Williamsburg. But of course Balkan fails, and repeatedly. The script for his fate has been written by a god who prefers farce over tragedy, Feydeau over Marlowe. When he goes to the funeral, he is beset by a series of contretemps ending in his being beaten up. Max is also an inventor. His most promising invention is bottled onion juice and his hopes soar when he receives word from Onagonda Onion Producers, Incorporated, but the word he receives is that bottled onion juice has already been invented. Finally, sadly, he becomes part-owner of a delicatessen.

 This humor is somewhat wry but not subtle. There is tremendous, ineluctable disparity between Max Balkan and his dreams—that is the joke, and the novel repeats it again and again, citing not only Max but also some of his friends and relations who similarly are obsessed by foolish dreams.

 There is after all an unexpected edge to this humor, however.

Imagination is not the will of things. Daniel Fuchs was not Wallace Stevens. But imagination is better than common labor. It does have its practical uses, when used shrewdly. In this novel as in the previous one the movies are a besetting sin of Williamsburg because they involve people, chiefly young women with courtship and marriage on their minds, in, precisely, foolish dreams. On the other hand, it is only the dreamers who might, just might, transcend Williamsburg.

At the end of this novel, when Max accepts defeat, his father mourns for him. His son is now dead, so he thinks, because he has resigned himself to living for bread alone, not that he was likely to do otherwise. The father, in this novel, has an authority. In his own youth he had been an actor. He now makes his living by dressing in a clown suit and carrying a sandwich board advertising Madame Clara's Scientific Beauty Treatments—a kind of work which wearies him but which has its traces of a past grandeur. Earlier in the novel he had presented his son with some startling advice.

> "Work," said Mr. Balkan in a softer voice, talking out the window, "two kinds of work there is, honest and not honest. Standing in a stationery store all day, pressing in a shop, cutting fur—that's honest work and it's no good. When I was a boy I ran away from it. I couldn't do it. It made me sick, too. That's why I went to Yudensky's and became an actor. . . .
>
> "The other kind a work is ganavish," Mr. Balkan went on. "You know what ganavish means, Max? To make a living not honestly, by tricks, by schemes, not with the hands. Gamblers, actors, poets, artists. This is good. It is easy, you can have a good time playing, but you need luck. Luck and good tricks."
> (231–32)

And to say that seriously—as he does and as, apparently, does Fuchs—is to render a quite sincere homage to the exemplary crook Blenholt. Blenholt was admirable because, given luck and good tricks, he had become the ruler of the sewers rather than one of the ruled. There are hidden ironies, as Fuchs will indicate. In the last line of the novel, at the point where the father is musing on the tragedy of the death of youthful dreams, we read: "But all the same the evening sun that day went down on time." (302) No one is tricky enough really to escape the order of things. Moreover, Blenholt had been only the commissioner of sewers, and not Tamburlaine—a not very extravagant tyrant even for a flat age. Nonetheless, and with all of the order of things against him, he had been what he was, namely, a modestly successful thief, and therefore he had suggested a marginal possibility for the good.

The father's elevation of the principle of the ganavish is obviously not unchallengeable, and in the next novel Fuchs does seem to have reconsidered, but not in ways which might have been anticipated in another author. From the perspective of the ghetto—now, in *Low Company,* Neptune Beach in Coney Island, but the change in locale is not very important—the trouble with dishonesty is not that it is wrong by definition, but that it is what it had indeed been for Uncle Papravel and in the aspirations of Max Balkan, namely, a mode of social climbing and therefore a betrayal of the ghetto. It had been a mode of cashing in on the promise of America, and therefore a betrayal of the ghetto.

In the penultimate scene a hitherto minor character—*Low Company* is not a well-made novel—is brought to the fore in order to moralize. He has just been made witness to the defeat of a gangster of Neptune Beach. A rival and more powerful gang has forced the gangster out of his brothel business and has threatened his life so that he has had to leave. Shoulders despairingly hunched, he is going to Troy, New York. The witness himself has been desperate to get away and begin a new life far from Neptune Beach, in Manhattan, and his particular plans, too, have suddenly been frustrated. This redoubled and absolute closing-in of the order of things brings him, like Max Balkan before him, to the point of resignation, but also to a feeling of relief. Guilt is lifted from him. We read that he realizes that "it had been insensible and inhuman for him . . . simply to hate Neptune and seek escape from it."

> This also was hard and ignorant, lacking human compassion. He had known the people . . . in their lowness and been repelled by them, but now it seemed to him that he understood how their evil appeared in their impoverished dingy lives and, further, how miserable their own evil rendered them. It was not enough to call them low and pass on.[23]

On the other hand, this declaration remains, for Fuchs, not more than a statement of intention. In the succeeding coda of a scene, Neptune is returned to its quotidian life in which the deadly business of ordinary business—catering to the beach crowd, in particular—usurps everything. Earlier in the novel the man who runs the ice cream and soda parlor has been robbed and murdered. Now, at the end, the weather has improved and business will be good. Fuchs reflects, terminally:

> The storekeepers of Neptune Beach put the papers aside and grew prepared for the rush. It was too bad about Spitzbergen, but after all, business was business and a man had to make a

living. It was a blazing sun, pouring thickly over the atmosphere
which was heavy with dampness. It was like a steamy blanket.
Their clothes were damp and chafing on their bodies. Going inside the stores, they scratched their chins thoughtfully and said
it was a pity the soda man wasn't alive to enjoy the wonderful
weather. (313–14)

—which is not to make Neptune Beach to be a name for the radiant
poor.

And despite these defeats and despite this ending, the major energy of the novel is in the portraying of the gangster. (The movie
version of the novel, written by Fuchs and produced in 1947, was
called *The Gangster.*) He is a figure of some genuine and unresolved
complexity, who apparently was genuinely problematic for Fuchs. In
the other novels, in his statements about the gangsters, Fuchs had for
the most part protected himself by his comic ironies. This gangster is
grotesque, but not funny. He is an unnaturally unwieldy, lumpish
man. He waddles when he walks because his legs are bowed. He is
startlingly ugly. Children call him King Kong, and the name he has
—Shubunka—has a sound which might frighten little children. At the
same time he is an elaborately generous and, even more, a courteous
and sensitive man. And he is elaborately neat. He barbers himself and
tailors himself, and carries himself with great dignity. Although in the
greater scheme of things he is a most minor gangster, he is a fearsome
presence in Neptune Beach, but he does his best—his insufficient
best, albeit—to make his presence easeful and anonymous.

Shubunka has triumphed, marginally, over a dismal ghetto past:

Shubunka remembered the poverty of Rivington Street in the East
Side, the steaming, relentless heat of the tenements in summer,
in winter the wretched cold when the only heat for the whole flat
came from the kitchen stove. . . .
   Shubunka remembered many meals of dry rolls, bought seven
for a nickel, eaten with salt for flavor, for his father had been a
poor man, a glazier everlastingly looking for broken windows to
mend. . . .
   Shubunka lay on the bed and remembered the cruelty of the
streets, the gang fights, the cops, the day when he fell off the
roof dodging one of them. Eight Ball, the boys called him, or
Nigger or Coke or Dopey Schmugguggle, because of his odd
gait, his squat bulk, the unnatural heaviness of his features.
(253)

He had once tried honest labor and of course had failed. He has worked
long and hard for what he now has, namely, money and the respect it

entails, no matter how grudgingly tendered. He has triumphed, marginally, even over his own repulsiveness.

Shubunka is a ghetto Gatsby, except that Fuchs made his case to be much more severe. He yearns not for romantic love, although he would like that, too, but simply for an acknowledged identity superior to his fatalities. And as a gangster he has achieved something of what he wants. As a gangster he is a *self-made* man, a matter of importance because both heredity and environment have conspired against him. The principle of the ganavish has been serviceable for him. But then it turns out that it is also his undoing because by his small triumph he has become something more than a neighborhood businessman. He is an American gangster, unfortunately recognized as such by other American gangsters, who are strangers. Shubunka's success has value only in reference to Neptune Beach, and as he trudges off to the subway which will eventually carry him to Troy, Fuchs recognizes in Shubunka's behalf that the worse fate is having to leave his city. Perhaps honesty would have been a better policy because, as an honest man, perhaps he would not have succeeded so well.

Fuchs himself went to Hollywood. The first movie for which he received story credits was called *The Day the Bookies Wept,* produced in 1939.

COMING OF AGE IN CHICAGO

In the spring of 1929 James T. Farrell wrote the short story called "Studs," from which the *Studs Lonigan* trilogy was to exfoliate. Farrell was, at the age of twenty-five, an undergraduate at the University of Chicago, and he was taking the course in advanced composition from Professor James Weber Linn. He had taken the beginning section of the course two years earlier, after which experience he had decided that he wanted to be a writer and had gone off to New York.[24] He had been reading ferociously and was writing voluminously, and in a small way was appearing in print. When, back again in Chicago, he wrote "Studs," Professor Linn was very enthusiastic. Farrell then asked Professor Robert Morss Lovett to read the story, and Professor Lovett was also encouraging and recommended specifically that Farrell expand upon the story and describe its milieu at greater length. Therefore, said Farrell himself in his introduction to the 1938 Modern Library edition of the trilogy, "In a sense, Professor Linn and Professor Lovett are the spiritual godfathers of *Studs Lonigan.*"[25]

And that acknowledgment, which most probably was appropriate and was, certainly, gracious, was after all surprising. *Studs Lonigan* is not a novel which would seem to have had a university beginning. It deals with low life. Although the three volumes are somewhat different from each other in formal ways—for one thing, the plot movement in the third volume is more emphatic than it is in either of the two other volumes—the novel is in no obvious way ambitiously literary; the novel sprawls, and there is very little (some, but very little) sense of an imposition upon the materials of a continuous literary intelligence. For many years, moreover, *Studs Lonigan* was to be a dirty book, of the sort which schoolchildren index and pass from hand to hand. It was not boldly so, in the manner of Henry Miller, but in a manner appropriate to this tale of arrested adolescence, it was tantalizingly so. Allowing Professors Linn and Lovett their evident shrewdness and literary progressivism, it is not likely that, when they laid hands on Farrell, *Studs Lonigan* was the book they had in mind.

But it is quite likely that what Farrell had in mind was an act of *writing*, by which he might use and compose and perhaps even settle scores with the materials he had. The original "Studs" is a story about the wake following upon Studs's death at the age of twenty-six. As in the novel to come, Studs has died of double pneumonia brought on by general dissipation. As in the novel to come, Studs's surviving pals are the fellows from the old Fifty-Eighth Street gang in Chicago, and they as much as Studs are the subject of the story because Studs had been exactly one of their stripe. What is to be known about Studs chiefly, as about the rest of the gang, is that finally he had been a "slob." The narrator says so, and he is to be believed. But in this story the subject is also and equally the narrator himself, engaged in making a judgment upon the old Fifty-Eighth Street gang. In the old days the narrator had been a kind of younger mascot to the gang, attached but not firmly attached, and then he had left. He says: "My associations with the corner gradually dwindled. I went to college, and became an atheist."[26] Subsequently he had gone to New York, like Farrell before him, "and stories of legendary activities became fact on the corner. I had started a new religion, written poetry, and done countless similar monstrous things." (228) If he is not precisely a certified artist, come back to reflect on the circumstances of his youth, he is as close to being so as Farrell's modesty would allow, and there can be little doubt that he is Farrell himself. "Studs" is a story of a writer writing about his story.

In Farrell's own version of his intentions, *Studs Lonigan* was, emphatically, not such a story. His ideal for the novel, said Farrell in the introduction to the Modern Library edition, was "the strictest possible objectivity." "In the early stages of writing this work," he said, "I analyzed my character as I considered him in his relations to his own world, his own background. I set as my aim that of unfolding the destiny of Studs Lonigan in his own words, his own actions, his own patterns of thought and feeling. I decided that my task was not to state formally what life meant to me, but to try and re-create a sense of what life meant to Studs Lonigan." He was studying Studs in relation to his particular time—the dates of the action in the completed trilogy are 1916–31—and his relation to the givens of his social institutions. "The important institutions in the education of Studs Lonigan were the home and the family, the church, the school, and the playground." This social milieu in all of its elements, said Farrell, had in Studs's time become degraded and Studs's environment was generally one of "spiritual poverty." He had authority to say so because he happened to come from that milieu. Studs had been "conceived as a normal American boy of Irish-Catholic extraction," and his fate, it followed, was exemplary: his demise was a dramatized instance of the effect of the spiritually impoverished times and institutions.[27]

But this was to say that at least in 1938, as probably also in 1929, the justification for the writing, for Farrell, was in the formulas of turn-of-the-century naturalism, according to which the phenomenon man was to be regarded by the novelist in the same manner as he/it might be regarded by the scientist, experimentally and objectively. "Metaphysical man" was dead, as Emile Zola had pointed out. The individual man was the product of the forces impinging upon him. The individual author was to be an affectless, nonmoralizing close observer. The ideal was, precisely, objectivity, but the ideal was also literary, in a recognized mode.

And in any event the novel Farrell wrote was both much more lyrical and much more moralizing than it was scientific. No doubt Farrell did want to look at Studs very objectively, and no doubt he wanted even more to objectify all of those institutions in which Studs had been educated and destroyed—even to think of home and family and church as "institutions" was to adopt a mode of distancing them. "Naturalism" would have been a natural technique. Meanwhile, however, in writing the novel, Farrell was inevitably revisiting the childhood and young-manhood in which he had himself lingered for a long time. Obviously he was not Studs. Studs was his opposite, but so exactly his opposite as in every paragraph of the novel necessarily to imply the existence of James T. Farrell. Studs and Farrell had shared the same "institutions," albeit there were differences in circumstance. In composing this version of a life engendered by these institutions, Farrell was in effect writing fictive autobiography, except that *he* had managed to outreach and outlive this life. He was in effect saying—as

in fact he did say explicitly in his essay about the novel in 1938—
"'There but for the grace of God go I.'"

He did in fact in the same statement add one more sentence.
"'There but for the grace of God,'" he said, "'go'—many others"—
which constituted an accurate if not necessarily searching assessment
of the moral of the tale, but it is to be noted that he was cautious in
saying "many others" and he did not say "everybody." Those institutions which Farrell had shared with Studs did have their particularities. And it is the testimony of the novel that Farrell had quite
contradictory feelings about them.

As Farrell himself pointed out in the 1938 essay, *Studs* is not a
story of a "slum neighborhood." It is a novel of social exposé of a
certain sort, but the subject is not economic privation. At least in the
first part of the trilogy, in *Young Lonigan,* the elder Lonigan, in 1916, is
contentedly looking forward to having a net worth of a hundred
thousand dollars, and it is not until the latter part of the end, in *Judgement Day,* that, with the onset of the Depression, money becomes a
pressing problem for either the father or the son. Farrell himself had
been born into a family which was desperately poor, but after the age of
three he had been raised by his maternal grandparents and by uncles
and aunts in circumstances which were middlingly, although waver-
ingly, bourgeois. It is the testimony of the novel that the Irish-Catholic
neighborhood from which he and Studs had come was a very insecure
place, but not because it had a population of Irish-Catholics without
money.

To the contrary, its failure adequately to provide for its progeny
was consequent upon the fact that it was just now in process of yielding
justification for its existence. It was being displaced. For one thing, in
the novel as in Farrell's own life, this ghetto was being displaced physically, ever moving a few city blocks southward in Chicago to escape the
expanding and encroaching black ghetto. On the other hand, its existence was being continuously threatened by its own success in
America, meaning its gradual dissipation into mores and values discrepant with its origins and functions. The institutions indeed did not
any longer sustain a growing boy, but were in process of becoming ever
more reified and absurd.

At the point when Studs graduates from grammar school, which is
the time of the action of *Young Lonigan,* Studs's mother wants him to
be a priest, and there is a triple irony here. First, Studs is a most unlikely
candidate for the receiving of the call. Second, the chief available model
of the priesthood, Father Gilhooley, is a very limited, and boring, man,
who is preoccupied, necessarily, with local boosterism. And finally,

while Studs is allowed once—just once, in the middle volume of the trilogy—to have a perception of mysteries and powers in Catholicism, in by far the greater part, the lessons offered by the Church and also truly learned by Studs are really limitations of knowledge. The Church has taught him that sex is wrong, and that is something he never forgets, unto his end when he is thirty years old. Therefore all of his sexual venturing is tainted and guilt-ridden and, indeed, dirty. The Church has presented Studs with the whole of his politics and ethics and even a curriculum for nonreading. In *The Young Manhood of Studs Lonigan* a visiting missionizing priest advises Studs and his crowd, redundantly, not to read Sinclair Lewis, H. G. Wells, or H. L. Mencken. The final irony is in the fact that Studs, in the very roteness of his life, is not far from being the priest his mother wants him to be.

The elders of the tribe meanwhile instruct Studs in ethnic pride and consequent xenophobia. The fourteen-year-old Studs particularly admires Johnny O'Brien's old man, who will not take any guff from anyone and who lays it on the line, and who reduces the whole of the problem of growing up Irish-Catholic in Chicago to a matter of prowess and tribal warfare. To be true to the heritage is to be skilled in battle, and vice versa. Old Man O'Brien speaks of the great fighters— prizefighters and other great men—of the old time:

> They didn't have fighters like that nowadays. None of 'em were no-fight champions like Jess Willard, and most of them were real Irish, lads who'd bless themselves before they fought; they weren't fake Irish like most of the present-day dagoes and wops and sheenies who took Hibernian names.... "But I ain't so much interested in sports as I used to be. Baseball's the only clean game we got left. The Jews killed all the other games. The kikes dirty up everything. I say the kikes ain't square. There never was a white Jew, or a Jew that wasn't yellow.... And now I'll be damned if they ain't comin' in spoiling our neighborhood. It used to be a good Irish neighborhood, but pretty soon a man will be afraid to wear a shamrock on St. Patrick's day, because there are so many noodle-soup drinkers around."[28]

Old Man O'Brien is the kind of Old Man whom fellows like because he can speak their language, but what he says is in fact repeated by most of the members of the generation of the parents and then duly repeated again by Studs's own crowd. Studs's father is a mild man who values decency and worries about his real-estate investments:

> When he'd bought this building, Wabash Avenue had been a nice, decent, respectable street for a self-respecting man to live with his family. But now, well, the niggers and kikes were get-

ting in, and they were dirty, and you didn't know but what, even in broad daylight, some nigger moron might be attacking his girls. He'd have to get away from the eight balls and tinhorn kikes. (24)

Ten years after the moment of this musing, when the boys of the Fifty-Eighth Street gang are in their mid-twenties, Red Kelley says to Studs, "'Well, I tell you, once the kikes get in a neighborhood, it's all over'"[29]

All of this, throughout the novel, was social exposé: to have grown up Irish-Catholic in Chicago was to have been educated by institutions which imposed repression, a curriculum for stupidity, and formulas of bigotry. The institutions had been demanding and irrelevant, and therefore harmful. Little wonder that Studs had turned out to be a slob.

But the novel at the same time speaks of the old neighborhood and its population and its ways in quite another fashion. The reigning emotion of the novel is melancholy, a yearning for something—a harmony and a closeness and an innocence—which has been lost and which is the only thing worth seeking in the future. Virtually all of the dozens of the characters in the novel participate in this feeling and none more pointedly than Studs himself, and in this, too, he is the exemplary son of the institutions. Nor was Farrell ironic or distant or objective in his regarding this feeling. Throughout the scores of the episodes the content of exposé is blended with a sympathy which amounts to something more than forgiveness.

Old Man O'Brien, in the brief episode devoted to him, obviously corrupts the youth. All of his adoption of the language of boyhood chumminess amounts to a device for inculcating what amounts to fascism. But it is a matter of equal obviousness that at heart he really is a boy, in a boy's book. All of his talk concerns his own lost and mythicized youth, and is elegiac. "'Hell,'"he says, "'you kids ain't as tough as kids used to be in my day. When we fought then, we fought. And we all had to use brass knuckles.'" (80) The underlying lesson in his teaching is that "times had changed. Even kids weren't like they used to be, they had none of the old feeling of other times, they didn't have that old barefoot-boy attitude, and they weren't as tough, either, and they didn't hang around knotholes at the ball park to see the great players, not the ones around Indiana anyway. Times had changed." (85) And there is a poignance in this, reinforced by the fact that Old Man O'Brien, as a man and no longer a boy, has been defeated by time and circumstance. He vends coal from a horse and wagon. Particularly, he vends coal to the sheeneys and the kikes, toward whom he must be pleasant and persuasive—"'You got to soft soap some of these Abie Kabbibles,'" he says. Times have changed, and his preferred time is a glamorous yesteryear, which most probably he misremembers.

And Studs's father, likewise, from beginning to end meditates upon the deprivations wrought by time, and all of his current efforts are devoted to preservation and stability. He resists those serial moves southward which he is forced to make. In the very first scene of the novel he is discovered to be meditating on his losses:

> Golly, it would be great to be a kid again!
> He said to himself:
> Yes, sir, it would be great to be a kid!
> He tried to remember those ragged days when he was only a
> shaver and his old man was a pauperized greenhorn. Golly, them
> were the days! . . . Golly, even with all that privation, them was
> the days. And now that they were over, there was something
> missing, something gone from a fellow's life. He'd give anything
> to live back a day of those times around Blue Island, and Archer
> Avenue. Old man Dooley called it Archey Avenue, and Dooley
> was one comical turkey, funnier than anything you'd find in real
> life. And then those days when he was a young buck in
> Canaryville. (19)

And so forth, at great length. In the last scene of the novel, as Studs lies dying, Paddy Lonigan does revisit the places of his own young manhood and childhood. Everything in the old neighborhoods has now changed, of course, but that return to childhood—that, plus getting drunk, which has the same effect—is his likely response to death, for the guiding principle of both his own life and the life he has given to his firstborn has been nostalgia.

Studs himself, from his very first moment in the novel, at the age of fourteen, is a captive of that principle, and although as he is moved forward through the years the objects of his nostalgia will have a few different identities, he goes through life to death looking backward. The total of the first volume of the trilogy has to do with Studs's graduation from grammar school and his wandering the streets during the summer months following. He has of course hated St. Patrick's and apparently with good reason, and in the first brief paragraphs of the novel he postures in front of the bathroom mirror, with a cigarette pasted in his mug, and says to himself, a couple of times, "Well, I'm kissin' the old dump goodbye," but very shortly thereafter he is brought, by Farrell, to the point of admitting, or imagining, that the old dump has had its loveliness, and he does not want to graduate. "He found himself suddenly sad because he wanted to stay in the eighth grade another year and have more fun.... He had long pants, and he wasn't just a grammar school punk any more, and he could walk down the street feeling he wasn't, but well . . . sometimes he wasn't so glad of it." (36, 38) And there is more here than merely a ritualistic sadness and fear, such as any youngster might be expected to know, because in fact reality for him hereafter will be almost entirely retrospective. Nothing lures him forward.

Fifteen years later, in *Judgement Day,* he is still engaged in binding himself back to the grammar school and the old Fifty-Eighth Street gang and the summer days. It is a peculiarity of this very long novel that despite the scores of episodes, nothing very much does happen in it except for the marking of time—only the enmity of time provides Studs with a continuous cause and a provocation to an imaginative life. Wedding bells break up that old gang of his, and that is cause for active melancholy. Demographic and geographic displacements are cause for active melancholy. Death breaks up that old gang, and that, again, is cause for ruminative melancholy. At the beginning of *Judgement Day,* when Studs is in his late twenties, he travels—as far as he ever does travel—to Terre Haute, to attend the funeral and wake of Shrimp Haggerty, meaning that this beginning of the end is another instance of looking backward. The survivors from the old time have assembled for the event, and they say, " 'Say what you like, our gang from the old neighborhood was the best damn gang of lads you'd want to see anywhere on Christ's green earth.' " (464) (It is Muggsy McCarthy who says so, and Studs silently wonders where he gets off with that *we* stuff because in fact McCarthy had not been central to the gang whereas he, Studs, had had special status—which is to tell us that Studs's engagement with the old gang contains an intensity quite beyond beery nostalgia.) Two events of his stripling youth particularly obsess Studs: the time when he had beaten up the bully in the gang, Weary Reilley, and a lyrical, innocent afternoon in the park, when he was fourteen years old, with Lucy Scanlan. Throughout his life, in one episode after another, Studs sustains himself and awards himself a place in the world by referring back to the brief moment of his social glory, when he had been acknowledged to be one tough guy. And throughout the novel his one significant image of love, purity, and salvation is Lucy, with whom in fact he has not had any significant romantic connection beyond that one afternoon. At the end, when he is engaged to Catherine, Studs sees only Lucy. His last coherent thoughts, as he lies in a coma, are of the old grammar school and of Lucy. He is not really going to die, so he thinks: "And next week he would be back in Sister Bertha's class at St. Patrick's telling kids in the class about how he had fooled them all by not dying at all, and he could hear Lucy Scanlan praying for him, and he would tell her, too, about this joke, and he wanted to sleep, he was so very, very, tired.'' (776)

Studs in this trilogy-length telling is still a slob. He is defined as such by the fact that he has allowed his life to slip away, rapidly, into lax dissipations. But the judgment is very considerably modified by the facts, first, that Studs does remain, precisely, a boy at heart, and second, that the novel is so very heavily freighted with nostalgia. The whole of the mood of Studs's imaginative connection with his life is yearningly conservative, implying that his heart's ultimate need is for some supposed status-quo-ante when the tribal institutions were harmonious with life and did sustain life and did constitute a formidable enclave wherein time stood still.

And it is the evidence of the text that Farrell, too, for lack of alternative, finally came to rest in the same longing for an antique stability. He wrote most of *Studs Lonigan* when he had already taken up permanent residence in New York, with an interim in Paris where at least until a few years earlier all of the good writers had gone. He was engaged with left-wing politics, but he defined himself as a writer. Just prior to the publication of *Young Lonigan* he had secured a passing endorsement from Ezra Pound, on the basis of a couple of stories,[30] and by that additional much he was an authentic writer. No matter that naturalistic ''objectivity'' might have seemed to him to be an important principle of literary virtue, he was perforce engaged in creating a coherence from the materials of and the problematics of his feelings about his own life. He might have ended in an invocation to revolution, in the manner of Mike Gold, or in an appeal to a kind of Lawrentian freedom such as might have been gleaned from Edward Dahlberg. That Farrell might well have considered just those possibilities is suggested by the fact that in *Judgement Day* he has Studs, most uncharacteristically, glance into a bookshop window, where he takes note of *Jews without Money* and *Bottom Dogs,* along with some other titles. And near the end of the trilogy, Paddy Lonigan in his melancholy wanderings in the old neighborhood is made to be observer of a Communist party demonstration, but this, too, is a brief episode, without further reverberation. Apparently Farrell could not discover the coherence he wanted in either socialism or Lawrentianism, or in any idea extraneous to the given materials.

At the end there is still all of that longing to return to an Ur-ghetto of the imagination, outside and prior to time, without further persuasive imaginative option. *Studs Lonigan* is an elegy. The polemical implication within the elegy is to the effect that sometime in a distant past the institutions of the Irish-Catholic ghetto had served truly to be the basis of a community—that ghetto community was better than the American and the time by which it was in process of being dispossessed.

In 1934, in a collection of fugitive reminiscences of his native Chicago which he called *On the Shore*, Albert Halper said that he had been "born in a raw slangy city, in a raw slangy neighborhood," on the West Side near the railroad tracks and the stockyards. Therein, he said, was an aesthetic imperative: "Just try to write in the classic tradition with that stink in your nostrils, sit down and spin out smooth poetic sentences."[31] He for one could not do it and would not try. To the contrary. "I'm not a snooper, I don't go around looking for stories, but I know what I know, I know what I have seen. If I was born in a raw slangy town, if I happened to see raw slangy things, why shouldn't my stuff be raw slangy?" (222–23).

At the time of this publication of the statement Halper had in fact been living in New York for five years, during which time he had become an established writer and his "stuff," while it had seemed often to be informed by a proletarian knowledge and while it was not necessarily shaped beautifully, was not in fact notably raw and slangy. The writer who here invoked the odor of the stockyards had come to print several years before under the auspices of Marianne Moore in her function as editor of the *Dial*,[32] a journal which did not print "stuff." Halper's first published novel, *Union Square*, had appeared in the year before he made this statement, and while that novel had attempted, among many other things, to define a folk aesthetic, even in that approach to an area of rawness and slang it had done its work by a process of very elegant, very self-conscious ironies.

On the Shore was merely a collection of tales and sketches, published on the basis of the success of *Union Square*, and it was not a new enterprise, but it must have suggested to Halper—this hard-working, certainly ambitious, not unimaginative writer—some question as to whether he indeed did know what he knew. His career up to this point had been nothing if not heterogeneous. He thought of himself as a serious writer, primarily. He was a quite successful commercial writer. He was just now, as a matter of achieving seriousness in literature, accepting the discipline of making fiction serve a frankly political purpose—his major new enterprise for the year was a frankly proletarian novel, *The Foundry*. Meanwhile he had but recently discovered, by coming to be a member of the circle of Elliott Cohen's *Menorah Journal*, that a literature of the Jewish experience had a certified literary value. His stories and sketches had appeared, heterogeneously, in *Dial, Pagany, Menorah Journal, American Mercury,*

Harper's, and *New Masses,* among numbers of other places.[33] In these
writerly circumstances his advertising of himself as a raw and slangy
roughneck from Chicago, that toddling town and hog butcher, was
evidently a momentary, simplifying, posturing indulgence, which
nonetheless suggested that he was hard at work looking for himself and
that he had not found himself.

He had had his ghetto-, seemingly just-not-quite impoverished
childhood in Chicago, and that should have meant something. He did
organize this book interpretively, and by that much *On the Shore* was a
current enterprise. In the first section he presented some tales, in the
first person, of his experiences as a small child. In the second section
he presented tales of a somewhat older child, eight to ten years of age,
told in the third person. In the final section he was retrospective, again
in the first person, moving from tales to essays and from his early
adolescence to his leaving Chicago in order to be a writer in New York.
The movement within this organization was meant evidently to suggest
a maturing in social awareness. In the title story, which occurs in the
final section of the book and which has to do with Halper's experiences
working nights at the post office, the "shore" refers grandly to the
division to be crossed when the adolescent becomes a man, but it also
refers specifically to this adolescent's coming to understand the position of blacks in the United States, by his becoming friendly with a
fellow employee who is black. And although the third-person tales in
the second section of the book are not quite so pointedly polemical, in
each of them there is a tutelary episode of social injustice, which in
each instance is comprehensible to little Dave Bergman but which calls
for an action beyond the capability and the courage of the young boy.

The tales of the first section, however, are not so comprehensible
to the first-person narrator, nor do they succumb so easily to Halper's
postulate of the nurturing of political sensitivities. There are four tales
here: "A Herring for My Uncle," "My Aunt Daisy," "A Parting in the
Country," and "The Penny-Divers." These compose the fundamental
experience from which the later, realized sensitivity is to be derived.
The tone of the tales is neither raw nor slangy, and their subjects
involve social injustice only, at most, at a remove of tenuous implication. They are genre pieces having to do with family and neighborhood
life, and the problem which in general they address has to do with
connectedness, or the lack thereof, in circumstances which are accepted as being quite ordinary. These tales provide little opportunity
for any kind of moralizing, and they validate themselves peculiarly by
the fact that they contain recollections which their author obviously
felt to be important but which, obviously, he was not able to shape into

didactic meanings. The first of the stories, "A Herring for My Uncle," would seem by reason of the title to point to a quaintness in the manners of old-world and hence ghetto family affection—the little boy, dressed in a new suit, goes to visit his Uncle Gustav, the cigar roller; he brings a herring as a gift and he spots his suit, and his uncle is fondly appreciative. But that is not what the story is about. And the other stories are even less discrete and definite and pointed.

The feeling they reflect, not unlike that of *Studs Lonigan,* is one of baffled yearnings and not-quite-apprehended failures and estrangements. The first three of the stories take the family for their subject, and what is continuously revealed but never quite said is that this family fails to be bonding and integrative. The father and Uncle Gustav are brothers who share an old-country past but who now seldom see each other and are uncomfortable with each other. "Aunt Daisy" is the mother's maiden sister from Boston, and while the children in the family are fascinated by her, an extended visit is not welcome because the feeding of her is after all costly and there is no room, and her needs—she wants a husband—constitute a problem in a situation in which there is no room for more problems. "A Parting in the Country" is a story about the boy's visiting his mother's relatives in the East and about the ending of the visit and the parting, and it is particularly about the boy's parting from his loving grandmother whom he scarcely knows. And even "The Penny-Divers," which does not take the family for its subject and which is a story with a certain charm, is nonetheless about a community which almost attains a structure and a coherence, and is then baffled. The boys in the neighborhood take to diving for pennies in a lake in one of the local parks and evolve a complicated, honorable system of competition, but then a girl gets into the business and the system collapses.

These are not stories about hardship, exactly, although the fact of the want of money is indeed present in them. The young protagonist in his various versions is more than anything else very lonely—that, finally, is his tale of a life in the ghetto. The narratives of the tales provide the protagonist with numbers of gestures toward a harmony and a security of affections, which have a poignance because they are always finally futile. The members of the immediate family scarcely seem to know each other. Much of the content of these stories and also that of some of the subsequent stories in the collection establishes the presence of lost relatives somewhere out there beyond the immediate family, who, when they are found, in their various ways confirm the lack of any possibility of relatedness.

And these early stories in the collection do after all anticipate both the writer Albert Halper and the rest of the book. Halper's making pretense in the book's terminal essay, called, blandly and blatantly, "Young Writer Remembering Chicago," to being "raw and slangy," which he was not, postulated an aesthetic definition of an experience which had been manifestly painful in its lack of definiteness. And if in both this collection of stories and his other writings in the 1930s Halper moved toward themes of a certified class significance, it was the case that for him as for many others the warfare of the classes provided an opportunity for a communal identity. The life of the ghetto had been disintegrative. It would have followed logically as a matter of longing that the future would be the opposite.

Meyer Levin was to say of *The Old Bunch,* which he had published in 1937, that he had intended to state a fundamental sociological observation of his own observing:

> While novelists emphasized the individual in the family unit as the determining human relationship, I saw the surrounding group, the bunch, as perhaps even more important than the family in the formative years. Particularly in the children of immigrants, the life-values were determined largely through these group relationships. It was this that I wanted to bring out in my novel, and I wanted to study it in the group I knew best, the Jews of Chicago.[34]

Formally, Levin's very long and very broad novel did make such a statement. His bunch consisted of an approximate dozen and a half commingled characters, each of an approximate equality of importance in the telling of the tale, although some three or four of the characters were better fabricated than the others for the uttering of Levin's own reflections. The members of the bunch are sons and daughters of West Side Jews. They are not in fact intensely or concentratedly or exclusively intimate with each other, but they have grown up with each other. The novel begins at the point when they have all just graduated from high school, just after the war, and then presents their individual fates and careers, period by period, through the subsequent decade and extending into the time of the early 1930s. Some members of the bunch marry each other, and some members of the bunch have other kinds of dealings with each other. The point made by the form of the novel is not quite that the bunch is an inevitable or inescapable or even a desirable community, but the bunch engages each of its individual members with a consistency of parallels of lives and circumstances according to which their "life-values" may be measured. Formally, each life is juxtaposed with each of the others, and in that way the bunch is determinative for each of its members. The characters are not permitted to escape from the novel; the novel prohibits apprehension of any of the characters apart from a knowledge of the rest of the old bunch.

But Levin's novel was in fact neither so programmatic nor so efficient as the idea of the novel. Levin himself, without ever doubting the abidingness of the meaning of the bunch, would seem to have had some difficulty in determining just what it was that pulled the bunch together and then in some way kept it together. By the evidence of the text, he had intended, or had hoped, that the given bunch would have a dynamic shape exactly like, and as mysterious as, the shapes of the molecule and the universe. In an episode in the first pages of the novel some members of the bunch come together for an evening of self-improvement and listen to a lecture on the uses of the microscope, and are fascinated. Levin says:

> For one small shivery instant the thought of the universe was clear to all of them; molecule and universe, from the largest to the most minute, the pattern was the same. And people, too! Each particle balanced among innumerable other particles, forces canceling each other, forces accidentally accumulating in a sudden direction, but throughout time the steadying, indrawing pull of the positive-charged nucleus.
>
> For one instant, to Alvin, Mitch, Joe, Harry, Rudy, Sylvia, Rose, it seemed clear how you could use these same construction pieces, these molecules, these chaotically assembled balances of positive and negative charges, female and male charges, static and erratic charges, you could put them together to build stone and to build flesh and to build thoughts; the relationship of people was in the same plan.[35]

Nor is the instant lost in time and linear narration. Some six hundred fifty pages later, near the end of the novel, the most philosophically inclined member of the old bunch is discovered reflecting upon and extending the same conceit:

> And if the electrons in a body-atom moved on the same general scheme as planets in a sky-system, why couldn't you say that the human being, on his social plane, moved in the same kind of pattern? Why couldn't you view society as a physical pattern, and people as these excited electrons, forming a social atom, joined in motion with similar atoms, forming a class of society; and the classes of society, whirled into a planetary unit, were humanity. (700)

And that, certainly, was to suggest that Levin really had a firm—
indeed, basic—model for his bunch. Science said. And if in this, too, as
in *Studs Lonigan,* there was a harking back to turn-of-the-century naturalism, perhaps there was connection in the fact that, like Farrell,
Levin had gone to the University of Chicago and had taken the writing
courses of Professors James Weber Linn and Robert Morss Lovett.

Levin's recollections, however, as contained in the telling of the
tale, said something else and something more subtle than was said by
science.

First of all, the conjectured nucleus of these materials was nothing if not problematic. The characters of *The Old Bunch* have grown up
in a particular place which is a Jewish place, and therein, certainly—in
the fact of the ghetto—should have been the singular, basic stuff by
which the bunch was defined. But Levin's ghetto was not the Lower
East Side at the turn of the century. The many protagonists are the
children of immigrants some of whom are intransigently old-fashioned
in their ways, but this is the West and the time is the 1920s, and these
immigrants are no longer tutelary elders of the tribe. They are more and
less acculturated and progressive; no one among the parents is entirely
an American, but those who are least American are not especially
honored for their traditionalism, either by any of the children or by the
author. Nor is this ghetto defined by poverty; some of the parents are
doing very well, and, broadly, in the matter of money, the neighborhood is middle class. Moreover, the life of the family is not likely to
be so determinative for the individual as is the persuasion of the bunch
for the reason, prior to Levin's sociological observation, that the family is no longer either besieged nor is it a haven. In the matter of
religion, some among the generation of the parents use the old ways on
special tragic occasions, as in the case of a death in the family, but in
general their Judaism is accommodative and is primarily a social fact.
Nor are the parents persuasive ethical models for the children, despite
the fact that all of them have known hardships. The father of Lou and
Celia Moscowitz, Rube Moscowitz, is a building contractor and is the
great financial success among the parents, but he is so because he has
made a place for himself in the dirty politics of Chicago. Lil Klein's
father, Marcus Klein, also is doing very well, but as a loan shark and a
gouging landlord, and furthermore he fails to convert accomplishment,
such as it is, into glamour: he wears a usual expression "of waiting for
small change." (228) There are more pleasant characters among the
parents, with less money, but they are equally remote.

The nucleus of the old bunch was a problematic quantity at best, and the motions of the many characters are not really centripetal. The old bunch is not a molecule, and the characters are not particles. What these characters do have in common is an increasingly ambiguous, increasingly tenuous cultural history, in which not one of them can find a stability of relationship and in which nevertheless they must make individual assertions.

What they have in common, more pointedly, is their seeking— their vain seeking, in all instances—for a wholeness of identity in a situation in which they are not so much culturally marginal as culturally nowhere. Except as a matter of technicality, they are the second generation of new native-born Americans. They have a lineage without having a distinct past. On the other hand, their engagement in the present is either continuously frustrated or at least challenged by the past they have not had. They go their various ways. The women in the bunch tend to marry within the bunch, although not without exception. Among the men, one becomes a six-day bicycle rider, one is a salesman, a couple are doctors, several become lawyers (of varying degrees of social consciousness), one is a sculptor, one is an inventor, and so forth. But in all instances their careers are metaphors for a constant, uncertain striving toward wholeness and reconciliation.

The striving is sometimes grotesque, embarrassing, craven, and comic. As time moves them forward the women begin to bear children, who are to be named, and the naming of the children is within this bunch a perilous kind of assertion. Rose (Skinny) Heller, who is desperate to be married and is not, says to one of her prospects by way of flirtation:

> "Mygod, the names some people give their kids! I was to a
> *briss* downstairs of us and they're old-fashioned Jews and they
> named the kid Mattashmayas or Shmatenyuh or some Bible
> name, it certainly sounded terrible. I don't see why people
> should persist in giving their children Jewish names. After all,
> we're Americans." (244)

But then in the next instant, desperately, playfully, and flirtatiously, she asks Manny Kassell to guess her own Jewish name: "She shook her head. Her eyes popped with laughter. 'Chayah-Shaynah!' Rose exploded." (244) And she feels that in the process of this dialogue she has made a conquest. Manny Kassell, on his side, says that "Clarence is a doggy name." When the time of Passover comes for the young marrieds of the bunch, Ev Goldberg has a Passover seder for young couples only. Her special guests for the evening are the McIlwains, whom everybody admires because he is "the son of a real drunken Irishman." Her special triumph for the evening is the place cards, which are "the cleverest things!"

> Each card was a cut-out of a biblical character, only Ev had
> fixed devilish little short skirts over the long gowns of the
> women characters, and put derby hats on the men. But the most
> comical thing she had done was to get pictures of movie stars
> and paste their faces on the biblical figures. (353)

And the goal of the striving is sometimes power within the larger civic community as the civil society is variously realized and assessed. The Law is in this instance a likely metaphor. Lou Margolis becomes a wealthy lawyer, but by means of being ingratiating at the upper levels of political power in Chicago. He never reaches too far, and he can make deals, realizing—somewhat against his wishes—that the law has very little to do with justice. Runt Plotkin, on the other hand, is a night-school lawyer who tries to insinuate himself at the lower levels. He knows some of the gangsters of Chicago, but, as it turns out, not the right gangsters. Sam Eisen, who is one of Levin's more spokesmanly characters, begins in ambitious cynicism as an admirer of the manipulative populism of Big Bill Thompson, and then develops left-wing consciousness of class identity. He is in fact honored by Meyer Levin for his achievement of consciousness, but not yet within this novel. In the next novel, *Citizens,* published in 1940, Sam Eisen will be awarded some heroism and, more to the point, some grateful recognition on the part of the oppressed classes, but within the bounds of *The Old Bunch* the striving itself is the issue and is a vector, merely, of yearning. Sam's social awareness indeed results in his separation from his wife and therefore from the old bunch, but on the other hand is at the end still abstract, wishful, tentative. In his last words in the novel Sam is found to be still struggling, against an assertion of evidence to the contrary, for a conception of a sentient "mass of the people." "'I know, I know,'" he says, "'yet a fellow can't help feeling the least people can do is realize what's going on, and think of themselves in relation to that—to that process.'" (262) That plaintiveness is the terminus and climax of his realizations.

And there is the character who is equipped to be an American hero after the model—albeit somewhat distantly—of Thomas Edison. He is imaginative and ingenious in the matter of electrical gadgets, but his name is Harry Perlin, and he is a poor and vulnerable Jew, and his most practical ideas are stolen from him and his other ideas cannot be capitalized. Heroism in industrial America, in the Century of Progress, is not available to a Harry Perlin.

And the goal of the striving is sometimes the putatively self-sufficient idealism of medical science. Mitch Wilner makes a fundamental discovery in the field of allergy treatments. Rudy Stone is a skilled and caring doctor. They proceed thus far toward the making of an integrity for themselves. But then of course they are led by their author to discover that the idealism of medical science is less ideal than they had anticipated it to be. Rudy Stone engages himself in an experiment in socialized medicine and thereby brings upon himself the wrath of a profession of which he can never really be a part. Mitch Wilner, equipped with credentials of genius, is denied the position in pure research at the Mayo Clinic which he should have, because he is a Jew. In the next novel, *Citizens*, Mitch Wilner will be Levin's major protagonist, on the basis of his being educated in the matters of social class, trade unionism, and politics, but in that next novel Levin was in general to be much more certain about the nature of his answers than about the nature of his questions. In the present novel Mitch Wilner ends by making cautionary adjustments between such rage as he is entitled to have, and such dignity as he has achieved, clinging to the relatively minor hospital position he has, but being not unsympathetic toward social conscience in medicine.

And there is artistic endeavoring for the purposes of self-realization, but the end of art for the artist—as art is both a career and a process of realization—is a greater confusion. Joe Freedman is another of the more spokesmanly of the characters of *The Old Bunch*. He becomes a sculptor. He becomes almost a recognized sculptor, and wins honors, but he is of course led to bitter knowledge of the circumstance that sculpture is a thing to be sold, and to be sold to customers who are manifestly ignorant in the matter of art. Sculpture, which should be recognized to be broadly integral to the national culture, is dependent on patrons of the type—one is named—of the fan dancer Sally Rand. Joe does see hope in the plans of the Federal Arts Project, but the novel ends just before the Arts Project gets going.

Joe Freedman, for the reason that he is the artist among the bunch, is Levin's primary seeker after a certainty and an integrity in tradition—which he does almost find in several kinds of perceptions, which, however, are in each case sabotaged by perplexing ironies. In Paris he meets a great sculptor who would seem about to give to Joe the purposiveness he wants. Like all of the parents of the Chicago bunch, the sculptor is an immigrant from the Jewish ghettos of eastern Europe.

Unlike the parents of the bunch, however, he has resisted the secularism of his new circumstances, and he has, rather, dug deep into the
lore of his heritage. The subjects of his sculptures are biblical ones,
rendered in such a way that they convey a powerful dignity. Once each
year the sculptor returns to the *stetl* where he was born. But the
sculptor's accomplishment is, as is discovered by another character,
not the absolute it seems to be, but an illusion of unity. The Jewish
sculptor, living in Catholic France, is in fact a Catholic convert,
wherefore it would follow that despite the man's intensity there is
within the sculpture a secret glibness. In any event, he is not the
answer to Joe's quest. Joe himself returns to the birthplace, which is a
little village near Kovno, and that journey is a failure. The village is
indeed untouched by the intervention of years, but it is not therefore a
source of allurement: "Here a brother of his grandfather still kept the
village inn. The inn was nothing more than an earthen hovel, where the
goyim came and got drunk. Though old Lazar had spent his eighty
years among them, they still cast taunts and insults at the Jew."(266)
All of the young people in the *stetl* want to get away, preferably to
America. And Joe, like the real Meyer Levin before him, goes to
Palestine, where he does find new inspiration for his sculpting, but only
temporarily because he is soon distracted by the immediate dangers of
Jewish life in Palestine and then by the ramifying contingencies of
realpolitik to which Zionism is subject.

Altogether the members of this latter-day generation of the West
Side Jews of Chicago find themselves in a history which contains no
definite past and which also confronts them with a perfectly ambivalent
present. Like Dos Passos, and adopting some of the devices of
U. S. A., Levin made public fact to be a part of the fiction, but the ironic
counterpointing which was available to Dos Passos with his more
exemplifying and more abstract idea of America was not really available to Levin. Much was to be made of such facts as the Leopold and
Loeb case and the Lindbergh kidnapping and the Chicago World's
Fair, but for Levin's special characters each of these American events
constitutes a peculiar challenge to identity. Leopold and Loeb are
Jews, and the members of the bunch must consider the probability that
the case has discouraged their own claim to being Americans. On the
other hand, Leopold and Loeb are South Side (that is, German,
established, Americanized) Jews, and the crime perhaps signals a social decay which in turn will mean an opportunity for the Jews of their
own West Side. On a third hand, Leopold and Loeb as Jews provide an
opportunity for an amount of pride, admittedly perverse, for they are

geniuses—one member of the bunch has read Nietzsche and tells the others that this is so. The Lindbergh kidnapping, as well, while it is offered explicitly as a symbol for the times in general—"when every man snatched what he could" (563)—has its special aspect as a problem for the bunch, for it is being rumored that the kidnapper is a Jew who has taken the baby for a ritual murder, and perhaps there are those who will believe the rumor.

The final section of the novel appropriates the Chicago World's Fair for the purpose of ironic symbolizing, together with the Fair's Century of Progress theme. The Fair with all of its tawdry boosterism coincides neatly with the early years of the Depression. Within this panoramic irony, however, the event of special significance for the bunch is Jewish Day at the Fair, coinciding with the commencement of the Jewish New Year. And what is dramatized in the series of fragmentary episodes and reflections is a renewed futile effort on the part of the bunch to overcome the fundamental knowledge of their own discrepancy. Jewish Day is for them, necessarily, a challenge to a demonstration of unity, which itself, like the music of the ram's horn, is perfectly ambiguous, an intermediacy between a wail and a brag. The thousands of Jews seated in the Stadium are first of all saluted by a flight of airplanes come all the way from Italy. Old Rube Moscowitz observes that a squad like that could wipe out Chicago, but his daughter says: "'Oh, why bring that up!...I think it was very nice of Mussolini to send them. It's a gesture of friendship.'" (635) For Lil Eisen, Jewish Day at the Fair is a provocation to some fleeting guilt; she resolves to send her little boy to a good modern Hebrew Sunday school. Lou Margolis, on the other hand, is provoked to new sarcasms; he doubts the authenticity of what is said to be real ancient Hebrew music, for what proof can there be that this is the real thing? Mrs. Abramson thinks about the fate of the Jews in Germany. "'I am not saying that Hitler is right,'" she says, "'but if it had to happen to Jews someplace, then they are the ones that deserve it most. So high class! A Russian Jew, to them, was to spit on.'" (638–39) Joe Freedman sees an intimation of the ideal Palestine in this gathering. Alvin Fox, the former reader of Nietzsche, says to his Gentile wife, "'Let's get the hell out of here.'" (640)

This lengthy, ambitious, deliberative tale of the ghetto is finally, explicitly and necessarily, a lyric to the fate of a generation of strays who are neither of the old bunch nor not of it. At the very end Harry Perlin, who had once had an idea for putting radios in cars, listens to a car radio. He hears a cowboy twang:

"Git along, little dogie, git along, git along,
Git along, little dogie, git along,
Git along, little dogie, git along, git along." (704)

All of these—Mike Gold, Henry Roth, Daniel Fuchs, James T. Farrell, Albert Halper, Meyer Levin, and the many others—were engaged in making a cultural assertion from utterly dubious cultural materials. In all of their instances the underlying truth of the ghetto was the dissolution of the ghetto—which, because America, too, was a dubious material, was not the same thing as a process of Americanization. On the other hand, their fabrications were not more arbitrary than those of, for random instances, Sherwood Anderson or James Agee or Ernest Hemingway or T. S. Eliot or William Faulkner. The underlying truth of America itself was its cultural dissolution, from which circumstance there followed necessity, in literature, for acts of artifice. The tales from the ghettos, those seemingly marginal quantities of American life, were of a piece with a general intention. In the circumstances of the 1930s the writers of these tales had the special advantage that they had intimate knowledge of cultural confusion.

Part Three

six lives

A lot of people take me for an American.
                        Jack Pearl, Baron Munchausen

Someone, obviously a Britisher, asked William Carlos Williams to name the source of that American language which he was defending, and Williams said that it came "from the mouths of Polish mothers."[1] The time was the early 1940s. Williams was once again claiming the integrity of a native poetical speech, and while there was nothing especially Polish in his own speech, it was to be understood that in using this hyperbole he was flaunting his own good, perverse, American credentials, in the face of all supposed literary-linguistic majesty and tradition. He was once again, like many a good man before him, making a declaration of the cultural independence of the United States. But he was also—whether or not the thought crossed his mind—touching upon a matter both larger and more immediate than that of lingering, snobbish British arrogation. By lineage and by the circumstances of his life, Williams did know something about the cultural pluralism, now, in the United States: enough to be certain that a singular, separate, reconciling language was a *new* necessity for an American poetry. There was an urgency which the American poetical forebears could not have realized. It would not have been the case prior to Williams's own time that the nominated source of American cultural independence would have been the mouths of Polish mothers. The figure would not have occurred to Ralph Waldo Emerson, who had been a radical in this area of assertion. Latter-day American independence was not what it had been.

Perhaps, however, Williams would have known that his response to the Britisher was after all just a bit cheeky, British-style, because along with the conviction that was in it there was an amount of posturing and of pretended authority. Williams would have known, deeply, that other Americans of his time did really have mothers who were Polish, or Hungarian or Sicilian or Rumanian or Lithuanian-Yiddish, or black, and he would have known that alongside of them he himself was almost a real American, old-style. These others had the original authority for saying what he had said.

On the other hand, as perhaps Williams would have realized, these others from whom he was borrowing his peculiar authority were not likely to make the same assertion in their own right, for they were likely to be very nervous about the matter of their cultural authority as Americans. To be an American such as they, and especially to be a writer as well, was to be confronted by a continuous struggle for an identity in culture with the result for literary speech of something quite other than Williams's own reconciling, studied plain-talk. They were likely to be extravagant in their styles of assertion, or intricately parodic and mocking, or violent, or brutal. The children of the real

229

barbarians had to write out of a knowledge that they were leading double lives at the least, albeit that, since in fact they were speaking to the prevailing actuality of culture in America, it was they who were effectively in charge of creating an American language and literature.

Their informative achievement, in these circumstances, was not the single poem or the individual novel, but the manifest striving for the making of poems and novels in America.

six

Itzok Granich and Michael Gold

In his ripeness Mike Gold, born Itzok Isaac Granich, came to be chief literary assassin for the Communist party of America and, as such, earned a somewhat abiding reputation, especially among anti-Stalinists of the literary left. Gold had a talent, an instinct, an enthusiasm, and a rhetoric. He was particularly impressive when, as time passed and political imperatives changed, he turned his talents upon erstwhile friends. Of John Dos Passos he said, "One cannot help seeing how important the *merde* is in his psychology, and how after a brief futile effort, he has sunk back into it, as into a native element." And of Robinson Jeffers:

> Poor Judas, poor Robinson Jeffers, poor little bourgeois neurotic, living safe as a bug in a rug on your little income, self-pent, in a self-made prison, fearful of sunlight, of women, of love of children . . . fleeing . . . all the passions, great and small, that produce Beethovens and Shakespeares, as well as Mayor Hagues. Poor sick man, poor hollow poet.

And "Edmund Wilson," he would write, "ascended the proletarian 'bandwagon' with the arrogance of a myopic, high-bosomed Beacon Hill matron entering a common streetcar." And: "These Mumfords, MacLeishes and [Waldo] Franks . . . go on spouting endless torrents of 'spirituality,' all the large, facile greasy abstract words that bookmen, like confidence men, are so perfect in producing." And again, not so insinuatingly but by way of brisk moral refreshment: "I have never turned away from a friend who lost his path through drink, disease, or personal weakness. But Max Eastman, former friend, you have sunk beneath all tolerance. You are a filthy and deliberate liar."[1]

In fact there was an amount both of plaintiveness and of justification in this practice which was not likely to secure contemporary notice. The period of Gold's ripeness comprised the years approximately 1933, when he was forty years old, to 1967, when he died. His major work for these many years was his newspaper column "Change the World!" from which he fulminated. His best enemies during these many years were not writers on the right, but, rather, the renegades, according to his own ideas—not necessarily the Party's—about what constituted reneging. He attacked Theodore Dreiser, for instance, on the issue of the latter's anti-Semitism when the Party was prone to protect Dreiser.[2] Nor did any purely political event ever inspire him to so fine an eloquence, and nothing in Gold's writings early or late suggests that he had ever been happy with intricacies of political thinking. And although he did serve the Party faithfully, he was not a determinative power in it in his own right, and it was the case, as Gold knew very well, that literature had not anyways ever been a matter of major concern to the Communist party in America. Everything—his style and the subject matter which secured his nicest exercises in style—might have suggested that the renegades were *his* particular opportunity, as also his particular problem. He was saying something about the shape and the honor of his own career as a writer.

Again, there was irony in the fact that he brought to his umbrage a personal—not a Party—authority which was plausible and discomforting, at least for so long a time as people remembered who he was. ("Change the World!" began in the *Daily Worker,* which people read, and ended in the *San Francisco People's World,* which few people read.) Having decided long before, along with many others, that literature was inextricable from politics and that the politics of reality was on the left, Gold—quite alone, so it must have seemed to him—had gone the whole way, making the requisite sacrifices and not without realization that sacrifice was demanded. He was saying in 1932 that "the Communist road is rough, dangerous, and often confusing, but it happens to be the only road that leads into the new world,"[3] and in approximately that moment many talented, goodwilled, and even famous fellow writers would have seemed quite plainly to agree, but the others had hedged and, curiously, perhaps pusillanimously, sometimes charmingly, had refused the acknowledged ultimate commitment. Gold's renegades were people whom he would have had very good reason to believe had been on his side, with much less opportunity for misinterpretation than they themselves might later have claimed, and if they did not go all the way and if later on they professed scruples, he peculiarly had the right to point out their failings.

In 1932 Sherwood Anderson, for one, was saying in response to a questionnaire, stoutly, that "the artist would . . . like to think of himself as ready to die for what he believes," but then he had said, when party affiliation was at issue, that the writer had ought to allow "plenty of room for the critical attitude." And John Dos Passos, answering the same questionnarie, was saying that he thought that becoming a socialist as compared with becoming a communist "would have just about the same effect on anybody as drinking a bottle of near-beer," but then he had looked inward and discovered that "some people are natural party men and others are natural scavengers and campfollowers.... I personally belong to the scavenger and campfollower section."[4] And again, there was Edmund Wilson, who, by chance in the same year, had ended his book *The American Jitters* with a statement almost anyone would have read as a formal conversion: "My present feeling is that my satisfaction in seeing the whole world fairly and sensibly run as Russia is now run, instead of by shabby politicians in the interests of acquisitive manufacturers, business men and bankers, would more than compensate me for any losses that I might incur in the process.... When the middle class upset the feudal landlords and the serfs and the slaves got free, we had the modern bourgeois-governed world; *now there is only one more step to go.*"[5] But with knee bent and thus seeming to yearn forward, he had not taken the step.

Apostasy had not always been Gold's favorite subject, but as his erstwhile companions would have likely appreciated, he had indeed tried throughout his writerly life to achieve an integrity for literature, according to which literature would have both a basis and a function within social reality. The episodes of his striving had frequently—not always—been arrogant, or otherwise immoderate, or bardic and banal, or weepy, or plainly silly; on the other hand, from the beginning back in 1914 when the *Masses* had accepted one of his poems, he had with rare consistency stood for an honored principle He had tried to fashion what he had been the first man in America to call a "Proletarian Art," which in his version implied, but was not synonymous with, a politics. He had, with reason, insisted on the exemplary importance of his own seemingly marginal experience in America. He had tried to make imposing cultural shape from the fact of and for the uses of the new masses who were the citizens of old America. And if, somewhat more fulsomely than others, he had joined his conception of the common man to communism, and if, somewhat more literally than others, he had identified communism with the Communist party, that progress, too, apparently demonstrated his faithfulness to the original principle. Unfortunately, as time passed and as the American Communist party itself came to seem to be more than anything else an invention of the FBI, the matter of Gold's lonely integrity, for itself, supported by nostalgia and emboldened by bitterness, came seemingly to be Gold's fundamental subject, but that happenstance did not cancel the fact that

at one time and for a long time he had been engaged in making fundamental discoveries about literature and life in America—at, it must be
added, various levels of his own awareness.

He was not a hero, but he was a symbol, and one of some complexity. Just what it was he symbolized had perhaps been broached
most succinctly when he who had been Itzok Isaac Granich became
"Michael Gold." The time was 1920.[6] Gold was later to suggest that he
took his new name for tactical, practical political reasons. The first of
the Palmer raids had occurred in January of 1920. Gold, writing as
"Irwin Granich," already had some prominence in the left press, and
perhaps for that reason he was in some danger. Moreover, he had
something in particular to hide: he had been a draft dodger, living in
hiding in Mexico in the years 1917 to 1919, and woe to him if he were
now to be exposed. But there must have been additional reason for his
naming himself anew. For one thing, had the troops of A. Mitchell
Palmer wanted Irwin Granich, they could have found him. For another
thing, Gold was not at all persistent in maintaining his new identity. For
the better part of a year after he became Michael Gold, he was still as
often calling himself Irwin Granich. It must have been the case that he
changed his name for the additional reason that all genuine revolutionaries did the same. Everybody had his Party name, by which few
usually were disguised. The name-taking was a ritualistic, emblematic
act: it signified imitation of, and honor to, the practice of the great
Bolshevik leaders in their exiles, and therefore implied a tradition,
specifically rebirth within the revolution.

But then beyond the act itself, there was the particular name,
which had to imply some personal conception of one's own role and of
one's personal choice of the revolution.

According to a memoir Gold wrote many years later, there had
been an original "Michael Gold" in his life. The first Michael Gold had
been the father of one of his boyhood friends on the Lower East Side.
The time was the 1890s, when, according to Gold (the second), recollections of the Civil War still had some living presence for a youngster. The principal of the public school was "a grand old white-bearded
Colonel Smith" who told anecdotes of the war at morning assemblies.
According to Gold (the second), this presence of the war—the war
against slavery—induced a personal, childhood involvement with social principle. And Michael Gold (the first) was, astonishingly, a veteran of the Union Army. He had been "Corporal Michael Gold."[7]

That is all that the second Gold ever said about the matter, and
that little bit—a single brief paragraph in an essay devoted to other

speculations—stopped short of explanation. Perhaps Corporal Michael Gold had been, simply, a very impressive man. There can be no knowing. But there also can be no doubt that he would have uniquely represented an ideal response to an intricate dilemma. He was a Lower East Side Jew, just like, say, Granich the elder, and he had fought with the Union Army against slavery. He might have known Abraham Lincoln. He testified to the reality of the democratic legend of America. He was a neighbor and a *landsman* in the Yiddish-speaking ghetto, and at the same time he was gloriously an American. He conjoined pieties. He must have suggested that one could indeed be both an immigrant Jew and an American, at least given a certain version of what an American was.

And that version was in fact discoverable in various representations, in the ambivalent circumstances of Gold's youth, and was fundamentally and continuously important to the Michael Gold who was a writer. According to the testimony of *Jews without Money,* the public school had for the most part been an alien place, but Gold had had the one inspiring teacher who had cried when he was forced to quit school, at the age of twelve, and had given him a copy of Emerson's essays, and had told him not to despair but to look back upon the example of Abraham Lincoln, that poor American boy, much like himself, who had made good. And there was Buffalo Bill, who looked like the Messiah, or vice versa. And—for in fact the real Itzok Granich would seem to have been a very bookish young fellow—there were literary discoveries available to him, chiefly Mark Twain and Walt Whitman. All of these were indisputably real Americans, of a certain sort: they were the American subverters of the pretensions to the American cultural authority which was represented, for instance, by the schoolteacher, also recalled in *Jews without Money,* who had addressed the young boy as "LITTLE KIKE."

Gold did remember and was inspired, from beginning to end. He was peculiarly loyal to the vision of the Young Abe studying by the light of the embers. Late in life, when Gold was writing for the *San Francisco People's World,* he was still referring to that vision and measuring his own lacking against it. "Education," he said, "haunts me."

> At the age of 12, I was forced to leave school and work in the hot hell of a New York factory making the gas-mantles of the time. Whatever education I later acquired was paid for with sweat and confusions. There were too many difficulties, it seems....

I was no Lincoln, unfortunately. I was just one of the many
who try and fail. But I always wanted an education, and kept
trying and failing again and again.[8]

And Gold was to recall, at the age of sixty, that as a boy he had
received virtual benediction from Mark Twain, precisely a laying on of
hands. As a boy, so he said, he had read everything that Mark Twain
had ever published. Mark Twain was popular on the East Side, being
known as a friend of the Jews. Gold particularly remembered the day
when Twain had come to the Educational Alliance to see a performance of *The Prince and the Pauper,* while he and all of the other little
paupers were rioting around the doors of the theater. "A carriage
rolled up and out stepped a magnificent old man with a crown of white
hair and a pirate mustache. He wore a white suit and smoked a big
cigar. We cheered him, and he smiled and put his hand on our heads in
passing."[9]

In the same instance of recollection Gold was to say that Walt
Whitman had been the greatest influence of his youth. "I have read him
so many different times," he said, "and in such varying moods that I
believe I could sit down and write a book about him without a moment
of research. He is part of me." And in fact from beginning to end there
had been at least a very frequent presence of Whitman in Gold's writings. In his initial conception of a "Proletarian Art," more than thirty
years earlier, Gold had taken his authority specifically from Whitman.
"The heroic spiritual grandfather of our generation in America is Walt
Whitman" he had said.

> That giant with his cosmic intuitions and comprehensions, knew
> all that we are still stumbling after. He knew the width and
> breadth of Eternity, and ranged its fearful spaces with the faith
> of a Viking. He knew Man; how Man was the salt and
> significance of Eternity, and how Man's soul outweighed the
> splendor and terror of the stars. . . . Walt dwelt among the mas-
> ses, and from there he drew his strength. From the obscure lives
> of the masses he absorbed those deep affirmations of the instinct
> that are his glory. . . . His individuals were those great, simple
> farmers and mechanics and ditch-diggers who are to be found
> everywhere among the masses—those powerful, natural persons
> whose heroism needs no drug of fame or applause to enable
> them to continue; those humble, mighty parts of the mass,
> whose self-sufficiency comes from their sense of solidarity, not
> from any sense of solitariness.[10]

And so forth. And in 1930 Gold was laying it down as a law of "proletarian Realism" that there would be "no straining or melodrama or

other effects." ("The great literatus will be known, among the rest, by his cheerful simplicity," Whitman had said, "and by the absence in him of . . . any strain'd and temporary fashion.") And a decade later, in an act of quick nostalgia for the supposed "renaissance" of the thirties just passed, Gold was again invoking Whitman, in Whitman's own words, to describe the ideal of culture: "Did you, too, O friend, suppose democracy was only for elections, for politics, for a party name? . . . I should demand a program of culture, drawn out . . . with an eye to practical life, the west, the workingmen, the facts of farms and jackplanes and engineers, and of the broad range of the women also of the middle and working strata, and with reference to the perfect equality of women."[11] The ideal for which Whitman stood did no doubt engage the affections of Michael Gold, just as he said, and deeply. His very style, at least when he was being idealistic, was plausibly Whitmaniacal, and he could, and in any event did, make Whitman's words to be his own.

Moreover, Gold did plausibly succeed in becoming the kind of American who was implicit in the myths, that American who was emblematic of the culture by virtue of being initially an outcaste of the culture. Gold had quit school at the age of twelve, when his father died, and had gone to work, but he did nonetheless, apparently, attend to the advice of the nice teacher who had recommended the example of Abe Lincoln. In his early young manhood he managed even to acquire an amount of advanced schooling, which he was later at pains to deny. He took a high school cram course at City College. In 1916, at the age of twenty-three, he became a freshman at Harvard, being admitted as a trial student. He left after the first semester, but that was because he could not support himself and attend school at the same time. He liked Harvard. He did well in his classes. He particularly liked the lectures of the nonrevolutionary Bliss Perry. He was bitter about having to leave.[12]

He was already a published poet and a journalist (working for the Socialist daily, the New York *Call*). Leaving Harvard, he in effect went to school in Greenwich Village. Particularly, he became one of the regulars in the *Masses* group. Max Eastman and Floyd Dell edited him, and he was exuberantly grateful. "*The Masses!*" he wrote in 1918. "One thrills at the name. It is hard to forget the blazing splendor of that meteor of art and revolution." The *Masses* was "a temple of freedom." Max Eastman was, at the same time, a man whose "vision is the complete fulfillment of every man's ego. . . . A fascinating figure in the ranks of democracy here in America, this long symmetrical Greek, with his slow voice and graceful leisurely limbs, and face radiating calm."[13] A few years later, in 1926, he was saying that Eastman and Dell were "the best teachers youth could have found during those years."[14]

And he did learn things about literary expression, from the *Masses* group directly and from the Village generally. Oddly enough, considering his later antagonism to any conception of literature as a matter of technical innovations, and the matter of accomplishment quite aside, Gold became an experimental writer, apparently adopting for himself the basic avant-garde idea that the language of literature demanded new freedoms.

In the manner of other experimentalists he tried, for instance, to write a poetry based on urban idiom, as in his poem of 1916 called "MacDougal Street":

> Bill, pipe all these cute little red doll's houses
> They are jammed full of people with cold noses
>   And bad livers
> Who look out of their windows as we go roaring by
>   Under the stars
> Disgustingly drunk with the wine of life
> And write us up for the magazines.[15]

He discovered suggestion in the new rhetoric of cinema, although not without some peculiarly highbrow embarrassment. There was a moment, in 1923, when Gold found himself liking a movie called *The Covered Wagon,* and he was sufficiently troubled by the event that he broached a question of genres. The people who made movies were despicable, of course. "The ideals of the movie industry in America," he wrote in an article in the *Liberator,* "are still those of a refined apartment-house prostitute." But still, he went on to say, it was quite possible "that the movies may eventually supersede all written fiction."[16] The reason for that was that movies could be more literal than fiction, but it must as well have been the case that he found something puzzling and attractive in the basics of the language of movies. On at least one occasion, in a story called "Faster America, Faster!" subtitled "A Movie in Ten Reels," he attempted a prose version of cinema by imitating the techniques of short single takes with their resulting episodic abruptnesses, and montage, and he made ironical use of the portentous titles of the silent films. The story is otherwise merely of the stock of Gold's usual convictions: a special train bearing some decadent movie people runs off the rails when the fireman, who is ridden by proletarian rages, goes crazy, and in that there is a lesson for the express train that is America. But the rhetoric of the story, with its brusque sequences and its dismissive carelessness of syntax and its refusal to go beyond abbreviations of dialogue and situation, was not polemical in its implications. It was, rather, ambitious, in the manner of writing trying to assert itself against an established literature.[17]

And he wrote mass recitations, the message of which would have been entirely political except that the message was in good part the style. The lines were to be chanted rather than spoken, as Gold said in his foreward to the recitation called "Strike!" and then the lines he provided were, studiedly, syntactically so minimal as to constitute an assault on traditional literary English.[18]

Another locale for education was the Provincetown Players, consisting of a group, at least in the beginning, almost identical with that of the *Masses*. Like the *Masses,* and most aptly for the needs of Itzok Granich, the Players wanted new, rude energies, *and* they were fiercely American. The guiding spirit of the Provincetown Players was Floyd Dell's Iowa friend George Cram Cook, whose dream, in his own words, was "a threshing floor on which a young and growing culture could find its voice."[19] Gold was an obvious candidate for the threshing. He was accepted, encouraged, and, again, very grateful. He wrote plays which Cook interpreted for him, and produced. Cook, said Gold later on, "talked as though he had known me for years. He made me feel like a god!"[20]

Politics was continuously an issue, of course, but not the main issue. Itzok Granich was becoming an American writer, eagerly, within such modes of Americanism as might encourage him. Such a one as he was being brought to cultural assertion, with the direct help of such real Americans as Max Eastman and George Cram Cook.

The cultural ambition was indeed not only separable from the political consideration, but also confused it.

One of the two full-length plays which Gold wrote by himself—he collaborated on others—was called *Hoboken Blues*, subtitled, doubly, "The Black Rip Van Winkle: A Modern Negro Fantasia on an Old American Theme." The subject was the American black proletariat as it is alternately assaulted and seduced by white American capitalism, and was thus expressly political. The hero, Sam Pickens, is a Harlem black. He is a loving husband, a loving father, and a banjo player. Hearing that there may be a job in Hoboken, he walks to Hoboken and there has a vision. A factory to which he goes is taken over by the workers, who make him their president because he is the finest singer among them. There are sunflowers around the factory door. The work day is three hours for everyone. All of this is a dream, as we know from the beginning. Actually, Sam was clubbed by some policemen over in

Hoboken, and has gone into a long sleep. Nonetheless, the dream has its vitality, and when Sam returns to Harlem twenty-five years later, he tries to speak of it to other blacks who, despite their own contemporary money madness, just might hear him. How comparatively little all of this was forceful propaganda, however—or how unsatisfactory or how muddled—was indicated to Gold when the Provincetown Players refused to produce the play, on political grounds. The leading black actor of the Provincetown Players was Paul Robeson, who would not play the part of a Harlem black who seemed to be defined primarily by his natural sense of rhythm. It was produced eventually by the "New Playwrights' Theatre," a company founded by Gold himself and some others and financed by Otto Kahn.

The play was, rather, an anthology of contemporary literary conceptions. The folk of the early Harlem, prior to the money madness of the mid-twenties, are pastoral figures, taken seemingly in good part from DuBose Heyward's *Porgy,* which had appeared in 1925, the year before Gold composed the play. They are joyous, simple, and loving, and their language mixes southern slurring with a mocking pedantry. The contemporary Harlem of the last act of the play is all cabarets and jazz—taken in large part, seemingly, from Carl Van Vechten's *Nigger Heaven,* which was published just when Gold was composing the play.

Prior to production, the play was accepted for publication in the *American Caravan,* for 1927, and Gold was to say much later that he was happily surprised by that acceptance,[21] but his surprise must have been, or should have been, mitigated by a knowledge that the play virtually repeated the editors' prescription for new American writing. The editors were Van Wyck Brooks, Alfred Kreymborg, Paul Rosenfeld, and Lewis Mumford, who together now for more than a decade had been urging the uses of the "usable past." They had specifically been urging the uses of American folk materials, such as the story of Rip Van Winkle. Brooks himself had found meaning in just that story for a climactic moment in his influential essay, "America's Coming of Age," and a meaning which Michael Gold must have found to be particularly impressive. Brooks had said:

> It is, in fact, the plain, fresh, homely, impertinent, essentially innocent old America that has passed, and in its passing the allegory of Rip Van Winkle has been filled with a new meaning. Hendrik Hudson and his men, we see, have begun another game of bowls, and the reverberations are heard in many a summer thunderstorm; but they have been miraculously changed into Jews, Lithuanians, Magyars and German socialists. Rip is that old innocent America which has fallen asleep and which hears

and sees in a dream the movement of peoples, the thunder of
alien wants. And when after twenty years he awakens again,
stretches his cold rheumatic limbs, and discovers the long white
beard, he will once more set out for home. But when he arrives
will he be recognized?[22]

The particular story had an established and accepted value. It was not
by chance that in 1926, as Gold was writing the play, Hart Crane was
writing the "Van Winkle" section of *The Bridge*. Gold's achievement
—a genuine one, in this context—was the closeness of his dependence
on Washington Irving. Sam Pickens has a scolding wife who insists that
he work. Sam is a dreamy kind of man. And so forth, in great detail.

The most startling component of *Hoboken Blues* was its directions for staging, but in this, too, Gold was learning and adapting
and deriving. In 1925 he had been in Russia and had been impressed by
the work of Meyerhold—the Jew from Tiflis, it may be noted, who had
risen through the social revolution to create the art of Moscow. He had
been excited by Meyerhold's "constructivist" settings with their
ramps and scaffoldings replacing conventional scenery, and by the
extremity of Meyerhold's symbolic devices. So in Gold's play the cast
was to be composed entirely of blacks, with whites being played "by
Negroes in white caricature masks." And the settings for the three acts
were to have a plot function, moving in three steps toward a freer and a
more furious symbolism. In the first act the stage was to be "a futurist
composition suggesting a corner of Harlem twenty-five years
ago . . . dynamic, yet with an old-fashioned peasant touch." The setting
for the fantasy in Hoboken, in Act Two, was to be "more extreme than
the last," with a multiple design "constructively adapted" to the action
in the hero's mind: an African jungle in one part, wheels and pulleys in
another, dollar signs elsewhere. Then, finally, the new Harlem in the
third act was to be "vastly more angular, confusing, colorful and jazzy;
a composition of sharp, outrageous lines, an ensemble of militant
statements by a drunken geometrician." And the whole was to be
performed on various planes with an effect of simultaneity, scenes
being made to overlap.

Obviously Gold did not think that, properly understood, the play
was politically offensive, and he would not have thought so because in
all probability Gold's fundamental, non-Party feeling about blacks was
that they, too, were outcastes necessarily engaged in making an assertion in American life. They were foreigners, like himself. To put blacks
in white face—that, in all probability, was for Gold the heart of the
polemics of the play.[23]

Indeed, much of Gold's imaginative writing dealt, with fine indiscriminateness, with varieties of foreigners, sometimes in their foreign places and sometimes in America, sometimes informed by some first hand knowledge and sometimes not. He wrote about Mexicans and Russians and Indians and Poles and Portuguese, as well as about blacks and Jews, all to the general purpose of making them present to the Americans.

Gold's second full-length play, *La Fiesta,* produced in 1929, was about the Mexican Revolution. Stark Young reviewed the play and did not like it, on the grounds that it was not realistic. There was the circumstance, beyond Gold's control, that all of his peons were played by Nordic actors, but beyond that, "Realism," said Young, "tackling such alien material must nearly always come a cropper." The diction, movement, volume and energy of emotion, transitions in feeling, and so forth, were so very different.[24] And that was doubly ironic, first of all because in this instance Gold did have some presumable intimate knowledge of his subject—he had done his draft dodging in Mexico— and, second, because it was not likely to have been the Mexican-ness of the Mexicans that was Gold's point, but, precisely, their incursion and their discrepancy and, in effect, their immigration onto an American stage. A more accomplished realism would no doubt have been serviceable to his purpose, but the likelihood of Gold's own basic commitment was that the play had very little to do with Mexicans as such.

In the play, revolutionary sentiment was motivated by the plight of an innocent, endangered young girl. That was the basic plot. Significantly, Gold had used essentially the same plot in a story he had written almost a decade earlier, "Champak—A Story of India." He had known nothing about India except what he had picked up from an Indian who had agreed to collaborate with him. Nonetheless he wrote with an authority quite sufficient to his purpose because what was important was the foreignness of the materials, merely. A great deal could be made to rest on brief ascriptions—on exotic names, on bits of geography, and on implication of a translated language:

> No one had seen him steal out of the home of Harish, he was
> sure. The gentle little clerk was trusted by the Raj, for no one
> who marked him puttering over the huge ledgers in the Sanitary
> Office could dream of the fiery visions of freedom which burned
> behind those placid eyes. . . . There were many ways of crossing
> the river back to Calcutta; there was the Howrah bridge, and
> several lines of ferries, moving like glowworms on the dark sur-
> face of the water. But Nanda avoided all these orthodox means
> and made his way to an old, rotting pier away from any houses

and people. There he leaned over the edge cautiously, and saw a small row-boat rocking idly on the broad bosom of the Ganges.[25]

This was costume drama, with the polemical implication that the foreign-born had a cultural beauty. And so with a hero named Kurelovitch, in a story of 1917 called "A Damned Agitator," about whom it was enough to say—perhaps to William Carlos Williams—that he spoke in "low, thrilling Polish."[26]

And Gold did succeed. He did convince many people that his generalized alien experience was the stuff of an exemplary Americanism. With his costuming of himself—in his dirty shirts and filthy black Stetson with the sombrero brim—and with his exaggerations of almost everything, he became the most perfervid proletarian in America, *and* he had an acknowledged authority. By 1921, at the age of twenty-eight, he was editor of the *Liberator,* which could make claim to being the leading left-wing journal in the United States. He, the barbarian, was the successor to Max Eastman himself, the long symmetrical Greek.

He also became a Bolshevik as soon as history allowed him to become one, but Gold's Bolshevism-communism-Stalinism, at least until the 1930s, was a trope of cultural assertion, not unlike the fascism, circa 1929, of T. S. Eliot. In his position as editor of the *Liberator,* in 1921, he could attack the various coteries of *Dial* and *Little Review,* and of *Nation* and *Freeman,* on the grounds, no longer paradoxical, of what he perceived to be their general anti-American bias. The *Nation* and *Freeman* groups were guilty of the error of pursuing "*the holy grail of a great American culture,*" which was a self-defeating contradiction in terms. And as for *Dial* and *Little Review*—their biases were clear, but especially piquant in the moment because *Dial* was just now offering a prize for the best contribution to its pages by an American, and there was a joke in that because no American author other than Sherwood Anderson ever seemed to be welcome to its pages. Gold's particular examples of a true American Bolshevik art, in this same moment, were very far from being examples of tractarianism: he nominated Floyd Dells' *Moon-Calf* and Sinclair Lewis's *Main Street.* These were novels, he said, which breathed "the dim, crude, pathetic American yearning for something beyond respectability and commercialism," and which thus foreshadowed the coming revolution.[27]

Gold's proletarianism, only tenuously attached to Marxism, achieved its clearest, most vivid, and most persuasive expression not when the issue at hand was narrowly political, but when, rather, a self-proclaiming high culture seemed to be imposing itself.

The real issue was joined perhaps most notably—and certainly, as events turned out, most notoriously—when, in 1930, in the *New Republic*, Gold published an essay-review called "Thornton Wilder: Prophet of the Genteel Christ."[28] The brief essay was conceivably the climax of his career. For two months the larger part of the "Correspondence" columns of the *New Republic* was given over to responses to Gold, latterly to responses to the responders, and the action no doubt would have gone on except for the deliberate suppression of it by the editors. The public was notified that the "Gold-Wilder controversy is hereby called on account of darkness. No further letters on this subject will be published."[29] But, nonetheless, two years later Edmund Wilson, who had already commented editorially on Gold's review, returned to the matter in a long, two-part article.[30] Gold's assault, said Wilson, had given rise to "one of the most violent controversies which the literary world has lately known."

In the later article, "The Literary Class War," Wilson went on to say that the response to Gold's review, rather than the review itself, now forced him to the conclusion that indeed there was a class issue involved in the dispute. Gold had been harsh in dealing with Thornton Wilder, but no more so than, for instance, had been Ernest Hemingway when he had mocked Sherwood Anderson in *The Torrents of Spring*. It had not been Gold's bad manners that had brought forth the violence of the controversy. Rather, it was the question of the justness or the appropriateness for the practice of literary criticism of, in the words of the title of Wilson's earlier editorial, an "Economic Interpretation of Wilder." "The people who applauded Gold," he said, "seemed to be moved by a savage animus; those who defended Wilder pleaded or protested in the tone of persons who had seen a dearly beloved thing desecrated. Strange cries from the depths arose, illiterate and hardly articulate." The whole of the affair "marked definitely the eruption of the Marxist issues out of the literary circles of the radicals into the field of general criticism," and indicated that "the economic crisis was to be accompanied by a literary one."[31]

The controversy did indeed demonstrate an engagement between large and mostly inarticulate forces of culture, and it did involve a class issue, but Wilson was in part, at least, mistaken. Gold's review could be defined as being an "economic" or "Marxist" interpretation of Wilder only by a kind of a priori implication—readers would know which side Mike Gold was on. The review in itself did not develop such an interpretation. Moreover, as Wilson would have known, Gold's review was something other than an abrupt act of terrorism. It was a last word in an in-house debate over at *New Masses*. Approximately six months before the appearance of the review, Gold had attacked

Wilder, in some brief and casual editorial notes, in connection with a more general assault on Humanism. Then "J. Q. Neets" had published an essay-review in which he had compared Wilder to Upton Sinclair and had suggested that after all Sinclair might learn something about the art of writing from Thornton Wilder. The issue within the dispute, discovered and agreed to by both parties, was, "Can We Learn Anything from the Bourgeois Writers?" A John Reed Club debate on that topic, between Kunitz and Gold, had accordingly been scheduled.[32] And in the very same moment Gold was busy defending *Jews without Money* from the strictures of his more dogmatically leftist colleagues. Altogether, within the context of its immediate history, the inevitable purpose of Gold's *New Republic* review was his assertion of the independence of a literary avant-garde which called itself Marxist, particularly its right and its duty to its own experience.

And Edmund Wilson's own peculiarly continued interest in Gold's review and in the subsequent controversy was not without its own probable ulteriority of purpose. Wilson, too, had been writing about Thornton Wilder, and not quite sympathetically. He had discovered that Wilder was the first American to be deeply influenced by Proust, and he had said that that was a good thing for art but, by the same token, America was not being served by her native son. "I wish," Wilson had said in 1928, "that [Wilder] would study the diverse elements that go to make the United States, and give us *their* national portraits. . . . we need him at home."[33] Wilson clearly was seeking resolution to that ambivalence which in this same movement he was also recording in *Axel's Castle*, between the lure of the modern movement which he called "symbolism" and his loyalty to his own nativity. Thornton Wilder himself, meanwhile, may or may not have realized that he was merely the occasion for other people's uses, but in fact his political sympathies happened to be all on the left. He had joined organizations.[34]

In his earlier editorial note in *New Masses*, Gold had been temporarily enraged by Wilder's "suavity, discretion and flawless rhetoric," and therein was a hint of the real point of the attack. The lucid elegance in Wilder's language in itself implied a spread of attitudes, all quite confirmable in Wilder's statements, which altogether composed just that cultural arrogation which would deny Mike Gold citizenship. The class issue involved in the dispute had nothing to do with the "economic interpretation" of literature except in a removed and accidental sense. The trouble with Wilder was that the area of his endeavorings was one of the ideal forms and eternal meanings. He wrote as one removed from this time and from every time. He wrote about characters whose engagements were merely moral, and beyond passion. His subject—a contemporary one, to be sure, but restricted in its relevance—was *malaise,* the ripeness beyond civilization, and his response was the Church.

In the *New Republic* essay, Gold contemplated Wilder but saw *class,* and a version of Wilder which looked very much like T. S. Eliot. "Mr. Wilder," Gold wrote, "wishes to restore, he says, through Beauty and Rhetoric, the Spirit of Religion in American Literature." And then, warming up:

> One can respect any writer in America who sets himself a goal higher than the usual racketeering. But what is this religious spirit Mr. Wilder aims to restore? Is it the crude self-torture of the Holy Rollers, or the brimstone howls and fears of the Baptists, or even the mad, titanic sincerities and delusions of a Tolstoy or Dostoievsky?
>
> No, it is that newly fashionable literary religion that centers around Jesus Christ, the First British Gentleman. It is a pastel, pastiche, dilettante religion, without the true neurotic blood and fire, a daydream of homosexual figures in graceful gowns moving archaically among the lillies. It is Anglo-Catholicism, that last refuge of the American literary snob.

"Let Mr. Wilder write a book about modern America," Gold concluded. "We predict it will reveal all his fundamental silliness and superficiality, now hidden under a Greek chlamys." Which was to say that nothing could be learned from the bourgeois writers because their prose, their manners, and their values were all of a piece, and alien to the lives of real Americans—real Americans such as, after all, Michael Gold.

The response, as it was to be measured by the thirty-odd letters printed by the *New Republic,* was confused if not quite illiterate, and was nothing if not disparate. It ranged from the comment of Mr. Walter S. Hankel, who said that he had the pleasure of the acquaintance of both Thornton Wilder and Michael Gold, and that contrary to what might have been implied by the essay, Wilder was a very contentious man while Gold was sweet in temperament, to the comment of Rabbi Charles Raddock, who accused Gold of slandering American Jews with his talk of whores, pimps, and bedbugs while daring to address a tirade against "a creative artist who is very capable of writing unadulterated English prose...who is concerned about sensitive souls like Uncle Pio, the Perichole, the Marquesa, the Woman of Andros and Pamphilus, etc."[35] But withal, the response did dramatize the class issue. In the guise of one problem or another (the proper role of a book reviewer, the question of universals in art, the question of the writer's *donnée,* and so on), the major theme in the letters had to do with the basic appropriateness or inappropriateness of Michael Gold's writing an essay about Thornton Wilder.

They were of different breeds. Gold was a Communist and a self-described proletarian. Could such a man criticize *literature?* Gold's defenders, constituting the minority, thought that the discrepancy did precisely qualify him because it made for a criticism which was *not* disinterested and which was not narrowly belletristic. But the majority felt otherwise:

> Mr. Gold's tirade . . . was an excellent outburst by a man with a myopic view of Communism against another man who is not ashamed of having an understanding of the world beyond his own confines of time and place. . . . It is almost as if he were enraged because he never caught Mr. Wilder saying "I seen" for "I saw."

> I have all respect for Mr. Gold and his work, but it strikes me that with his capitalist-communist complex he is as utterly unqualified to judge Mr. Thornton Wilder's work as the average man of the street.

> Michael Gold's diatribe against Wilder is unkind. Or is his stand made as the expected defender of crude Communism?

> I am sure Mr. Gold wrote by the best light he had. But, sir, would you ask a drummer, however competent on his own instrument he may be, to play the violin in your orchestra?

But the response to Gold went still deeper, plunging in one instance to utter revelation. A Miss Jeannette Peabody of Cambridge, Massachusetts, wrote to the editors:

> Why did you allow such an unfair, vulgar, tainted, poisonous review to be printed? Why did you allow a Jew to write a review of books written by a man who acknowledges himself the apostle of Anglo-Catholicism? A Jew naturally has no sympathy with this point of view. Thornton Wilder would have given a much fairer picture of Zionism! This review seems to me entirely unworthy of your standards of criticism. It is scurrilous, profane, dirty. The writer shows his vast ignorance of any comprehension of the vision, beauty, ideal for which Thornton Wilder stands. I am not an Anglo-Catholic, nor a parlor Christian, but I heartily resent, as do many of my liberal friends, this attack on a man who we consider has done some lovely things and who we believe is endowed with a very lovely nature.[36]

There, finally, was the class issue plain. Miss Peabody justified
Michael Gold. Her insistence on a harmless loveliness involving necessarily a smidgen of anti-Semitism, her gentility calling itself liberalism,
her vague address to vision, beauty, and the ideal, her small sense of
hurt, and her intractable knowledge of the nature of vulgarity created
the bad manners of Michael Gold, because she was out there in mul-
titudes in America before she ever wrote her letter. After Miss Peabody, Gold's sneering and blatancy and histrionic crudeness, and sentimentality, were most appropriate. His manners constituted the way in
which he could tell Miss Peabody that he was the American.

seven

Nathan Weinstein and Nathanael West

The small truth was that he had a cousin named Sam Weinstein who had already made "Weinstein" into "West," and he had another cousin, Nathan, who had previously become at least a sufficiently American "Nathaniel" with an "i," if not quite an antique "Nathanael" with an "a." [1] So sometime in 1926, at approximately the moment he was deciding that he would be a writer, Nathan Weinstein named himself Nathanael West. Appeal to legend came later. When his friend William Carlos Williams asked him why he had changed his name after such fashion, he said that he had simply followed the advice of Horace Greeley: "Horace Greeley said, 'Go West, young man.' So I did."

That was a bit of joshing, but very much his own. The Weinstein who made the joke was a young man who was slight of build, saturnine in complexion, heavy-lidded with slightly protuberant eyes and rather a bulbous nose and lacking in chin, and generally drooping in appearance, and who was preternaturally and obsessively knowledgeable about the comedy of social pretensions. In this instance he would have known that there were at least two jokes in his joke, one on himself and the other on Horace Greeley, not to mention general reflection on the matter of the quality of cliché in all cultural identity. He would have known that no Weinstein could ever be or could ever go West. Weinsteins were not within the provenance of the legend of the pioneers. They did not look the part. They were too Jewish. On the other hand, here he was, and Horace Greeley and the other Yankees were to know that they had secured a client of such a type as they could not initially have had in mind. This Weinstein answered Horace Greeley's generous advice with a nice parody.

The tone of West's assertion was always, certainly, much less clamorous than that of his sometime friend Mike Gold. Unlike Gold, West was a calculating novelist and was equipped with an intricate, discriminating literary intelligence. He was a modern artist, in the modern movement. Moreover, the experience from which he wrote novels was in obvious ways the opposite of that which secured Michael Gold's loyalty. West had grown up as an Uptown Jew, with plenty of money. He had, as a lad, been steeped in Culture, in a version which was perhaps ambiguous but which was nonetheless distinct in being high-class. But for all of that he was Gold's superior in his knowledge of the endless, reflexive frustration of cultural assertion, and he was also, by far, more strenuous than Michael Gold, the professional revolutionary, in his imaginative grasping of the desirability, finally, of violence.

West wrote novels about heroes whose authority was in the fact that with all naive or desperate eagerness, they did not quite belong. They were not outcastes, exactly, nor were they spokesmanly satirists, nor were they figures for the proving of a deep ontological despair. And West did not try to make jokes after the manner of his brother-in-law S. J. Perelman, although he was related to Perelman by more than family connection and although, according to testimony, he wrote with Perelman in mind as his first audience. Using clearly cognate materials, Perelman was blatant, forcing sharp discordances between baroque English prose and Yiddish homeliness. West would not have written *Dawn Ginsbergh's Revenge*. West's protagonist would in fact have been rescued by the perception of any absolutes of discrepancy: he would have had the satisfaction of a static role for himself, whether as a tragic outcaste or as a stock figure in a vaudeville routine, or whatever. As he was, he had no certainty of definition whatsoever other than, in three of the four novels, a comic, whimsically anomalous name: Balso Snell, Miss Lonelyhearts, or Lemuel Pitkin. This protagonist's typical adventure consists in his being lost in a strange country where, in his eagerness, he is constantly baffled by the signs. He is all too willing to be a citizen and have a role, and his adventures therefore turn sinister—because he cannot be easy with the idiom of the country, because he tries to literalize everything, because he tries to discover substance in signs. Therefore that which is casually spurious for everyone else—be it literature or Christianity or democracy or Hollywood—becomes overbearing and grotesque. Engaged with phantoms, he wants a decisive phenomenality—something he can really feel himself to be and do—which is to be discovered ultimately, in each of the four novels, only in reductive violence, along with sex.

There were no prior ideas or values of any determining importance. West's hero was so situated, merely, as to transform everything into parody, without mercy or hindrance or principle of selection. Everywhere this hero goes, equipped as he is with his privileged displacement, he encounters roles rather than people and clichés rather than things. The fiction proceeded headlong from item to item, mimicking and mocking as it went, and discovering, by so doing, that everything could be mimicked and mocked and that therefore all ideas and values and principles are arbitrary and fantastic. West's hero was so situated as to reveal that nothing, save perhaps violence, has an original reality, and then even the violence was just a matter of terminal and unargued relief.

It was a kind of knowledge for which Nathanael West had been peculiarly well prepared when he had been Nathan Weinstein. He had been a boy and then a young man who, precisely, did not quite belong but who, rather, had occupied an uncertain middle place between plausible aspirations and genteel rejections.

He, too, had been the son of eastern-European immigrants, and by so much, according to the implications of the Americans, he had been a child of the barbarians. His parents were Lithuanian Jews. His father, like so many other Russian Jews of the Great Immigration, had come to America in flight from the conscription laws of the czar and by so much had been eligible for citizenship in the American ghetto. But Max Weinstein was different from those other Russian Jews, first of all because he did, quickly, become well-to-do in America, as a building contractor, and second because he did not have to think of himself as a Russian Jew, downtown-style. Back in Kovno Gbernya the Weinsteins had had some small social standing. The family of Max's wife, the former Chana-Mindel Leizerovna Vollenstein, of Kovno, had had quite superior social standing, which was understood, acknowledged, and subsidized both by Max and by the children to come. The Wallensteins had been very wealthy, and they had been a cultivated family in the highest manner of the time and the place, meaning that they were more Jewish than Russian but that most of all they were Germans. German thought and art and civilization and language had constituted the style of true aristocracy in Lithuania for centuries past, although in fact that arrangement which had permitted the so-called German Home Rule had been nullified just when West's parents were coming of age in Lithuania. Nonetheless the Wallensteins and the Weinsteins could and apparently did think of themselves as heirs to a nobility. They were not immigrants, but emigrés. Come to America, and having money, they were loyal to the grand German manner.

The style of the home of West's growing-up was that of Greater Europeans. His parents knew the languages, including English, but their preferred language was German. That was the language they taught their children. They had German-speaking friends and German-speaking servants. Their friends included painters and musicians, who were in touch with culture in the European way. The parents went to the Metropolitan Opera regularly.

They were upper-crust Litvaks—inhabiting therefore a social position which was almost totally artificial in the United States in the twentieth century. They were outside any recognized American mode of social pretension, but nevertheless thay had caste. They were better than other people, as was indicated by their tastes and their restraints even more than by their money. The Weinsteins dressed very well—and even in later years West himself was always to take great care to be fashionable, even elegant. They were Jews and identified themselves as Jews, but they were not ghetto Jews. Judaism had its place as a thing to be guarded and honored, but not obsessively. And they were, perforce, petitioners in America and acknowledged the necessity of their being Americans, but they petitioned on their own terms. So, according to West's biographer Jay Martin, one of the cousins was to recollect that the family was "not going to be American peasants, we were going to be American gentlemen"—thereby, assuming an accuracy in the vocabulary of the recollection, creating a distinction which in itself had meaning for an antique nobility, no doubt, but which had little relevance in New York. New York in 1903, when West was born, was divided in many social ways, but not between a gentleman class and a peasant class.

A young boy growing up amidst these odd pretensions did have something to gain, namely, cultivation after the Greater European fashion. At the age of ten West was reading Tolstoy. As a boy he owned fine sets of the nineteenth-century Russian masters—Turgenev, Dostoevski, Chekhov; and he had good editions of Pushkin, Thackeray, Dickens, Maupassant, Balzac, Thomas Hardy, and Shakespeare the celebrated German *Dichter*. But as the pretension of the parents became the ground of cultural identity for the next generation, its meaning necessarily became the more ambiguous. The social function of the caste system in which the parents took high place was at best very limited. It was limited absolutely to those few who knew about and could believe in the system, those whose memory of courtly Lithuania was more active than their knowledge of the cultural exigencies of the present. The next generation would have had the position of a minor nobility after the revolution, trained in arrogance but subject to doubts and given to irony.

Given a perspective altered ever so slightly by American social reality, American nativism, and the passing of time, it was very funny that the family should have entertained some claim to actual lineage of the blood, as it did—the basis of the claim being Schiller's *Wallenstein,* which was taken to be, conceivably, a family chronicle. The claimancy was funny because it provided a parody of what was the basic case of the family: it emphasized the discrepancy between the family's style of assertion and its field for assertion. The Wallenstein-Weinsteins not only were of the better sort but had the caul, and what meanwhile they had to show for their true rank was a Litvak invention of a relic of the beau monde.

West himself, far from detaching himself from these affectations, retained them in all of their exaggeration. His first nom de plume, used in his college years, was "Nathaniel von Wallenstein Weinstein." Apparently until the end, moreover, he continued to rehearse a manner which would be appropriate to the joke of the secret of his birth. On the basis of late acquaintance, Lillian Hellman was to recall that West played the part of a Middle-European baron, "certainly not delicate and not quite aristocratic, but . . . both distinguished and casual." Earlier, and as a mere stripling, he seems to have cultivated beautiful failure. At the boys' summer camp to which he was sent, he was called "Pep"—with great irony because on the playing fields he displayed no pep. Instead, he was the boy who drew sarcastic cartoons for the camp newspaper. In his schooling he failed more efficiently, by refusing the gift of his interest in or attendance at school, absenting himself as many as thirty times in a semester. It is not a likelihood that he was simply too smart to go to school, and it was not the case that his schoolmates, had he bothered to be in school with them, would have been intellectually unsatisfying for him. There were among them, it happened, a surprising number who in the future were to be important people in American letters and learning.[2] Nor was it the case, either, that he lacked encouragement. Formal education was important to the elder Weinsteins. They fretted. They bribed teachers. Max located his apartment houses specifically so that the best schools in New York would be available to his son. West as a boy lacked neither encouragement nor potential reward, but still he refused to go to school, no doubt because failure was more distinguished, more cavalier, more insouciant.

He did have companions, and, according to testimony, he was something of a leader among them. He failed not because he was a retiring sort of a boy. But his companions seem to have been restricted to just those few who were in a position to share his irony. Not surprisingly, the Weinsteins and the Wallensteins were exceptionally

clannish, and not surprisingly, West's own constant companions were
his Weinstein and Wallenstein cousins. Among them his two closest
friends were two other Nathans, one Weinstein and one Wallenstein,
the three Nathans composing virtually a select order. They did nothing
very unusual. They roamed New York. They did an amount of secret
observing in Central Park. Meanwhile, however, they must have provided an unusual amount of insulation for each other, sufficient to
prevent risk of exposure of their superiority, for certainly their
superiority would have been neither accepted nor understood by random outsiders. The three Nathans would have shared a wonderful and
an almost inexplicable joke, together with a wonderful precariousness.
Their circumstances made them to be unacknowledged princes of the
blood and also utter frauds. As they roamed New York together, they
would have been *flanneurs*, taking in the scene, and by the fact of their
companionship sustaining their aloofness.

But West's insulation could not have been total, of course, and
there is evidence that at the same time that he was nourishing his
genealogy, he was trying hard to be a regular American boy. At the
same time that he was deriving himself from Schiller, he was also
reading Horatio Alger and the Boy Scout manual. From the time of
his early boyhood into the time of his career as a writer, he would seem
to have been particularly obsessed by baseball and the more particularly by his failure to be a good player of baseball. Repeatedly in those
cartoons for the camp newspaper the subject was silly mistakes in
baseball. Failure on the field was the subject of one of his early short
stories, "Western Union Boy." Baseball was not just a game, evidently, or merely a locale of competition with other boys. It would
have been for West, as indeed for the other boys he knew—the sons of
Jewish immigrants—an arbitrary and foolish but nonetheless actual test
of naturalization. Baseball would have been a device of access to an
American boyhood, and indeed it must have terrified him just because
it was so unimpeachable an expectation, so plainly and so much by
universal assent what American boys were interested in.

West was to find a literary career in recognizing the essential
emptiness in all social signs and tokens, but not before—in his fiction as
in his life—acknowledging their imperiousness. Baseball was a token
for his youth; others were forthcoming. When he went to college (first
Tufts and then Brown, in both instances with fraudulent transcripts, as
would have been a prerogative of nobility), he was among the first to
know that there was more to college than classes and a curriculum of
study. He would seem most of all to have been a ready convert, to a
discrepant everything.

He was to be remembered as a snappy dresser. He wore Brooks Brothers suits and argyle socks and, according to a classmate, "Whitehouse and Hardy brogues, Brooks shirts and ties and Herbert Johnson or Lock and Co. hats."[3] He dressed as a College Man to the point of parodic comment, as he could not have failed to know, but also greatly respecting what was being parodied, for otherwise he would not have kept up the masquerade. And presumably with the same kind of aggressive ambivalence he became an energetic dancer, and he learned to play the banjo, and he drove a red Stutz Bearcat, and he went to the football games.

And presumably along the same line of endeavor he became anti-Semitic—or, more to the point, an anti-Semitic snob: witty, mannered, and gracefully disdainful. According to his own later testimony, he wanted desperately to be pledged to a fraternity. He was not and could not be because the fraternities of his choice, which would have been to say the genuine, really collegiate fraternities, simply did not admit Jews, or Catholics, but West could and did try on their manners, including the manners of their racial purity. He never denied his antecedence and his name was Nathan Weinstein, but he let it be known that he, too, did not like Jewish Jews and pushy Jews. He did not like "Bronx intellectuals," and he had great fun, according to his friend John Sanford, née Julian Shapiro, in referring to Jewish girls as "bagels." According to Sanford, "he did everything possible to create the impression in his own mind—remember that, in his own mind—that he was just like Al Vanderbilt. It never quite came off."[4] And if West never denied that he was Jewish, he characteristically went further and denied the fact that Jews were. Another friend was to recall that West knew more about the history of anti-Semitism than any man he had ever met. West had concluded that contemporary anti-Semitism contained theoretical error, because Jews as such simply did not exist. "He held, and underwrote his opinion with facts and figures, that the original Jewish people had wandered so far and blended so deeply into the blood of the countries they found that it was senseless to identify them as a blood strain. He did not regard himself as a Jew at all, but as an American."

On the other hand, the young man with the banjo was also "Nathaniel von Wallenstein Weinstein," a name which he wrote again and again in his college notebooks, indicating at the least that the name was very pleasing to him. Stutz Bearcat and all, he was a very aesthetic young man, prone to burning with a hard, gemlike flame and fueling himself with amounts of esoteric reading. He had a group of friends of like disposition to whom he referred, with multiple ironies, as the

"Hanseatic League." These others were not themselves necessarily boy barons, but they must have constituted an appropriate companionship for West's secret nobility. They were a self-nominated elite, and therefore not at all American college boys. They constituted, precisely, a cabal. Their taste ran to mystery and ritual and high decadence. They tried opium. They read a great deal in ancient and secret learning and developed a secret language. In the rooms of one and another member of the group, they practiced black magic and conducted the Black Mass, and when they went to the movies together, they laughed at the sad parts and cried during the funny parts.

West received what was altogether a very good education at college. He learned some new categories of cultural identity. Moreover, while still in college, he began to write the little novel which eventually would be *The Dream Life of Balso Snell,* "Literature" in itself being a category of cultural identity. He did, apparently, read widely and eagerly, and was excited by his discoveries and told his friends about them, but what he was discovering after all was that literary avant-gardism which would have been most available to a bright undergraduate in the early 1920s, which implied manners and attitudes and which encumbered a certain knowledge which in turn created virtually a social definition. As certainly West did know at some level of realization, Literature was as ill-befitting to him as the image of Al Vanderbilt, or the name Nathanael West, but it presented him with intricate possibilities for the kind of learning he was good at. Literature was a richer and broader and more compelling stuff for both emulation and dismissive parody.

After college and after the publication of his first novel, West was to tell an interviewer that the literary life at Brown had been split between Catholic mysticism and French surrealism, but it is unlikely that while at Brown he was making that distinction or any such distinction. He would seem rather, according to the evidence of *Balso Snell,* to have been discovering a comically amalgamated idea of the sources of the imagination, via a general set of instructions derived from Pound and Eliot and Joyce and Gertrude Stein and Wallace Stevens, all of whom he was reading. And he was in part simply recapitulating the literary educations of these leaders of the modern moment, who were his slightly older contemporaries. He read Huysmans with particular diligence, and via Huysmans was able to amaze his friends with his knowledge of the lives of minor Catholic saints. He struggled with Baudelaire and Mallarmé and Verlaine and Rimbaud and Villiers de l'Isle Adam and Corbière and Laforgue—the whole of the symbolist *équipe* as particularly recommended by Arthur Symons. And he read

French fiction; among his friends he repeatedly confided his admiration for the first scene of *A la recherche du temps perdu*. He was also a faithful purchaser of the *Mercure de France* and of *Nouvelle revue française*, albeit that his French was shaky. He was impressed as well by the writers of the Celtic Twilight, a number of whom gave lectures at Brown: AE, Padraic Colum, and James Stephens. Like everybody else, he was reading James Branch Cabell, and, also, Walter Pater and Oscar Wilde and Arthur Machen and James Gibbons Huneker. The singular, composite idea which he could have drawn from all of these would have been, moreover, one which would have particularly suited his own prior knowledge; he would have learned a piquancy of weary decadence mixed with aesthetical cynicism. He would have learned that the life of art was privileged, that it derived from ancient and unsuspected tradition (involving Church history with curious frequency), that the tradition was available chiefly in arcane learning, and that art had its own logic and language which might be understood only by a select few in this barbarous time and place.

There can be no doubt that at least initially, as West was beginning to put himself to the actual task of writing, he regarded Literature as being something classy and glamorous before it was either a job of work or a visitation of the muse, or self-expression, or whatever, but there can be no doubt, either, that in the same moment, characteristically, he quite saw through the affectations of literary life. Shortly after college he went to Paris, as he was likely to do because that is where all of the real writers went and also because his father could afford to send him to Paris. The year was 1926. In fact he stayed in Paris for only a brief three months because his father suffered abrupt financial reverses—the forthcoming Depression reached the building business somewhat in advance of depressing the rest of the country, and hereafter West would have to work for a living. But those three months were important to him, specifically by way of refining his knowledge of the absurdities of his aspirations. He did no actual writing, but he did try to lead the literary life and he did apparently deeply know that he was very much out of place. In later years he was to tell many tales about his adventures in Paris, frequently with the implication that he had spent a considerable amount of time among the celebrities and that he had been one of them, but the probable truth both of his situation and of his perception of his situation was contained in the interstices of a short story which he wrote several times, called variously "L'Affaire Beano," "The Fake," and "The Impostor." It was a story about an American artist in Paris who was an impostor. The artist thinks—mistakenly—that in order to be an artist, one must live and look like one, and he has had his difficulties because by

1926, in Paris, all of the obvious roles have been exhausted. "Long hair and a rapt look wouldn't get you to first base," he says. "You had to have something new on the ball." "But," he says, "I made a lucky hit."

> Instead of trying for strangeness, I formalized and exaggerated the costume of a bond salesman. I wore carefully pressed Brooks Brothers clothing, sober but rich ties, and carried gloves and a tightly-rolled umbrella. My manners were elaborate and I professed great horror at the slightest breach of the conventional. It was a success. I was asked to all the parties.[5]

Numbers of those stories he told his friends in later years were for that matter just sartorial reverses on the same theme. Underneath his Brooks overcoat, he said, he was dressed in tatters or he was naked. In all of the versions the bedeviling point was whether or not he had looked the part, from which it followed—for all of these tales were variations on a single joke—that Literature was a kind of dress-up. Therefore it was a thing to be ridiculed, but at the same time dressing-up was of course important to West. Everything was eventually a kind of dressing-up.

He would die young. He was killed in an automobile crash in 1940 shortly after his thirty-seventh birthday. During the few years when he was seriously a writer, he would know new circumstances, and even mentors and influences and sources of ideas. Returned from Paris to New York, where for most of the time he worked as a hotel manager, he was variously acquainted with a good many authors, none of whom had derived from decadence, including Dashiell Hammett, Lillian Hellman, Erskine Caldwell, James T. Farrell, Dorothy Parker, Josephine Herbst and her husband John Herrman, Mike Gold, and William Carlos Williams. Gold offered West tutorials on how to write salable articles, and Williams was directly responsible for getting *Balso Snell* into print. West also became a member of a very serious, Russianized discussion group consisting of Russian Jews exactly of the kind of those "Bronx intellectuals" whom he still professed to despise. For the final five years of his life, he was in Hollywood, which he did indeed despise. Both East and West, most of his friends were involved with the political left, and so, then, was he, but not to the point of a commitment much beyond companionable sympathy. How generalized and distant was his political knowledge was to be indicated by his one political novel, *A Cool Million,* published in 1934.

And altogether, except as a matter of providing him with occasional subjects, the circumstances and the influences he was to know during his writerly life seem by the testimony of the books not to have influenced him very deeply. The books did not arrive at values, but were, comically and desperately, processes of perception, of a kind which he had had and which he had been refining since the beginning.

He began to write Literature, reasonably according to the kind of his perception, by imitating most—or in any event an astonishing amount in a narrow space—of what he knew of Literature, thereby trying it on and disposing of it in one motion. *The Dream Life of Balso Snell,* published in 1931, was obviously by intention a precious little joke, packed with more and less overt intellectual-artistic references ranging from Euripides to Joyce, and including, at random, Gide, Freud, Picasso, Rimbaud, Daudet, Gertrude Stein, the Marquis de Sade, George Moore, Aldous Huxley, and Dostoevski, among many others, with some special consistency of allusion to Huymans and to James Branch Cabell's *Jurgen.*[6] Balso Snell, a poet, has a dream. In his dream he comes upon and enters the famous Trojan Horse. Wandering through the bowels of this source of the myths, he meets characters all of whom have an artistic-literary turn of mind, who tell him stories. He meets a Jewish tour guide, who is perhaps Gertrude Stein and certainly is himself, who tells him a tale of the philosopher saint Appolonius of Tyana, who had a snake in his anus. He meets Maloney the Areopagite, a Catholic mystic, naked except for a derby bedecked with thorns, who composes verses, so he says, in imitation of Notker Balbus, Ekkenard le Vieux, and Hucbald le Chauve. Maloney tells Balso the story of Saint Puce, who had lived in the armpit of our Lord. Balso meets John Gilson, a twelve-year-old schoolboy who has written a journal in which he has cast himself in parts after the manners of Iago, Nietzsche, Rimbaud, and mostly Raskolnikov. Balso dreams that he falls asleep and has a dream about a young man named Beagle Darwin and a young woman named Janey Davenport who imagine themselves—it is not clear at this level who is doing the imagining—in the parts of a weary Hamlet and Ophelia, perhaps as conjointly transmitted by Rimbaud and Gide. They realize and are cynical about the amount of their own literary posturing. And Balso meets Mary McGeeney, a schoolteacher who is writing a biography of Samuel Perkins, the man who wrote the biography of E. F. Fitzgerald, who wrote the biography of Hobson, the biographer of Boswell, the biographer.

For all of its intricacy, *Balso Snell* was not a deft job of satirical work. The jokes were alternately very arcane and leeringly scatological. Balso enters the Trojan Horse from the rear, a circumstance which announces much of the thematics of the novel, for it is to be known what he is likely to discover, but then the circumstance also prompted puns West was unable to resist. "O Anus Mirabilis!" says Balso, in his very first utterance, and thereafter there is a great deal of the same. Had West been able to resist, then certainly the novel would have been a nicer and a more amusing and altogether a more exquisite anthology of parodies than in fact it turned out to be.

The novel was the work of a young man who was learning how to be a writer, and without doubt it was the work of a young man who had not yet learned good techniques of control. On the other hand, West had written and repeatedly rewritten the brief novel over a period of something more than six years and without doubt he did have a very fine ability for sensing stylistic and tonal discrepancies, for otherwise he could not have written this novel at all. There can be little doubt that where the novel was raw and blatant and dirty-minded, he wanted it to be so, and the novel after all contained an energy and an anger, as well as a problematics, which could not have been contained merely in a nice accuracy of parody of the masters. The first target of the novel's satire is not the masters at all, but their parodists, often unwitting but sometimes witting. The novel in this aspect is a parody of parodists, the ultimate target inevitably being West himself as a would-be writer deriving himself, inevitably, from writers whose entire knowledge is derivatively literary. Entering that Trojan Horse, which should be a place of origins, Balso finds himself pressingly surrounded and besought by the posturing dead who pretend to be alive. Balso comes to realize that the wooden horse "was inhabited solely by writers in search of an audience," and, West adds, "he was determined not to be tricked into listening to another story."[7] The horse is a mare and is appropriately—to name the one pun which West did not pursue—the locus of nightmare.

If this, in the bowels of the Trojan Horse, is what the literary imagination is all about, then obviously there is something feculent in the literary imagination. Moreover, by obvious extension, all writers are sexual perverts. Balso's dream of literature begins in sodomy, recapitulated almost immediately in the tale of the saint with the snake in his anus. Maloney the Areopagite, engaged when Balso comes upon him in trying to crucify himself with thumbtacks, is a masochist, and that derby of his, with the thorns stuck into it, suggests the same. John Gilson, in the most elaborate of his imaginings of roles for himself, imagines himself to be a male prostitute, and meanwhile, cynically and therefore with seeming rationality, he justifies his writing by saying that he is merely trying to seduce his English teacher. And the same general theme is instanced forth, with variations, in each of the other characters and in each of the characters invented in the dreams of the other characters.

But Balso does finally awaken, thereby providing West with an escape from this literary nightmare, in an ending which is abrupt but is neither illogical nor insignificant. West was himself at this point embracing a career. Balso, meanwhile, embraces Mary McGeeney, who has suddenly been revealed to be his old sweetheart. Poised in the precoital moment, with Mary McGeeney on her back with knees spread apart and Balso standing over her, the two hold back in order to consider a catalog of standard attitudes ranging from Isadora Duncan to Molly Bloom, but everything comes down to plain, unmediated sex, as by now we know, and Balso finally goes to the saddle. The dream of Literature has turned out to be a wet dream, with some multiple implications of relief. The dreaming has been terminated in behalf of its opposite—a palpability and an actuality. All of the posturing and perversion have been terminated in behalf of straightforward animal coupling. And mounted upon Mary McGeeney, schoolteacher that she is and heiress of the pedantry of the ages, Balso has found the proper end of learning and knows what to do with it. At the beginning the Jewish tour guide had presented him with an old adage, "A hand in the Bush is worth two in the pocket." That is the only good advice he has received, and he now discovers the truth that is in it.

That ending is, specifically, a release into reductiveness. We read: "His body broke free of the bard. It took on a life of its own; a life that knew nothing of the poet Balso." Thus unencumbered, Balso's body enacts a true art, namely, the ceremony of its base elements: "A ceremony whose ritual unwound and maneuvered itself with the confidence and training of chemicals acting under the stimulus of a catalytic agent." (61)

The novel was truly and importantly an apprentice work. In his years of laboring at it West did apparently learn formal skills requisite to his privileged perception of the delusions of cultural identity, and hereafter he would be much more efficient in saying basically what he had said in *The Dream Life of Balso Snell*. "Literature" was one of the delusions by which he had been particularly beckoned, but there were many others, all equally and in the same way delusive. All cultural constructs were false, and only sex and violence were real.

Miss Lonelyhearts, published in 1933, followed logically from *Balso Snell*. It began not precisely with the relief of sex and violence, but with the same qualities expressed so compactly and so bluntly and in a manner so certified by pain as to mock all cultural pretensions and social roles. The protagonist, "Miss Lonelyhearts," is in the first instance not "Miss Lonelyhearts," but a newspaperman making a living at a role, the falsity of which everyone of any sophistication is ready to accept. He is challenged by "Sick-of-it-all" and "Desperate" and "Harold S." and "Broad Shoulders," with their letters testifying to that which is genuine—disfiguration, rape, the pathology of sadism and victimization, and so forth.

> *I am sixteen years old now and I dont know what to do and would appreciate it if you could tell me what to do. When I was a little girl it was not so bad because I got used to the kids on the block makeing fun of me, but now I would like to have boy friends like the other girls and go out on Saturday nites, but no boy will take me because I was born without a nose—although I am a good dancer and have a nice shape and my father buys me pretty clothes. . . . Ought I commit suicide?*

> *I am writing to you for my little sister Gracie because something awfull hapened to her and I am afraid to tell mother about it. I am 15 years old and Gracie is 13 and we live in Brooklyn. Gracie is deaf and dumb and biger than me but not very smart on account of being deaf and dumb. . . . Last week a man came on the roof and did something dirty to her. She to'd me about it and I dont know what to do as I am afraid to tell mother on account of her being lible to beat Gracie up. I am afraid that Gracie is going to have a baby and I listened to her stomack last night for a long time to see if I could hear the baby but I couldn't. If I tell mother she will beat Gracie up awfull because I am the only one who loves her and last time when she tore her dress they loked her in the closet for 2 days and if the boys on the block hear about it they will say dirty things.*[8]

What follows in this novel which in itself is reduced to its basics is a catalog of clichés of cultural response to such reality. And at the end the only adequate response to sex and violence is sex and violence.

Numbers of obvious clichés are disposed of very quickly, by parody. The primary parodist is the newspaper's hard-boiled feature editor, blatantly named "Shrike." In his principal set scene, consisting of approximately a half-dozen paragraphs, Shrike runs through a range of socially acknowledged posturings. He speaks of the life of the soil:

> So you buy a farm and walk behind your horse's moist behind, no collar or tie, plowing your broad swift acres. As you turn up the rich black soil, the wind carries the smell of pine and dung across the fields and the rhythm of an old, old work enters your soul. To this rhythm, you sow and weep and chivy your kine, not kin or kind, between the pregnant rows of corn and taters. Your step becomes the heavy sexual step of a dance-drunk Indian and you tread the seed down into the female earth. You plant, not dragon's teeth, but beans and greens. (107)

And so, rapidly, for the "South Seas," "Hedonism," "Art," and suicide and drugs. All of these are escapes, as Shrike himself says, the proof being in the parodies. If all of these idealized attitudes are merely mannerisms—the life of the soil in this respect being not different from suicide and drugs—then they are already secondhand and they prevent rather than encourage original apprehension.

But in fact the proffered clichés are more numerous and occasionally more plausible than those of Shrike's catalog. Shrike himself, as cynical newspaperman, is playing a role. There are some other newspapermen who make an appearance in the novel, and they, too, are appropriately hard-drinking and hard-boiled. Shrike has a wife who plays, blowzily and ineptly, at being sexually liberated. Miss Lonelyhearts has a fiancée, wholesomely named Betty, who loves him and who offers him a standard version of domestic bliss, at the reasonable expense of his being a standard husband with a job in advertising. There is indeed some suggestion of the secondhand even in the letters which bespeak the agonies of "Sick-of-it-all," "Desperate," and the others. What is said in the letters is so brutal that it must be real, but the letters come in at the rate of more than thirty a day and they have a sameness, "all of them alike," as Miss Lonelyhearts says in a particularly violent metaphor, "stamped from the dough of suffering with a heart-shaped cookie knife." (66)

The writers of the letters are in effect praying to Miss Lonelyhearts. He is the Christ of the New York *Post-Dispatch,* and what he calls the "Christ Dream" is in this novel the chief means for West's perceptions. By taking his job very seriously, Miss Lonelyhearts can—and in fact does—enact Christ. West, too, takes the job seriously, and he does not mock it. He does dispose of it, however, by reduction. The "Christ Dream," as an initial postulate, is itself a partial disencumbrance; it is a stepping-forth from the cliché of Christianity. But at the end the "Christ Dream" not only is not a cliché but has no social or institutional or ritual or mythical quality whatsoever. In an early chapter Miss Lonelyhearts has dreamed of a college prank in which he and his roommates had sacrificed a lamb, the point of the dream being his realization that the sacrifice really was a piece of butchery. In what there is of a main action in the novel, Miss Lonelyhearts becomes engaged in the domestic troubles of a pair of his petitioners: Fay Doyle—"legs like Indian clubs, breasts like balloons and a brow like a pigeon. . . . she looked like a police captain" (100)—and her husband, Peter Doyle, who is a cripple. Enacting Christ, Miss Lonelyhearts bequeathes himself to Mrs. Doyle—some while thereafter he will attempt to preach Christ's love to her, but she wants action on the mount, not sermons. He then becomes the lover of Peter Doyle, if not quite actually at least tantamountly, and at the very end, in the chapter called "Miss Lonelyhearts Has a Religious Experience," in an action composed of confused intentions, the two struggle together in an erotic-deathly embrace. We have just read that in his rushing toward Peter Doyle, Miss Lonelyhearts has been plunging as well toward "Desperate," "Harold S.," "Catholic-mother," "Broken-hearted," and all of the others. Peter Doyle shoots Miss Lonelyhearts unto death, by way of justifying the chapter heading. The "Christ Dream" is now corporealized, activated, freed from the lethargy of sleep. We are to know that the components of its actuality are sex and violence.

A Cool Million; or, The Dismantling of Lemuel Pitkin, published in 1934, was conceived by West to be a satire on the American Dream of Success, especially as codified by Horatio Alger. West wrote it very quickly, and not well. The novel turned toward topical political statement: when fascism comes to America, it said, it will be tricked out like a typical American and will wear a coonskin cap—which statement no doubt had an accuracy, but West did not probe deeply for a deep paradox, as to say that the American Boy and Horst Wessel were the same boy despite acknowledged differences. The portion of his materials which obviously most besought West was the 100 percent Americanism and not the fascism: the novel was not a warning but a mannerist's joke, the base of the joke being the pretentious and anachronistic and otherwise foolish myth of the Yankee. And at the end and despite the misdirections in the novel, the perception in it was of a piece with that of *Balso Snell* and *Miss Lonelyhearts:* what happens in the novel is that a deep dreamer obsessively literalizes his dreams and is then seized by the genuine—"drilled through the heart by an assassin's bullet."[9]

Our hero, Lemuel Pitkin, a plucky lad and an American Boy, is unwittingly martyred to a cause invented by ex-president of the United States Nathan (Shagpoke) Whipple, a character modeled loosely after Warren G. Harding, Calvin Coolidge, and Adolf Hitler. As ultimate cliché of the American Dream, Lemuel Pitkin serves to prove that the American Dream is ultimately exploitable for purposes of demogoguery—that is the essential part of the political message of the novel. At the same time, however, and quite aside from his usefulness to fascist exploitation, Lemuel Pitkin is an emblem of a social quantity quite like that of the literary life of *Balso Snell* and of the Christianity of *Miss Lonelyhearts,* and as in the other instances the social quantity is created in order to be at once parodied and violently reduced. Lemuel Pitkin was for that matter something like baseball—a faith to which everybody who seemed to be culturally at home seemed to subscribe, and which was compelling beyond mere allurement for a young man who had never been culturally at home anywhere, and which was so obvioulsy ill-befitting to everything he knew as to be ridiculous.

In that more important aspect, everything that West had to say was present in the first few paragraphs of the novel. The Widow Pitkin, mother of young Lem, loses her Vermont farmstead when Squire Bird forecloses. That, so far, was plausibly a parody of a Horatio Alger story. Lem must go forth to seek his fortune. But Squire Bird has foreclosed, so we learn, because a New York decorator named Asa Goldstein has decided to promote Colonial and has offered a price for what is really a decayed shack. That was not parody of Horatio Alger, but rather an abrasive assertion of an actuality which included Jews, the evident hypocrisy of interior decorating, and, by way of multiplying the irony, the successful commercialization by Jews of an essentially valueless American heritage.

The novel immediately skitters off in several other narrative directions, but that conflict which is discovered in the first few paragraphs—in effect between the American Boy and the New York Jew, both of whom were Nathanael West at several removes of parody—is the model for the real politics of the novel. Every character, every thing, and every incident is a cultural cliché ripe for undermining. It is in that respect rather than as a matter of ideology that Shagpoke Whipple can be seen to be an American Hitler, for we know that presidents of the United States really are self-serving opportunists; as we should have known, Shagpoke Whipple's sole ambition is to line his own pockets, and the presidency is a confidence game. When Betty Prail, our heroine, is sold into prostitution in Wu Fong's "House of all Nations," interiors meticulously created by Asa Goldstein, that, several times over, is an undermining along the same order. Into these pages there comes a westerner who talks like Davy Crockett and rapes poor Betty. There are Indians who talk Indian talk, one of whom owns an oil well and a gold mine, and the other of whom, Chief Israel Satinpenny, is a sophisticated terrorist: "He had been to Harvard and hated the white man with undying venom." (231) A Barnum kind of "Chamber of American Horrors" provides West with opportunity to catalog the American artifacts, which are gadgets cunningly made to look like other gadgets: "pencil sharpeners that could be used as earpicks, can openers as hair brushes ... flower pots that were really victrolas, revolvers that held candy, candy that held collar buttons." (239)

What is to be discovered, in brief, is that there is no reality in the

American myth, as presented in a range of its typicalities. And Lemuel is the appropriate intelligence of the novel because, although offered many fine opportunities for knowing what is real, he persists in being the American Boy, at least until the assassin's bullet reaches him. The habit of Lemuel's intelligence is in fact derived not from Ragged Dick, that shrewd urban confidencer, but from Gulliver and from Rasselas and most of all from Candide. Terrible things happen to Lemuel, and he refuses to disbelieve. He is dismantled. Sequentially, he loses: his home, his mother, his girl, his cow, his money, his teeth, his eye, his thumb, his scalp, and his leg. Penultimately, he is a comedian's stooge in a vaudeville act, which indeed is what he is for Nathanael West. He is the true emblem of the American Dream of Success because he is at once crippled and stupid, and it is West himself who hits him over the head, repeatedly, with a rolled-up newspaper, in a vain effort to tell him that there is no such thing as a Yankee—as previously there had been no such thing as a Jew. But some people just never learn, and so West shoots him. And if at the very end Lemuel Pitkin is the hallowed martyr of the triumphant National Revolutionary party, that was to say that all of those Yankees out there probably would never learn.

A Cool Million was a cartoon of a novel.[10] *The Day of the Locust*, published in 1939, was much more novelistic than any of the previous novels: West invented characters of a certain depth, and he had a somewhat determinative plot in addition to a set of situations, and he had a protagonist who was not merely the butt of a jest. *The Day of the Locust* was also more distinctly autobiographical than any of the previous novels, as a matter of its circumstancing—the protagonist, Tod Hackett, is a set and costume designer in Hollywood, and West was now a screenwriter in Hollywood—and as a matter of its interiority: Tod Hackett thinks about others and about himself at a level of reflection which evidently was West's own. He did not have a funny name. He is a serious character.

And Hollywood was, seriously, the perfect summary metaphor for the main part of the materials of West's previous novels. Both as a dream dump and as California, it was the ultimate institutionalized fraud. Hollywood was not only the locale of deception, but the locale of truly cultural deception. It was a place in which everyone cooperated to the end of being adequately deceived. Actors become roles and caricatures of roles, as West several times pointed out, in order to meet the demands of an audience which itself has turned to Hollywood for the beauty and romance it needs and does not have. The audience is continuously disappointed, but then continuously turns to seek another and another figure of its dreaming. Hollywood is the place where everyone can be anything because everything is a fake, unto the houses which people inhabit and the clothes they wear. It is a place where pretense to identity has become more than identity, wherefore, for instance, a character who has happened really to have been a cowboy, transforms himself into a movie version of a cowboy.

Given West's exquisite knowledge of pretentions, Hollywood was the perfect object for his satirizing, but in fact what West wrote in *The Day of the Locust* was only in small part a revelation of Hollywood. Tod Hackett is indeed sent forth to be a satirist. He is a serious painter, in his spare time, who at least at the beginning of the novel acknowledges his masters to be Goya and Daumier. And within the first few paragraphs of the novel, West himself does a remarkably swift job of revealing both the lie and the desperation in the lying. On the other hand, Tod Hackett is implicated in that lying, and more intricately than perhaps West would have realized. Tod, we are told at the beginning, is "really a very complicated young man with a whole set of personalities, one inside the other like a nest of Chinese boxes,"[11] and while the novel does not then proceed to an exploration of his personalities, as the sentence would seem to promise, the ascription is important to the novel. The basic concept of "personality" in it—West's own, and without irony—is of something rigidified and reified and constructed, and it would follow that Tod's task, which in any event he does not pursue, would be to discover not a fluency of life within himself but the innermost box. Tod, too, that is to say, like everyone else around him, is self-encrusted in standardized versions of identity. And his real task, which is beyond his conscious knowing, is to escape from all of his imputed "personalities." Personality, with its inevitability of social definition, is a role and is the enemy.

And if that realization is not explicit in the pages of the novel, the passion to escape from all social prescriptions certainly is, and the method is the usual one, namely, sex and violence. Tod works throughout the novel on the large painting to be called *The Burning of Los Angeles*, which is to say that as a painter his ambition is extravagant beyond satire. He wants holocaust—literally, a total burning—which will be apocalypse—literally, a revelation and particularly of one's self. The novel ends with Tod lying in a police car, screaming in imitation of a siren, suggesting the hysterical—literally, the uterine—nature of his passion. Tod, moreover, is the appropriate intelligence of the novel because he is attuned to everybody else's yearning for the something which will destroy their personalities. Tod expends much effort in pursuit of Faye Greener, who has "platinum" hair and is a starlet and who is in other ways as well an ambulatory organization of clichés. He knows, as he says several times, that for the love of Faye Greener only rape will do: "Her invitation wasn't to pleasure, but to struggle, hard and sharp, closer to murder than to love. If you threw yourself on her, it would be like throwing yourself from the parapet of a skyscraper. You would do it with a scream." (271)

That is to say something about Tod's own habit of loving, probably beyond West's intention, but Tod is also right about Faye. She can be brought into original life only by some kind of undeniable assault. She is finally bedded by a Mexican who pits fighting cocks. And as with Faye, so with her father, an ex-vaudeville comic who has become an automaton of his various roles and who can be brought into a quietude of life only by death. And as with Faye's father, so with this novel's Candide—in this instance a young man from Iowa with unimpeachable midwestern credentials: he knows but one song, "The Star-Spangled Banner," he is named Homer Simpson, and he is a man whose impulses are so unaided by imagination that he might as well be dead. He is a pathetic stooge, but unlike, for instance, Sherwood Anderson's Wing Biddlebaum, from whom West freely borrowed in making the character, he is present on the page not merely so that he might be understood but also so that the way of his salvation might be indicated. He is betrayed and taunted, and finally a nasty little boy hits him in the face with a stone. At that point he jumps onto the back of the little boy, landing with both feet, and then jumps again. That is his one positive action in the novel, and is his life.

In *The Day of the Locust* West allowed himself a latitude for interpretation. Tod reflects on the meaning of his painting and therefore on the meaning of the novel. But what he sees is only a portion of what the novel finally says. In his final paragraphs of message in the novel, Tod discovers, as he has earlier, that the Hollywood personnel, including himself, are victims of that mob "of the people who come to California to die . . . all those poor devils who can only be stirred by the promise of miracles and then only to violence." (420) It is the expectations of the mob, which is to say the audience for the Hollywood dreams, which have made grotesques of Faye Greener and her father and of Tod himself to a degree, and some others. In fact, however, it was West who had created the roles for everybody, including the audience, and what was to be discovered was that, as usual, no roles contained a satisfactory reality. Only the violence, after the frustration of the acting of the roles, had the feel of a reality. Tod ends his discourse, prior to his screaming, by laying blame. The general action of the novel ends in a general riot.

There had been an occasion several years earlier when West had opined editorially that "in America violence is idiomatic."[12] He had been associate editor of the little magazine *Contact*, briefly, and therefore had temporarily been in a position to be a pundit. American writing, he said, had to contain more violence than an Englishman or a European would be likely to understand because in America there was so much more of it. The statement was self-evidently glib, nor could West bring any personal testimony to it. For most of his years he had lived a singularly protected life. But the statement was not unprovoked. Particularly, West was responding to a mention of *Contact* in the "Foreign Periodicals" section of the *Criterion*, in which the reviewer had said of a certain story—not West's own—that the thing was incredible, lacking what the reviewer called "an emotional description." And it must have been the case that, beyond the little desirability of advertising the accomplishments of his own magazine, West would have found in that comment and especially in the source of that comment still another instance of that certainty of cultural manner and that security of condescension to which Nathan Weinstein, the boy baron, had repeatedly and futilely pretended, and to which the only imaginable adequate response was violence unmitigated and total. Therein was his security.

eight

Black Boy and Native Son

Richard Wright became a spokesman, inevitably although not necessarily against his wishes. His audience was predominantly white, from beginning (discounting the audience for his juvenilia) to end, and in all goodwill it wanted spokesmanship from him. He had most of his learning in the actual making of literature in the years approximately 1927 to 1936, in Chicago, which is to say in a time and in a place in which social protest in literature was an orthodoxy. He achieved his first recognition—of a sort which he himself could recognize—in a milieu, moreover, which virtually prohibited any other kind of literary ambition: more than anyone else, and perhaps uniquely, Wright discovered himself through association with the John Reed Clubs, the local chapter of which he joined in 1933. The white folks there more than welcomed him. The club offered him editors, discussion, instructors, friends and publication—instant and international publication. Prior to this moment he had published two tales, both of them in black journals, neither of them having anything to do with plight or protest or politics; they were both of them bits of stagy Gothic horror, and he had published the first when he was sixteen years old.[1] Now, abruptly, for a period of about three years, 1933 to 1936, poems poured from him, and they were published in *Left Front*, which was the Chicago club's journal, and in Jack Conroy's *Anvil* and *New Masses* and *Midland Left* and *International Literature* and *Partisan Review*. The poems had such titles as "A Red Love Note," "I Am a Red Slogan," "Red Leaves of Red Books," "Rise and Live," "Strength," and "I Have Seen Black Hands." In fact in only a few of these poems did Wright take specifically black protest to be his subject-matter, but he did in this moment of his maximum learning take spokesmanship to be the proper form for poetry. Therein was the obvious importance of literary expression.

This early arena of his trying was evidently important to Wright to the point of being determinative, although in multiple and paradoxical ways. His major career would so indicate. The John Reed Clubs created his basic knowledge of the readers to whom he could write—not the great proletariat of the vision of the founder, Mike Gold, but the membership and friends of the John Reed Clubs. And the clubs gave him his conception of his materials, which happened to be not entirely native to him, and gave him his knowledge of what his circumstances demanded that he say, which constituted quite a different matter. It was a likelihood, as apparently Wright realized, that the local club was eager at once to provide him with the promise of a career and also to use him. So Wright said in the early 1940s, when he was writing his autobiography.[2] He was the club's conspicuous black, At the very beginning, Wright recalled, the editor of *Left Front* had told him that his poems were indeed crude, but "good for us." "We write articles about Negroes," he had said, "but we never see any Negroes."[3] In 1934, within a few months of his joining, Wright was elected executive secretary of the club, and as such, and having now some national standing within the organized left, in the same year he joined the Communist party. In later years Wright would repeatedly and in various voices slur and obfuscate and utterly deny the significance of his association with the Party, and he would recall—accurately, without doubt—instances of the Party's stupidity and arrogant boorishness in its treatment of him. Nonetheless, his major and best fiction was addressed to the organized left as he had known it, in its friendship and realism and hypocrisy and vulgarity.

In the early 1940s, in the book which would eventually be the second volume of his autobiography, Wright was already telling the tale of his disillusion with the Party. That book, *American Hunger*, was not to be published in its entirety until 1977, long after Wright's death, but during the 1940s he did print edited sections of it dealing with his leaving the Party: in a two-part essay in *Atlantic Monthly*, in 1944, called "I Tried to Be a Communist," and, in 1949, as his contribution to Richard Crossman's *The God That Failed*. He said in each of these instances of the same story that he had been on his way out almost as soon as he had entered. Since the point of his entry had been the John Reed Clubs, he was stunned by the decision of the Party to dissolve the clubs, which decision was being formulated as early as the summer of 1934 in accordance with the policies of the Popular Front. In general, and almost immediately, so he said, he was confronted by Party strategies which disvalued and virtually disallowed his writing. So soon as 1935 he was being slandered within the Party by the Party's chief theoretician of the black problem, presumably John P. Davis. It was said that he was a "'smuggler of reaction'" and a "'petty bourgeois degenerate.' '" In 1936, at a unit meeting, he had asked to be dropped from membership, but it was not the Party's way to allow anyone to resign. One had to be expelled. In either 1936 or 1937 the Party had prohibited him from marching in the May Day parade.[4]

On the other hand, as Wright did not bother to recall, when the Party had faced its greatest crises during the 1930s, namely, the Moscow Trials and the event of the Nazi-Soviet Pact, he had been one of the few of the acknowledged "intellectuals" who had been loyal. In 1938 he had signed a statement, appearing in the *Daily Worker*, in defense of the Trials.[5] In 1939 he had written an essay—which, however, he did not publish—not precisely in defense of the Pact, but in any event assailing those many who were fleeing the Party because of the Pact. His title for the essay was suggestive: "There Are Still Men Left." Not unlike his elder colleague Mike Gold, he had discovered that the issue was not the tactics of the Party, with which in this instance Wright in fact seemed to disagree, but courage and the grander vision. "The rightness or wrongness of a given set of tactical actions by the Communist Party," he had said, "does not strike me as being of any great ultimate importance. What does fasten my attention upon communist action is whether it overcomes settled and ready-made reality, whether it effectively pushes outward and extends the area of human feeling." And sometimes, he had said, he felt himself to be most attracted to the Party just when most other people were repelled, as at the present juncture. Those who remained among the "faithful" were true "rebels against the limits of life, the limits of experience as they know it."

> Just as Lenin turned from the men who went mystic after the failure of 1905, just as the Bolsheviks pushed on relentlessly after the first war and set up a dictatorship to retain power for the common masses . . . so the men who today stay do so because they are living more meaningfully (as they *must!*). They tense themselves for another push. Those who left make it easier.[6]

He did not publish that statement perhaps because after all it was too mystical, but in fact he had participated very actively in the brief season of the Party's pacifism. He had served as a vice-president of the front group called "American Peace Mobilization." He had made speeches and written articles upon request.

He did leave the Party sometime in 1942, although without public announcement. He was now a famous man and therefore perhaps capable of an independence not available to him just a few years before, and now apparently he did believe that tactics mattered. In any event, the general issue which prompted his leaving had little to do with ideology and nothing whatsoever to do with a rebellion, in any wonderful metaphysical sense, against the limits of life. Simply, the Party was busy with the war and seemed no longer to be concerned with—nay, seemed to be opposed to—actions having to do with black causes. The *Daily Worker* was advising its readers, for instance, that a lynching in Mississippi, in 1942, was wrong because it was an act of sabotage against the war effort. The Party opposed a march on Washington, organized by A. Philip Randolph, to protest discrimination and segregation in armaments factories and in the military services. Wright was pained and enraged, and he knew that he was more black than red.[7]

But that was something which really he would have seemed to have known from the beginning, and something which, moreover, while no doubt it had involved him in ambiguities, had provided him with his essential subject. He had been telling the tale of black folks to white folks who were also red, whose expectations and whose errors of stereotyping he could at once exploit and correct. In leaving the Party, that is what he left, and indeed for the remaining eighteen years of his life he would seem to have been engaged largely in either talking back over his shoulder to the people of the Party, as in his testimonies to his disillusion and in the accounts of the actualities of his own life prior to and outside of the Party, or roaming in search of some kind of new concordance of audience and personal authority, as in the schematic, very French existentialism of *The Outsider,* in 1953, or in the punditry of his series of statements about the rising of the colored peoples of Africa and Asia: *Black Power,* in 1954, and *The Color Curtain,* in 1956, and *White Man, Listen!* in 1957. His achieved subject had been a black peasantry in America, in the rural South and the ghettoized North, about which progressive white people wanted to learn something and about which they thought that they knew something, and about which they did not know.

Wright had found his authority not indeed in his superior personal knowledge of that peasantry—he was not himself a peasant, and he had had to do research—but in his perception of his being truly an outsider: what he truly knew, according to the testimony of the fiction, was the necessity of his inventing some kind of a certified origin for himself. In the circumstances in general of his wanting to be a writer in America, and in the circumstances especially of his having readers who were all too willing to make him a black writer, he had had to discover a cultural definiteness by virtue of which his blackness was an assertion and had a uniqueness and was not merely a local symbol of victimization, serviceable primarily to others. And it was that perception of his need, and not necessarily the blackness, which had in fact related him to a community.

The particular audience may or may not have understood him. Party considerations often enough encumbered understanding. Wright's kind of engagement with the particular audience, on the other hand, paradoxically associated him not only with that audience but with all of the other writers of his moment who were attempting to fabricate a cultural identity. For Wright the matter of color would inevitably be basic to cultural definition, but in his apparent realization of his need in the first place for creating some kind of home place in which he might have residence and which he might register against competing plausibilities of culture in America—in that matter, as a writer, he was not at all a member of a minority. Like the many others, moreover—including ones so otherwise opposite in temperament and situation as, for instance, Allen Tate and Nathanael West, and ones so similar as, for instance, his friends Jack Conroy and James T. Farrell—his relationship to the cultural materials with which he could work was really quite equivocal. Tate had not been able simply to inherit the antebellum South. Farrell had had to make a myth of Irish Catholicism in America, which at the same time he was busy rejecting. Wright was not an exemplary black American, even presuming the existence in America of an exemplary black American—and, both lacking and needing a sure knowledge of his cultural difference, he was in the mainstream.

Like the so many others, he both was and was not what he ought to have been for the purposes of glib representation. Almost opportunely he had in fact been born on a plantation in Mississippi and was the son of an illiterate sharecropper. On the other hand, his immediate experience of the sharecropping black South had come to an end in 1911, when he was three years old, at which time he had been moved to Natchez to live with his mother's family, and how little he actually knew of that rural black South which was to be the locale of his fiction prior to *Native Son* was to be indicated directly by the fact that when he came came to write autobiographically about his childhood, in *Black Boy*, he began with the fourth year of his age. In *Black Boy* Wright was, among some number of other things, a streetwise urchin.

But then he was not quite that, either. *Black Boy*, which he wrote in the 1940s after fame had come to him, was of course a version of himself. This volume of the autobiography was primarily a portrait, by an acknowledged artist, of the artist as a young man: quite after the manner of Joyce, Wright recorded the dawning of consciousness despite suppressions. He testified to the anguish of his childhood. He had seldom had enough to eat. His father had deserted the family, and his mother was ill, and he had lived in too many places on the charity of too many of his maternal relatives and also for a while in an orphanage, and he had never known a stable home life. He had been surrounded by and subjected to a constancy of irrational violence. His attempted expressions of individuality had been suppressed automatically, reflexively, not only by white folk but by blacks as well, especially including the members of his family. He had lived in fear, yearning for flight. That, he said in effect, was the truth of what it was to be a Black Boy in America, and that life, almost although not quite entirely unremitted by any charm or any lightsome moments, constituted his credentials. He had become a writer, so he directly suggested, because of the something within him which impelled him to fight back: *Black Boy* begins with an episode in which the four-year-old Richard sets fire to his house, and ends with the nineteen-year-old Richard setting off for Chicago armed with his sudden discovery that words could be weapons. Particularly (and like numbers of other young would-be writers in the South), he had discovered Mencken: "Yes, this man was fighting, fighting with words. He was using words as a weapon, using them as one would use a club. Could words be weapons? Well, yes, for here they were. Then, maybe, perhaps, I could use them as a weapon? No. It frightened me. I read on and what amazed me was not what he said, but how on earth anybody had the courage to say it."[8] He himself had had to struggle even to attain literacy, and when once earlier, in his sixteenth year, he had dared to compose a story, his companions had been suspicious and his family had accused him of doing the devil's work. No doubt that these others had indeed sensed that written words could be a weapon. Particularly, so Wright suggested, literary imagination was a behavior which escaped the community's censorship and which therefore was feared because it might well upset the complex, tenuous balance of relationship between blacks and whites.

Black Boy justified Richard Wright, the writer, by making a coherence of the harshnesses by which he had been created. Having had such a life, he had a truth to tell to his goodwilled but ignorant readers.

That coherence had had to be purchased, however, at the cost of some editing and some shifts of emphasis and some suppressions of his own. There were other salient facts of his life, aside from the horrors, which would not have served his purposes had he allowed them any prominence, for they would have—needlessly—modified his claim to

being an exemplary Black Boy. In the text Wright's mother is a cook in
the kitchens of the white folks—when she is able to work at all. In life,
as Wright did not say in the text, she had also been a schoolteacher, in
the years prior to and just after her marriage, and that fact must have
had some influence on young Richard by way of establishing not only
an acceptance but an expectation of literacy. By the standards set forth
by the place and the time and, of course, by the conditions of race in
the South, his mother would seem to have been a learned woman. By
the same standards, moreover, almost all of the members of this family
with which he had struggled, sometimes violently, were persons who
had had some claim to achievement or to what should have been
recognized to be a consequentiality. There were eight uncles and aunts.
One of the uncles had gone to sea, and Wright had never known him,
but each of the others had had a kind of distinction beyond caste and
class. Two others among the uncles had been schoolteachers, and one
of these two was a Methodist minister in a town in Ohio during the time
of Wright's childhood. The other was out of work, and he is portrayed
in *Black Boy* as being one of the special villains of Wright's childhood,
but in terms which suggest that what Wright considered to be a drama
of tyranny and victimization was not always quite so raw a matter as he
otherwise indicated. Uncle Thomas was a failure—he was temporarily
employed as a chair-stuffer—and that was held against him. His major
fault of character was his insistence on a punctiliousness of respectful
manners. And he in particular had been critical of Wright's juvenile
efforts to compose fiction, but on grounds which were after all literary,
although Wright did not emphasize the matter. He had been contemptuous, in Wright's recollection, but not appalled. Richard's story,
he had said, had no point, and he did not like the title, *The Voodoo of
Hell's Half-Acre*.

And there had been two aunts who were also schoolteachers, one
of them—with whom, again, Wright particularly fought—having the
quite unusual credential of a completed secondary-school education.
One uncle, in whose home Wright had resided for a while, was a
contracting carpenter and seems absolutely to have been well-to-do.
The grandmother, according to accounts other than Wright's own,
seems to have been the dominant member of the family. She was
illiterate, and therefore of course she was not likely to have nurtured
the literary ambitions of young Richard when he came to have such
ambitions. She was also very religious, and in an odd and discomforting mode: within a mostly Baptist population, she was a strict
Seventh-Day Adventist, and she enforced a regimen of prayer and
other observation which of course would have been irritating for any

young boy. But it must have made a great difference to this young boy's knowledge of his definition in the world that his grandmother was, first of all, white, except as a matter of technicality in the codes of the South, and that she was not merely, severely respectable, but that she was respected, among both whites and blacks. She was a midwife-nurse. When her own family had settled in Natchez, just prior to the turn of the century, she had been an assistant to a white doctor in the town. The house she lived in and which the boy Richard had set afire was located, according to Wright's biographer Michel Fabre, in "the neighborhood reserved at that time for the best mulatto society of the city, where, for instance, the white aristocrats used to establish their mistresses and the colored bourgeoisie aspired to live."[9] Later, in considerably lesser surroundings, she was still "*Mrs*. Wilson," and never anybody's "Auntie."

Again, the purposes of *Black Boy*—polemical, cultural, and literary—required that Wright would recall that the oppression of blacks by whites in the South had been systematic, automatic, and continuous. To learn how to be a Black Boy in the South had been to learn the strategies of being afraid of whites. Among whites, only an occasional misplaced northerner might, tentatively, have signaled a feeling of common humanity. But Wright's own, actual experience had seemingly not been either so unmitigated or so simple. He recorded the murder, by whites, of one of his uncles by marriage. He recorded several instances of random, jesting cruelty on the part of whites. He recorded a great many instances of the servile proprieties practiced by blacks, along with the subterfuges—petty thefts, for the most part—by which they attempted to deny their servility. On the other hand, in this quite detailed account of fifteen years of his childhood and adolescence, Wright did not mention the fact that for almost two years—his fifteenth through his seventeenth, when certainly he was of an age to have realizations—he had worked for a very kindly white family, to whom, according to testimony he was later to give to one of his biographers, he had felt free to address his problems and in whose home he had found an understanding better than that of his own family.[10]

Black Boy was the work of a writer who was engaged in making an assertion of his credibility as a writer, and credibility in his case as in that of the many others of his moment would not accommodate the confusions of the full truth. Wright had read H. L. Mencken and, consequently, hated the white man with an undying venom.

Following upon this resolved version of his childhood in several southern towns—Natchez, Jackson, Elaine (Arkansas), Memphis—literary propriety demanded that the North would signify uncertainties and instabilities, and losses. And so it was. In the penultimate paragraph of *Black Boy* Wright had written:

> Yet, deep down, I knew that I could never really leave the South, for my feelings had already been formed by the South, for there had been slowly instilled into my personality and consciousness, black though I was, the culture of the South. So, in leaving, I was taking a part of the South to transplant in alien soil, to see if it could grow differently, if it could drink of new and cool rains, bend in strange winds, respond to the warmth of other suns, and, perhaps, to bloom. (228)

Arriving in Chicago in the first paragraph of the next installment of the autobiography, *American Hunger,* Wright said: "My first glimpse of the flat black stretches of Chicago depressed and dismayed me, mocked all my fantasies. Chicago seemed an unreal city whose mythical houses were built of slabs of black coal wreathed in palls of gray smoke, houses whose foundations were sinking slowly in the dank prairie." (1) "Everything," he said, "seemed makeshift, temporary. I caught an abiding sense of insecurity in the personalities of the people around me." (3) Indeed, at this point he might have been Faulkner's Quentin Compson, hating the South and knowing well the evil that was in it, but being nonetheless the true heir of his knowable culture.

The whole of the strategy of his subsequent literary and political life consisted of his entering various mainstreams with a retained and aggressive sense of his own difference. Arriving in Chicago in 1927 with literary ambitions, he would inevitably have been attracted to the organized political left and especially to its organized activity for the making of literature. The John Reed Club provided him with a companionship, which of course he needed, and also with a paradigm of cultural integration. The details of the route of his entry into the party aside, it was apparently the case that he became a Communist quite willingly and gratefully, and for essentially the same reason that, for instance, Henry Roth, the emigré from the Lower East Side, was to join the Party. For Roth the Party was to be the larger thing with which to identify beyond Judaism. Wright had been impressed, so he said in *American Hunger,* by Stalin's *The National and Colonial Question:* "Stalin's book showed how diverse minorities could be welded into unity. . . . Of all the developments in the Soviet Union, the method by which scores of backward peoples had been led to unity on a national scale was what had enthralled me." (81–82) (In making this statement, it may be noted, Wright was, in the immediate context, denying accusations of Trotskyist deviationism. He had been a loyalist and not a deviator.) The Party had been attractive to him, as he also said, because it had seemed to him "that here at last in the realm of revolutionary expression was where Negro experience could find a home, a functioning value and role." (63)

But despite a most generous loyalty, he had not found that the Party was a home, although it did provide him with a functioning value and role. He was, precisely, different. He was different from the true believers among the other black Communists, who patronized him and despised him for being an intellectual. He was different from the white Communists in being black, insistently and from the beginning and prior to ideology. Except perhaps at the level of theoretics, the Party did not integrate him, and could not, as Wright seems to have known, because the Party in itself was culturally a mess. It was at least as foreign a thing as Richard Wright, wherefore it followed that blacks who tried to be good Communists ended by being ridiculous, not in their ideas, necessarily, but in their postures and bearing and manner. He had had his first glimpse of communism in action, he said in *American Hunger,* in his early days in Chicago. He had taken to visiting Washington Park and listening to the Communist speakers, and he had been particularly baffled and angered by the black Communists because of the way they acted—which was like people who actually were Communists. They were "deliberately careless in their personal appearance, wearing their shirt collars turned in to make V's at their throats, wearing their caps—they wore caps because Lenin had worn caps—with the visors turned backward, tilted upward at the nape of their necks." He was offended by their aping gestures—thumbs in their suspenders or left hands in their shirt bosoms. And their speech—not necessarily what they said—was grotesque:

> In speaking they rolled their "r's" in Continental style, pronouncing "party" as "parrrtee," stressing the last syllable, having picked up the habit from white Communists. "Comrades" became "cumrrrades," and "distribute," which they had known how to pronounce all their lives, was twisted into "distrrribuuute," with the accent on the last instead of the second syllable, a mannerism which they copied from Polish Communist immigrants who did not know how to pronounce the word. (37–38)

Here, in effect under the sign of the unity of backward peoples on a national scale, were southern Blacks trying to be eastern Europeans—eastern Europeans who themselves, as Wright must soon have known, were trying to assert their own distinction as Americans.

He was not going to be one of the Communist party's captive blacks, and he was not going to be a black Communist; logically enough, his "functioning value and role" was to be discovered in his being a black representative to those who would listen to him, who in the first instance were those whites in the Communist party who wrote articles about blacks but never saw any.

He read and he wrote. In 1935, when he was employed by the Illinois Federal Writers' Project and thus had an unaccustomed amount of time for himself, he was writing the stories which would eventually be collected in *Uncle Tom's Children*. When the first of them, "Big Boy Leaves Home," was published in 1936 in the anthology *The New Caravan* edited by Lewis Mumford and others, Wright abruptly had a larger audience, but prior to the publication he had been presenting readings of the story to people he knew, and in any event the writing of the stories had been done in a milieu which was defined by what was now his familiar audience. He was by 1935 a somewhat established writer on the left, in Chicago. It was in 1935, according to the accounts in *The God That Failed* and *American Hunger,* that he had been particularly both slandered and solicited by the Party. He was in this year suspected of the heresy of nationalism, among some other things, because he had been discovered taking notes on the life of a certain member of the Party, David Pointdexter, who was a southern black and who was himself accused of nationalism. Wright claimed to be innocent, but he seems in fact to have been fascinated by the tales Pointdexter told him, and those tales had much to do with the daring of southern blacks and with the tricks they played upon whites, and therefore certainly implied at least a troublesome differentiation between blacks and whites.[11] Drawing upon Pointdexter's stories, and perhaps upon those of some other black Communists, Wright was going to compose an account of the typicalities of race. "I felt," said Wright in the autobiography, "that if I could get his story I would make known some of the difficulties inherent in the adjustment of a folk people to an urban environment" (78)—which was to say, at the level of Party rhetoric, that he was going to tell the whites he knew something about the blacks whom they thought that they knew.

Drawing upon Pointdexter's stories, Wright used the materials which became "Big Boy Leaves Home." That tale was perhaps open to a variety of moralizing interpretations. Eleanor Roosevelt, for one, wrote a letter to Wright when the story appeared in *Uncle Tom's Children,* to say that she admired the collection and that what had struck her about "Big Boy Leaves Home" was the fact that "little things bring such tragic results," in this instance "a silly woman's fear—really an accident in almost every case that could be so easily understood if every one kept his head"[12] But clearly what Wright had described had nothing to do either with "the adjustment of a folk people to an urban environment," except perhaps in the most ironic sense of adjustment, or with the necessity for people's keeping their heads, except perhaps in the most literal sense. The fourteen-year-old hero of the tale leaves his home in the South in order to escape being lynched. He has witnessed murders and lynching. He has also committed a murder, which perhaps technically was an accident, but such an accident as it is the point of the story to reveal is the logical expression of the relationship between whites and blacks in the South. The tale begins in pastoral with four young boys gamboling and singing in the woods, and in their folk way also playing the dozens, but it moves very quickly toward exploitation of quite another kind of folk material, namely, that of white folk. The young boys trespass across the line which has been established by white folks, and one thing quickly leads to another. They trespass literally by using a swimming hole which is the property of a white man. They are naked, they are surprised by a white woman, they try to reach their clothing, the white woman thinks rape—the story does not say so, but of course it need not—and two of the boys are immediately shot by the woman's companion, and a third is lynched a few pages later. In the struggle at the swimming hole, Big Boy has shot the white man, *but he escapes.*

It is Big Boy's getting away that is important—page by page, it was on that point that the story concentrated its energies. Big Boy is obviously a victim of the southern mythology, but his very name suggests that he is not totally a victim. During the course of the story he has a very bad day, but not totally an unprofitable one. He has learned several things: by crossing the line, he has certified the existence of the line, and by engaging family and friends in his escape, as he does, he has further and more clearly established the division between whites and blacks as a division of communities, not merely of persons, and he has learned both the necessity and the justice of getting away with murder. During his flight he entertains fantasies of grandiose and well-publicized revenge: if the lynch mob were to find him, where he lies huddled in a cave, and if he had a shotgun, then he would shoot one after another, and the newspapers would say "NIGGER KILLS DOZEN OF MOB BEFO LYNCHED!" or maybe "TRAPPED NIGGER SLAYS TWENTY BEFO KILLED!" and he smiles at the notion.[13] In a later incident he is in fact discovered by a dog, which he strangles, and Wright intended the singularly brutal scene to be symbolic—he had invented it and inserted it into the story after learning some techniques of symbolic representation from a reading of Henry James.[14] "Big Boy Leaves Home" was a shocking and ominous story, or would have been were it not for the intransigent goodwill of Wright's readers. It transformed the confusion of racial relationship as Wright had known it into the indubitableness of violence, and then went one step further. Big Boy, equipped with his experiences, leaves home, which is to say the South which Wright was to say that he would never forget, and, in leaving, is coming North—and so much for the probabilities of "the adjustment of a folk people to an urban environment."

The four stories plus a preface, and then later the five stories which were to be included in *Uncle Tom's Children*, were composed separately, but nonetheless they had a singleness of condition and apparent intention. (The first edition of the book was published in 1938. The second, expanded edition appeared in 1940.) In 1937 Wright moved to New York and met some new people, who must have implied to him the same demands as those he had known in Chicago. Despite the later suggestions to the contrary, and perhaps despite his deepest wishes, he was still an active member of the Party. For a period of about seven months in 1937, until he was able to get an appointment to the New York Writers' Project, he had an official, paid position with the Party, as director of the Harlem Bureau of the *Daily Worker*. And the fiction he was writing or had recently written had, still, its peculiar relevance for people who were too anxious at once to hear from him and to define him, and to whom he could be a black representative.

The stories were fabricated. They deal with peasant materials, borrowing from an available mythology which both Wright and his audience could think to be substantial. Members of the Communist party in America had always wanted to believe that America owned a peasantry. (It is said that a banner borne in one of the Party demonstrations in the early days had beckoned to the putative masses with the words, "Workers and Peasants of Brooklyn, Unite!")[15] Here, perhaps, in the black South, was the real thing. The stories created a cultural artifact for an audience and an author who needed one. And Wright went further toward satisfying desire by creating blacks, in community, who at once were victims of whites and who learned lessons in militance. That was the essential plot line of each of the stories. In "Down by the Riverside," the second story in the collection, during a flood a black peasant who is burdened with his own family crisis finds among whites in this time of universal trouble not understanding but provocation beyond measure, and he kills and is ready to kill again, and is killed. In "Long Black Song" a black peasant kills the white slicker who has raped his wife, and at the end stands ready to kill everyone else. In "Fire and Cloud," the only one of the tales in which there is a beating but no actual killing, a black minister dares and conquers the white rulers of the town by leading a Communist demonstration. In "Bright and Morning Star" a black mother avenges the death of her son—who is a Communist organizer—by shooting one of his lynchers.

But each of these stories was relevant for an audience by way of being also admonitory, to the point of being antagonistic, for which reason perhaps the official left received the collection with some moderation of enthusiasm. In the *Daily Worker* review of the 1938 edition, Alan Calmer liked the fact that "the book is laid in the locale of lynching and serfdom" and dealt "with characters who are not meek Uncle Toms but a courageous, fighting lot," but he felt that after all the book did not "dig down" far enough.[16] But the book did dig down so far as to undermine the Party position, precisely by dealing in representations in black and white. In the final story of the collection, which had not been included in the 1938 edition, Wright's tendency to heretical advices indeed became very clear. The mother in "Bright and Morning Star" is as sympathetic to her son's Communist activities as in her antique and peasant way she can possibly be. She might be Maxim Gorki's *Mother*. But in her antique and peasant way she is in fact more knowing than her son. She realizes as her son does not, or on principle will not admit, that the presence of whites in the local Communist organization presents a danger. There is a traitor in the group, and she knows that he must be white. And he is, and she shoots him.

Native Son was published in early 1940, and Wright, at the age of thirty-one, was suddenly a famous man. *Native Son* was a Book-of-the-Month Club selection. It was praised by *Time* and *Newsweek*. Wright's name was inscribed on the Wall of Fame at the New York World's Fair. It was said widely that he had written the black *Grapes of Wrath*.

There was obvious, albeit pleasant, irony in the range of the novel's success, however, for *Native Son* was much more ambitious and a much more specific book than Steinbeck's ecological parable. Bigger Thomas was Big Boy come to Chicago with all of his innocence and his ominousness intact, ready to undergo his frightening adjustment to an urban environment. The book's subject was not social plight, except as a kind of accepted fact of background, but cultural individuation involving murder, in the North as it had in the South. The book was about the relationship of blacks to whites, with Wright stressing the reality of the color line just at the place where it would have seemed to be most obscure, among liberals and Communists. Quite like the stories of *Uncle Tom's Children,* prior to *Native Son,* and like *Black Boy,* forthcoming, it created a version of black life in America for the sake of people who thought that they knew, and were sympathetic, and did not know, and if at the end of the novel Bigger Thomas does extend a friendly hand, it is he who is making the gesture.

Native Son cannot and does not begin in pastoral, but in fact it begins in a mode which is not altogether different. Bigger is at home, albeit that his home is a horribly crowded and rat-infested tenement flat, and in his first action in the novel he demonstrates perfect competence in dealing with his environment. He kills a rat. It is passingly a matter of social exposé that the slum dwellings occupied by blacks in Chicago are infested, but so they are, and Bigger easily does something which it is necessary for him to do and which it is expected that he will do. The novel begins, that is to say, with Bigger in his place, within a known community, and therefore in a condition of certitude. The number of brief episodes which constitute the beginning movement of the novel say essentially the same thing, although with foreshadowing ironies attached and with some prosy warnings by the author. Bigger knew, says Wright, "that the moment he allowed himself to feel to his fullness how [his family] lived, the shame and misery of their lives, he would be swept out of himself with fear and despair. . . . He knew that the moment he allowed what his life meant to enter fully into his consciousness, he would either kill himself or someone else."[17] Nonetheless, as he and his friend Gus "play 'white,'" and as they watch an airplane and want to be aviators, and as Bigger and his pals go to the movies, and even as they contemplate robbing Blum's Delicatessen, we may know that Bigger's life, while it is restricted and defined by the power of whites all around, is meanwhile safe and stable within itself. The brief number of episodes at the beginning compose a ritual in which Bigger is fully a participant and even something of a leader. The one truly discordant datum within these opening scenes is in the fact that Bigger is not actually a boy in the time of gamboling, but is twenty years old and is at or past the age when he must move on.

It is Bigger's exemplary misfortune that, leaving the ghetto, he comes to be among whites who are well disposed and who are anxious, in some varying ways and degrees, to solve the Negro problem. In all of the remainder of the long novel, villainy is in fact correlated not with amounts of white racism, but the opposite. It is the niceness of some very nice and also very vulnerable people that drives Bigger to murder. while those few characters who should obviously be his major enemies—the cynical detective, Britten, and the state's attorney, Buckley, and the anonymous newspaper reporters who suggest that he is an ape—are not more than incidental presences in Bigger's narrative. Bigger's employer, Mr. Dalton, on the other hand, with his vague and certainly inadequate but nevertheless at least token awareness of the troubles of Bigger's people, does qualify for villainy. His awareness is limited, however, and by so much the novel absolves him, by dispensing with him. Mrs. Dalton is the more important in determining Bigger's actions and fate because she is more actively engaged in trying to do good. She has "a very deep interest in colored people." (41) She wishes to confound the whole of the history of the relationship between the races by offering Bigger kindness and manifest confidence. She wants to send Bigger to night school, thus perhaps to raise him up from slavery. And she is blind, and, more pointedly, she is a purveyor of blindness. She is "a white blur" and "a flowing white presence," but for whom Bigger would have been safe at the levels of both the action of the story and the symbology of the story. It is Mrs. Dalton who invites Bigger to disregard what he knows is the reality of the color line.

The more direct responsibility for Bigger's actions and fate lies, of course, with Mary Dalton, whom he will murder, and with her friend Jan Erlone, whom not without reason he will try to blame for the murder. They are sweet-tempered and rather playful young Communists, who in their utter ignorance totally and willfully attempt to eliminate the color line. They will not treat the chauffeur of the Dalton household as though he were a chauffeur. They insist upon entering Bigger's cultural life. At Ernie's Kitchen Shack, where with all high principle of goodwill they are intruders, they play black, and Jan goes so far as to make an attempt at the lingo of the place. Their gestures toward common humanity are grotesque and, as the event turns out, portentous. They are the major culprits of the novel, at the basic level of the plotting of the novel—had they not forced Bigger to be companionable against all of his instincts, then the initial murder would not have happened—and they are appropriately guilty because they are whites who, in all privileged arrogance, think that they know and who do not know.

There was a message here which was addressed to some people more particularly than to others. With whatever ambivalences, Wright, as he was writing *Native Son*, was a faithful and active member of the Party. There can be little doubt that as he was writing, he had certain people and relationships in mind. Bigger, first of all, was a reincarnated Big Boy, whom he had already found to be useful, and he was a mix of several Black Boys whom he had known in the South, as Wright himself pointed out in his essay "How 'Bigger' Was Born." This Bigger had in all of his preceding identities been a young man who had been, simply, bigger than others, and a bully, and in his relationships with whites, when he had had any, had been a "bad nigger." [18] In this novel this Bigger, who was more black than Wright, was sent forth to meet Mary Dalton and Jan Erlone, who were not just anybody. "Mary Dalton" was in fact the Party name of one of the officials whom the New York Communists had sent to Chicago. It would have been most unlikely that in creating "Jan Erlone,' Wright would not have had in mind the young painter named Jan Wittenber who had been a Chicago Communist and who had been the person who had initially interested Wright in the John Reed Club. According to his biographers, Wright had liked Wittenber and had heartily disliked "Mary Dalton," [19] and it is not to be thought that Wright's invocation of the two was merely spiteful or personal, but together they did stand, as in the novel, for the kind of principle of cultural integration which Wright could not help but find attractive, and which was in the practice a denial of cultural identity.

The novel ends not far from where it began. Bigger has committed murder, twice, and in a thematics clearly borrowed from Dostoevski he has discovered self and freedom. "In all of his life," says Wright in Bigger's behalf, "these two murders were the most meaningful things that had ever happened to him." "He was living, truly and deeply, no matter what others might think, looking at him with their blind eyes. Never had he had the chance to live out the consequences of his actions; never had his will been so free as in this night and day of fear and murder and flight." (203) And at the very end, in jail and facing execution, Bigger says approximately the same thing in his own voice: "'What I killed for must've been good!' Bigger's voice was full of frenzied anguish. 'It must have been good! When a man kills, it is for something. . . . I didn't know I was really alive in this world until I felt things hard enough to kill for 'em.'" (358)

But the community, white and black, has after all paid a dear price for Bigger's self-contentment, and were his moments of self-discovery less circumstanced, then the message would have been glibly literary, at best, or, at worst, morally fatuous. Bigger has from the beginning, however, been not merely a self in search of proofs in his unique existence. He has been a Black Boy, who at the beginning of his story was a Black Boy without doubt and who latterly has had to assert the distinction of his blackness, finally at the cost of adopting—by his sympathetic author's manipulation, of course—the most frightening of available white clichés of blackness. Within a context not of warfare but of niceness in which all things are blurred, he has done good by being a bad nigger.

The irony is reduplicated in the fact that this bad nigger is said to be a native son.

Conclusion

Enough.

I have wanted to say that the American literature of this century has been created by people who have known themselves to be marginal Americans, sometimes by an act of imagination and sometimes by right of birth. The cultural fact of America has consequently been either rejected or, repeatedly, created—but never merely accepted because in an abruptly urbanized, industrialized, radicalized, and ghettoized society, there has been no American culture available for mere acceptance. Approximately at the moment of the turn of the new century, America vanished, and that fact created a fine opportunity both for some literary people who had lived in the place for generations and for some greater number of literary people who felt themselves to be just arriving. History presented both kinds of Americans with a problem for exploitation: Richard Wright equally with, say, T. S. Eliot, discovered motif and drama in his construction of a home place for himself, or of a tradition, and hence in his assertion of a cultural right and a cultural authority.

For both old Americans and new Americans the presented problem extended beyond literature to include social vision and political expression—or, to be more precise, history created a situation which suggested to everyone that "both politics and the arts must derive their power from a common center of energy." Allen Tate's statement, uttered in 1936, may or may not contain transcendent truth, but it was urgently true in the year of its utterance and it was generally and informatively true for American writers, as I have tried to indicate, in the years approximately of the first half of this century.

In my attempt to locate the category which would express at once and all together the sense of and the striving for roots and tradition and manners and class and art and politics, I have no doubt too often repeated the word "culture," but not without knowing that the word itself is both vague and various in its meanings and that it has been the subject of important dispute. My dictionary advises me that "culture" in the sociological sense means, merely, "the sum total of ways of living built up by a group of human beings which is transmitted from one generation to another," and therefore advises me implicitly not to fret about how much is included in the sum total, nor about what, if anything, is left out, and advises me implicitly not to worry about the processes and the ways by which "the sum total of ways of living built up by a group of human beings" is actually built up and then transmitted. Of course it has suited my convenience not to pursue these matters. Had I done so, however, I suspect that I would have discovered that "culture" in the period and place which I have taken for my subject was still another metaphor, without any absolute meaning but interesting as an indication of the attempt by the users of the word to comprehend a meaning.

I have heretofore referred to the influential essay "Reality in America," first published in 1940, in which the critic Lionel Trilling attacked Vernon L. Parrington's *Main Currents in American Thought*. Trilling said: "Parrington's characteristic weakness as a historian is suggested by his title, for the culture of a nation is not truly figured in the image of the current. A culture is not a flow, nor even a confluence; the form of its existence is struggle, or at least debate—it is nothing if not a dialectic." And had I pursued the matter—I would simply have agreed with Trilling up to this point. But Trilling went on to say, "And in any culture there are likely to be certain artists who contain a large part of the dialectic within themselves, their meaning and power lying in their contradictions; they contain within themselves, it may be said, the very essence of the culture, and the sign of this is that they do not submit to serve the ends of any one ideological group or tendency." Had I pursued the matter, I would have wanted to argue that this notation toward the definition of culture had meaning in itself *only* as an expression of ideology or tendency— in this instance, literary anti-Stalinism. In later years, and for more than three decades, the word "culture" was to have a singular importance for Trilling and was to secure quite other connotations, but in this early instance he was speaking—so I would have argued—from within a problem and not with lexicographical prerogative. He, too, was asserting his "cultural" authority by drawing upon the resources of his felt marginality to "culture." Lionel Trilling, son of an immigrant Jewish tailor, wrote the standard study of Matthew Arnold, apostle of culture.

Had I wished to carry this study forward in time, I think that I would not have lacked for materials. I might have contemplated the long career of the poet Louis Zukofsky, beginning with his participation in the invention of "Objectivism" circa 1931, and concentrating on his later, strange identification with Henry Adams. I would have contemplated the career of Delmore Schwartz, whose knowledge of his cultural marginality was without doubt crucial to his accomplishment. I would have considered Norman Mailer as the fabricator of *An American Dream*, and Saul Bellow, who yawped—at a fictive remove, to be sure—"I am an American, Chicago born—Chicago, that somber city—and go at things as I have taught myself, free-style, and will make the record in my own way." And I would have considered the case of Lionel Trilling.

Certainly I would not have claimed anything more imperative than one perception, among many other possible ones, of a progress of the making of American literature in the twentieth century. Had I carried my account forward to the moment of this writing, I would have suggested only that it is possible to see that our literary history has had a coherence: we began with the opportunities afforded by cultural chaos, and latterly we have improved upon our inheritance.

Notes

CHAPTER ONE

1. T. S. Eliot, "Mr. Barnes and Mr. Rowse," *Criterion* 8 (July 1929): 683, 690–91.

2. Ibid., pp. 689–90.

3. John Gould Fletcher, "Recent Books," *Criterion* 6 (Sept. 1927): 265–66.

4. F. S. Flint (trans.), *Criterion* 4 (Apr. 1926): 224–43.

5. The subscription list of the *Criterion* never exceeded eight hundred. See John D. Margolis, *T. S. Eliot's Intellectual Development 1922–1939* (Chicago: University of Chicago Press, 1972), p. 34.

6. T. S. Eliot, "Swinburne as Poet," *Selected Essays: 1917–1932* (New York: Harcourt, Brace & Co., 1932), p. 285.

7. Ezra Pound, "A Retrospect," in T. S. Eliot (ed.), *Literary Essays of Ezra Pound* (1918; New York: New Directions, 1968), p. 3.

8. T. E. Hulme, "Romanticism and Classicism," *Speculations* (1924; New York: Harvest Books, n.d.), p. 122.

9. "A Retrospect," p. 12.

10. T. S. Eliot, "Tradition and the Individual Talent," *Selected Essays: 1917–1932*, p. 4.

11. Ibid., pp. 5, 10.

12. He certainly would have read the review by John Gould Fletcher, *supra*, of Harold Laski's *Communism*, and perhaps he had looked at the book itself. Eliot's *Criterion* editorial for July 1929 was a response to two essays which had appeared side by side in the immediately prior issue of the magazine, one by Mr. Barnes on fascism and the other by Mr. Rowse on communism. See A. L. Rowse, "The Literature of Communism: Its Origin and Theory," *Criterion* 8 (April 1929): 422–36. In the postscript to *After Strange Gods*, published in 1934, Eliot refers to John MacMurray, *The Philosophy of Communism*.

13. "Mr. Barnes and Mr. Rowse," p. 688.

14. It should be said that my purpose here is to establish the political tendency of a literary generation, not reductively and half a century too late to serve up an indictment. Among the major modernist writers, only Pound devoted a substantial amount of energy to formal political spokesmanship, and it might be argued that just by the amount that Pound shifted his energies to political spokesmanship, he was authentically crazy. Certainly it is to be borne

in mind also that the Italian fascism which both Pound and Eliot endorsed had a historical meaning which is still open to interpretation and is not identical with Nazism. Eliot's commitment to fascism, moreover, like his anti-Semitism, while certain, was something less than a platform. It is not to be explained away, but the various statements in prose do in each instance have contextual nuances by which they are both complicated and modified. The question has been addressed several times heretofore. See William M. Chace, *The Political Identities of Ezra Pound and T. S. Eliot* (Stanford: Stanford University Press, 1973), especially pp. 136ff.; Roger Kojecky, *T. S. Eliot's Social Criticism* (London: Faber & Faber, 1971), especially pp. 12ff.; and Margolis, *T. S. Eliot's Intellectual Development,* especially pp. 38ff., 152ff. It is my intention to suggest that precisely the casualness of the fascism and anti-Semitism in Eliot's self-conscious literary spokesmanship reveals social assumptions in modernism.

15. Some such logic, by which a device was transformed into an idea, would seem to have been decisive in the case of Eliot himself. The now-published original manuscripts of *The Waste Land* show more clearly than before that in the early 1920s Eliot's intentions for poetry were in large part satirical; the prominent trick in the poem called at first *He Do the Police in Different Voices* consists in placing fragments of contemporary idiom within a formal literary context, thereby revealing the debasement of the contemporary. But then it was the context, the device by which the revelation occurred, that obviously became important for Eliot. T. S. Eliot, *The Waste Land: A Facsimile and Transcript of the Original Drafts Including the Annotations of Ezra Pound,* ed. Valerie Eliot (New York: Harcourt Brace Jovanovich, 1971).

16. Ernest Hemingway, *The Sun Also Rises* (New York: Charles Scribner's Sons, 1926), pp. 152–53.

17. For further discussion of the chronology of the generation, see John McCormick, *The Middle Distance: A Comparative History of American Imaginative Literature: 1919–1932* (New York: Free Press, 1971).

18. See Ezra Pound, *Indiscretions; or, Une revue de deux mondes* (Paris: Three Mountain Press, 1923), pp. 18, 34.

19. "Eliot reacted against an emotional inertia, a moral blight, and in *The Waste Land* located it in England after the First World War. That war *did* provide a 'waste land' experience, but its dramatic reality for Eliot belonged to his youth in America at the beginning of the century." Lyndall Gordon, *Eliot's Early Years* (Oxford and New York: Oxford University Press, 1977), p. 16.

20. Harold Stearns (ed.), *Civilization in the United States: An Inquiry by Thirty Americans* (New York: Harcourt, Brace & Co., 1922), pp. 285–96. Harold Stearns (ed.), *America Now: An Inquiry into Civilization in the United States by Thirty-Six Americans* (New York: Charles Scribner's Sons, 1938), pp. 385–94.

21. See E. V. Stonequist, *The Marginal Man* (New York: Charles Scribner's Sons, 1937), p. 97; Maldwyn Allen Jones, *American Immigration* (Chicago: University of Chicago Press, 1960), chapters 7–8; statistical tables in Samuel Eliot Morison and Henry Steele Commager, *The Growth of the Ameri-*

can Republic (New York: Oxford University Press, 1950) 2: 908; Dixon Wecter, *The Age of the Great Depression* (New York: Macmillan, 1948), p. 123.

22. Writing in 1924, Horace Kallen was observing that "Cultural Pluralism" was not a popular idea in America. "Both American tories and American intellectuals reject it. They reject it because they find themselves all at once undermined in all their customary securities—in their securities of habit, of thought, of outlook—by the shift of the social facts upon which the securities were postulated." Horace M. Kallan, *Culture and Democracy in the United States: Studies in the Group Psychology of the American Peoples* (New York: Boni & Liveright, 1924), pp. 11–12. The best general account of the response of old Americans to the new immigration is John Higham, *Strangers in the Land: Patterns of American Nativism 1860–1925* (New York: Atheneum, 1968). See also Barbara Miller Solomon, *Ancestors and Immigrants: A Changing New England Tradition* (Cambridge: Harvard University Press, 1956).

23. Henry Adams, *The Education of Henry Adams* (1907; New York: Random House, Modern Library, 1931), p. 238.

24. Pound, *Indiscretions*, pp. 13, 58. Note that Pound was writing this series of autobiographical essays early in the 1920s, prior to his conversion to Social Credit and fascism.

25. T. S. Eliot, *After Strange Gods: A Primer of Modern Heresy: The Page-Barbour Lectures at the University of Virginia, 1933* (London: Faber & Faber, 1934), pp. 15–16, 19–20.

26. Herbert Read, "T. S. E.—A Memoir," in Allen Tate (ed.), *T. S. Eliot: The Man and His Work* (New York: Delacorte Press, 1966), p. 15.

27. E. E. Cummings, "One XVII," *Is Five* (New York: Liveright, 1926), p. 26. (For a brief discussion of Cummings in the Lower East Side ghetto, see Judd L. Teller, *Strangers and Natives: The Evolution of the American Jew from 1921 to the Present* [New York: Delacorte Press, 1968], p. 51.)

28. For a more extensive list of the number of Jews prominent in American literary circles in the 1930s, see Daniel Aaron, "Some Reflections on Communism and the Jewish Writer," in Peter I. Rose (ed.), *The Ghetto and Beyond: Essays on Jewish Life in America* (New York: Random House, 1969), pp. 253, 266.

29. William Dean Howells, *Impressions and Experiences* (New York: Harper & Brothers, 1896), pp. 138–39.

30. T. S. Eliot, "A Commentary," *Criterion* 12 (Jan. 1933): 244–49.

31. See Higham, *Strangers,* pp. 9–12, 131–57. See also Solomon, *Ancestors and Immigrants,* chapter 4, and Oscar Handlin, *The Uprooted* (Boston: Little, Brown, 1951), chapter 10. For a more contemporary account, see Kallen, *Culture and Democracy in the United States,* pp. 23ff.

32. Ezra S. Brudno, *The Fugitive: Being Memoirs of a Wanderer in Search of a Home* (New York: Doubleday, Page & Co., 1904), p. 276.

33. M. E. Ravage, *An American in the Making: The Life Story of An Immigrant* (New York: Harper & Brothers, 1917), p. 61.

34. See Handlin, *Uprooted,* especially chapters 2, 4, 6, 9.

35. Especially in the case of the eastern European Jews, direct evidence of the disintegration of family and community life, except in memoirs and fictive autobiography, is extremely resistant to discovery. Writers on the subject early and late have tended to accept and eulogize the myth of the peculiar stability of Jewish family life. Some figures and other data are available, however, and also some seemingly neutral observations from which deductions can be made. In 1898 a survey of arraignments in the Essex Market Court was divided by nationalities. The court's jurisdiction included but was not limited to the Lower East Side, and extended to portions of the Bronx and also included the high-crime area of the Bowery. One of the nationality groupings, of a total of seven, was "Russian," which may be taken largely to indicate Jewish. The survey revealed that "Russians" committed fewer than their proportionate share of such crimes as assault and public intoxication, but were conspicuous for certain other kinds of crimes, among them specifically failure to support wife or family. That abandonment was a problem of community-wide dimension seems moreover to have been known and acknowledged: the *Jewish Daily Forward* ran a column called the "Gallery of Missing Husbands," with pictures.

It seems also to have been an accepted fact that Jews were particularly liable to "diseases of the nervous system": neurasthenia, hysteria, and insanity. A report of 1905 stated, "Recent statistics show that the Jews in [New York City] supply a greater number of insane to the asylums than any other race living here." In 1907 a Yiddish newspaperman was estimating that "there are six Jewish suicides on the average weekly in New York City."

Walter Scott Andrews, "Law and Litigation: New York," and Maurice Fishberg, M.D., "Health and Sanitation: New York," both in Charles S. Bernheimer (ed.), *The Russian Jew in the United States: Studies of Social Conditions in New York, Philadelphia, and Chicago, with a Description of Rural Settlements* (Philadelphia: John C. Winston Co., 1905), pp. 336ff., 282ff.; Isaac Metzker (ed.), *A Bintel Brief* (New York: Ballantine Books, 1972), p. 10; Ande Manners, *Poor Cousins* (New York: Coward, McCann & Geoghegan, 1972), p. 231.

36. See E. Franklin Frazier, *The Negro in the United States*, rev. ed. (New York: Macmillan, 1957), pp. 440ff.

37. See Frank V. Thompson, *Schooling of the Immigrant* (New York: Harper & Brothers, 1920), chap. 2.

38. Mary Antin, *The Promised Land* (Boston: Houghton Mifflin Co., 1912), pp. xii, 271.

39. Abraham Cahan, *The Rise of David Levinsky* (1917; New York: Harper Torchbook, 1960), pp. 243, 252.

40. Milton Herbert Gropper and Max Siegel, *We Americans* (New York: Samuel French, 1928), pp. 3, 96–97.

In his autobiography Morris Raphael Cohen speaks of the impact wrought upon family life by the general secularization of the learning of the children: "What ensued was a struggle between the old and new ideals, resulting in a conflict between the older and younger generations fraught with heartrending consequences. Homes ceased to be places of peace and in the ensuing discord much of the proverbial strength of the Jewish family was lost. As the home ceased to be the center of interest, the unity of life, nurtured by pride in the achievements of one's forbears and by parental pride in the achievements of children, was broken. There was scarcely a Jewish home on the East Side that was free from this friction between parents and children." Morris Raphael Cohen, *A Dreamer's Journey,* in Milton Hindus (ed.), *The Old East Side: An Anthology* (Philadelphia: Jewish Publication Society of America, 1969), p. 47.

41. See, e.g., Bernheimer, *Russian Jew in the United States,* section 6, "Educational Influences."

42. Even in the very best instances of non-public-school education as well, the attitude incorporated in the learning was likely to be ambiguous, perhaps confused, and in any event patronizing. Probably the very best was New York City's People's Institute presided over by the philosopher Thomas Davidson. Davidson was a man of great learning and by all accounts a man of large energy and charity. He reflected on some of his work at the institute and the Educational Alliance as follows: "In these discussions I had come to know to some extent the character, aspirations, and needs of the young people whom I undertook to instruct. I saw that they were both able and earnest, but carried away by superficial views of a socialistic or anarchist sort, greatly to their own detriment and to that of society. My first object, therefore, in taking up this class was to induce its members to study and think out carefully the problems of sociology and culture, in accordance with the historic method, and so to impart to their minds a healthy attitude towards society, to do away with the vengeful sense of personal or class wrong, and to arouse faith in individual effort and manly and womanly self-dependence. I desired, moreover, to give them such an outlook upon life as could lift their lives out of narrowness and sordidness and give them ideal aims. Finally, I wished to train them in the use of correct English, both written and spoken." Cited in William Knight, *Memorials of Thomas Davidson* (Boston and London: Ginn & Co., 1907), p. 80.

43. Frances Blascoer, *Colored School Children in New York* (1915; New York: Negro Universities Press, 1970), pp. 84–90.

44. Frazier, *Negro in the United States,* pp. 440ff.

45. J. K. Paulding, "Educational Influences: New York," in Bernheimer, *Russian Jew in the United States,* pp. 191, 189.

46. Moses Rischin, *The Promised City: New York's Jews 1870–1914* (New York: Corinth Books, 1964), p. 87; Robert W. DeForest and Lawrence Veiller (eds.), *The Tenement House Problem* (New York: Macmillan, 1903), 1: 303ff., 2: 33ff.

47. Lawrence A. Cremin, *The Transformation of the School* (New York: Alfred A. Knopf, 1961), p. 71. The initial statement of the matter was made by Jacob Riis: "The majority of the children seek the public schools, where they are received sometimes with some misgivings on the part of the teachers, who find it necessary to inculcate lessons of cleanliness in the worst cases by practical demonstration with wash-bowl and soap. 'He took hold of the soap as if it were some animal,' said one of these teachers to me after such an experiment

upon a new pupil, 'and wiped three fingers across his face. He called that washing.' In the Allen Street public school the experienced principal has embodied among the elementary lessons, to keep constantly before the children the duty that clearly lies next to their hands, a characteristic exercise. The question is asked daily from the teacher's desk: 'What must I do to be healthy?' and the school responds:

I must keep my skin clean,
Wear clean clothes,
Breathe pure air,
And live in the sunlight.

"It seems little less than biting sarcasm to hear them say it, for to not a few of them all these things are known only by name." Jacob Riis, *How the Other Half Lives: Studies among the Tenements of New York* (New York: Charles Scribner's Sons, 1891), p. 113.

48. See, e.g., the series of vignettes in Myra Kelly, *Little Aliens* (New York: Charles Scribner's Sons, 1910). Kelley was a schoolteacher. The vignettes in this volume and others were obviously based on her own experiences. She was as understanding as might be, but a basic ambiguity of attitude is nonetheless there, as when she says that in the classroom she was a *Krisht*.

49. Anzia Yezierska, *Bread Givers* (1925; New York: George Braziller, 1975), p. 8.

50. Victor N. Paananen, "Rebels All: The Finns in America," *In These Times* (5–11 Apr. 1978), p. 19.

51. Cited in Cremin, *Transformation of the School,* pp. 68–69.

52. Peter Roberts, *The New Immigration: A Study of the Industrial and Social Life of Southeastern Europeans in America* (New York: Macmillan, 1920), p. 307.

53. Woodrow Wilson, *Reunion and Nationalization,* vol. V of *A History of the American People* (New York: Harper & Brothers, 1901), pp. 212–13.

54. Quoted in Manners, *Poor Cousins,* p. 136. See also Oscar Handlin, *Adventure in Freedom* (Port Washington, N.Y.: Kennikat Press, 1954), p. 158: the fundamental aim of the Educational Alliance was to elimate the "Oriental" elements in the life and culture of the new immigrants.

55. Quoted in Manners, *Poor Cousins,* p. 109. Antin does seem to have been a very pretentious person. For a firsthand account, by a contemporary Jewish madam, see Ruth Rosen and Sue Davidson (eds.), *The Maimie Papers* (Old Westbury, N.Y.: Feminist Press, 1977), pp. 158–67.

56. Rischin, *Promised City,* pp. 130ff.

57. Joseph Freeman, *An American Testament* (London: Victor Gollancz, 1938), pp. 30, 35.

58. Frederic M. Thrasher, *The Gang: A Study of 1,313 Gangs in Chicago* (Chicago: University of Chicago Press, 1927), chapters 1, 12.

59. Rischin, *Promised City,* chapter 5.

60. Harry Roskolenko, *When I Was Last on Cherry Street* (New York: Stein & Day, 1965), pp. 2–3.

61. Boxing seems to have provided a particularly available opportunity

for Russian-Jewish immigrants and their children. The opportunity was appreciated, moreover. The phenomenon of a Jewish boxer confounded a stereotype, and by that much the phenomenon might even be confused with ideas of progress and enlightenment. In 1925 a writer for the *Jewish Daily Forward* provided a list of some twenty-two Jewish prizefighters, including besides the famous Benny Leonard, Kid Lavigne, Louis (Kid) Kaplan, Battling Levinsky, Soldier Bartfield, and Corporal Izzy Schwartz, concluding: "After all, the people who are certain about the alleged congenital cowardice of the Jewish race are the selfsame upholders of law and order and defenders of the constitution that pass laws to banish Darwin from college textbooks. We can afford to be in the same boat with the author of *Origin of Species.*" Cited in Louis Wirth, *The Ghetto* (1928; Chicago: University of Chicago Press, 1960), p. 253. Wirth himself, writing in 1928, used the reference to suggest not only a route of emergence from the ghetto, but virtual transcendence. "As he emerges from the ghetto," Wirth writes, "the Jew loses his distinctive personal appearance. This change in facial expression and in bearing is most apparent in the young people. The second generation becomes self-assertive, straightens out its spine, and lifts its head." Ibid., p. 252.

62. Especially in the case of the eastern European Jews, direct evidence is, again, hard to come by. (See note 35 above.) Again, however, some statistics and some seemingly neutral observations are available. In the 1898 survey of arraignments in the Essex Market Court, cited above, there were one hundred fifty-four cases of prostitution, this small total number indicating that this crime was for the most part overlooked by the police. Within the small total, however, the "Russians" were prominent—forty cases out of the whole. A few years later, in 1905, a doctor was noting an increase in cases of gonorrhea among Russian Jews in New York, suggesting an increase in the incidence of prostitution. See Walter Scott Andrews, "Law and Litigation: New York," and Maurice Fishberg, M.D., "Health and Sanitation: New York," both in Bernheimer, *Russian Jew in the United States*, pp. 336ff., 282ff. The two-volume report of the New York State Tenement House Committee published in 1903 included testimony on the prevalence of prostitution. Testimony by Dr. Felix Adler made specific reference to the Lower East Side: "In any proper, careful consideration of the subject I should think that the economic causes would be mentioned first, especially the evils of the sweat shop system on the East Side, which produce a condition of things that render these poor unfortunate girls more susceptible ... to temptation than they otherwise would be. I have known directly of cases where young women refused to share the poverty of their families, saying that life at best under the prevailing conditions was a continuous series of privations, and that if they could, even for a short time, escape from this horror of the tenement house and of the poverty-stricken home in the tenement house, to the streets, or to the gay saloons, or to the company of such companions as they had access to, they preferred the latter." DeForest and Veiller, *Tenement House Problem*, 2: 18. Ironically, reform effects in themselves seem to have had the effect of domesticating prostitution while eliminating brothels. In 1895 the report of the New York State Tenement House Committee stated: "The presence of many

immoral women in the tenement houses . . . forms a most deplorable condition. There has been a manifest increase in this condition during the past year or 18 months, and there is no doubt that the influx of prostitutes into actual residence in tenement-houses is due to the police raids, which have closed most of the houses of ill-fame in the tenement-house districts. . . . At present [prostitutes] form a part of the life of the great tenement-houses, and thus their contaminating influence is felt far more directly by the general public than was formerly the case." New York State, *Report of the Tenement House Committee* (Albany, 1895), p. 88.

Cahan's David Levinsky is made to offer comment to the same effect: "The fact that these wretched women were not segregated as they were in my native town probably had something to do with [his] resorting to prostitutes. . . . Instead of being confined to a fixed out-of-the-way locality, they were allowed to live in the same tenement-houses with respectable people, beckoning to men from the front steps, under open protection from police." Cahan, *Rise of David Levinsky*, p. 125. It is to be noted that Cahan's intention for the novel was sociological before it was fictional. See Jules Chametzky, *From the Ghetto: The Fiction of Abraham Cahan* (Amherst: University of Massachusetts Press, 1977), chapter 9.

Again, Lincoln Steffens, in the section of his *Autobiography* dealing with "The Ghetto," recounts an episode of children watching a prostitute at work in a tenement-house apartment. When Steffens interviews the prostitute, she complains—the time is the nineties—that she has been driven into the tenement by the Parkhurst reform movement. Lincoln Steffens, *The Autobiography of Lincoln Steffens* (New York: Harcourt, Brace & Co., 1931), 1: 245–46.

63. See: Denis Tilden Lynch, *Criminals and Politicians* (New York: Macmillan, 1932); Handlin, *Uprooted,* chapters 3, 6, 8; Thrasher, *Gang,* chapter 21 ("The Gang in Politics"); Jacob Riis, *The Battle with the Slum* (New York: Macmillan, 1902), chapter 9; Teller, *Strangers and Natives,* pp. 89–90. See also Albert Fried, *The Rise and Fall of the Jewish Gangster in America* (New York: Holt, Rinehart, & Winston, 1980), for discussion of the "culture" of vice and criminality within the Lower East Side in the time of the Great Immigration and thereafter. The criminals—gamblers, prostitutes and their cadets, thieves, hired thugs, labor racketeers, and vote enforcers—were young people, for the most part. In the earlier time they were likely to have privileged connections with Tammany Hall. Fried suggests that these criminals tended to regard themselves as being the ghetto's special elect.

64. Michael Gold, *Jews without Money* (1930; New York: Avon Books, 1965), p. 17.

65. Samuel Ornitz, *Haunch Paunch and Jowl* (New York: Boni & Liveright, 1923), pp. 183, 295.

66. Liveright's testimony is included in the flap copy of early printings of the book.

67. For material on Yiddish theater see especially Irving Howe, *World of Our Fathers* (New York: Harcourt Brace Jovanovich, 1976), chapter 14. See

also Handlin, *Adventure*, pp. 140ff.; Bernheimer, *Russian Jew in the United States*, pp. 221ff.

68. "The positive, creative role of the Jew as modern American, and above all as a modern American writer, was in the first years of this century being prepared not in the universities, not even in journalism, but in the vaudeville theaters, music halls, and burlesque houses where the pent-up eagerness of penniless immigrant youngsters met the raw urban scene on its own terms. . . . it was the Marx Brothers, Eddie Cantor, Al Jolson, Fannie Brice, George Gershwin, Jewish clowns, minstrels, songwriters helped to fit the Jew to America, and America to the Jew, with an *élan* that made for the future creativity in literature as well as for the mass products of the 'entertainment industry.'" Alfred Kazin, "The Jew as Modern Writer," in Rose, *Ghetto*, pp. 422–23.

69. Anzia Yezierska, *Children of Loneliness: Stories of Immigrant Life in America* (New York: Funk & Wagnalls Co., 1923), p. 25.

70. The complete original version of this longest of Stevens's poems was published by Alcestis Press, 1936. In its subsequent publication, in the volume *The Man with the Blue Guitar,* 1937, it was edited and shortened, and it is not included at all in the *Collected Poems*. The original version is reprinted in *Opus Posthumous*, ed. Samuel French Morse (New York: Alfred A. Knopf, 1957), pp. 39–72.

71. Stevens, *Opus Posthumous*, p. 219.

72. See Rischin, *Promised City*, p. 127; Teller, *Strangers and Natives*, pp. 45ff.

73. In fact in the 1920s the majority of American workers were foreign born. See Nathan Glazer, *The Social Basis of American Communism* (New York: Harcourt, Brace & World, 1961), p. 76.

74. See Alfred Kazin, *On Native Grounds: An Interpretation of Modern American Prose Literature* (New York: Reynal & Hitchcock, 1942), chapter 16.

CHAPTER TWO

1. The forthcoming change in attitudes is suggested in *The Life of Emerson*, published in 1932, and is manifest in *The Flowering of New England,* published in 1936. The reasons for the change are intricate with personal problems suffered by Brooks, and will never be fully available to explanation. Some speculations are offered by Brooks himself in the second volume of his autobiography, *Days of the Phoenix: The Nineteen-Twenties I Remember* (New York: E. P. Dutton, 1957).

2. Van Wyck Brooks, *The Wine of the Puritans: A Study of Present-Day America* (London: Sisley's, 1908), p. 138.

3. Ibid., p. 121.

4. Ibid., pp. 15, 142.

5. Van Wyck Brooks, "America's Coming-of-Age," 1915, in *Three Essays on America* (New York: E. P. Dutton, 1934), pp. 99, 108–9, 105.

6. Van Wyck Brooks, "Letters and Leadership," 1918, ibid., pp. 146–47, 184, 187, 153.

7. The point is made by William Wasserstrom, *The Legacy of Van Wyck Brooks: A Study of Maladies and Motives* (Carbondale: Southern Illinois University Press, 1971).

8. Van Wyck Brooks, *The World of H. G. Wells* (New York: Mitchell Kennerly, 1915), p. 40.

9. Van Wyck Brooks, "The Parvenu Intellectuals," in *Sketches in Criticism* (New York: E. P. Dutton, 1932), p. 52.

10. Edmund Wilson, Jr., "Imaginary Conversations: Mr. Van Wyck Brooks and Mr. Scott Fitzgerald," *New Republic* (30 Apr. 1924), pp. 249–54.

11. Lewis Mumford, *The Golden Day: A Study in American Literature and Culture* (1926; Boston: Beacon Press, 1957), p. 144.

12. Randolph Bourne, "Twilight of Idols," 1917, in *The History of a Literary Radical & Other Papers* (New York: S. A. Russell, 1956), pp. 258–59.

13. "An Expression of Artists for the Community," *Seven Arts* (Nov. 1916), pp. 52–53.

14. Jane Heap, "Lost: A Renaissance," *Little Review* (May 1929), p. 5.

15. Bourne, "Twilight of Idols," p. 257.

16. Messages from or essays by Pound appear in the issues for Dec. 1926, Mar. 1927, and June 1928. Joseph Freeman comments on Tate's early relationship with *New Masses* in his autobiography, *An American Testament* (London: Victor Gollancz, 1938), pp. 304–5. Tate appears in the magazine in the issues for Jan. 1927 and Sept. 1927.

17. Van Wyck Brooks, "The Critical Movement in America," 1921, in *Sketches in Criticism*, p. 25.

18. Brooks, *The World of H. G. Wells*, p. 15.

19. In Max Eastman, *Love and Revolution: My Journey through an Epoch* (New York: Random House, 1964), p. 217.

20. See Theodore Draper, *The Roots of American Communism* (1957; New York: Viking Press, Compass Books, 1963), pp. 284–93.

21. The essays are reprinted in Max Eastman, *The Literary Mind: Its Place in an Age of Science* (New York: Charles Scribner's Sons, 1932), pp. 57–78, 93–122. Eastman's comments on the consequences of the essay for his career are in *Love and Revolution*, p. 518.

22. Max Eastman, *Enjoyment of Living* (New York: Harper & Brothers, 1948), p. 416.

23. For discussion of the ideology and practice of the *Masses*, see William L. O'Neill, *Echoes of Revolt: The Masses 1911–1917* (Chicago: Quadrangle Books, 1966), pp. 18–19, 27–28.

The relationship between Eastman and Goldman seems to have been continuously tentative at best, the discrepancy between them being a matter of ideology only in part—his Marxism and her anarchism. In her autobiography Goldman was to accuse Eastman of a series of betrayals and then, finally, with nice sarcasm, to dismiss him: "Lack of fairness to an opponent is essentially a sign of weakness. And, truth to tell, Max Eastman was neither strong nor brave. . . . Well, what of it? He possessed other gifts worthy of king's ransom: he was a poet and handsome. Better a Napoleon in his own domain than a common soldier in the social battle." Emma Goldman, *Living My Life* (1931; Richard and Anna Marie Drinnon [eds.], New York: New American Library, 1977), pp. 689–90. Eastman, the poet, was to say that the trouble with Goldman's anarchism was that it had no practicality to it: "Her whole life-wisdom consisted of comparing reality with an absolute ideal, and breaking her neck, and if need be all necks, in some obviously desperate leap for the idea." Moreover: "I never liked Emma Goldman very well. Her force and eloquence impressed me less than her impermeability to humor and logic." Eastman *Enjoyment of Living*, p. 423, and see also p. 235.

24. In Eastman, *Enjoyment of Living*, p. 421. See also Art Young, *Art Young: His Life and Times* (New York: Sheridan House, 1939), p. 276. It should be added that the *Masses* group had some clear relationship to the Progressives who had come of age in the 1890s, and indeed they were to be damned on that score, too. A succeeding generation could, luxuriously, accuse Progressivism of inconsistency, timidity, and bad conscience, and so by association the *Masses*. But whatever the amount of truth in the general accusation, the *Masses* group also inherited from these immediate forebears a feeling for latitudes in revolution and the idea of a happy rebellion. Eastman and Reed's manifesto for the *Masses* was, for instance, quite similar to the statement of purpose published in *American Magazine*, founded in 1906 by a group of Progressive muckrakers. That magazine promised "the most stirring and delightful monthly book of fiction, humor, sentiment, and joyous reading that is anywhere published. It will reflect a happy, struggling, fighting world, in which, as we believe, good people are coming out on top." Cited in Richard Hofstadter, *The Age of Reform* (New York: Vintage Books, 1955), p. 197. Even in the early 1930s, when distinctions in the attitudes underlying political commitments were to become very strict, the single most successful of the converting ordinances of the Communist party was the *Autobiography* of the old muckraker Lincoln Steffens.

25. See Draper, *Roots of American Communism*, pp. 11–13.

26. Quoted in Richard Hofstadter, *Anti-Intellectualism in American Life* (New York: Vintage Books, 1963), p. 289.

27. See John E. Hart, *Floyd Dell* (New York: Twayne Publishers, 1971), pp. 35–37.

28. Quoted in Van Wyck Brooks, *John Sloan: A Painter's Life* (New York: E. P. Dutton, 1955), p. 77.

29. See Ira Glackens, *William Glackens and the Ashcan Group: The Emergence of Realism in American Art* (New York: Crown Publishers, 1957), pp. 78, 90.

30. For discussion of Debs's background and the kind of his appeal, see Ray Ginger, *The Bending Cross: A Biography of Eugene Victor Debs* (New Brunswick: Rutgers University Press, 1949).

31. See Young, *Art Young*, p. 275. Eastman himself was to say that his leaving Columbia was his own decision and had nothing to do with his politics. Cf. Eastman, *Enjoyment of Living*.

32. Eastman, *Enjoyment of Living*, pp. 411–12.

33. Young, *Art Young*, p. 275.

34. Hart, *Floyd Dell*, p. 105.

35. Ibid., pp. 19–29.

36. Floyd Dell, *Moon-Calf* (1920; New York: Sagamore Press, 1957), p. 112.

37. See Eastman, *Enjoyment of Living*, pp. 354–55; *Love and Revolution*, chapters 2, 18, 28.

38. In Young, *Art Young*, p. 351.

39. Floyd Dell, *Intellectual Vagabondage: An Apology for the Intelligentsia* (New York: George H. Doran, 1926), pp. 258–59. In its first version the book was a series of articles, "Literature and the Machine Age," in the *Liberator*, 1919.

40. Quoted in Eastman, *Enjoyment of Living*, p. 559.

41. Michael Brewster Folsom, "The Education of Michael Gold," in David Madden (ed.), *Proletarian Writers of the Thirties* (Carbondale: Southern Illinois University Press, 1968), p. 230.

42. Freeman, *An American Testament*, pp. 60–61.

43. See Eastman, *Love and Revolution*, pp. 69ff.

44. Max Shachtman, review of *James Joyce: His First Forty Years* by Herbert S. Gorman, *Liberator* (June 1924), p. 33.

45. See Claude McKay, *A Long Way from Home* (New York: Lee Furman, 1937), pp. 140–41.

46. See Eastman, *Enjoyment of Living*, p. 418, for an account of a relevant exchange of letters between Eastman and Minor. Minor had gone to Russia in 1918 and had become involved in the defense of anarchists against Communist party persecutions, going so far as to petition Lenin directly. For a while thereafter, until he was taught better, he continued publicly to sympathize with anarchism. See Joseph North, *Robert Minor: Artist and Crusader* (New York: International Publishers, 1956). In his hagiographic account, North has obvious difficulty in attempting to explain away the formal elements of Minor's politics prior to 1921.

47. Freeman, *An American Testament*, pp. 273, 274.

48. *Liberator* (Apr. 1920), p. 49.

49. Freeman, *An American Testament*, p. 277.

50. Ibid., p. 287.

51. Bertha Fenberg, "A Test of Beauty," *Liberator* (Apr. 1924), p. 11. Mary Heaton Vorse, "Fraycar's Fist," *Liberator* (Sept. 1920), pp. 17–24. Roger Baldwin, "The Living Dead," *Liberator* (Apr. 1919), p. 38. John Dos Passos, "Farmer Strikers in Spain," *Liberator* (Oct. 1920), pp. 28–30. Edmund Wilson, Jr., "The New Patriotism," *Liberator* (June 1920), pp. 26–27.

52. Stanley Boone, "Friends of American Freedom," *Liberator* (Aug. 1922), pp. 30, 32. Ralph Chaplin would have been a particularly available figure

for this reviewer's loyalty. Chaplin was an authentic American, born in Ames, Kansas, in 1887. He was a friend of Debs. He had been through many of the adventures of the left, as a leader of the Socialist party of America, as a worker in behalf of the Mexican revolution, and as an IWW organizer. He was at this time, moreover, one of the few Wobblies who had joined the Communist party. He had also written the lyrics to "Solidarity Forever." Ironically, he was soon to suffer disgrace on the left. He had been jailed in 1918 with more than a hundred other Wobblies under terms of the Espionage Act. In 1923 he was to be one of the forty-five members of the group who accepted Warren G. Harding's offer of clemency. As the most prominent of the "clemency hounds," he received the most abuse.

53. Allen Tate, "Preface to Reactionary Essays on Poetry and Ideas, 1936," in *On the Limits of Poetry: Selected Essays* (New York: Swallow Press & William Morrow, 1948), p. xiv.

54. Freeman, *An American Testament*, p. 185.

55. Leon Trotsky, *Literature and Revolution* (1924; New York: Russell & Russell, 1957), p. 14.

56. Freeman, *An American Testament*, p. 285.

57. *New Masses* (26 Jan. 1937), p. 29.

58. Quoted in Daniel Aaron, *Writers on the Left: Episodes in American Literary Communism* (New York: Harcourt, Brace & World, 1961), pp. 100–101.

59. See Irving Howe and Lewis Coser, *The American Communist Party: A Critical History* (1957; New York: Frederick A. Praeger, 1962), pp. 239–43.

60. Freeman, *An American Testament*, p. 342.

61. *New Masses* (May 1926), p. 6.

62. There is mystery here, with inference that Williams was all too true to his sources. When the story appeared, Williams was sued for libel; he eventually settled out of court for five thousand dollars. In the *Autobiography* he said that the story had been told to him by a young person of his acquaintance, that he had rushed home and pounded it out on his typewriter, and that when he had sent it out he had neglected to change the names. Hence the libel action. He said also that he had had to use real names in order "to write convincingly." He was sued by the young person who had told him the story. But in fact the only name which appears in the story is that of the Gas and Oil Company. William Carlos Williams, *The Autobiography of William Carlos Williams* (New York: Random House, 1951), pp. 241–43. Williams did not note the title of the story in question; it is identified in Reed Whittemore, *William Carlos Williams: Poet from Jersey* (Boston: Houghton Mifflin Co., 1975), pp. 206–7.

63. Herman Spector, "Liberalism and the Literary Esoterics," *New Masses* (Jan. 1929), pp. 18–19.

64. John Dos Passos, "A Lost Generation," ibid. (Dec. 1926), p. 26.

65. Dos Passos and Gold quoted in Freeman, *An American Testament*, pp. 342–43.

66. "America Needs a Critic," *New Masses* (Oct. 1926), p. 7.

67. Ibid. (Oct. 1926), p. 9.

68. Ibid. (Aug. 1926), pp. 5–7, 28.

69. Ibid. (June 1926), pp. 15–17.

70. Ibid. (Aug. 1926), p. 2.

71. See Barbara and Arthur Gelb, *O'Neill* (1962; New York: Delta, 1964), pp. 348–49.

72. Circa 1910 the editor of the *Bintel Brief* column of the Yiddish-language *Forward* was saying to potential contributors: "Under your tenement roofs are stories of the real life-stuff; the very stuff of which great literature can be made. Send them to us. Write them any way you can. Come and bring them, or tell them to us." Quoted in Moses Rischin, *The Promised City: New York's Jews* (1962; New York: Corinth Books, 1964), p. 131. In that moment Gold had been a teenager, with literary ambitions, living on the Lower East Side. The basic idea that it was the vulgar who owned literature would have come to him from everywhere, but it is a likelihood that this particular exhortation, with all of the implications in its address to that Lower East Side population from which he came, would have suggested a special militance and a special justification. Certainly he would have been familiar with it.

73. V. F. Calverton, "Proletarian Art," in *The Newer Spirit: A Sociological Criticism of Literature* (New York: Boni & Liveright, 1925), pp. 139–49.

74. Quoted in Granville Hicks, *Part of the Truth* (New York: Harcourt, Brace & World, 1965), pp. 100–101. See also Aaron, *Writers on the Left*, p. 209.

75. See Freeman, *An American Testament*, p. 225, and Eastman, *Love and Revolution*, p. 265.

76. *Liberator* (June 1922), pp. 25–26.

77. In Eastman, *Love and Revolution*, p. 255.

78. "Towards Proletarian Art," *Liberator* (Feb. 1921), pp. 20–24.

79. See Calverton, "Proletarian Art," p. 143.

80. Trotsky, *Literature and Revolution*, p. 14. My italics.

81. "America Needs a Critic," p. 8.

82. For further discussion of this shift in the magazine, See Aaron, *Writers on the Left*, pp. 209–13.

83. See "Floyd Dell Resigns," *New Masses* (July 1929), pp. 10–11.

84. For further discussion, see Aaron, *Writers on the Left*, pp. 219ff.

85. See William Phillips and Philip Rahv, "In Retrospect," in *The Partisan Reader: Ten Years of Partisan Review 1934–1944* (New York: Dial Press, 1946), pp. 679ff.

86. See Aaron, *Writers on the Left*, pp. 213–30.

87. See Howe and Coser, *American Communist Party*, pp. 283ff.

88. Eastman, *Love and Revolution*, p. 467.

89. Williams, *Autobiography*, pp. 146, 174–75. My italics.

90. Michael Gold, "Go Left, Young Writers!" *New Masses* (Jan. 1929), pp. 3–4.

INTRODUCTION TO PART TWO

1. Franklin Delano Roosevelt, "Extemporaneous Remarks before the Daughters of the American Revolution, Washington, D.C., April 21, 1938," *The Public Papers and Addresses of Franklin D. Roosevelt* (New York: Macmillan, 1941), 7: 259.

2. See Nathan Glazer, *The Social Basis of American Communism* (New York: Harcourt, Brace & World, 1961), pp. 34–64.

3. See Earl Browder, *The People's Front* (New York: International Publishers, 1938), especially "Democracy and the Constitution," pp. 235–48, and "Revolutionary Background of the United States Constitution," pp. 249–69.

4. See Theodore Draper, *The Roots of American Communism* (1957; New York: Viking Press, Compass Books, 1963), pp. 307–8; Irving Howe and Lewis Coser, *The American Communist Party: A Critical History* (1957; New York: Frederick A. Praeger, 1962), chapter 8.

5. Quoted in W. C. Brownell, *Democratic Distinction in America* (New York: Charles Scribner's Sons, 1927), p. 26.

6. Statistics are to be found in Glazer, *Social Basis of American Communism*, pp. 38, 94, 100.

7. Eric F. Goldman, *Rendezvous with Destiny: A History of Modern American Reform* (1952; New York: Vintage Books, 1956), pp. 67, 102–3. Henry Adams, *The Degradation of the Democratic Dogma* (1919; New York: Capricorn Books, 1958), pp. 104–9; Brownell, *Democratic Distinction in America*, p. 14.

8. See *New Masses* (12 May 1936), p. 25.

9. See, e.g., Frank Sullivan, "The Cliché Expert Testifies as a Roosevelt Hater," reprinted in Milton Crane (ed.), *The Roosevelt Era* (New York: Boni & Gaer, 1947), pp. 237ff.

10. Roosevelt's "Forgotten Man" campaign speech, in 1932, was addressed particularly, in point of fact, to the plight of farmers. Franklin Delano Roosevelt, "The 'Forgotten Man' Speech. Radio Address, Albany, N.Y. April 7, 1932," *Public Papers and Addresses of Franklin D. Roosevelt*, 1:624–27. But the phrase obviously had a general applicability, and it entered into a common usage. In 1933 a certain E. G. Shinner, a man who had been in the meat business for twenty-five years in Chicago, published a book called *The Forgotten Man* in which he complained about the chain system and approved of New Deal intervention in business. Cited in Arthur M. Schlesinger, Jr., *The Coming of the New Deal*, vol. 2, *The Age of Roosevelt* (Boston: Houghton Mifflin Co., 1958), p. 493. No doubt Roosevelt, or whoever it was who wrote Roosevelt's speech, had some recollection of a once-celebrated address by William Graham Sumner, titled "The Forgotten Man," delivered in 1883. Sumner's address, ironically given the use of the phrase in the 1930s, postulated the noble Forgotten Man who was the victim in effect of charitable enterprises, government and private, which were being wasted on the nondeserving poor. "Now, if we have state regulation, what is always forgotten is this: Who pays for it? Who is the victim of it? There always is a victim. The

workmen who do not defend themselves have to pay for the inspectors who defend them. . . . Here, then, you have your Forgotten Man again. The man who has been careful and prudent and who wants to go on and reap his advantages for himself and his children is arrested just at that point, and he is told that he must go and take care of some negligent employees in a factory or on a railroad who have not provided precautions for themselves or have not forced their employers to provide precautions, or negligent tenants who have not taken care of their own sanitary arrangements, or negligent householders who have not provided against fire, or negligent parents who have not sent their children to school." William Graham Sumner, *The Forgotten Man and Other Essays* (New Haven: Yale University Press, 1919), pp. 482–83.

CHAPTER THREE

1. H. L. Mencken, "The Sahara of the Bozart," reprinted in *A Mencken Chrestomathy* (New York: Alfred A. Knopf, 1949), pp. 185–86. For discussion of attitudes toward Mencken in the South, see John L. Stewart, *The Burden of Time: The Fugitives and Agrarians* (Princeton: Princeton University Press, 1965), pp. 114ff.

2. Mencken, "Sahara of the Bozart," p. 185.

3. For a short history of the Piedmont strikes, see Irving Bernstein, *The Lean Years: A History of the American Worker 1920–1933* (1960; Baltimore: Penguin Books, 1966), pp. 1–43.

4. Harvey O'Connor, "Carolina Mill Slaves," *New Masses* (May 1929), p. 7.

5. Frederic Cover, "Carolina," *New Masses* (July 1929), p. 5.

6. Ella Ford, "We Are Mill People," *New Masses* (Aug. 1929), p. 3.

7. Grace Lumpkin, *To Make My Bread* (New York: Macaulay Co., 1932), pp. 7–8.

8. Fielding Burke [Olive Dargan], *Call Home the Heart* (New York: Longmans, Green & Co., 1932), p. 2.

9. Ibid., p. 392.

10. A fourth Gastonia novel, *Gathering Storm,* by Dorothy Myra Page, was published in the same year, 1932, but it was exceptional both for its comparative lack of fictiveness—the novel names real places and people and events—and for the parochialism of its propaganda. An emphatic part of the action is given over, for instance, to the rivalry between the AFL's National Textile Union and the Party-sponsored National Textile Workers Union. More particularly, the novel deals with race, discovering that in the heat of the struggle black and white will discover each other and then unite and fight. The subtitle of the novel is "A Story of the Black Belt," which might have indicated a fundamental distortion of the story of Gastonia except that Page insisted otherwise, no doubt following upon the insistences of the Party.

The mechanisms of the plotting of the novel are, however, suggestive. Page does begin, quite like Burke and Lumpkin, with a tale of the mountain folk, and the novel harks back, in appropriate dialect, to the ways and the health of the folk in the time before the coming of the mills. But Page apparently could not generate from such materials either the novel or the revolution she wanted. An outside agency of learning was needed, especially in the matter of race. The major characters therefore go traveling, to New York City, to Chicago, and, by means of the World War, to Europe, in all instances learning class solidarity and a little bit of Lenin. When they return to awaken the masses at home—using simple language unlike the remote and pompous leaders of the NTU—the masses fall very quickly into enlightenment but at the expense of whatever social and psychological specificity was in the first chapters of the novel. Dorothy Myra Page, *Gathering Storm: A Story of the Black Belt* (New York: International Publishers, 1932).

11. Quoted in Walter B. Rideout, "Introduction," Sherwood Anderson, *Beyond Desire* (1932; New York: Liveright, 1970), p. vii.

12. Cleanth Brooks and Robert Penn Warren, *Understanding Poetry*, 3d ed. (New York: Holt, Rinehart, & Winston, 1960), p. xiv.

13. Tate quoted in Stewart, *Burden of Time*, p. 41. See Stewart passim for a detailed account of the history of the Fugitive group. See also Louise Cowan, *The Fugitive Group: A Literary History* (Baton Rouge: Louisiana State University Press, 1959).

14. See Stewart, *Burden of Time*, pp. 25, 26, 114.

15. John Crowe Ransom, "Reconstructed but Unregenerate," in Twelve Southerners, *I'll Take My Stand: The South and the Agrarian Tradition* (1930; New York: Harper Torchbooks, 1962), p. 14.

16. George Marion O'Donnell, "Looking down the Cotton Row," in Herbert Agar and Allen Tate (eds.), *Who Owns America? A New Declaration of Independence* (Boston: Houghton Mifflin Co., 1936), pp. 167–68.

17. Frank Lawrence Owsley, "The Irrepressible Conflict," *I'll Take My Stand*, p. 71.

18. Andrew Lytle, "The Hind Tit," *I'll Take My Stand*, pp. 208, 244, and passim.

19. Ransom, "Reconstructed but Unregenerate," p. 25.

20. Herbert C. Nixon, "Whither Southern Economy?" *I'll Take My Stand*, p. 188. Lytle, "The Hind Tit," p. 207. Owsley, "The Irrepressible Conflict," pp. 65–66.

21. Lytle, "The Hind Tit," p. 205.

22. Robert Penn Warren, "The Briar Patch," *I'll Take My Stand*, pp. 260–61.

23. Owsley, "The Irrepressible Conflict," p. 62. Ransom, "Reconstructed but Unregenerate," p. 14. John Gould Fletcher, "Education, Past and Present," *I'll Take My Stand*, p. 121.

24. Tate told Donald Davidson that the particular line in the poem had been the germ of the Stonewall Jackson book. Letter from Tate to Davidson, Mar. 1928, quoted by Cowan, *Fugitive Group*, pp. 242–43.

25. Allen Tate, *Stonewall Jackson: A Narrative* (New York: Minton, Balch & Co., 1928), p. 3.

26. Allen Tate, *Jefferson Davis: His Rise and Fall* (New York: Minton, Balch & Co., 1929), pp. 207–8, 299.

27. Ibid., p. 251.

28. See Thomas Daniel Young, "Introduction," Allen Tate, *The Fathers* (1938; Baton Rouge: Louisiana State University Press, 1977). See also Stewart, *Burden of Time,* pp. 334ff.

29. This interpretation of the ambiguous ending of the novel is Tate's own. See his "Note" written as an afterword to the 1977 edition of *Fathers,* cited above, p. 314.

30. Tate, *Fathers,* pp. 125–26.

31. Agar was the London correspondent to the *Louisville Courier* and an admirer of the British Distributists, "a small, loosely organized group led by G. K. Chesterton and Hilaire Belloc which wanted to break up large corporations and land holdings, distribute the property among small owners who would live mainly by sibsistence farming, and extend the authority and ceremonies of churches—particularly the Roman Catholic church—throughout the life of the community." He was interested in the similarities of the proposals for reform in Agrarianism and Distributivism. Stewart, *Burden of Time,* pp. 180ff.

32. Donald Davidson, "Lands That Were Golden," *American Review* (Oct. 1934), pp. 554–55, 561.

33. Allen Tate, "Remarks on the Southern Religion," *I'll Take My Stand,* p. 175.

34. Ransom, "Introduction," *I'll Take My Stand,* pp. xxix–xxx.

35. Ransom, "What Does the South Want?" *Who Owns America?* p. 183.

36. I am indebted to Professor William Fischer for this information and for other speculations on what he calls the "Sewanee Swindle."

37. James M. Cain, *The Postman Always Rings Twice,* 1934, in *Cain Omnibus* (New York: Sun Dial Press, 1943), p. 136.

38. Ibid., p. 136.

39. Ibid., p. 22.

40. Edmund Wilson, "The Boys in the Back Room," 1940, in *A Literary Chronicle: 1920–1950* (New York: Doubleday, 1952), p. 240.

41. See David Madden, *James M. Cain* (New York: Twayne Publishers, 1970), pp. 50–51.

42. James M. Cain, *Serenade,* 1937, in *Cain Omnibus,* p. 4.

43. See Madden, *James M. Cain,* passim, for various testimonies to this effect.

44. Dashiell Hammett, *Red Harvest* (1929; New York: Vintage Books, 1972), pp. 3–4.

45. Ibid., p. 39.

46. Dashiell Hammett, *The Dain Curse* (1929; London: Cassell, 1974), p. 191.

47. *Red Harvest,* p. 199.

48. Ibid., pp. 41, 107–8, 142–43.

49. Horace McCoy, *They Shoot Horses, Don't They?* (1935; New York: Avon Books, 1966), pp. 19, 128.

50. Ibid., pp. 23, 126, 86.

51. See Thomas Sturak, "Horace McCoy's Objective Lyricism," in David Madden (ed.), *Tough Guy Writers of the Thirties* (Carbondale: Southern Illinois University Press, 1968), pp. 140, 162. See also Robert M. Coates, "Afterword," *They Shoot Horses, Don't They?* edition cited above.

52. *They Shoot Horses Don't They* p. 23.

53. See Sturak, "Horace McCoy's Objective Lyricism," p. 148.

54. *They Shoot Horses, Don't They?* and *I Should Have Stayed Home* are thematically and structurally similar: the latter novel, published in 1938, is another exposé of the lives of Hollywood extras: once again McCoy's male protagonist is very innocent although equipped with some small aptitude for cynicism; once again, the female protagonist is swifter and bolder in apprehension, and offers lessons in utter cynicism. The novel is, however, much more circumstantial than *They Shoot Horses, Don't They?* and politically is much more explicit. The protagonists are invited to consider the relevances of contemporary events including the war in Spain, the case of the Scottsboro Boys, and Nazism (as a direct influence in the motion picture industry). The female protagonist leads a strike. On the other hand, the hero of the tale, who is twenty-three years old and is a farm boy from Georgia and is a virgin and has never touched liquor, is invited equally to become aware of a range of quite nonpolitical sordidnesses: liquor and lesbianism and pornography and the predations of aging wealthy women, etc. There is a general moral in all of this, having to do with self-respect, but that moral is inevitably qualified by all of the many contingencies.

55. *They Shoot Horses, Don't They?* pp. 21, 124.

56. "This is an uneven novel written by an uneven man in the most uneven of American times." Nelson Algren, "Preface," *Somebody in Boots* (1935; New York: Berkeley Publishing, 1965), p. 9.

57. *Somebody in Boots*, pp. 18, 103, 107, 243, 245.

58. Ibid., p. 16.

59. Ibid., p. 8.

60. Ibid., pp. 249, 214.

CHAPTER FOUR

1. Malcolm Cowley, *Exile's Return: A Literary Odyssey of the 1920's* (1934; New York: Viking Press, 1956), pp. 286, 287. For discussion of attitudes of public officials and of writers in the 1930s toward the values of the previous decade, see William E. Leuchtenburg, *Franklin D. Roosevelt and the New Deal* (New York: Harper Torchbooks, 1963), pp. 337ff. Leuchtenburg cites an especially suggestive statement by Horace Gregory. Reviewing the works of D. H. Lawrence in 1932, Gregory declared, "The world is moving away from Lawrence's need for personal salvation; his 'dark religion' is not a substitute for economic planning" (p. 342).

2. Thomas Wolfe, "The Company," *New Masses* (11 Jan. 1938). Reprinted in Joseph North (ed.), *New Masses: An Anthology of the Rebel Thirties* (New York: International Publishers, 1969), pp. 115–29.

3. For an account of Henry Miller's literary ambitions—reconstructed,

ordered, and interpreted from Miller's own accounts—see Jay Martin, *Always Merry and Bright: The Life of Henry Miller* (Santa Barbara: Capra Press, 1978), especially pp. 70ff.

4. Archibald MacLeish, "Invocation to the Social Muse," *New Republic* (26 Oct. 1932), p. 296; "The Social Cant," *New Republic* (21 Dec. 1932), pp. 156–58. For some of the immediate responses to "Invocation to the Social Muse," including poetical responses by Allen Tate and Selden Rodman, see *New Republic* (14 Dec. 1932), pp. 125–26.

5. Archibald MacLeish, *The Irresponsibles: A Declaration* (New York: Duell, Sloan & Pearce, 1940), p. 34.

6. The Marxian theorist John Strachey addressed MacLeish's dilemma at length, and then resolved it with facility. Strachey's *Literature and Dialectical Materialism* was devoted in large part to an analysis of the apparent duality of attitude in "Frescoes." "On the one hand," Strachey said, "there is this perfectly genuine emotion of revolt against the great bankers, and on the other hand, in the last section of the poem, there is the equally strong revulsion against the actual masses—against the urban masses in particular. For these masses are largely either Jewish, or ill-educated, or foreign born.... Now where have these two emotions of revolt—of revolt against the bankers and of revolt against anything foreign—appeared together before? The answer is that they have appeared in the rank and file of every fascist movement in the world." Strachey insisted, however, that MacLeish did not know that he was a fascist, but was rather an example of what Michael Gold had called the "Fascist Unconscious." John Strachey, *Literature and Dialectical Materialism* (New York: Covici-Friede, 1934), pp. 22–23, 27–28.

7. For a personal account of the effect of this change in the Party line, see Granville Hicks, *Part of the Truth* (New York: Harcourt, Brace & World, 1965), pp. 134–35.

8. The "N. L. D." was the National Labor Defense, a legal-defense unit of the Communist party. It had challenged the NAACP for the right to defend the Scottsboro Boys, and it was to that challenge that Wexley was referring. John Wexley, "They Shall Not Die," in *Proletarian Literature in the United States: An Anthology* (New York: International Publishers, 1935), p. 317.

9. *Proletarian Literature in the United States*, pp. 33, 28.

10. "Introduction," *Proletarian Literature in the United States*, pp. 19–20, 23, 27.

11. William Phillips and Philip Rahv, "Recent Problems of Revolutionary Literature," *Proletarian Literature in the United States*, pp. 367–73.

12. David Wolff, "Remembering Hart Crane," *Proletarian Literature in the United States*, pp. 201–2.

13. Meridel LeSueur, "I Was Marching," *Proletarian Literature in the United States*, p. 224.

14. James T. Farrell, *A Note on Literary Criticism* (New York: Vanguard Press, 1936). See especially chapter 4, "Left-Wing Dualism." The attack on Granville Hicks is continuous throughout the book.

15. For biographical material on Farrell, see Alan M. Wald, *James T. Farrell: The Revolutionary Socialist Years* (New York: New York University Press, 1978). Hicks recalls his attitudes toward the Party in *Part of the Truth,* pp. 92–128, and passim.

16. See Walter B. Rideout, *The Radical Novel in the United States; 1900–1954* (1956; New York: Hill & Wang, 1966). Rideout names seventy proletarian novels—his concern is with novels only—published during the 1930s by approximately fifty authors. See pp. 295–98.

17. Clara Weatherwax, *Marching! Marching!* (New York: John Day Co., 1935), pp. 208, 276.

18. Rideout, *Radical Novel,* pp. 179–80.

19. Weatherwax, *Marching! Marching!* pp. 32, 197, 61.

20. Albert Halper, *The Chute* (New York: Viking Press, 1937), p. 67.

21. Myra Page, *Moscow Yankee* (New York: G. P. Putnam's Sons, 1935), p. 255.

22. Thomas Bell, *All Brides Are Beautiful* (Boston: Little, Brown, 1936), p. 330.

23. Edward Dahlberg, *Bottom Dogs* (1930; San Francisco: City Lights, 1961), p. 207.

24. Kenneth Burke, "The Writers' Congress," *Nation* (15 May 1935), p. 571.

25. Albert Halper, *Union Square* (1933; New York: Belmont Books, 1962), pp. 53, 229–34.

26. Ibid., pp. 46, 219.

27. Ol'ga Nemerovskaja, cited in Deming Brown, "Soviet Criticism of American Proletarian Literature of the 1930s," *American Contributions to the Fourth International Congress of Slavicists, Moscow, September 1958* (The Hague: Mouton & Co., 1958), p. 8.

28. Jack Conroy, *The Disinherited* (1933; New York: Hill & Wang, 1963), pp. 286, 289.

29. Jack Conroy, "Home to Moberly," *MLA Quarterly* (Mar. 1968), p. 42.

30. Jack Conroy, "Introduction," *Writers In Revolt: The Anvil Anthology 1933–1940,* ed. Jack Conroy and Curt Johnson (New York: Lawrence Hill, 1973), p. x.

31. *Disinherited,* p. 13.

32. Philip Rahv, "Proletarian Literature: A Political Autopsy," *Southern Review* (Winter 1939), pp. 623, 628.

33. Jack Conroy, letter to Marcus Klein, 29 Mar. 1968.

34. Daniel Aaron, *Writers on the Left: Episodes in American Literary Communism* (New York: Harcourt, Brace & World, 1961), p. 300.

35. See, e.g., Irving Howe and Lewis Coser, *The American Communist Party: A Critical History* (1957; New York: Frederick A. Praeger, 1962), pp. 273ff.

36. Michael Gold, "Notes of the Month," *New Masses* (Sept. 1930).

37. A. B. Magil, letters to Marcus Klein, 14 Nov., 6 Dec. 1977.

38. Magil's poem "Angelina" (*New Masses* [Sept. 1928], p. 15) began with the following lines, and was typical:

Angelina, turn your face away.
Let dark hands flutter over floors.
Scrub them bright and clean, Angelina, bright and clean.
Make them glitter in the sun so the rich will be happy
And pity you and smile at the bright clean floors.
Turn your face away, don't be standing at the window.
You will see the park with the green trees shining;
You will see the young men walking and the children playing.
(Why do your lips quiver so, Angelina?)

Your eyes are little dark birds, but they'll never fly away
To the green trees and the children and the young men walking
        in the street.
Say this over to yourself a thousand times.

. . . .

39. Isidor Schneider, "Sectarianism on the Right," New Masses (23 June 1936), p. 25.

40. Isidor Schneider, "Home Girl Makes Good," *New Masses* (27 Nov. 1934), pp. 21–22.

41. See John Unterecker, *Voyager: A Life of Hart Crane* (London: Anthony Blond, 1969), pp. 617–21.

42. Isidor Schneider, "Their Books," *New Masses* (16 June 1936), p. 21.

43. Gertrude Stein to Isidor Schneider in "Home Girl Makes Good," cited above.

As for Wallace Stevens, Stanley Burnshaw was undoubtedly approximately correct when, in an essay published in 1961, he said that Stevens in the thirties was "a man not in the least ignorant of the issues or, for that matter, of the controversies and the codes." There had been a particular controversy. In 1935 Burnshaw had reviewed Stevens's *Ideas of Order* for *New Masses*. By *New Masses* standards, the review was not really unfriendly. Stevens was seen to be a potential ally. *Ideas of Order,* coming after *Harmonium,* revealed that Stevens had discovered discord in his harmonious cosmos. "Acutely conscious members of a class menaced by the clashes between capital and labor, these writers [the other writer under consideration was Haniel Long] are in the throes of struggle for philosophical adjustment. And their words have intense value and meaning to the sectors within the class whose confusions they articulate." But of course Burnshaw concluded by saying that Stevens had not yet achieved a valid Idea of Order. Stevens was provoked—significantly, because it might well have been the case that he would have found the review to be simply irrelevant. Apparently he found in the review an exaggerated and distorted usage of an idea with which he had felt himself to be sympathetic. A week after the review appeared, Stevens was writing to a friend: "I hope I am headed left, but there are lefts and lefts, and certainly I am not headed for the ghastly left of MASSES. The rich man and the comfortable man of the imagination of people like Mr. Burnshaw are not nearly so rich nor nearly so comfortable as he believes them to be. And, what is more, his poor men are not nearly so poor.... MASSES is just one more wailing place and the whole left now-a-days is a mob of wailers. I do very much believe in leftism in every direction, even wailing. These people go about it in such a way that nobody listens to them except themselves; and that is a least [*sic*] one reason why they get nowhere. They have the most magnificent cause in the world."

Sometime within the subsequent three weeks Stevens was writing the long poem called "Mr. Burnshaw and the Statue," which was to be published as the second section of the original edition of *Owl's Clover*. (In later editions the poem was called "The Statue at the World's End.") Insofar as the poem did directly refer to Burnshaw and those whom Stevens would have thought to be of his ilk, it suggested that literal, practical communism was the death of the imagination.

There is significance in the fact that Stevens in the mid-thirties was trying to affiliate his thoughts with some kind of generally formulated expression of the issues and controversies of the moment. He must have realized that the circumstances of life for poetry, too, had indeed been revised. The conclusion of *Owl's Clover* so testifies, as does—just as Burnshaw had maintained—the publication of *Ideas of Order* following upon *Harmonium*. But Stevens's politics as a matter of declared affiliations was even more confused than Burnshaw had supposed. At about the same time Stevens was saying that he hoped he was headed left, he was telling the same correspondent that he was "pro-Mussolini," and a few days after that, perhaps in more serious vein, he was saying that he believed in "'up-to-date capitalism.'"

And there can be little doubt that Stevens, of the Bucks County Stevenses who had been in Pennsylvania longer than the Penns, was fundamentally out of touch with what Burnshaw called the "codes." As Burnshaw pointed out in the 1961 essay—not the 1935 review—the longest poem in *Ideas of Order* was "Like Decorations in a Nigger Cemetery." Burnshaw to the contrary, it would seem to be entirely likely that Stevens did *not* know "that the word 'nigger' was scrupulously avoided by white people who had now become acutely aware of its extreme offensiveness." In the private letter in which he declared himself to be pro-Mussolini, Stevens justified his position by saying that "the Italians have as much right to take Ethiopia from the coons as the coons had to take it from the boa-constrictors." That expression was a private one and also glib, but the section of *Owl's Clover* which deals with Mussolini's bombing of Ethiopia (section V of "The Greenest Continent") transforms the war into high spectacle and grand symbol, in which there is no possibility of regard for individual human sufferings and certainly not for racial sensitivities:

Forth from their tabernacles once again
The angels come, armed, gloriously to slay
The black and ruin his sepulchral throne.
Hé quoi! Angels go pricking elephants?
Wings spread and whirling over jaguar-men?

See: Stanley Burnshaw, "Wallace Stevens and the Statue," *Sewanee Review* (Summer 1961), pp. 355–66. Burnshaw here reprints his 1935 review of *Ideas of Order,* called "Turmoil in the Middle Ground." Letters from Wallace Stevens to Ronald Lane Latimer, 9 Oct. 1935, 31 Oct. 1935, 5 Nov. 1935, in Holly Stevens (ed.), *Letters of Wallace Stevens* (New York: Alfred A. Knopf, 1966), pp. 286–87, 288–89, 290–93.

44. Edmund Wilson, *The American Jitters: A Year of the Slump* (New York: Charles Scribner's Sons, 1932), p. 303.

45. Sherman Paul says of *The American Jitters* that "it is a book of voices." Sherman Paul, *Edmund Wilson: A Study of Literary Vocation in Our Time* (1965; Urbana: University of Illinois Press, 1967), p. 113.

Upon publication of the book, Christian Gauss wrote to Wilson: "The first stage in the fight for the new social order is to make larger and larger numbers see that Hamfishism and Henryfordism are obsolete and that the farmer holding out his hand for the Red Cross dole and the man at the machine have deserts that are being denied them. I don't know any book that has done this more tellingly than you have by your realistic presentments. You have made them all so simply reasonably human. As an adventure in realism your book is an amazingly good size-up of the American comedy in 1932." Katherine Gauss Jackson and Hiram Haydn (eds.), *The Papers of Christian Gauss* (New York: Random House, 1957), p. 283.

Wilson, *American Jitters,* p. 50.

46. Sherwood Anderson, *Puzzled America* (1935; Mamaroneck, N.Y.: Paul P. Appel, 1970), p. ix.

47. Erskine Caldwell, *Some American People* (New York: Robert M. McBride, 1935), pp. 4–5.

48. Louis Adamic, *My America: 1928–1938* (New York: Harper & Brothers, 1938), p. xiii.

49. *American Jitters,* p. 313.

50. Benjamin Appel, *The People Talk* (New York: E. P. Dutton, 1940), p. 502.

51. Appel, *The People Talk,* p. 497. Louise V. Armstrong, *We Too Are the People* (Boston: Little, Brown, 1938), p. 16. Nathan Asch, *The Road: In Search of America* (New York: W. W. Norton, 1937), p. 11. Anderson, *Puzzled America,* pp. xv–xvi.

52. For extended discussion of differences between these photographers, and especially between Margaret Bourke-White and Walker Evans, see William Stott, *Documentary Expression and Thirties America* (New York: Oxford University Press, 1973), passim.

53. Sherwood Anderson, *Home Town* (New York: Alliance Book Corp., 1940), pp. 144, 9.

54. James Agee, *Let Us Now Praise Famous Men,* photographs by Walker Evans (1941; New York: Ballantine Books, 1966), pp. xiv–xv; 12, 121, 182–83.

55. James Agee, *Letters of James Agee to Father Flye,* 2d ed. (Boston: Houghton Mifflin Co., 1971), pp. 104–5.

56. *Let Us Now Praise Famous Men,* pp. 304, 85, 128, 133–34.

57. A detailed, authoritative, and anecdotal account of the Federal Writers' Project is Jerre Mangione, *The Dream and the Deal: The Federal Writers' Project, 1935–1943* (New York: Avon Books, 1972).

58. Some of the writers employed at various times by the Project were Lionel Abel, Conrad Aiken, Nelson Algren, Nathan Asch, Saul Bellow, Maxwell Bodenheim, Arna Bontemps, Sterling Brown, John Cheever, Jack Conroy, Edward Dahlberg, Floyd Dell, Loren Eisely, Ralph Ellison, Kenneth Fearing, Vardis Fisher, Joe Gould, Zora Neale Hurston, David Ignatow, Orrick Johns, Weldon Kees, Claude McKay, Willard Motley, Roi Ottley, Philip Rahv, Kenneth Rexroth, Harold Rosenberg, Isaac Rosenfeld, Eli Siegel, Studs Terkel, Dorothy Van Ghent, Margaret Walker, Richard Wright, Frank Yerby, and Anzia Yezierska.

59. Federal Writers' Project, "Literary Groups and Movements," *Massachusetts: A Guide to Its Places and People* (Boston: Houghton Mifflin Co., 1937), p. 109. "Literature," ibid., p. 99.

60. J. S. Balch, *Lamps at High Noon* (New York: Modern Age, 1941), pp. 35–36, 229.

61. Norman MacLeod, *You Get What You Ask For* (New York: Harrison-Hilton Books, 1939), p. 209.

62. The great vision was no doubt so emphatically and continuously prescribed by the administrators of the Project as to inspire cynicism, particularly among writers who had some other ideas about the nature of literature. "This search for cultural unity," Harold Rosenberg was to recall, "was the 'dream' that the Project substituted for a concern with American writing. As early as 1937, Bernard de Voto complained that the Guides 'are all cluttered up with our cultural heritage,' and among the Washington staff a joke went the rounds that parodied Göring: 'When I hear the word "culture," I reach for my unity.' " Harold Rosenberg, "Anyone Who Could Write English," *New Yorker* (20 Jan. 1973), p. 102.

63. Federal Writers' Project, *These Are Our Lives* (1939; New York: W. W. Norton, 1975), pp. 185, 46–47.

64. Federal Writers' Project, *American Stuff: An Anthology of Prose and Verse by Members of the Federal Writers' Project* (New York: Viking Press, 1937), p. viii.

65. Bernard Smith, *Forces in American Criticism: A Study in the History of American Literary Thought* (New York: Harcourt, Brace, 1939), pp. 386–87.

66. Vernon L. Parrington, *Main Currents in American Thought: An Interpretation of American Literature from the Beginnings to 1920* (New York: Harcourt, Brace, 1927, 1930), 1: iii; 3: xxix.

67. F. O. Matthiessen, *The Achievement of T. S. Eliot: An Essay on the Nature of Poetry,* 3d ed. (1935, 1947; New York: Oxford University Press, 1959), pp. vii, ix.

68. F. O. Matthiessen, *American Renaissance: Art and Expression in the Age of Emerson and Whitman* (New York: Oxford University Press, 1941), pp. ix, xiv–xv, 626ff.

69. For discussion of directions in American historical writing in the 1930s, see Alfred Haworth Jones, "The Search for a Usable American Past in the New Deal Era," *American Quarterly* (Dec. 1971), pp. 710–24.

70. See Constance Rourke, *The Roots of American Culture and Other Essays,* ed. Van Wyck Brooks (New York: Harcourt, Brace, 1942), especially pp. 22ff.

71. Stanley Edgar Hyman, *The Armed Vision: A Study in the Methods of Modern Literary Criticism* (New York: Alfred A. Knopf, 1948), pp. 134ff.

72. Allen Tate reviewed *In the American Grain* for *New Masses,* and seemed to be of two or three minds about it. The date of the review is 1927, by which time Tate himself was deeply engaged in trying to fashion his own version of his American tradition—he was just then composing his biography of Stonewall Jackson. He thought that Williams's book was appropriate to the moment, but unfortunate, "significant, rather than important." The book, he said, "is an instance of the very disease under diagnosis; in a living culture supporting satisfactory art-forms the immediate production is the exclusive interest of criticism, for the tradition is taken for granted. Dr. Williams believes that we are not sustained by a living tradition, and he has written a historical survey of the American spirit in search of one." While despairing of the enterprise, Tate was prone to agree to its necessity in these times, nor did he disagree with the main question he thought to have been raised by the book: "Why we are spiritually conditioned to hatred of life—what is the origin of the obsession." But he also seemed to think that the book was self-indulgent, was frustratingly lacking in analytical insight, and in general did not go about answering the question in the right way. "Dr. Williams' appeal to origins is the uneasy attempt of an individual to define his tradition. (It *is* uneasy: his prose, which can be economical and sustained, is seldom explicit; it breaks off into purple writing and obscure divination.) . . . his method of getting to what Mr. Brooks has called a usable past is like Mr. Brooks' own method to that end; it is usually its own frustration. It succeeds chiefly as recapitulation, and it sterilizes whatever it heroically tries to resuscitate." Allen Tate, "Our Will-to-Death," *New Masses* (Jan. 1927), p. 29.

73. Constance Rourke, *Audubon* (New York: Harcourt, Brace, 1936), p. 126. Rourke had used the same story several years before, in *American Humor: A Study of the National Character* (New York: Harcourt, Brace, 1931), p. 51.

74. *American Humor,* pp. 179ff., 186ff., 235ff., 266ff.

75. Dahlberg, *Bottom Dogs,* pp. 4, 88.

76. Tom Kromer, *Waiting for Nothing* (1935; New York: Hill & Wang, 1968), pp. 188, 22.

77. Hart Crane, *The Letters of Hart Crane, 1916–1932,* ed. Brom Weber (New York: Hermitage House, 1952), letter to Otto Kahn, p. 223.

78. Hart Crane, *Letters,* p. 303.

79. John Dos Passos, *U. S. A.* (1930, 1932, 1936; New York: Random House, 1937), pp. vi–vii; 3: 560.

CHAPTER FIVE

1. Jerre Mangione, *The Dream and the Deal: The Federal Writers' Project, 1934–1943* (New York: Avon Books, 1972), pp. 62–63, 92, 54ff.

2. See Melvin P. Levy, "Michael Gold," *New Republic* (26 Mar. 1930), pp. 160–61; Michael Gold, "A Proletarian Novel," *New Republic* (4 June 1930), p. 74. Since Gold was one of the founding editors of *New Masses,* that journal of course reviewed the novel favorably, although not without some objections by the reviewer, Joshua Kunitz, to the style of the novel. J. Q. Neets, "Jews without Money," *New Masses* (Mar. 1930), p. 15.

3. Michael Gold, *Jews without Money* (1930; New York: Avon Books, 1965), p. 224.

4. For factual data of the life of Michael Gold, see, chiefly, two essays by Michael Brewster Folsom: "The Education of Michael Gold," in *Proletarian Writers of the Thirties,* ed. David Madden (Carbondale: Southern Illinois University Press, 1968), pp. 222–51, and "Introduction," *Mike Gold: A Literary Anthology,* ed. Michael Folsom (New York: International Publishers, 1972), pp. 7–20.

5. According to Flynn herself, Flynn had been an extraordinarily attractive woman. In her autobiography she recalled the time the theatrical producer David Belasco had sought her out. She had been speaking at a rally in the theater district, and Belasco had caught her act. He had then and there, so she recalled, offered to make her a star. See Elizabeth Gurley Flynn, *I Speak My Own Piece* (New York: Masses & Mainstream, 1955).

6. Carlos Baker, *Ernest Hemingway: A Life Story* (New York: Charles Scribner's Sons, 1969), p. 4.

7. For the factual data following I am largely indebted to Bonnie Lyons, *Henry Roth: The Man and His Work* (New York: Cooper Square Publishers, 1976).

8. Roth has so testified on a number of occasions. See, for example, Bonnie Lyons, "Interview with Henry Roth, March, 1977," *Studies in American Jewish Literature* (Spring 1979), pp. 50–58.

9. Roth quoted by Marsha Pomerantz, "A Long Sleep," *Jerusalem Post International Edition* (23 Sept. 1977), p. 9.

10. Roth quoted in Lyons, *Henry Roth,* p. 163.

11. See Pomerantz, "A Long Sleep."

12. Henry Roth, "Where My Sympathy Lies," *New Masses* (2 Mar. 1937), p. 9.

13. Reviews quoted in Lyons, *Henry Roth,* pp. 16–18.

14. For a history of the rediscovery, see Lyons, *Henry Roth,* pp. 27ff.

15. Ibid., p. 19.

16. Roth quoted in Pomerantz, "A Long Sleep."

17. Roth quoted in Lyons, "Interview with Henry Roth, March, 1977," p. 53.

18. Henry Roth, *Call It Sleep* (1934; New York: Avon Books, n.d.), p. 141.

19. Henry James, *The American Scene* (1907; New York: Horizon Press, 1967), pp. 131–39.

20. The three novels were published together for the first time in 1961, as a single volume called *The Williamsburg Trilogy*, with an introduction by Fuchs.

21. Daniel Fuchs, *Summer in Williamsburg*, in *The Williamsburg Trilogy* (New York: Avon Books, 1972), pp. 11–12.

22. Daniel Fuchs, *Homage to Blenholt*, in *The Williamsburg Trilogy*, p. 55.

23. Daniel Fuchs, *Low Company*, in *The Williamsburg Trilogy*, p. 311.

24. For the biographical data following, I have relied largely on Edgar M. Branch, *James T. Farrell* (New York: Twayne Publishers, 1971).

25. James T. Farrell, *Studs Lonigan* (New York: Random House, Modern Library, 1938), p. xi.

26. James T. Farrell, "Studs," reprinted in Albert Halper (ed.), *This Is Chicago: An Anthology* (New York: Henry Holt, 1952), p. 228.

27. See "Introduction" to Modern Library edition, passim.

28. James T. Farrell, *Young Lonigan* in *Studs Lonigan* (1932, 1934, 1935; New York: Avon Books, 1977), pp. 82–84.

29. James T. Farrell, *The Young Manhood of Studs Lonigan* in *Studs Lonigan*, p. 401.

30. See Branch, *James T. Farrell*, pp. 172–73.

31. Albert Halper, "Young Writer Remembering Chicago," *On the Shore: Young Writer Remembering Chicago* (New York: Viking Press, 1934), p. 221.

32. See Albert Halper, *Good-bye, Union Square: A Writer's Memoir of the Thirties* (Chicago Quadrangle Books, 1970), p. 11.

33. Ibid., passim.

34. Meyer Levin, *In Search: An Autobiography* (Paris: Authors' Press, 1950), pp. 75–76.

35. Meyer Levin, *The Old Bunch* (1937; New York: MacFadden Books, 1962), p. 35.

INTRODUCTION TO PART THREE

1. William Carlos Williams, *The Autobiography of William Carlos Williams* (New York: New Directions, 1951), p. 311.

CHAPTER SIX

1. References to Robinson Jeffers, Edmund Wilson, Lewis Mumford, Archibald MacLeish, and Waldo Frank in Michael Gold, *The Hollow Men* (New York: International Publishers, 1941), passim. *The Hollow Men* appeared originally as a series of articles in the *Daily Worker* under the title, "The Great Tradition: Can the Literary Renegades Destroy It?" Reference to John Dos Passos is quoted in Irving Howe and Lewis Coser, *The American Communist Party: A Critical History* (1957; New York: Frederick A. Praeger, 1962), p. 308. Reference to Max Eastman is quoted in Max Eastman, *Love and Revolu-*

tion: My Journey through an Epoch (New York: Random House, 1964), pp. 602–3.

2. See Michael Gold, "The Gun Is Loaded, Dreiser," *Change the World* (New York: International Publishers, 1936), pp. 50–59.

3. "Why I Am a Communist," in Michael Folsom (ed.), *Mike Gold: A Literary Anthology* (New York: International Publishers, 1972), p. 214.

4. Sherwood Anderson and John Dos Passos cited in Daniel Aaron and Robert Bendiner (eds.), *The Strenuous Decade: A Social and Intellectual Record of the Nineteen-Thirties* (New York: Anchor Books, 1970), pp. 292, 293.

5. Edmund Wilson, *The American Jitters: A Year of the Slump* (New York: Charles Scribner's Sons, 1932), pp. 312–13. My italics.

6. My chief source for biographical information is two essays by Michael Folsom: "The Pariah of American Letters," in *Mike Gold: A Literary Anthology*, pp. 7–20, and "The Education of Michael Gold," in David Madden (ed.), *Proletarian Writers of the Thirties* (Carbondale: Southern Illinois University Press, 1968), pp. 222–51. In the latter essay Folsom says that Itzok Granich became Michael Gold in 1921, but he is apparently mistaken in this detail. The new name appears under an article about a convention of the Amalgamated Clothing Workers, in the *Liberator* in 1920. See Michael Gold, "In the Shell of the Old," *Liberator* (July 1920), pp. 30–34.

7. Michael Gold, "The Writer in America," in Samuel Sillen (ed.), *The Mike Gold Reader* (New York: International Publishers, 1954), p. 183.

8. Quoted in Folsom, "The Education of Michael Gold," p. 224.

9. "The Writer in America," p. 182.

10. Ibid., pp. 182–83.

11. "Towards Proletarian Art," *Liberator* (Feb. 1921), p. 22. "Proletarian Realism," Sept. 1930, reprinted in Folsom, *Mike Gold: A Literary Anthology*, p. 208. "The Second American Renaissance," address to Fourth Congress of American Writers, 1941, printed in Folsom, ibid., p. 251.

12. See Folsom, "The Education of Michael Gold," pp. 225 26.

13. Quoted in Max Eastman, *Love and Revolution*, p. 266.

14. Quoted in Folsom, "The Education of Mike Gold," p. 230.

15. *Masses*, May 1916, reprinted in Folsom, *Mike Gold: A Literary Anthology*, p. 23.

16. "Rouge and Redskins," *Liberator* (Dec. 1923), p. 31.

17. *New Masses* (Nov. 1926), pp. 7–8.

18. *New Masses* (July 1926), pp. 19–21.

19. See Barbara and Arthur Gelb, *O'Neill* (1962; New York: Delta, 1964), chapters 26–30. Cook quoted, 304.

20. In 1917 the Provincetown Players produced two of Gold's one-acters: *Down the Airshaft* and *Ivan's Homecoming*. In 1920 it produced his one-acter called *Money*. Gold quoted in Gelb, ibid., p. 359.

21. See Folsom, "The Education of Mike Gold," p. 234.

22. Van Wyck Brooks, "America's Coming-of-Age," 1915, in *Three Essays on America* (New York: E. P. Dutton, 1934), p. 37.

23. At the point of production, however, the director of the play turned

the device around completely: all of the parts were played by whites, with blacks being played in blackface. The director also had the actors mingle with the audience during intermission, dispensing balloons.

24. Stark Young, "Two Special Openings," *New Republic* (9 Oct. 1929), pp. 205–6. Produced at the Garrick Theatre, New York, 18 Sept. 1929. Gold's typescript title for the play was *La Fiesta: A Comedy of the Mexican Revolution, in Three Acts and a Prologue.*

25. Irwin Granich and Manabendra Nath Roy, "Champak—A Story of India," *Liberator* (Feb. 1920), pp. 8–11.

26. Reprinted in Folsom, *Mike Gold: A Literary Anthology,* pp. 24–32.

27. "Two Critics in a Bar-room," *Liberator* (Sept. 1921), pp. 28–31. My italics.

28. *New Republic* (22 Oct. 1930), pp. 266–67.

29. *New Republic* (17 Dec. 1930), p. 141.

30. Edmund Wilson, "The Economic Interpretation of Wilder," *New Republic* (26 Nov. 1930), pp. 31–32. Edmund Wilson, "The Literary Class War: I & II," *New Republic* (4 May 1932), pp. 319–23, (11 May 1932), pp. 347–49.

31. "The Literary Class War: I," pp. 319, 320.

32. For the record of the exchanges, see *New Masses* (Apr. 1930 to July 1930).

33. Edmund Wilson, "Thornton Wilder," 1928, reprinted in Edmund Wilson, *The Shores of Light: A Literary Chronicle of the Twenties and Thirties* (New York: Harcourt, Brace & World, 1961), p. 243.

34. See Daniel Aaron, *Writers on the Left: Episodes in American Literary Communism* (New York: Harcourt, Brace & World, 1961), p. 243.

35. Hankel: *New Republic* (5 Nov. 1930), p. 325; Raddock: *New Republic* (17 Dec. 1930), p. 141.

36. *New Republic* (12 Nov. 1930), p. 353.

CHAPTER SEVEN

1. Except as otherwise noted, all biographical and some background materials in this chapter have been appropriated from Jay Martin's authoritative biography, *Nathanael West: The Art of His Life* (New York: Hayden Book Co., 1970).

2. The school was De Witt Clinton High School. During the time of West's attendance, or nonattendance, other students enrolled at De Witt Clinton included Mortimer Adler, Countee Cullen, Ernest Nagel, and Lionel Trilling. See Martin, *Nathanael West,* p. 35.

3. Quoted in James F. Light, *Nathanael West: An Interpretive Study,* 2d ed. (Evanston: Northwestern University Press, 1971), p. 9.

4. Quoted in Light, *Nathanael West,* pp. 68, 144.

5. The story was not published. This version is quoted in ibid., pp. 39–40. A final version of the same is quoted in Martin, *Nathanael West,* pp. 88–89.

6. For a detailed explication of West's sources, see Randall Reid, *The Fiction of Nathanael West* (Chicago: University of Chicago Press, 1967), pp. 13–40.

7. Nathanael West, *The Dream Life of Balso Snell*, 1931, in *The Complete Works of Nathanael West* (New York: Farrar, Straus & Co., 1957), p. 37.

8. Nathanael West, *Miss Lonelyhearts*, 1933, in ibid., pp. 67, 68.

9. Nathanael West, *A Cool Million; or, The Dismantling of Lemuel Pitkin*, 1934, in ibid., p. 253.

10. West might well have thought of the novel as being a cartoon precisely. According to his own testimony he considered writing *Miss Lonelyhearts* after the fashion of a comic strip: "The chapters to be squares in which many things happen through one action. The speeches contained in the conventional balloons. I abandoned this idea, but retained some of the comic strip technique: Each chapter instead of going forward in time, also goes backward, forward, up and down in space like a picture. Violent images are used to illustrate commonplace events. Violent acts are left almost bald." Nathanael West, "Some Notes on Miss L.," 1933, in Jay Martin (ed.), *Nathanael West: A Collection of Critical Essays* (Englewood Cliffs, N.J.: Prentice-Hall, 1971), p. 66.

11. Nathanael West, *The Day of the Locust*, 1939, in *The Complete Works of Nathanael West*, p. 260.

12. Nathanael West, "Some Notes on Violence," 1932, in Martin, *Nathanael West: A Collection of Critical Essays*, p. 50.

CHAPTER EIGHT

1. The title of the first of the tales was either "Hell's Half Acre" or "The Voodoo of Hell's Half Acre," and was published in the *Southern Register* in 1924. The text has disappeared, but a version of it has been reconstructed by Michel Fabre. Fabre relies on the recollection, many years after the event, of the *Southern Register's* typesetter, and therefore it is not likely that his text is accurate, and indeed it is not fully accordant with Wright's own recollection of the story in *Black Boy*, as is noted by Fabre. But the title of the story—in either version of the title—suggests what must have been its general tone. According to the typesetter, it may be noted, the name of the hero of the story was "James 'Bigger' Thomas." See Michel Fabre, *The Unfinished Quest of Richard Wright*, trans. Isabel Barzun (New York: William Morrow & Co., 1973), pp. 48ff. The second of the tales was called "Superstition" and appeared in *Abbot's Monthly Magazine*, (Apr. 1931). Fabre summarizes the story, pp. 84ff.

2. Richard Wright, *American Hunger* (New York: Harper & Row, 1977), p. 68.

3. Ibid., p. 67.

4. According to Wright's recollection, in *American Hunger*, the date was 1936. Fabre says that the year was 1937. See *American Hunger*, pp. 131ff; Fabre, *Unfinished Quest*, pp. 137–38.

5. See Fabre, *Unfinished Quest*, p. 163. For a brief discussion of Wright's attitude toward the issue of the Trials, apparently based on interviews with Wright, see Constance Webb, *Richard Wright: A Biography* (New York: G. P. Putnam's Sons, 1968), p. 147.

6. Quoted in Webb, *Richard Wright*, pp. 149–50.

7. Since Wright did not make any public announcement of his break with

the Party at the time he apparently decided to leave, the precipitating causes of his decision are not recorded in primary documents. However, both of Wright's major biographers, using various sources, say that the racial matter prompted the decision. See Fabre, *Unfinished Quest,* pp. 228ff.; Webb, *Richard Wright,* p. 410.

8. Richard Wright, *Black Boy: A Record of Childhood and Youth* (New York: Harper & Brothers, 1945), p. 218.

9. Fabre, *Unfinished Quest,* p. 5.

10. The family's name was Wall. Mr. Wall was a foreman in a sawmill, and apparently in genuine kindness he advised Wright, on an occasion, not to try to find work in a sawmill. A version of the occasion appears in *Black Boy,* where Wall is called "Bibbs," but there is no account in *Black Boy* of Wright's close and long-term association with the Walls. See Fabre, *Unfinished Quest,* pp. 46ff.

11. Webb spells the name "Poindexter." In *American Hunger,* as also in the extract from *American Hunger* which appeared in *The God That Failed,* Wright refers to him as "Ross." For accounts of the kind of information Wright was likely to have received from Pointdexter, see Fabre, *Unfinished Quest,* pp. 106–7, and Webb, *Richard Wright,* pp. 125ff.

12. Quoted in Webb, *Richard Wright,* p. 168.

13. Richard Wright, "Big Boy Leaves Home," *Uncle Tom's Children* (1940; New York: Harper & Row, Perennial Library, 1965), p. 44.

14. See Fabre, *Unfinished Quest,* p. 110.

15. I am indebted to the recollection of Irving Sanes for the salvaging of this anecdote.

16. Alan Calmer, *New York Daily Worker* (4 Apr. 1938), p. 7, in John M. Reilly (ed.), *Richard Wright: The Critical Reception* (New York: Burt Franklin & Co., 1978), pp. 12ff.

17. Richard Wright, *Native Son* (New York: Harper & Brothers, 1940), p. 9.

18. Richard Wright, "How Bigger Was Born," *Saturday Review of Literature* (1 June 1940), pp. 3–4, 17–20.

19. See Fabre, *Unfinished Quest,* p. 170; Webb, *Richard Wright,* pp. 117ff.

Index